THE PACIFIC RIM

As the importance of the Pacific Rim as a global centre of large-scale investment, development, and trade continues to increase, so do the potential benefits that Canada and other countries could reap as a result of an increased presence in this diverse region. This book, a revised, and to a large extent new, version of *The Pacific Rim: Investment, Development, and Trade* (1987), integrates a broad range of current economic data concerning the Pacific Rim with some of the more important theoretical issues in the area of economic development and trade. It demonstrates the paradoxical combination of strength and fragility that characterizes the emerging integrated Pacific Rim economy and attempts to clarify the nature of the framework and constraints that face foreign investors and trading partners.

New contributions outline in detail the nature of, and rationale for, the profound change in Japan's foreign direct investment in the 1980s; deal with the policy environment for Pacific strategic management; compare the financial centres of Hong Kong and Singapore as these face the challenge of strategic adjustment and repositioning in international financial markets during the 1990s; and present a new theoretical framework for comparing United States and Japanese trade policies.

The second part of the book examines the critical role of energy in the future development of the Pacific Rim and its interdependence with other global regions. New articles discuss the progress and prospects for energy co-operation in the Pacific Basin and the potential for further development of nuclear power, while those dealing with the British Columbia coal industry and the changes in the energy systems of Japan and China have been updated to reflect current data. Another new contribution seeks to explain the excess capacity in the coal industry.

Looking beyond its traditional ties with Europe and the United States, Canada is in a particularly advantageous position to participate in the dvelopment and integration of the Pacific Basin. Canada's geographic location, coupled with its increasing economic and cultural ties to East Asia, suggest that this country can have a profound effect upon, and will be profoundly affected by, Pacific Rim development in the coming decade. While the risks may be high and the payback period long, the potential return on investment is significant.

PETER N. NEMETZ is an associate professor and former chairman of the Policy Analysis division of the Faculty of Commerce and Business Administration at the University of British Columbia. He is also the editor of the *Journal of Business Administration*, where earlier versions of many of the articles in this book have appeared.

The Pacific Rim: Investment, Development, and Trade

Second Edition

Edited by
Peter N. Nemetz

University of British Columbia Press
Vancouver

Printed in Canada on acid-free paper ∞

ISBN 0-7748-0360-6

Canadian Cataloguing in Publication Data

Main entry under title:
The Pacific Rim

Includes bibliographical references
ISBN 0-7748-0360-6
1. Pacific Area - Commerce. 2. Pacific Area - Economic conditions.
3. Investments, Foreign - Pacific Area. 4. Power resources - Pacific Area.
I. Nemetz, Peter N., 1944–
HC681.P34 1990 338.95 C90-091386-X

University of British Columbia Press
6344 Memorial Road
Vancouver, BC
V6T 1W5

Contents

Tables

Figures

The Pacific Rim: Investment, Development, and Trade

Second Edition

CHAPTER ONE

Investment, Development, and Trade in the Pacific Rim: Introduction and Overview

Peter N. Nemetz

INTRODUCTION

One of the world's most diverse geographic areas, the Asia-Pacific, has been transformed within the last two decades into a global centre of large-scale investment, development, and trade. Manifesting a remarkable diversity of area, population, and wealth (see Table 1), the twenty-six countries that comprise this region can be divided into at least seven distinct national subgroupings: Oceana, ASEAN, the newly industrializing states (NICs), Japan, island states, the People's Republic of China, and four smaller independent communist countries — Kampuchea, Laos, North Korea, and Vietnam. The economic vitality of the Pacific Rim is demonstrated by the dramatic increase in gross domestic product, trade, and industrial activity characteristic of the region's twelve most prominent nations (see Tables 2, 3, and 4).

With average growth in both Gross Domestic Product (GDP) and GDP per capita well in excess of the world's market economies (UN [1988], *1985/6 Statistical Yearbook*: 10-11), the Asia-Pacific bloc is viewed by many investors as an engine of growth that will play a major role in sustaining continued global economic expansion. Because of its blend of plentiful and increasingly sophisticated labour force, capacity for technological innovation, and extensive resource base, this vast and diverse region is expected to be an indispensable source of primary commodities and manufactures for the developed world as well as an

Table 1
Basic Economic, Geographic, and Demographic Data by Country, 1987–8

Grouping	Population (million)	GDP (US$ billion)	GDP/ CAPITA (US$)	Area (sq. km)	Population/ sq. km
OCEANIA					
Australia	16.5	$182.500	$11,061	7,692,300	2.1
New Zealand	3.3	$25.000	$7,576	269,063	12.3
ASEAN					
Indonesia	177.4	$57.000	$321	1,906,240	93.1
Malaysia	17.0	$33.050	$1,944	332,556	51.1
Philippines	63.2	$33.940	$537	300,440	210.4
Singapore	2.6	$19.040	$7,323	618	4207.1
Thailand	54.7	$48.200	$881	514,820	106.3
Brunei	0.3	$3.422	$11,407	5,765	52.0
NICS					
South Korea	42.6	$121.300	$2,847	98,913	430.7
Taiwan	19.8	$91.330	$4,613	35,981	550.3
Hong Kong	5.7	$46.550	$8,167	1,064	5357.1
JAPAN	122.7	$2,387.000	$19,553	381,945	321.3
ISLAND STATES					
Fiji	0.73	$1.099[b]	$1,514	18,376	39.5
Kiribati	0.07	$0.023	$350	690	97.4
Naura	0.01	$0.160[a]	$19,753	21	391.3
Papua New Guinea	3.70	$3.150	$851	475,369	7.8
Western Samoa	0.16	$0.087[b]	$539	2,934	54.9
Solomon Islands	0.29	$0.116[b]	$403	29,785	9.7
Tonga	0.10	$0.100[b]	$1,000	997	100.3
Tuvalu	0.01	$0.004[a]	$444	26	346.2
Vanuatu	0.14	$0.079[b]	$545	14,763	9.8
PRC	1087.0	$295.000	$271	9,600,000	113.2
SMALLER COMMUNIST COUNTRIES					
Kampuchea	7.6	n.a.	n.a.	181,083	41.9
Laos	4.3	$2.826[b]	$653	236,860	18.3
North Korea	21.9	$20.500	$936	121,730	179.9
Vietnam	65.2	$18.100	$278	329,707	197.8

Sources: UN, *Statistical Yearbook;* ADB, *Key Indicators of Developing Member Countries of ADB; Far Eastern Economic Review;* US CIA, *World Factbook*

[a]1984; [b]1986

area with extraordinary new market opportunities for exports from the industrialized nations.

The central issues of trade, investment, and development — their past patterns and prognosis for the future — provide the focus for the first eight chapters of this book. What is perhaps most remarkable

Table 2
Annual Growth Rate in GDP for Major Asia-Pacific Nations (%)

Country	1970	1977	1982	1988
Australia	6.5	2.9	3.1	4.0
New Zealand	3.6[a]	7.6	4.0[d]	1.4[f]
Indonesia	3.6	8.0	7.9	3.6[g]
Malaysia	5.8[a]	9.2	7.8	8.1
Philippines	5.1	6.3	5.5	6.4
Singapore	10.0	8.6	9.6	8.8[g]
Thailand	8.4	6.9	6.8	7.1[g]
South Korea	10.4	10.2	4.6	11.1[g]
Taiwan	12.9[b]	9.9	7.2[e]	11.1[g]
Hong Kong	5.0[a]	1.2	2.4	13.6[g]
Japan	11.5	4.6	4.8	5.6
PRC	n.a.	12.0[e]	3.0[d]	10.3[g]

Sources: UN, *Statistical Yearbook;* World Bank, *World Tables;* US CIA, *World Factbook;* Republic of China, *Handy Economic Data Kit;* IMF, *International Financial Statistics;* ADB, *Key Indicators of Developing Member Countries of ADB*

[a]1970/71; [b]1971; [c]1978; [d]1980/81; [e]1983; [f]1986; [g]1987

Table 3
Total Industrial Activity as Percentage of GDP of Major Asia-Pacific Nations

Country	1970	1977	1982	1986
Australia	33	30	30	34
New Zealand	26	26	27	33
Indonesia	15	29	36	37
Malaysia	24/13.4[a]	20[a]	21.3[a]	25[a]
Philippines	26	28	29	32
Singapore	23	27	32	38
Thailand	19	22	23	30
South Korea	24	30	32	42
Taiwan	37	44	43	43
Hong Kong	33	27[c]	27[d]	29
Japan	39	33	34	41
PRC[e]	40[b]	44.2[a,c]	42.3[c]	46

Sources: UN, *Statistical Yearbook;* Republic of China, *Statistical Yearbook;* World Bank, *World Tables; Far Eastern Economic Review;* ADB, *Key Indicators of Developing Member Countries of ADB*

[a]manufacturing only; [b]percentage of net material product; [c]1978; [d]1980; [e]1981

about this impressive record of economic activity is that it came in a period marked by global economic disruption caused to a large degree by the energy crises of 1973, 1979, and 1986. Yet it would be incorrect to assume that energy is incidental to the economic vitality of this region. The second part of this volume examines in closer detail the

Table 4
Merchandise Exports from Major Asia-Pacific Countries, FOB (US $ million)

Country	1970	1977	1982	1987
Australia	4,770	13,351	22,002	25,035
New Zealand	1,225	3,198	5,524	6,350
Indonesia	1,108	10,853	22,293	16,780
Malaysia	1,687	6,079	12,030	17,930
Philippines	1,142	3,127	4,968	5,220
Singapore	1,554	8,241	20,788	28,692
Thailand	710	3,490	6,945	11,654
South Korea	835	10,047	21,853	47,282
Taiwan	1,481	7,520	21,872	53,534
Hong Kong	2,514	9,616	20,984	48,476
Japan	19,319	80,493	138,911	229,221
PRC	2,260	7,520	21,872	34,100

Sources: UN, *Statistical Yearbook*; Republic of China, *Statistical Yearbook*; ADB, *Key Indicators of Developing Member Countries of ADB*; US CIA, *World Factbook*

critical role of energy supply and demand in the future development of the Pacific Rim and its interdependence with other global regions.

JAPAN, ASEAN, AND THE NICs

A significant proportion of the economic vitality associated with the Pacific Basin has been attributable both directly and indirectly to one nation, Japan. Viewed by some as the next, and perhaps preeminent, global superpower (Brown et al. 1986; Vogel 1979), Japan has, in the postwar period, built a dynamic and resilient economic system despite a considerable reliance on imports for basic necessities (see Table 5).

Japan has become, and will continue to be in the indefinite future, the most significant driving force in the development and integration of the Western Pacific. In many respects, the process of Japanese industrial development and concomitant trade has had a profound influence on the evolution of other major developing countries in the Far East, such as Korea and Taiwan. This chain of influence, or "ladder of development," extends downward to encompass the ASEAN nations of Indonesia, Malaysia, the Philippines, Singapore, and Thailand. The effect of Japanese development has been pervasive; it has contributed significantly to the expansion of Australia's resource industries and, more recently, played a central role in the international participation in Chinese industrial expansion. This accomplishment is remarkable given Japan's relative scarcity of many important resource commodities, most notably energy.

Much analytical research generated in the past few years has

Table 5
Japan's Reliance on Offshore Resources

Commodity	Reliance (%)	Date	Reference
Bananas	100.0	1986	Hitachi
Bauxite and alumina	100.0	1986	Keizai
Cobalt	100.0	1985	U.S. Interior
Coffee beans	100.0	1986	Hitachi
Columbium	100.0	1985	U.S. Interior
Corn	100.0	1987	Keizai
Cotton	100.0	1986	JETRO
Mica (sheet)	100.0	1985	U.S. Interior
Nickel	100.0	1987	Keizai
Oranges	100.0	1986	Hitachi
Phosphate	100.0	1985	U.S. Interior
Potash	100.0	1985	U.S. Interior
Silicon	100.0	1985	U.S. Interior
Strontium	100.0	1984	Morgan
Tanatalum	100.0	1985	U.S. Interior
Wool	100.0	1980	JETRO
Iron ore	99.9	1987	Keizai
Crude oil	99.7	1987	Keizai
Tin	99.7	1987	Keizai
Chromium	99.0	1984	Morgan
Manganese	99.0	1985	U.S. Interior
Molybdenum	99.0	1985	U.S. Interior
Asbestos	98.0	1985	U.S. Interior
Copper	97.4	1987	Keizai
Platinum group	97.0	1985	U.S. Interior
Soybeans	96.0	1986	Hitachi
Natural gas	94.7	1987	Keizai
Gold	94.0	1985	U.S. Interior
Tomatoes	90.0	1986	Hitachi
Coal	88.9	1987	Keizai
Lead	87.2	1987	JETRO
Aluminum	86.0	1985	U.S. Interior
Wheat	86.0	1987	Keizai
Honey	83.0	1986	Hitachi
Buckwheat	81.0	1986	Hitachi
Mercury	79.0	1984	Morgan
Tungsten	79.0	1986	Hitachi
Zinc	76.2	1987	Keizai
Lobsters/shrimp	74.0	1986	Morgan
Octopus	72.0	1986	Hitachi
Wood and lumber	64.3	1986	JETRO
Barite	40.0	1985	U.S. Interior
Salmon	37.0	1986	Hitachi
Cow's milk	22.0	1987	JETRO
Meat	22.0	1987	Keizai
Squid	17.0	1986	Hitachi

Table 5 (continued)

Commodity	Reliance (%)	Date	Reference
Textiles and clothing	9.4	1977-9	Bunge
Fats and oils	9.0	1987	Keizai
Chemicals	6.8	1977-9	Bunge
Iron and steel	5.7	1977-9	Bunge
Gypsum	4.0	1984	Morgan
Rubber	4.0	1977-9	Bunge
Hen eggs	3.0	1987	Keizai

Sources: Bunge 1982; JETRO 1982, 1987; US Department of the Interior 1988; Hitachi 1986; Keizai Koho 1989

attempted to explain the Japanese phenomenon, attributing its success in whole or in part to such internal variables as cultural homogeneity, an excellent educational system, close government-business co-operation, the provision of low-cost capital to selected industries, long-term business strategy, a preoccupation with labour peace, consensus decision-making and quality control in the industrial system, a low level of defence expenditures, a high rate of personal savings, postwar industrial reconstruction, extensive participation by banks in the industrial sector, various tariff and non-tariff barriers, and a pronounced need to compensate for domestic deficiencies of vital foodstuffs and raw materials.[1]

Understanding the Japanese experience also requires, however, a clear knowledge of external factors, particularly the pattern of Japan's investment and trade with other nations. It is this task which *Yoko Sazanami* of Keio University undertakes in this volume. Her analysis of Japanese economic interdependence with other Pacific nations describes the remarkably dynamic phasing of economic activities among groups of countries within the region. Professor Sazanami records several shifts in the pattern of Japanese foreign investment and trade from the late 1960s to the early 1980s: first, a focus on investment in offshore resource development to guarantee a supply of relatively inexpensive raw materials; second, a shift to investment in foreign manufacturing to take advantage of low production wages and to avoid trade barriers in developing countries; third, a growth in investment in specific foreign energy projects and a shifting of energy-intensive manufacturing offshore in the period following the 1973 oil crisis; and, fourth, a diversified strategy which included, for example, a shift of investment from resource development in such areas as ASEAN to materials processing.

As Professor Sazanami recognizes, the lack of corporate data frequently increases the difficulty of assessing the impact of investment patterns on the changing Japanese import mix. Clearly, however, such an impact exists, and it is potentially very large. The broad linkage between investment and trade is indisputable, and as Sazanami concludes: "The development of Japanese direct investment in Pacific Rim countries between 1973 and 1983 generally corresponded to the development of trade interdependence."

Tracey Redies updates the study of Japanese international economic policy by outlining in detail the nature of, and rationale for, the profound change in Japan's foreign direct investment in the 1980s:

> For over three decades Japanese foreign direct investment was largely utilized as a means of protecting the cost and availability of critical imported natural resources, maintaining access to export markets, and compensating for the inevitable loss of sectoral comparative advantage that accompanied the country's economic evolution. From the mid-1980s onwards, the macroeconomic characteristics of the Japanese economy, international balance of payments surpluses, and massive appreciations in the value of the yen have created a huge, usable pool of capital in excess of domestic needs. This capital has combined with the needs of the large Japanese financial and industrial companies for international market "elbow room" for their products and services to unleash a flood of foreign direct investment. These investments are different from their defensive predecessors. They are targeted at establishing a substantial international presence. The leading investor companies intend to establish manufacturing facilities for their products or delivery centres for their services that are optimally located to serve the major global markets in the most efficient and profitable way attainable. As with their export strategies of the past, the major Japanese companies will seek dominance or, at least, significant influence in their fields of activity.

The nature of export composition and performance of Japan's trading partners is the subject of a complementary study by *Rod Tyers and Prue Phillips*, who focus their analysis on ASEAN. The trends in international trade studied by the authors are "dominated by major shifts in the distribution of factor endowments (particularly physical and human capital) between countries in the Pacific Basin and their associated impacts on specialization in exports." The authors document the shifts in production patterns in the Basin that respond to changing factor availability and prices.

> There has been a striking decline in the relative importance of labour-intensive exports from Japan. ... Correspondingly, Japan has developed a significant comparative advantage in technology- and human-capital-

> intensive goods. . . . A similar but more subdued pattern is observable for the Asian NICs. . . . As real wages continue to grow in the Asian NICs, their degree of export specialization in labour-intensive goods can be expected to decline further. Although this trend should see an expansion in the role of labour-intensive manufacturers in ASEAN exports, the gap left by the Asian NICs is more likely to be filled by China. . . .
>
> As the capital endowments of the ASEAN countries continue to rise, these countries should specialize increasingly in manufactured exports. Relative to their principal trading partners, the ASEAN countries have a growing comparative advantage in labour-intensive goods. Relative to China, however, their comparative advantage remains in natural-resource-based goods. In the world market for labour-intensive manufactures China may be a formidable competitor. The degree to which ASEAN manufactured exports are labour-intensive may depend, therefore, on the pattern and growth of China's exports.

This analysis suggests a dynamic and healthy evolutionary pattern where groups of nations are passing through successive stages of industrialization relatively rapidly in response to changing patterns of investment, factor availability, and prices. The generally increasing wealth associated with this process is no small reason why many of the other global trading blocs have looked to the Pacific Rim as a strong and continuing source of imports and as a market for exports.

A cogent example of these evolutionary changes in production and trade is provided by Figures 1-3, which focus on clothing exports, aluminum production, and shipbuilding. These data illustrate in particular how several critical adjustments in Japan's industrial base have been accompanied by compensatory changes in other Pacific Basin nations. The best example is provided by clothing exports, the production of which has been traditionally labour-intensive and consequently highly sensitive to wage rates. Figure 1 demonstrates how Japan's decreasing role in this market has been followed by the successive entry of Korea, China, and several of the ASEAN countries. In a somewhat similar manner, Japan's sensitivity to energy costs and environmental concerns has prompted a shift away from aluminum production (Figure 2) — a change that has been accompanied by increased output in China and Indonesia, although trading patterns have not demonstrated as marked a change as of yet. Finally, Figure 3, while illustrating Japan's continuing pre-eminence in the shipbuilding industry, also demonstrates the increasing role in this field of a newly industrializing country like Korea. In moving away from such basic goods as clothing, aluminum, and petrochemicals, Japan has opted for more human capital- and technology-intensive commodi-

Figure 1 Clothing Exports of Selected Pacific Rim Countries (SITC # 84)

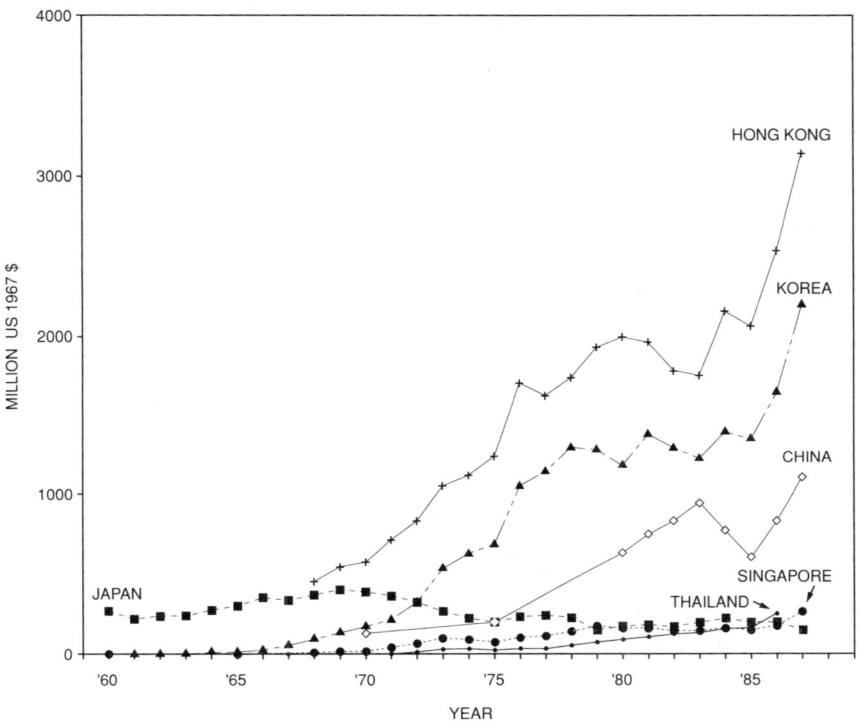

ties, for example, road vehicles and electrical machinery including computers. (See Kodama 1986; and Figure 4.) In fact, one of the first tangible indicators of the emerging strength of the Japanese economy in the postwar period was the growth in production of its automobile industry, particularly with respect to the United States. (See Halberstam 1986; and Figure 5.)

In light of the extraordinary and interrelated opportunities that accompany the rapid economic expansion of the Pacific Basin, what are appropriate strategies for the countries in the process of economic development? In his contribution to this volume, Professor *Theodore Panayotou* shows that the lessons derived from Thailand "are of relevance ... to other developing countries in the region, such as the Philippines, Indonesia, and Malaysia, which have been following similar development strategies." In his view, the problem is that:

Figure 2 Primary Aluminum Production of Selected Pacific Rim Countries

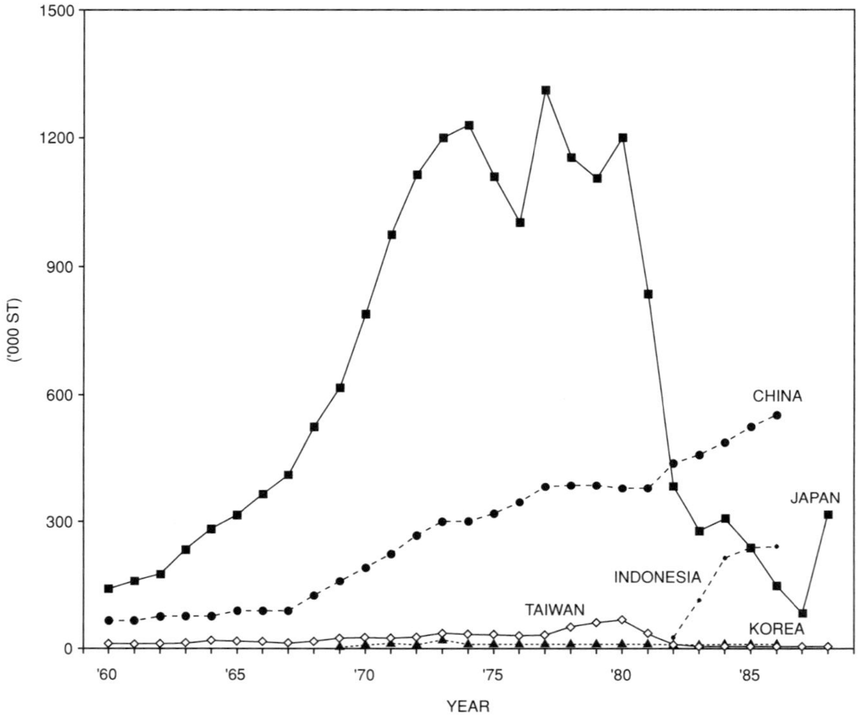

Agriculture, which receives the lion's share of development assistance, faces absorptive capacity constraints at home and depressed prices abroad. Industrial exports, which enjoy generous promotional privileges, face increasing protectionism from developed countries, at a time when foreign exchange earnings are needed to service a rising foreign debt and to contain a growing balance of trade deficit. Equally disturbing is the growing employment deficit at home. Agriculture is increasingly becoming labour-saving as it shifts from the extensive to the intensive margin, while urban-based industry is becoming increasingly capital-intensive because of factor-price distortions and promotional incentives.

Panayotou makes the case for "investment in the development of labour-intensive rural industry to support and supplement agricultural development, which faces absorptive capacity constraints, and to compete with the capital intensive urban-based industry, which

Figure 3 Merchant Vessels: Tonnage Launched in Selected Pacific Rim Countries

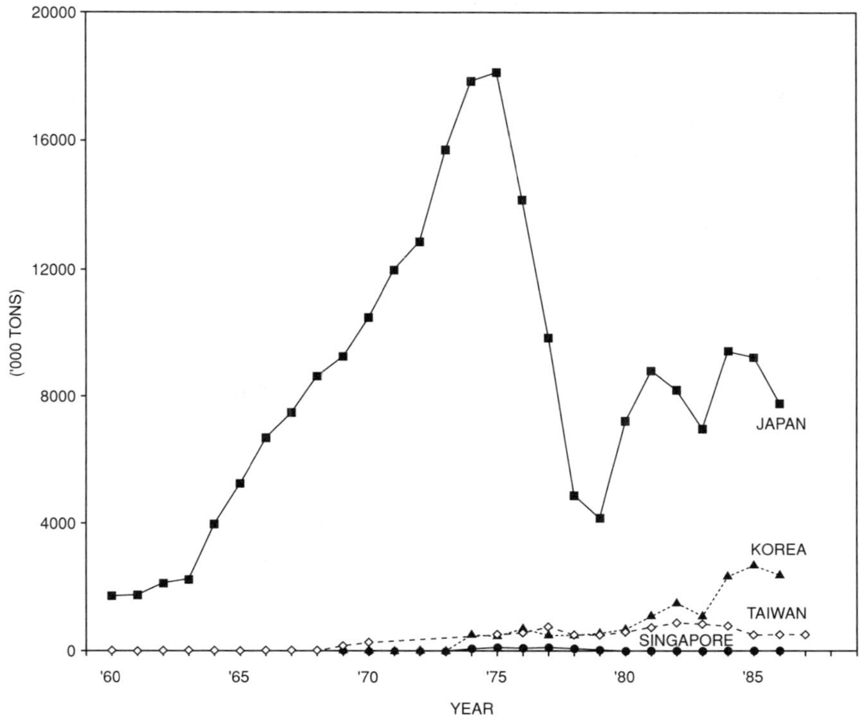

has been overpromoted with little regard to employment, market demand, and balanced growth."

There are two areas of concern mentioned by the author that are particularly relevant to the discussion of the continuation and stability of the process of economic growth in Southeast Asia and in many other developing countries. The first is the ecological price frequently associated with population growth and economic development. In Thailand, "rapid expansion into watershed areas and marginal lands has brought about second-generation problems (erosion, floods, droughts) that pose a threat to the resource base and hence to the sustainability of Thai agriculture."

Unfortunately, the problem is not confined to Thailand, as is illustrated by the selected data on global deforestation rates in Table 6. The reasons are multifold, but, in essence, they are attributable to several basic pressures: a need for greater fuelwood supply for domestic

Figure 4 Electrical Machinery Exports of Selected Pacific Rim Countries (SITC #75, #76, #77)

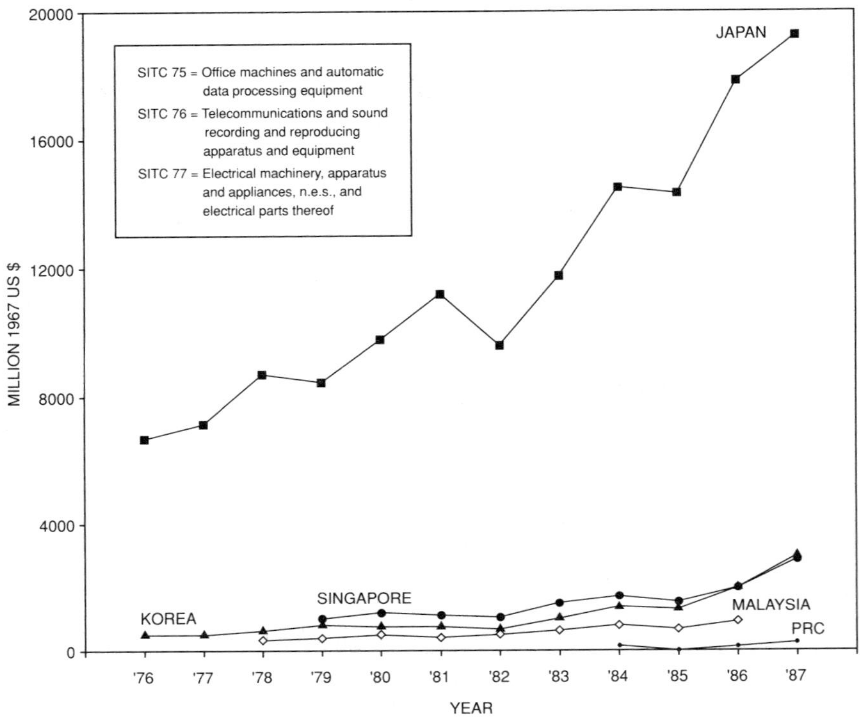

heating and cooking; a requirement for greater land area for agriculture; and a demand for domestic and foreign exchange earnings from tropical wood products. Deforestation has approached the crisis level in the developing world, and it has prompted several major studies of possible policy reforms (see, for example, World Resources Institute et al. 1985).

The second critical issue touched on by Panayotou is socioeconomic and political stability. The events of the past two decades have begun to offer the prospect of improvement in the living conditions for hundreds of millions of people. The process of economic growth has a profound impact on social and political institutions and can create a momentum of expectations, which, should that growth falter, can ultimately lessen the stability of these institutions and their inherent processes.

While the slowing or loss of economic growth may portend social

Figure 5 Automobile Production in Selected Pacific Rim Countries

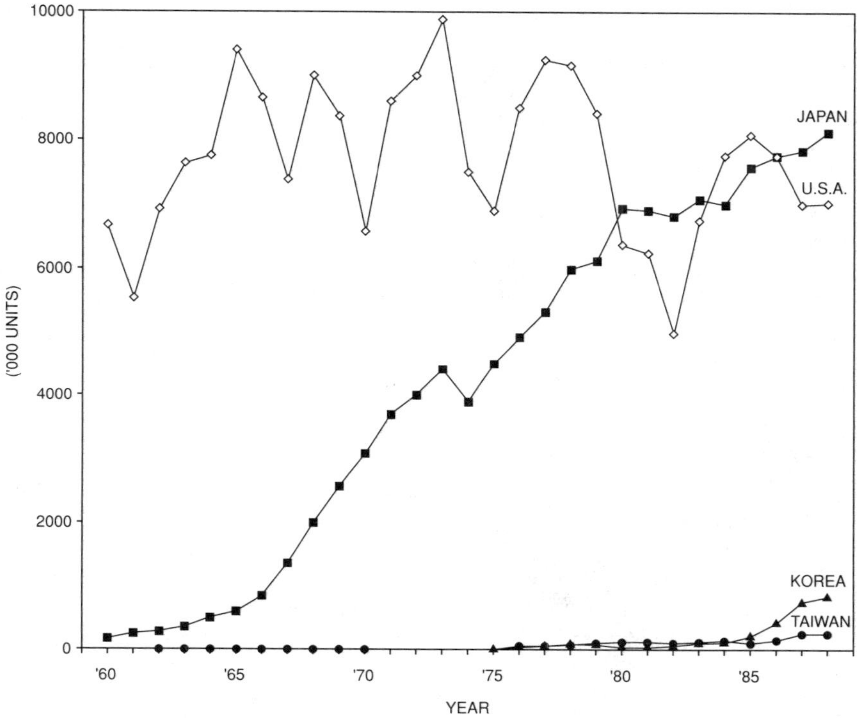

and political dislocation on a national scale, it is frequently smaller population subgroupings that first feel the brunt of these difficulties. An example of such a group is the Nanyang (or Overseas) Chinese, who have played a central role in the commercial development of Southeast Asia. The treatment of Nanyang Chinese, and indeed any significant minority, can provide a bellwether of the social, economic, and political health of a nation. Past events in Indonesia and more recent stresses in Malaysia are indicative of this phenomenon.

While offering the tempting promise of revitalization for a stagnant world economy, the economic situation in the Western Pacific is more complex and uncertain and, indeed, unstable than it may first appear. There are several symptoms that lead to this more cautious prognosis: falling prices for commodities like rubber, tin, palm oil, timber, sugar, copra, rice, and tapioca (see Tables 7 and 8); growing protectionist sentiments in such large and crucial markets as the United States

Table 6
Rates of Deforestation in Selected Countries (1980s)

PACIFIC RIM	Average annual extent ('000 hectares per year)	Per cent per year	Reforestation (1980s) ('000 hectares per year)
Thailand	397	2.5	31
Vietnam	173	1.7	36
Philippines	143	1.5	63
Malaysia	255	1.2	25
Indonesia	920	0.8	164
Papua New Guinea	23	0.1	2
SELECTED OTHER COUNTRIES (for comparative purposes)			
Costa Rica	124	6.9	1
Côte d'Ivoire	510	5.2	8
Nepal	84	4.0	5
Haiti	2	3.8	0
Sri Lanka	58	3.5	16
Argentina	1550	3.5	40
Malawi	150	3.5	1
El Salvador	5	3.2	0
Jamaica	2	3.0	1
Brazil	9050	1.8	561

Source: WRI, *World Resources 1988–9 and 1990–1*

sentiments in such large and crucial markets as the United States concerning critical goods like textiles and automobiles; and "shake-outs" in specific international industries, for example, computers and related microelectronics.

Underlying the potential difficulties that face several of the Southeast Asia nations are political and social factors whose contribution to instability can increase in an adverse economic environment. Included among these are communist insurgency and military rebellion in the Philippines, racial and religious friction in Malaysia, and political instability of Thailand's neighbours, Kampuchea and Myanmar (formerly called Burma).

RISKS

A critical factor in the record of economic growth in the Asia-Pacific region has been the achievement of full sovereignty and independence by many nations in the postwar period. The remarkable political, social, and economic diversity that, in many respects, contributes to the area's strength, also generates risks — a continuing potential for disruption and the concomitant threat to the edifice of investment and trade.

The last half century of the Pacific Rim's history has been marked by

Table 7
Major Commodity Exports of Selected Pacific Rim Countries
(1984–5 by 3-digit SITC code) (as percentage of all exports)

Country	First (%)	Second (%)	Third (%)	Fourth (%)
Australia	#321 coal, coke, briquettes 15.9	#041 wheat, etc. unmilled 9.4	#262 wool & animal hair 8.3	#281 iron ore, concentrates 6.4
Hong Kong	#841 clothing, not of fur 32.6	#894 toys, sporting goods 8.1	#724 telecommunications equipment 6.8	#864 watches & clocks 6.8
Indonesia	#331 crude petroleum 47.6	#341 natural gas 17.7	#631 veneers, plywood 4.3	#231 rubber, crude, synthetic 4.1
Japan	#732 road motor vehicles 22.6	#724 telecommunications equipment 6.7	#891 sound recorders and parts 6.6	#729 electrical machinery nes 5.8
Korea	#735 ships & boats 16.3	#841 clothing, not of fur 14.5	#724 telecommunications equipment 5.4	#729 electrical machinery nes 5.0
Malaysia	#331 crude petroleum 22.9	Other fixed vegetable oil 13.3	#729 electrical machinery nes 12.5	#231 rubber, crude, synthetic 8.6
New Zealand	#011 meat fresh, chilled, frozen 19.6	#262 wool & animal hair 13.0	#023 butter 6.0	#022 milk and cream 5.0
Philippines	#422 other fixed vegetable oil 9.4	#729 electrical machinery nes 6.0	#841 clothing not of fur 5.2	#051 fruit fresh, nuts fresh, dry 4.8
PRC (in 1987)	yarn, fabrics, manufactured goods and related products 14.7	petroleum, petroleum products & related materials 10.2	clothing and garments 9.5	textile fibres and their waste materials 3.8
Singapore	#332 petroleum products 25.8	#729 electrical machinery nes 7.8	#714 office machines 5.4	#724 telecommunications equipment 5.4
Taiwan (in 1984)	electrical machinery 21.6	textile products 20.0	metal products and machinery 9.5	plastic products 8.3
Thailand	#042 rice 13.4	#054 vegetables etc. fresh, simply preserved 9.1	#841 clothing not of fur 7.8	#231 rubber, crude, synthetic 7.3

Source: Bunge, F.M., ed. (1984). *Malaysia: A Country Study;* Keizai Koho Center, Japan (1988). *An International Comparison, 1977;* People's Republic of China (1988). *China Statistical Yearbook;* Republic of China (1985). *Handy Economic Data Kit;* UN (1988). *Handbook of International Trade and Development Statistics;* UN, *Statistical Yearbook, 1983/84*. Table 166; US CIA (1984). *The World Factbook;* World Bank (1983). *China, Socialist Economic Development*. Vol. 1

Table 8
Price Indexes of Major Commodity Exports of the Asia-Pacific (1985 = 100)

Commodity	Location	1980	1986	1988
Food		133.5	87.8	114.9
Beverages		113.2	115.3	82.8
Agricultural raw materials		128.7	101.6	148.5
Metals		142.9	94.1	166.0
Bananas	Latin America	99.2	101.0	117.8
Beef	All origins (US ports)	128.2	97.3	116.9
Butter	New Zealand (London)	149.2	113.5	138.5
Coal	Australia	113.5	98.4	90.9
Cocoa beans	New York & London	115.5	91.7	70.2
Coconut oil	Philippines (New York)	114.0	50.2	95.7
Coffee	All (New York)	112.9	127.6	86.2
Copper	UK (London)	154.2	96.7	183.4
Copra	Philippines (Europe)	117.2	51.1	102.5
Hides	Australia	179.8	123.4	224.5
Iron ore	Brazil (North Sea ports)	120.2	96.6	102.0
Lamb	New Zealand (London)	157.0	110.8	131.0
Logs	Malaysia (Tokyo)	143.5	111.0	171.4
Maize	Thailand	158.8	86.1	122.7
Palm oil	Malaysia (Europe)	116.4	51.3	87.3
Pepper, black	Malaysia (New York)	52.2	126.5	n.a.
Phosphate rock	Morocco (Casablanca)	137.7	101.3	102.5
Plywood	Philippines (Tokyo)	129.8	130.0	170.1
Rice	Thailand (Bangkok)	199.5	96.7	138.7
Rubber	Malaysia (Singapore)	187.8	106.3	156.2
Sawnwood	Malaysia (France)	133.8	96.4	110.9
Sugar	Australia	360.8	136.4	163.8
	Philippines	108.6	117.8	127.3
Tin	Malaysia (Penang)	137.3	49.9	59.0
Wheat	Australia (Sydney)	202.4	81.1	118.9
Wool	Australia–New Zealand (UK)	142.6	108.1	155.1

Source: IMF, *International Financial Statistics*

of these nations emerged with new political structures in the aftermath of World War II and the colonial era. Two major wars, one on the Korean Peninsula and the other in Southeast Asia, have provided particularly strong evidence of the volatility of this region and it susceptibility to superpower conflict as well as of continuing historical animosities. In addition to these two most obvious and destructive events, there has been a progression of potentially disruptive developments that contribute either directly or indirectly to a range of risks faced by the nations in this region today.

Table 9 provides a short summary of some of the most important of these historical events by country. What is noteworthy about this information is the extent of the impact of these events upon the

Table 9
Major Historical Events, by Country

Country	1940s	1950s	1960s	1970s	1980s
Hong Kong			1967 riots		1983 rioting in response to price increases in food and other basics Sept. 1983 concern over political future placed severe downward (but temporary) pressure on HK$ July 1986 Hong Kong/US Textile & Apparel agreement curtailing exports 1989 increased capital flight in reaction to events in PRC; and concern over UK-PRC agreement to pass control to PRC in 1997
Indonesia	17 Aug. 1945 Sukarno declares independence 27 Dec. 1949 formal transfer of sovereignty	March 1957 minor local coups plus continuing Islamic resistance to central government 14 March 1957 martial law Dec. 1957 46,000 Dutch expelled 15 Feb. 1958 revolt at Bukittinggi 16 Nov. 1959 Chinese forbidden from trading in rural areas	1960 Indonesian-Dutch military engagement in W. New Guinea Sept. 1963 military activity initiated against Malaysia Feb. 1965 govt. seizes US rubber plants Sept. 1965 abortive communist coup attempt; result was anti-communist & anti-Chinese violence. Estimated 500,000 killed March 1967 Sukarno removed from office	Jan. 1974 "Malari Affair" — riots against Japanese and Chinese economic influence 7 Dec. 1975 Indonesian troops land on East Timor. Guerrilla war continues until 1978	1984 violent demonstration by Islamic fundamentalists

Table 9 (continued)
Major Historical Events, by Country

Country	1940s	1950s	1960s	1970s	1980s
Japan	3 May 1947 new constitution	April 1952 US military occupation terminated; full independence restored		1973 embargo by OPEC of Japanese oil purchases	7 Jan 1989 Emperor Hirohito dies 25 May 1989 US labels Japan as unfair trading partner under provisions of 1988 Trade Act Prime Ministers Takashita and Uno resign
Korea	15 Aug. 1948 republic proclaimed	25 June 1950–27 July 1953 Korean War 1956 martial law	26 April 1960 President Rhee resigns after student revolt over fraudulent March election 16 May 1961 coup by Park June 1964 Seoul under martial law in response to riots April 1965 student riots in Seoul	Dec. 1971 Park declares national emergency Oct. 1972 martial law Aug. 1979 "Y.H. Incident" worker demonstrations 26 Oct. 1979 Park murdered by KCIA	May 1980 coup foiled 1987 anti-government demonstrations prompt electoral reforms and presidential election Nov. 1988 student protest demonstrations
Malaysia	1 Feb. 1948 Federation of Malaya Agreement 18 June 1948 state of emergency following communist attacks on rubber plantations 1949–51 major communist armed offensive	31 Aug. 1957 independence	Jan. 1963 Indonesia announces confrontation policy against proposed federation 16 Sept. 1963 Malaysia formed, followed by some border incidents and sabotage 1964–5 attempted trade embargo by Indonesia 9 Aug. 1965 Singapore separates 11 Aug. 1966 peace with Indonesia May 1969 ethnic riots follow election		1989 Communist rebels abandon armed struggle

Table 9 (continued)
Major Historical Events, by Country

Country	1940s	1950s	1960s	1970s	1980s
Philippines	4 July 1946 Independence 1949–50 height of peasant Huk rebellion based on tenant-landlord grievances		1965 Marcos elected president	Jan. 1970 anti-corruption demonstrations 1970–2 growing communist insurgency plus religious strife and Muslim insurgency 21 Sept. 1972 Marcos declares martial law 1978 Marcos assumes premiership	Aug. 1983 Benigno Aquino murdered 1983 demonstrations by opposition lead to political instability, economic crisis, capital flight Feb. 1986 Marcos departs; Corazon Aquino in office 1986 & series of coup attempts, strikes, and guerrilla attacks 1989 abortive coup attempt by army dissidents
PRC	1 Oct. 1949 PRC founded	Oct. 1950 intervention in Korean War 1958–60 Great Leap Forward 1959 beginning of Soviet technicians' withdrawal 1959 Indo-Chinese border dispute	Oct. 1962 Sino-Indian border clash 1966–8 Cultural Revolution Sept. 1967 Sino-Indian artillery duel 1969 Sino-Soviet border clash	1971 coup attempt by Lin Biao Early 1976 (prior to Mao's death) — temporary resurgence of radicalism 1976 Mao dies; followed by "coup attempt" by his widow, Jiang Qing	Oct. 1986 some urban disturbances over inflation June 1989 Tiananmen Square massacre

Table 9 (continued)
Major Historical Events, by Country

Country	1940s	1950s	1960s	1970s	1980s
Singapore		1950 ethnic riots 1955 some communist-inspired internal unrest (riots & strikes) 1956 further riots and strikes 1957 home rule	16 Sept. 1963 Singapore joins Malaya, Sarawak and Sabah to form Malaysia Oct. 1963 government forestalls general strike June & Sept. 1964 race riots 1964–5 attempted trade embargo by Indonesia 9 Aug. 1965 Singapore separates from Malaysia 1968 British announce pullout 1969 ethnic riots		1989 Prime Minister Lee announces plans to step down in 1990
Taiwan	Dec. 1949 seat of Nationalist government moved to Taiwan	1954–8 sporadic military activity by PRC against Nationalist islands	June 1965 US ends economic aid	1975 US withdraws last combat aircraft 5 April 1975 Chiang Kai-shek dies	13 January 1988 death of President Chiang Ching-kuo (son of Chiang Kai-shek)
Thailand	Nov. 1947 military coup	1951 government-engineered coup 1952–3 anti-communist campaign focused on local Chinese Sept. 1957 coup by army	1960s communist insurgency from Malaysia in south; Muslim insurgency; Meo insurgency in north; communist insurgency in NE	Nov. 1971 government-inspired coup 1973 student demonstrations bring end to military dictatorship July 1976 US completes troop withdrawal 6 Oct. 1976 military coup Oct. 1977 military junta seizes control	April 1981 and Sept. 1985 coup attempts by army dissidents

national economies. In data (albeit incomplete) on GDP levels and growth by country over the postwar period, the instances where GDP actually declined are relatively infrequent and short-lived (see Table 10). The most precipitous drop in national GDP in the Pacific Rim was associated with China's Great Leap Forward. Its impact and the subsequent Cultural Revolution are depicted in Figure 6. From a strategic management perspective on investment opportunities, the pattern of national GDP growth rates in the Pacific Rim is at least one indication of the potential resilience within this global economic subsystem.

Table 11 attempts to summarize some of the major short/medium and medium/long-term country-specific risks within the Basin. It is apparent that the roots of some of these potential threats to economic growth and stability can be traced directly to the historical events in Table 9. A dichotomous typology of risks is presented in Table 12. This type of analysis also provides some guidance with respect to strategic investment opportunities, for it helps to identify the nature and extent of country-specific risks that may be minimized by a diversified investment strategy.

It is the generic/global risks, however, that are significantly less amenable to such a diversified portfolio protection approach. For example, American protectionism is of particular concern to many nations of the Pacific Rim. Several basic economic indicators can be utilized to identify potential protectionist disputes by country. The first of these is the balance of trade between the United States and selected Pacific Rim nations over the period 1972-88 (see Table 13). Countries running significant trade surpluses with the US, such as Japan, Korea, Hong Kong, and Taiwan, have experienced increasing American pressure and restrictive and/or retaliatory measures. A cogent example of such a response was the American decision of 29 January 1988 to end special trade preferences to Taiwan, South Korea, Hong Kong, and Singapore (*New York Times*, 30 January 1988).

Second, it is possible to identify a subset of Pacific Rim countries that, because of chronic current account deficits (Table 14), can be expected to consider the use of tariff or nontariff barriers and other forms of government intervention in trade to ameliorate their economic situation. At least two nations, Malaysia and Indonesia, have pursued such a policy despite the risks of retaliation (Nemetz 1990).

It is the other three generic/global risks, namely, the continuing vulnerability of the US dollar, Third World debt, and oil price instability, that may pose the greatest threat to economic vitality in the Pacific Rim. With respect to recent exchange rates for the major Pacific Rim nations against the US dollar, the Taiwanese NT$ and Japanese yen have performed the best, with the Chinese yuan, Indonesian rupiah,

Table 10
Some Decreases in GDP and Associated Events

Country	Dates	Related events
Indonesia	1963	Gross economic mismanagement marked by hyperinflation and high foreign debt
Japan	1974	OPEC oil price increase
Korea	1980	Recession induced by oil price increases and attempted government restructuring of economy, including stabilization measures entailing lowering of growth rate and stringent tight-money policy, and shift of investment from heavy to light industry
Malaysia	1952–3*	58.5% decrease in the price of rubber from the high associated with the Korean War
	1958*	Culmination of a 25% drop in the price of rubber over the previous three years. (9% in 1957/8)
	1985	Country's key export commodities (esp. oil, LNG, tin, rubber, palm oil, and timber) experience depressed world prices
New Zealand	1967	Sharp recession as a result of a severe drop in the price of wool on world markets. The terms of trade index which stood at 107 in 1965/6 fell to 86 in March 1967. UK devalued sterling by 14%; NZ felt compelled to follow with 19.5% devaluation
	1975	NZ's terms of trade reach lowest level since WWII. Price of oil had major role in the decline of the terms of trade index from its peak of 124 in June 1973 to 70 in March 1975
Philippines	1984, 1986	Political and economic aftermath of Aquino murder
PRC	1959–61	Great Leap Forward
	1967	Cultural Revolution
	1976	Temporary resurgence of political radicalism prior to Mao's death and subsequent power struggle, plus moderate contraction in agricultural sector
Singapore	1964	Indonesian "confrontation" policy and attempted trade embargo imposed on Singapore by Indonesia
	1985	Recession attributed especially to labour shortages and wage increases in 1980s

*Only nominal GNP data are available for Malaya/Malaysia in the period prior to 1972. The three years listed in the table (1952, 1953, and 1958) represent decreases in these nominal values. It is likely that decreases in GNP also occurred in several other years, such as 1956 and 1957, when rubber prices fell substantially and nominal GNP rose only marginally.

and Philippine peso the worst (see Table 15). At least one major caveat is required in the interpretation of these data. In some cases, governments play a very active role in the foreign exchange market either by

Table 11
Some Current and Future Country-Specific Risks

Country	Short-medium term	Medium-long term
Hong Kong	Uncertainty over PRC control post-1997 Concern over US protectionism, esp. with respect to textiles & apparel	Uncertainty over PRC control post-1997 Rising real wages leading to lower competitiveness in labour intensive & low-technology goods
Indonesia		Social unrest from labour force growth outstripping job creation; income maldistribution
Japan	Concern over US protectionism in response to trade surplus Adverse foreign response to continuing difficulty of access to domestic markets	Concern over US protectionism Increasing competition from NICs
Korea	Transition to pluralistic society from authoritarian society (esp. concern over political role of military, labour-management relations, regional animosities, distributional shares); US response to Korean protectionism; world protectionism (esp. on steel)	Concerns over military intentions of N. Korea
Malaysia		Ethnic & racial tensions related to distribution of income & state of economy; religious fundamentalism
Philippines	Continuing threat of military coups; US protectionism (e.g., sugar)	Communist insurgency
PRC	Concern over US & European protectionism, esp. textiles Reestablishing confidence of foreign investors after Tiananmen Square incident	Succession to new generation of leadership Transition to more market-oriented system, esp. resistance of conservatives; effect on social fabric of accompanying inflation in key commodities from price realignments, unemployment, new personal wealth differentials
Singapore	Political succession	External protectionism; low birth rate; cost-competitiveness; interethnic balance & peace
Taiwan	Political succession and relationship between native Taiwanese and older mainlander power blocs; US concern over large trade surplus (e.g., textiles)	PRC desire for ultimate reunification
Thailand	Khmer Rouge insurgency in Cambodia and destabilizing influence of refugees; Karen insurgency in Burma; US protectionism (e.g., textiles, rice); territorial dispute with Malaysia in S. China Sea concerning hydrocarbons	Maldistribution of income esp. rural/urban split; deforestation

Figure 6 PRC National Income (1980 prices)

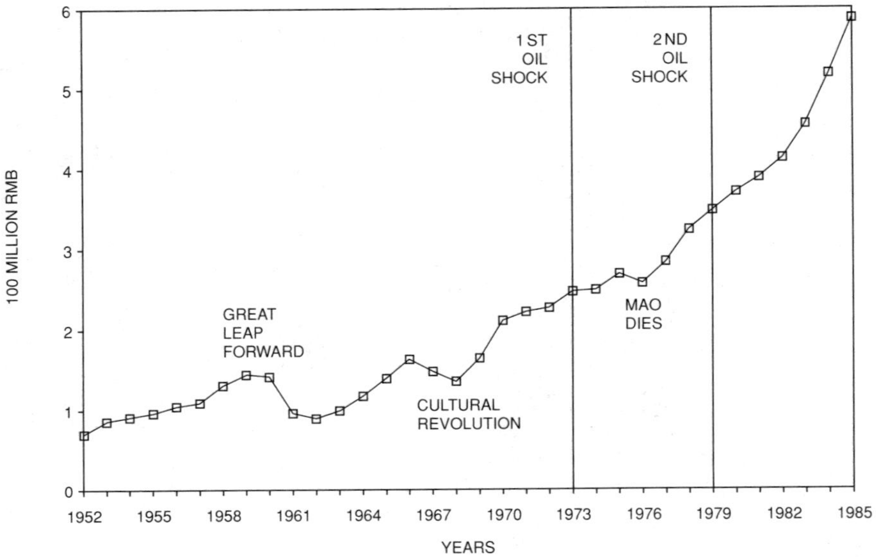

PRC National Growth

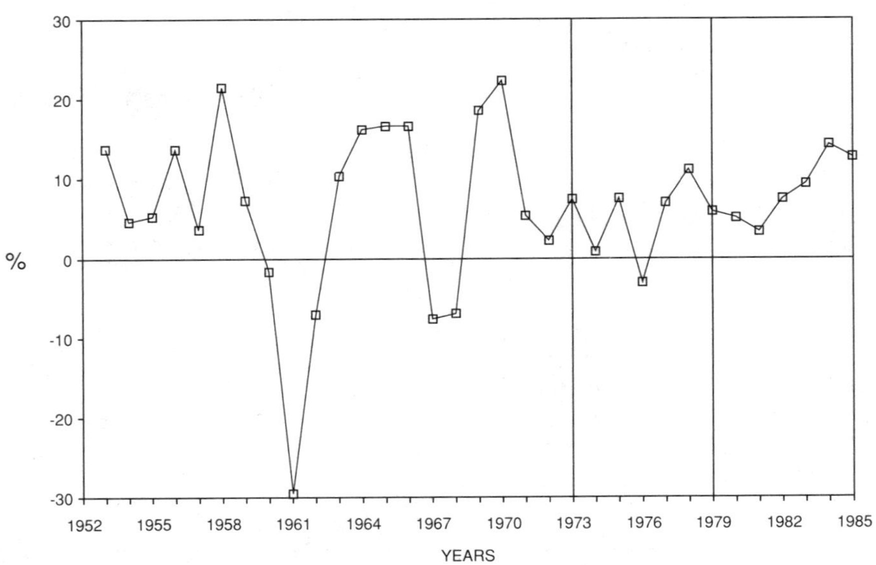

Table 12
Country-Specific and Generic Risks

	China	Hong Kong	Indonesia	Japan	Korea	Malaysia	Philippines	Singapore	Taiwan	Thailand
COUNTRY-SPECIFIC										
Political transition	X	X						X	X	
Radical changes in economic system	X									
Income distribution			X			X	X			X
Unemployment/underemployment			X				X			X
National tariff and nontariff barriers			X	X	X	X			X	
External military threats					X				X	X
Ethnic racial tensions						X		X		
Political role of military					X		X			X
Religious fundamentalism						X				
Insurgency							X			X
Population size & growth (high or low)	X		X					X		
Changing cost-competitiveness		X		X				X		
Environmental stresses	X	X		X						X
Territorial disputes						X				X
Refugees		X								X
High sensitivity to commodity price changes			X			X	X			X
GENERIC/GLOBAL										
US protectionism	X	X	X	X	X	X	X	X	X	X
Vulnerability of US dollar	X	X	X	X	X	X	X	X	X	X
Third World debt	X	X	X	X	X	X	X	X	X	X
Oil price instability	X	X	X	X	X	X	X	X	X	X

Table 13

Balance of Trade between US and Selected Pacific Rim Nations (in US $ billions)

Country	X-M	1972	1973	1974	1975	1976	1977	1978	1979	1980	1981	1982	1983	1984	1985	1986	1987	1988
Japan	X	4.963	8.318	10.679	9.563	10.150	10.532	12.885	17.597	20.790	21.823	20.966	21.894	23.575	22.631	26.882	28.249	37.732
	M	9.618	10.264	13.339	12.341	16.928	20.203	26.471	28.173	32.973	39.904	39.931	43.559	60.371	72.380	85.457	88.074	93.168
	NET	-4.655	-1.946	-2.660	-2.778	-6.778	-9.671	-13.586	-10.576	-12.183	-18.081	-18.965	-21.665	-36.796	-49.749	-58.575	-59.825	-55.436
Korea	X	0.735	1.237	1.546	1.762	2.015	2.371	3.160	4.191	4.685	5.116	5.429	5.925	5.983	5.956	6.355	8.099	11.290
	M	0.750	1.032	1.561	1.586	2.646	3.162	4.087	4.349	4.433	5.475	6.011	7.657	10.027	10.713	13.497	17.991	21.209
	NET	-0.015	0.205	-0.015	0.176	-0.631	-0.791	-0.927	-0.158	0.252	-0.359	-0.582	-1.732	-4.044	-4.757	-7.142	-9.892	-9.919
Hong Kong	X	0.489	0.740	0.882	0.808	1.115	1.291	1.625	2.083	2.688	2.636	2.453	2.563	3.062	2.786	3.030	3.983	5.691
	M	1.325	1.538	1.752	1.735	2.638	3.135	3.767	4.307	5.029	5.758	5.895	6.825	8.899	8.994	9.474	10.490	10.810
	NET	-0.836	-0.798	-0.870	-0.927	-1.523	-1.844	-2.142	-2.224	-2.341	-3.122	-3.442	-4.262	-5.837	-6.208	-6.444	-6.507	-5.119
PRC	X	0.064	0.690	0.807	0.304	0.135	0.171	0.824	1.724	3.755	3.603	2.912	2.173	3.004	3.856	3.106	3.497	5.039
	M	0.035	0.068	0.123	0.171	0.223	0.224	0.357	0.656	1.164	2.062	2.502	2.477	3.381	4.224	5.241	6.910	9.270
	NET	0.029	0.622	0.684	0.133	-0.088	-0.053	0.467	1.068	2.591	1.541	0.410	-0.304	-0.377	-0.368	-2.135	-3.413	-4.231
Thailand	X	0.173	0.256	0.369	0.357	0.347	0.510	0.629	0.961	1.263	1.170	0.915	1.063	1.113	0.849	0.936	1.544	1.964
	M	0.122	0.149	0.198	0.240	0.307	0.380	0.478	0.646	0.866	1.007	0.956	1.035	1.426	1.543	1.873	2.387	3.424
	NET	0.051	0.107	0.171	0.117	0.040	0.130	0.151	0.315	0.397	0.163	-0.041	0.028	-0.313	-0.694	-0.937	-0.843	-1.460
Malaysia	X	0.128	0.157	0.377	0.393	0.536	0.561	0.728	0.932	1.337	1.537	1.736	1.684	1.856	1.539	1.730	1.897	2.139
	M	0.319	0.466	0.826	0.812	0.994	1.390	1.596	2.252	2.688	2.272	1.959	2.205	2.825	2.399	2.534	3.053	3.853
	NET	-0.191	-0.309	-0.449	-0.419	-0.458	-0.829	-0.868	-1.320	-1.351	-0.735	-0.223	-0.521	-0.969	-0.860	-0.804	-1.156	-1.714
Indonesia	X	0.308	0.442	0.531	0.810	1.036	0.763	0.751	0.981	1.545	1.302	2.025	1.466	1.217	0.795	0.946	0.767	1.056
	M	0.297	0.535	1.826	2.528	3.288	3.738	3.906	3.927	5.539	6.413	4.509	5.657	5.867	4.933	3.675	3.719	3.494
	NET	0.011	-0.093	-1.295	-1.718	-2.252	-2.975	-3.155	-2.946	-3.994	-5.111	-2.484	-4.191	-4.650	-4.138	-2.729	-2.952	-2.438
Singapore	X	0.385	0.684	0.988	0.994	0.965	1.172	1.462	2.331	3.033	3.003	3.214	3.759	3.675	3.476	3.380	4.053	5.770
	M	0.280	0.495	0.590	0.564	0.728	0.922	1.119	1.535	1.985	2.195	2.274	2.969	4.121	4.412	4.884	6.395	8.226
	NET	0.105	0.189	0.398	0.430	0.237	0.250	0.343	0.796	1.048	0.808	0.940	0.790	-0.446	-0.936	-1.504	-2.342	-2.456
Philippines	X	0.366	0.495	0.747	0.832	0.819	0.876	1.040	1.570	1.999	1.787	1.854	1.807	1.766	1.379	1.363	1.599	1.880
	M	0.520	0.710	1.169	0.834	0.994	1.236	1.346	1.648	1.913	2.161	1.958	2.160	2.622	2.334	2.150	2.481	2.906
	NET	-0.154	-0.215	-0.422	-0.002	-0.175	-0.360	-0.306	-0.078	0.086	-0.374	-0.102	-0.353	-0.856	-0.955	-0.787	-0.882	-1.026
Australia	X	0.843	1.439	2.157	1.815	2.185	2.356	2.910	3.617	4.093	5.242	4.534	3.954	4.793	5.440	5.551	5.495	6.981
	M	0.856	1.132	1.119	1.298	1.369	1.339	1.854	2.387	2.782	2.707	2.552	2.422	2.899	3.067	2.873	3.287	3.856
	NET	-0.013	0.307	1.038	0.517	0.816	1.017	1.056	1.230	1.311	2.535	1.982	1.532	1.894	2.373	2.678	2.208	3.125
New Zealand	X	0.135	0.247	0.452	0.411	0.415	0.403	0.405	0.530	0.595	0.922	0.897	0.620	0.708	0.728	0.881	0.819	0.942
	M	0.293	0.433	0.370	0.288	0.379	0.413	0.605	0.794	0.793	0.820	0.870	0.828	0.880	0.969	1.097	1.181	1.303
	NET	-0.158	-0.186	0.082	0.123	0.036	-0.010	-0.200	-0.264	-0.198	0.102	0.027	-0.208	-0.172	-0.242	-0.216	-0.362	-0.361
TOTAL NET		-5.826	-2.117	-3.338	-4.348	-10.776	-15.136	-19.167	-14.157	-14.382	-22.633	-22.480	-30.886	-52.566	-66.534	-78.595	-85.966	-81.035

Source: IMF, *Direction of Trade Statistics* X = exports M = imports

Table 14

Current Account Balances of Selected Pacific Rim Countries (in US $ millions)

	1971	1972	1973	1974	1975	1976	1977	1978	1979	1980	1981	1982	1983	1984	1985	1986	1987	1988
Australia	-833	462	407	-2,836	-1,065	-2,010	-3,133	-4,560	-2,660	-4,248	-8,507	-8,514	-5,946	-8,549	-8,717	-9,724	-8,772	-10,946
Hong Kong[a]	n.a.	n.a.	n.a.	n.a.	n.a.	n.a.	n.a.	n.a.	n.a.	n.a.	n.a.	-1,087	-557	1,413	1,869	1,758	2,480	2,012
Indonesia	-372	-334	-476	598	-1,109	-907	-51	-1,413	980	2,864	-566	-5,324	-6,338	-1,856	-1,923	-3,911	-2,098	-1,189
Japan	5,814	6,666	-120	-4,719	-690	3,741	10,910	16,530	-8,740	-10,750	4,770	6,850	20,800	35,000	49,170	85,831	87,000	79,630
Korea	-848	-362	-299	-2,019	-1,889	-310	12	-1,085	-4,151	-5,321	-4,646	-2,650	-1,606	-1,372	-887	4,617	9,854	14,161
Malaysia	-108	-248	105	-543	-496	580	436	108	929	-285	-2,486	-3,601	-3,497	-1,671	-613	52	2,572	1,884
New Zealand	-20	164	-122	-1,803	-1,167	-802	-692	-486	-824	-926	-1,116	-1,612	-968	-1,748	-1,411	-1,481	-1,758	-761
Philippines	-2	5	473	-208	-923	-1,105	-753	-1,094	-1,496	-1,917	-2,096	-3,212	-2,748	-1,268	-18	971	-498	-373
PRC	n.a.	n.a.	n.a.	n.a.	n.a.	n.a.	n.a.	n.a.	n.a.	n.a.	n.a.	5,823	4,487	2,509	-11,417	-7,034	300	n.a.
Singapore	-724	-495	-519	-1,021	-584	-567	-295	-453	-736	-1,563	-1,470	-1,296	-610	-385	-4	542	553	1,660
Taiwan	n.a.	n.a.	n.a.	n.a.	-589	292	911	1,639	181	-913	519	2,248	4,452	6,976	9,195	16,217	18,057	n.a.
Thailand	-175	-51	-46	-87	-625	-440	-1,098	-1,153	-2,086	-2,070	-2,569	-1,003	-2,874	-2,109	-1,537	247	-365	-1,671

Source: IMF (various years), *International Financial Statistics*; Republic of China (various issues), *Statistical Yearbook*; Republic of China (various issues), *Industry of Free China*

[a]visibles and non-visibles; n.a. not available

creating loosely linked rates between currencies (the "adjusted peg") or by adopting a policy of keeping their currencies relatively weak against the dollar in order to encourage exports. The United States had indicated its concern to several Pacific Rim nations, including South Korea and Taiwan, about this issue (*New York Times*, 6 May 1989).

It is the relationship of the dollar to the yen that poses the most serious risks, however. Significant erosion of the American currency could have a major destabilizing effect on world financial markets and trade. Evidence of this effect was decisively illustrated by the October 1987 and subsequent global stock market responses to US trade data. The foreign exchange rate situation could be exacerbated by concern on the part of Japanese investors over financial losses on American investments. In fact, it has been reported that there was heavy selling by Japanese investors in the bond market crash on 26 March 1988 and the subsequent stock market plunge on 16 October (Nakagama 1988; *Wall Street Journal*, 22 April 1988). As Satoshi Sumita (1989), governor of the Bank of Japan, has stated:

> Recently, we have heard the opinion that the existence of external imbalances should not be considered excessively burdensome, as the deficit in the US balance of payments is being smoothly financed by Japanese institutional investors. Such a view, however, is a source of concern for the following reasons: External imbalances give rise to protectionist pressures, as symbolized by recent movements in the US Congress to pressure Japan through the possible application of Super 301. In the long run, stability of the international financial system could be jeopardized if the stability of the dollar is endangered, reflecting the fact that the United States, the key currency country, has become a net debtor country and that the stable foundation for the dollar as the key currency is being undermined.

This situation is also addressed in this volume by *Gavin Boyd*, who observes that "Japanese monetary cooperation is needed by the US to keep the dollar at an acceptable level. Any major contraction of Japanese lending to the US government would tend to force increases in American interest rates, causing upward pressure on the dollar but diminishing general confidence in the US economy and threatening to cause a recession."

The current state of international indebtedness (Table 16) also has a potentially major destabilizing influence. While the debt load of the Pacific Basin countries is by no means small, direct, debt-related threats to the world's financial system, and indirect threats to the

Table 15
National Exchange Rates (on US Dollar)

Country	1983	1984	1985	1986	1987 (31 Dec.)	1988 (22 Feb.)	1990 (11 Jan.)	% change from 1983
Currencies appreciating against the dollar								
Japan	232.20	251.10	200.50	158.10	123.30	129.40	145.40	37.38
Taiwan	40.26	39.49	39.39	36.76	28.50	28.56	25.87	35.74
Currencies remaining approximately stable against the dollar								
Korea	795.500	827.400	890.200	861.400	795.100	771.600	673.100	15.39
Singapore	2.127	2.178	2.105	2.175	1.993	2.010	1.895	10.91
Hong Kong	7.782	7.821	7.810	7.788	7.758	7.793	7.810	-0.36
Thailand	23.000	23.000	26.650	26.130	25.190	25.340	25.600	-11.30
Malaysia	2.338	2.425	2.427	2.580	2.488	2.585	2.700	-15.48
Currencies depreciating against the dollar								
Philippines	14.00	19.76	19.03	20.52	20.70	20.85	21.77	-55.50
Indonesia	994.00	1074.00	1125.00	1641.00	1650.00	1662.00	1790.00	-80.08
PRC	1.98	2.80	3.20	3.72	3.72	3.72	4.72	-138.38

Sources: *New York Times, Wall Street Journal, Globe and Mail*

Table 16
Total Debt and Debt Service Ratios, 1986

Country	Total L.T. Debt ($ millions)	as % of GNP	Interest ($ millions)	Debt Service as % of GNP	Debt Service as % of Exports
Brazil	$97,164	37.6	$7,516	4.1	41.8
Mexico	$91,062	76.1	$7,737	10.2	51.5
Argentina	$43,012	51.7	$3,698	6.8	64.1
Indonesia	$35,279	49.7	$1,394	7.3	33.1
Korea	$34,304	36.1	$2,896	10.8	24.4
Philippines	$21,622	72.2	$1,092	6.1	21.3
Malaysia	$19,650	77.0	$1,394	12.7	20.0
PRC[a]	$17,193	7.0	n.a.	n.a.	8.0
Thailand	$14,130	35.2	$1,031	7.7	25.4
Singapore	$138	n.a.	n.a.	n.a.	n.a.

Sources: World Bank, *World Development Report;* WRI, *World Resources 1988–9; Far Eastern Economic Review*

[a]disbursed long-term public debt

economies of the Pacific Rim, are more likely to emerge from unresolved problems in Latin America and Eastern Europe.

The continuing instability of world oil prices is the fourth major generic risk, and energy-related issues are the subject of the second half of this volume.

In sum, it appears that the greatest threats to the continued growth and strength of the Pacific Rim may lie largely outside the region, and much of the concern centres on the policies and performance of the American political and economic systems.

THE CHANGING ROLE OF THE UNITED STATES

While Japan has been instrumental in the vitalization of the Pacific Basin, the United States has played an equally important although slightly different role. Like Japan, the US has provided extensive import and export opportunities to the Pacific Rim nations, but the nature of its investment activities has been somewhat more contentious. The central issue is the purported role of American "deindustrialization." The extent, or even existence, of this phenomenon is controversial (e.g., Abernathy et al. 1983; Bluestone and Harrison 1982; Fallows 1980; Lawrence 1984; Reich 1983; US OTA 1981), but a forceful expression of the case has been presented by Hajime Karatsu of Matsushita Communication Industrial Company in an article that first appeared in Japanese in the September 1985 issue of the journal *Voice*:

"Shooting oneself in the foot" is an American expression for rash, self-destructive actions. It is an apt description of what the United States does when it takes the high-technology industries that it has successfully developed and sends them overseas just to reduce production costs. . . .

Much more serious than US-Japan issues is the effect of allowing American industry to stampede out of the country, thereby destroying the domestic industrial base. . . . Look at the steel industry, for example. Coddled into self-complacency by import quotas, steel has lost any hope of recovery. And other US industries are marching merrily down the same path. Domestic television manufacturing has failed, and such flagships of high technology as semiconductors and personal computers may also be on the verge of fleeing the country. . . .

The deindustrialization of America now in progress is evident from recent US labor statistics, which shows that every month 20,000-30,000 manufacturing-industry workers lose their jobs. This is an alarming figure. . . .

The abnormally strong dollar is doubtless one of the factors that has gutted manufacturing activity of its substance. There is another cause, though, that bears mentioning, namely, the stance taken by American business leaders.

These are strong words, and some critics might suggest that such a harsh analysis is provided at least in part to shield Japanese trade practices from critical commentary. To so dismiss Karatsu's analysis would be a mistake, however, for he has identified a phenomenon which has already generated domestic American debate.

In a special issue devoted to the problems facing American manufacturing, *Business Week* (3 March 1986) focused on what it called the new "hollow corporation":

A new kind of company is evolving in the US — manufacturing companies that do little manufacturing. Instead, they import components or products from low wage countries, slap their own names on them, and sell them in America. Unchecked, this trend will ultimately hurt the economy — retarding productivity, innovation, and the standard of living. And even the rise of a strong service economy is not likely to offset the decline in manufacturing.

The misplaced faith in the capacity of the service industries to maintain the strength of the American economy has also been criticized by Lester Thurow (1985: 56-9) in his book, *The Zero-Sum Solution*:

The current plight of American industry is sometimes dismissed as a sign of the second industrial revolution. The first industrial revolution saw a shift from agriculture to industry; the second industrial revolution represents a

> shift from industry to services. . . . Between 1977 and 1982 . . . thirty-seven percent of all those new service workers went into health care. Whatever you believe about the desirability of more health care, Americans are not going to generate a high standard of living giving each other heart transplants. . . . Another 33 percent of all those new service workers went into business or legal services. . . . Suing each other is good clean fun and generates a lot of jobs, but it is not productive. . . . One has only to look at Great Britain to see what happens to service industries when manufacturing collapses. . . . While the pattern of industrial activity is indeed changing, as it must, America is not now experiencing a benevolent second industrial revolution but a long-run economic decline.

What is the import of Karatsu's and Thurow's conclusions for the economic vitality of Pacific Basin economic activity? First, as explicitly stated by Karatsu, through the export of capital and accompanying jobs, the US "boosts the industrial potential of the recipient countries, giving them a weapon that sooner or later will be turned against it." This is clearly not an argument against trade or investment per se in the Pacific Basin. What it does imply is that, *in extremis*, a deindustrialized United States, should it materialize, might lack the purchasing power to sustain this trade and investment. Ultimately, Karatsu argues for a revolutionary change in US management practices that can recreate an American competitive position in world markets. In this sense, Karatsu is far from alone. (See, for example, *Globe and Mail*, 5 May 1989; and Dertouzos et al. 1989.)

Second, while the process of foreign investment in Southeast Asia promises increased employment opportunities in the short run, rapidly shifting investment patterns (see, for example, *Economist*, 5 November 1988) may have a disruptive impact on local economic structures and activity, with potentially negative social and political effects.

Third, a comparison of Japanese and American investment in the Pacific Rim reveals some notable differences. While to some analysts the process of offshore investment and the shifting of manufacturing activity is weakening the American economy, only recently has there been any suggestion that Japanese investment activity may have a similar type of effect, and some concerns have been expressed over future investment patterns (Yamada 1982; *Globe and Mail*, 2 December 1986).

To return once again to Karatsu's analysis, the answer lies in management attitudes and practices. Inherent in the reformulation of American management should be a realization that North America cannot and should not compete against the less developed countries on the basis of near-starvation wages, but on the basis of higher quality manufactures, its traditional strength. This necessary concern over American industrial policy is not just of relevance to the United States. As Karatsu concludes: "the collapse of [US] manufacturing industry . . . may lead to the breakup of the free-world community." The devastating impact of such an event on the Pacific Rim requires no elaboration.

Alan Rugman and Alain Verbeke present in this volume a new theoretical framework to compare US and Japanese trade policies, and they put in contrast the failure of American structure and trade strategy and the Japanese experience. The authors conclude that

> the main problem associated with the present system of US decentralized administrative protection is that it provides shelter. It does not permit discrimination between protecting potential growth sectors and sunset industries that face an inevitable decline because of weakening FSAs [firm-specific advantages]. The escalating number of countervailing duty and anti-dumping cases suggests that a non-free trade strategy has become the new trade strategy of the United States.

To Rugman and Verbeke, such a sheltering strategy is "bound to fail in the long run in the presence of global competition." While the US response is by no means predetermined, outspoken critics such as Lester Thurow (1985) and Cohen and Zysman (1987, 1988) have predicted that fundamental and pervasive shifts in American management attitudes and practices are the *sine qua non* of the preservation of economic prosperity and, indeed, survival as a major international player in an increasingly competitive global environment.

In the international economy, a partial vacuum has emerged in the light of the recent US economic performance and uncertain prospects, and we are already witnessing a significant shifting of economic power into the Pacific Rim, principally to Japan, but also, to a lesser extent, to the other emerging and dynamic economies. Two chapters in this volume describe the development of competing institutions, most notably within the critical international financial arena. As *Colin Dodds* states,

> with the end of the Pax Americana Epoch and with it US hegemony in the world economy, we have witnessed the emergence of other centres of economic power, including the Pacific. The increased globalization and integration of world financial markets that has occurred, and the volatility that continues to exist in them, has brought with it challenges and opportunities. . . .

The Pacific has emerged as a major economic base in terms of exporting both capital and goods. In this region, Japan is playing a pivotal role as it moves in an evolutionary way with the shifting patterns of trade and investment. With the emergence of Tokyo and the increasing importance of Japanese banks and securities houses, North America and Europe both face a challenge that extends beyond the manufacturing sector to financial services. Japanese banks are already the largest in the world, and the yen in taking on an increasing international function. . . .

Just as Japan is seen to have developed a comparative advantage in many industrial sectors, it is quickly developing such an advantage in financial services. This is both a threat and a challenge. If, as some commentators predict, we are now in the Pacific Century, then financial institutions from outside of the region wishing to participate will have to meet the challenge as well as the threat to their own domestic markets from Japanese financial institutions.

Kam-Hon Lee and Ilan Vertinsky focus their analysis on "two important Pacific Rim international financial centres that face the challenge of strategic adjustment and repositioning in international financial markets in this decade: . . . Hong Kong and Singapore." The authors conclude that "both Hong Kong with its reactive, noninterventionist, market-sensitive strategy of environmental management, and Singapore's proactive anticipation of a changing market environment, can respond effectively to changing needs that the more complex regulatory systems in other larger IFCs [international financial centres] fail to identify or choose to ignore."

Much of the focus of this book, and indeed of global economic attention, centres on Japan, China, Australia, ASEAN, and the Pacific Basin NICs. Of lesser immediate concern because of their dispersion and low levels of population and resource endowments are the multitude of island states and dependencies scattered across Melanesia, Micronesia, and Polynesia. What prospects does the success or failure of the Pacific Rim economy hold for these disparate entities?

The economic fortunes of many of these islands have depended largely on tourism, basic raw materials and foodstuffs, and some onshore mineral deposits. Recent discoveries of undersea minerals may hold the promise for significant increments of wealth in the future. The potential extent and importance of manganese nodules, cobalt-rich manganese crusts, and polymetallic sulphide deposits are just now beginning to be assessed under the leadership of research institutes such as Hawaii's East-West Center. In their chapter, *Charles Johnson, Allen Clark, and Robert Yonover* conclude that while no full-scale, private-sector financed commercial operation is likely to occur before the early part of the twenty-first century . . . the potential economic importance to small island nations is large, and the present state of knowledge about the extent of crust resources and other seabed resources is so limited, that priority is justified in evaluating the crust potential of the EEZs [Exclusive Economic Zones] of all Pacific countries and territories known to contain favourable geologic and physical environments for crust, nodule, and sulfide deposits.

The final group of papers in this volume address several critical energy-related issues in the recent development of the Pacific Basin. The discussion of these issues not only promotes our understanding of the relevant decision processes in the Asia-Pacific, but also informs the policy-making process by external corporations and governments who wish to engage in trade and investment activities in this region. Before addressing these specific issues, however, it is instructive to review the impact of the energy crises of 1973, 1979, and 1986 on the major nations of the Western Pacific.

ENERGY IN THE PACIFIC RIM

The critical role of energy in economic development has become a central concern of economic planning since 1973; and it is this subject that provides the principal focus of the second half of this book. As Table 17 shows, there is a wide disparity in energy resources among the nations of the Western Pacific, with seven countries holding the bulk of the reserves of crude oil, natural gas, and coal. An assessment of the long-term importance of these resources to each nation requires additional information, however, such as a comparison of reserves to current production (see Table 18). While these R/P ratios, or supply/demand surrogates, are a useful first approximation to anticipated reserve life, any detailed utilization of these data in energy policy analysis must incorporate at least five major adjustments for: (1) anticipated growth in final demand associated with increases in population, industrialization, and general economic well-being; (2) lower growth rates in energy demand stemming from increased energy efficiency and changes in industrial mix in response to increasing prices; (3) projected patterns of interfuel substitution in response to price signals, the availability of competing fuels, and environmental constraints; (4) expected exports of fuel; and (5) anticipated accretions to reserves through additional exploratory activity. Each one of these forecasts is a complex and subjective undertaking fraught with uncer-

Table 17
Proved Energy Reserves of the Major Asia-Pacific Nations (1986, except where noted)

Country	Oil (million bbl)	Natural Gas (TCF)	Coal (million metric tons)
Australia	1,692	18.6	74,263
Brunei	1,420	7.0	—
Hong Kong	—	—	—
Indonesia	8,400	73.0	3,000
Japan	57	1.0	1,015
Korea	—	—	751[a]
Malaysia	2,900	52.2	311
New Zealand	160	5.2	243
Philippines	16	0.1	255
PRC	18,400	30.7	168,115[a]
Singapore	—	—	—
Taiwan	5	0.9	200
Thailand	99	3.7	487-900

Sources: *Financial Times* 1985; Sycip et al. 1983; Republic of China 1985; BID 1983; US Department of Interior 1988; *International Petroleum Encyclopedia* 1988; BP *Review of World Gas*; BP *Statistical Review of World Energy*

[a]1988

Table 18
Reserve to Production (R/P) Ratios of the Major Fuels by Country

Country	Oil	Natural Gas	Coal
Australia	9	31	554
Brunei	26	38	n.a.
Hong Kong	n.a.	n.a.	n.a.
Indonesia	16	68	1154
Japan	12	19	95
South Korea	n.a.	n.a.	31
Malaysia	16	92	[a]
New Zealand	17	31	110
Philippines	6	n.a.	206
PRC	19	64	376
Singapore	n.a.	n.a.	n.a.
Taiwan	7	21	116
Thailand	12	27	323

Sources: BP, *Statistical Review of World Energy*; BP, *Review of World Gas*; ADB, *Energy Indicators of Developing Member Countries*; UN, *Energy Statistics Yearbook*

[a]production is minimal

tainty, but they are essential to the design and implementation of an effective national energy policy.

In fact, a systematic analysis of long-term energy supply security for any nation must also include a comparison of reserves and levels of current consumption (R/C). R/P and R/C ratios can frequently differ by a

Table 19
Major Energy Trade in the Pacific Rim
(entries are included only if Pacific Rim nations are either exporters or importers)

Natural Gas (1988, billion cubic metres)

	Importer	
Exporters	Japan	Korea
Abu Dabai	3.2	
Alaska	1.3	
Brunei	7.2	
Indonesia	21.9	2.7
Malaysia	8.3	

Oil (1988, million tonnes)

	Importers							
Exporters	Western Europe	Africa	Southeast Asia	Japan	Australasia	US	Latin America	Others
Australasia			3.6	1.7	n.a.	2.6		
Canada			0	0.2	0.1			
Japan			0.7	n.a.	0			
Latin America			1.7	9.3	0			
Middle East			101.9	138.3	7.2			
North Africa			6.3	2.8	0			
PRC	0.5		7.4	15.2	0.1	4.5	2.5	4.6
South Asia			0.1	1.8	0.1	1.4		
Southeast Asia	1.1		0.6	44.7	3.9	12.0	0.3	1.6
US			4.5	2.4	0.9			
USSR			14.1	0.5	0			
West Africa			1.3	0.3	0			
Western Europe			0.6	0.4	0.1			

Hard coal (1987, '000 metric tons)

	Importers			
Exporters	Hong Kong	Japan	S. Korea	Others
Australia	2972	47126	7821	26740
Canada	313	16845	3991	
PRC	1963	4301		607
South Africa	2559	7560	4800	
US		9256	3624	
USSR		6367		

Sources: BP, *Statistical Review of World Energy*, *Review of World Gas*; UN, *Energy Statistics Yearbook*

significant magnitude. For example, a country that is extracting oil, gas, or coal at a low rate from a rather limited resource base may have a relatively high R/P ratio because of its principal reliance on energy imports to satisfy domestic demand. Under these circumstances, the

R/C ratio would be considerably lower and would provide a more accurate measure of that country's ability to meet future energy demand from domestic reserves.

The marked discrepancies in energy resource endowments in the Pacific Rim have led, as they have throughout the globe, to a significant international trade in energy commodities, most notably, crude oil, natural gas, and coal (see Table 19). With respect to coal, it is important to make a distinction between "thermal" or "steaming" varieties used by utilities and industry to produce electricity and/or process heat, and "metallurgical" or "coking" coal utilized principally as a reducing agent in the production of steel.

In characterizing the energy demands and economic capacities of East Asian countries to meet their anticipated fuel requirements, it is important that the fundamental diversity of these nations be recognized. From the point of view of energy analysis, this heterogeneity is manifested on at least two major dimensions: first, the availability of domestic energy resources; and second, national wealth, or the capability to pay for imported energy if required. The diversity is explicitly addressed in Figure 7 and Table 20 by a typology of countries used to structure the analysis of energy supply and demand patterns and opportunities. The typology can be represented in its simplest form by the following matrix:

	Energy-poor nations	Energy-rich nations
Developed nations	A	C
Developing nations	B	D

The only anomalous entry in Figure 7 is that of New Zealand — an economically developed nation whose GDP per capita was surpassed by two of the NICs, Singapore and Hong Kong, in the period following 1983.

In a more detailed energy analysis, it would be necessary to differentiate, for each country, among specific fuels and between short-term problems of energy supply and demand imbalance and longer-term prospects. The typology does, however, identify characteristics that differentiate countries with energy surpluses and deficits. These differences play a central role in delimiting the policy

Figure 7 A Typology of Energy and Development, 1987

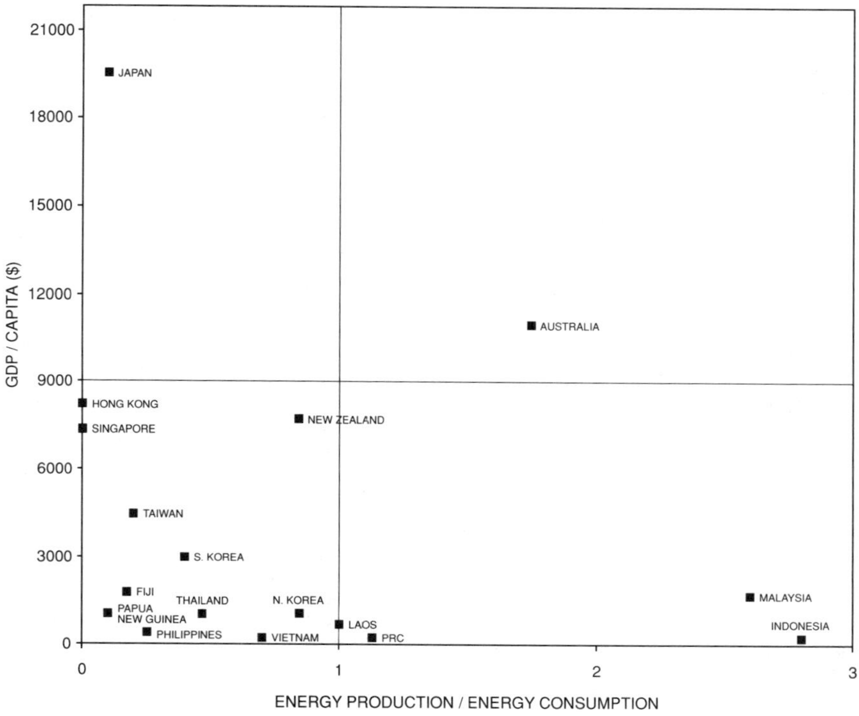

options available to each nation in addressing its respective energy problems and/or opportunities.

The study of energy use in industrial production and economic development began in earnest after the OPEC price shock of 1973, although pioneering work on this issue had been conducted by such research groups as Resources for the Future prior to that date (e.g., Darmstadter 1971). One of the earliest analytical devices developed in an attempt to probe the energy-economy linkage was the double logarithmic comparison of energy consumption and gross domestic product, both expressed per capita. An example of this approach for the Pacific Rim is provided in Figure 8. Canada and the United States have been included for comparative purposes, since they are among the highest per capita users of energy in the world.

Initial conclusions from this type of analysis suggested a strong linear relationship between these two variables, leading, in turn, to an equally strong conclusion that increasing industrialization and wealth

Table 20
Typology of Energy and Development
(1987 commercial energy only — '000 terajoules, i.e., petajoules)

Country	GDP/Capita (US $)	Energy production (P)	Energy consumption (C)	Energy consumption per capita (gigajoules/capita)	P/C
Brunei	$11,407	680	71	293	9.58
Indonesia	$321	3,863	1,382	8	2.80
Malaysia	$1,944	1,525	609	38	2.50
Australia	$11,061	5,671	3,243	201	1.75
PRC	$308	25,930	23,469	22	1.10
Laos	$653	4	4	1	1.00
North Korea	$936	1,482	1,698	79	0.87
New Zealand	$7,576	323	373	113	0.87
Vietnam	$278	171	217	3	0.79
Thailand	$881	343	770	14	0.45
South Korea	$2,847	628	2,173	52	0.29
Philippines	$537	70	450	8	0.16
Taiwan	$4,613	141	1,038	53	0.14
Fiji	$1,514	1	8	11	0.13
Japan	$19,553	1,440	13,367	110	0.11
Papua New Guinea	$851	2	34	9	0.06
Cambodia	n.a.	0	6	1	0
Hong Kong	$8,167	0	311	55	0
Nauru	$19,753	0	2	222	0
Samoa	$539	0	2	12	0
Singapore	$7,323	0	366	140	0
Solomon Islands	$403	0	2	7	0
Tonga	$1,000	0	1	9	0
Vanuata	$545	0	1	7	0

Sources: UN, *Energy Statistics Yearbook, 1987;* ADB, *Energy Indicators of Developing Member Countries of* ADB

would inevitably entail a comparable increase in the demand for scarce energy resources. In the post-1973 world of rising energy prices and increasing concern over the finite limits to fuel supplies, this early conclusion had serious policy implications for the process of industrialization in the Third World.

Fortunately, there are several reasons why the early conclusions from this type of analysis have turned out to be overly pessimistic. First, as Corazon Siddayao (1982) has demonstrated, there are numerous and major conceptual problems in the generation of commensurable estimates of cross-national GDP and diverse forms of energy; and second, the oil crisis of 1973 had a profound effect on the Pacific Rim, as well as other national economies, leading to a significant slowing of growth and, in the case of Japan, to a minor and short-lived

Figure 8 Energy Consumption per Capita versus GDP per Capita, 1987

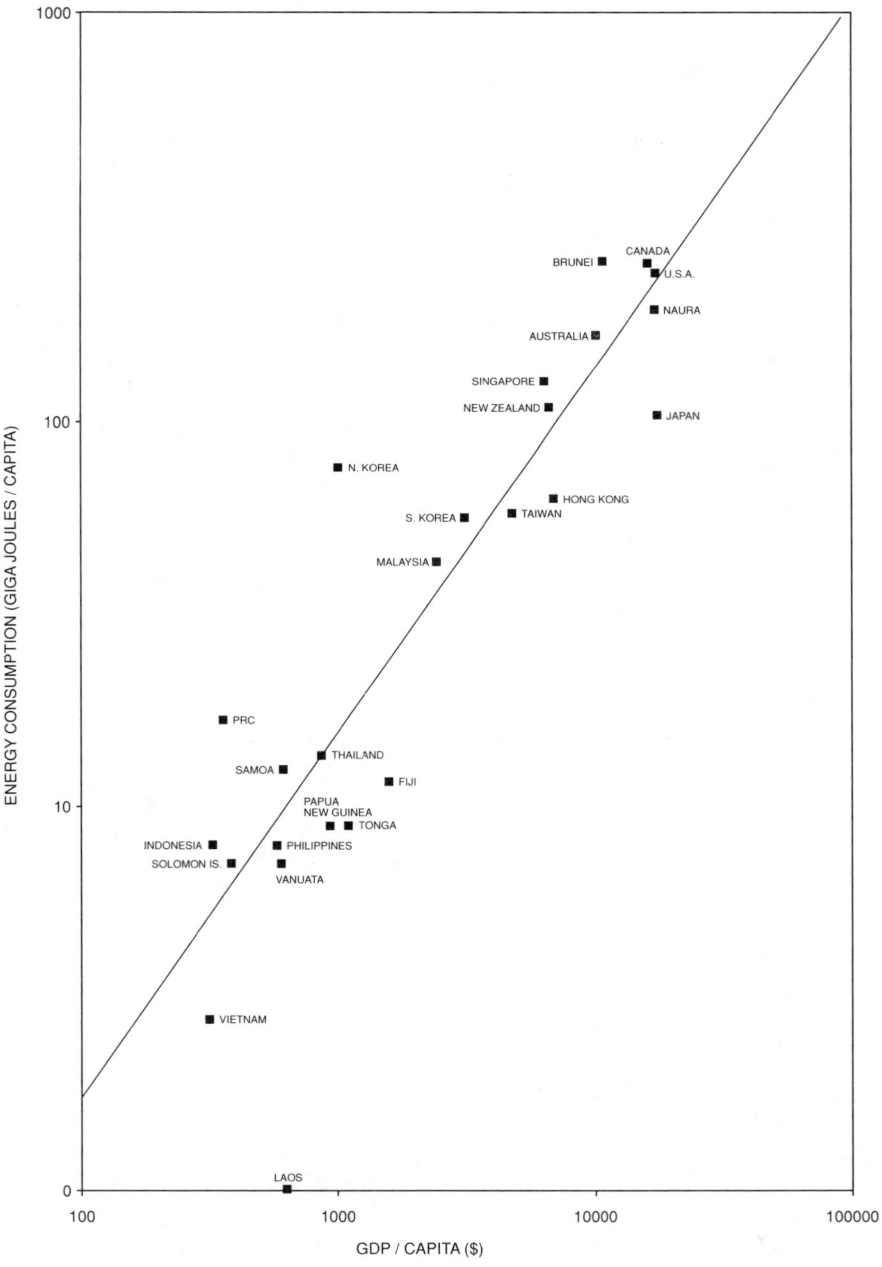

contraction in total output (see Table 21). The impact on levels of unemployment is difficult to discern, but the effect on inflation is unambiguous, considering the critical role of energy in modern economies (Nemetz 1988). In virtually every case, the impact of the second crisis of 1979 was much less pronounced, although the oil price only doubled in 1979-80 in contrast to the quadrupling of 1973-4. From the viewpoint of risk, however, it is especially critical to track the response of the Pacific Basin countries in their patterns of energy use; doing so provides potentially useful insight into how each nation might fare in the face of another global energy crisis.

Three energy-related variables are of particular interest in assessing the impact of the three energy shocks: total use, a utilization index as a measure of efficiency, and oil consumption (see Table 22). With only one exception—the Philippines—total energy use continued to increase in the wake of the first two energy crises. This phenomenon tends to reflect the continuing economic growth of the Pacific Rim. What is more informative is an examination of the efficiency of energy use, represented by an energy-use index based on total energy consumption per real currency unit for each nation. On this dimension, the inter-country differences are quite remarkable. With the exception of China, the three other major energy-rich nations (Australia, Indonesia, and Malaysia) seem to have achieved little in the way of increased energy efficiency. China has historically been burdened with extraordinarily inefficient production and distribution systems (Smil 1978, 1987), but it has made remarkable improvements in energy efficiency.

Except for Singapore and New Zealand, the six other major energy-poor nations (Japan, Hong Kong, Korea, Philippines, Taiwan, and Thailand) have achieved some degree of increased energy efficiency. The most remarkable accomplishments are those of Japan, which has not only tended to shift away from highly energy-intensive industries, such as petrochemicals and aluminum production (Samuels 1983), but has also developed significantly more efficient production processes (Nemetz et al. 1984-5; Nemetz and Vertinsky 1984). Some caution should be exercised in the interpretation of these phenomena, however. From a global perspective, the transference of energy-intensive manufacturing from one country to another does not, in itself, represent aggregate energy savings. These can only be achieved if new processes are adopted and/or if new products emerge that displace older, energy-intensive goods, as they have in Japan.

With respect to long-term risk, one of the more important factors is oil consumption; the continuing prospect of international crises in the production, availability, and price of this commodity casts a pall over

Table 21
Some Economic Impacts of the Oil Crises of 1973 and 1979

	GDP change		Inflation		Unemployment	
Country	1973+	1979+	1973+	1979+	1973+	1979+
DEVELOPED, ENERGY-POOR						
Japan	drops by 1.4%	slows by 2% pts.	+18% pts.	+4% pts.	+0.7% pts.	little impact
New Zealand	slows by 3% pts., then drops by 17%	slows by 2% pts.	+10% pts.	+5% pts.	little impact	+1.8% pts.
DEVELOPING, ENERGY-POOR						
Hong Kong	0 growth	slows by 9% pts.	+12% pts.	+9% pts.	n.d.	+1% pt.
Korea	slows by 8% pts.	drops by 3% pts.	+22% pts.	+14% pts.	no effect	+2% pts.
Philippines	slows by 5% pts.	slows by 5% pts.	+26% pts.	+11% pts.	no effect	+2% pts.
Singapore	slows by 7% pts.	little effect	+20% pts.	+4.5% pts.	no effect	no effect
Taiwan	slows by 11% pts.	slows by 5% pts.	+44% pts.	+13% pts.	n.d.	no effect
Thailand	slows by 4% pts.	slows by 0.25% pts.	+19% pts.	+12% pts.	n.d.	n.d.
DEVELOPED, ENERGY-RICH						
Australia	slows by 5% pts.	slows by 2% pts.	+9% pts.	+3% pts.	+3% pts.	little impact
DEVELOPING, ENERGY-RICH						
China	slows by 7% pts.	slows by 2% pts.	+0.5% pts.	+5% pts.	n.d.	n.d.
Indonesia	slows by 5% pts.	little effect	+34% pts.	+12% pts.	n.d.	n.d.
Malaysia	slows by 11% pts.	slows by 3% pts.	+14% pts.	+4% pts.	n.d.	n.d.
WORLD	slows by 6.3% pts.	slows by 3% pts.	+9.4% pts.	+6% pts.	n.d.	n.d.

n.d. no data

projections of uninterrupted economic dynamism over the next few decades (see, for example, US GAO 1988). In this category of energy use, the results are not particularly encouraging. With the exception of Australia, the energy-rich nations increased their crude use by a significant degree over the period 1973-85, although this increase was tempered in China and Indonesia after the second oil crisis. Even the few Pacific Basin nations blessed with major petroleum deposits will face the pressure of increasing demand in the next few decades.

Table 22
Some Energy-Related Impacts of the Oil Crises of 1973 and 1979 (percentage changes)

	Total energy use			Energy use index			Oil use		
Country	1973-8	1979-84	1973-85	1973-8	1979-84	1973-85	1973-8	1979-84	1973-85
DEVELOPED, ENERGY-POOR									
Japan	4	4	11	-11	-14	-29	-5	-22	-33
New Zealand	11	31	20	14	16	5	-27	-10	-47
DEVELOPING, ENERGY-POOR									
Hong Kong	65	38	126	12	-4	-2[a]	66	9[b]	81[b]
Korea	53	27	136	-5	-5	-2	62	10	92
Philippines	17	-9	25	-14	-13	-13	5	-25	-13
Singapore	99	73	331	43	15	91	27	21	62
Taiwan	68	28	130	12	-1	-3	99	15	168
Thailand	33	32	101	-8	1	-3	11	-13	5
DEVELOPED, ENERGY-RICH									
Australia	11	12	4	-1	-2	2	7	-7	5
DEVELOPING, ENERGY-RICH									
China	48	16	88	15	-23	-19	86	-1	89
Indonesia	74	33	138	22	-1	15	29	4	51
Malaysia	42	94	251	4	39	n.d.	9	47	63
WORLD	13.5	4.2	25.7	-2.5	-5.5	-7.9	10.2	-9.4	0.4

[a]1973-84
[b]1979-82
n.d. no data

The developing and energy-poor countries, except for the Philippines, generally experienced a similar pattern of increased oil use over the period 1973-85, but there was a slowing after the second crisis of 1979. Several of the countries in the Basin are making pronounced efforts at interfuel substitution, moving away from excessive reliance on liquid fuels and toward coal, hydropower, natural gas, nuclear power, and a range of nonconventional sources, including bagasse, garbage, micro-hydro, biogas, and geothermal energy (Carley et al. 1985a, b; Riek et al. 1985a, b). Most noteworthy among these are Japan and New Zealand, which have achieved significant decreases in total crude use. New Zealand has undertaken a pioneering project in the production of synoil from its natural gas deposits (Nemetz et al. 1984, Kanetkar et al. 1983).

The oil price crash of early 1986 had serious economic impacts on many global oil producers, including Indonesia. Table 23 summarizes available data on GDP growth, inflation, energy utilization, and oil consumption for the major Pacific Rim nations in 1986. It could be expected that such a precipitous decrease in the price of oil (from

Table 23
Some Effects of the Oil Price Crash of 1986 (percentage changes)

Country	GDP Growth	Inflation	Energy Use Index (change in 1986) (%)	Oil Use (1986) (1985 in brackets) (%)
DEVELOPED, ENERGY-POOR				
Japan	slowing by 2.2% pts.	slowing by 1.4% pts.	−2.3	+0.5 (−4.0)
New Zealand	increase by 0.8% pts.	slowing by 5.4% pts.	+8.0	+2.0 (−6.0)
DEVELOPING, ENERGY-POOR				
Hong Kong	increase by 8.1% pts.	slowing by 1.2% pts.	−2.0	+4.3 (+5.0)
Korea	increase by 6.5% pts.	slowing by 0.2% pts.	−6.9	+7.1 (−0.4)
Philippines	increase by 5.7% pts.	slowing by 22.3% pts.	no change	+3.1 (−0.2)
Singapore	increase by 3.7% pts.	deflation of 1.4%	+15.7	+17.9 (+0.6)
Taiwan	increase by 6.5% pts.	increase by 0.3% pts.	−2.2	−0.6 (−7.8)
Thailand	increase by 0.2% pts.	slowing by 0.6% pts.	+4.0	+8.3 (+4.1)
DEVELOPED, ENERGY-RICH				
Australia	slowing by 3.1% pts.	increase by 2.4% pts.	+6.4	+1.4 (−3.3)
DEVELOPING, ENERGY-RICH				
PRC	slowing by 5% pts.	slowing by 0.6% pts.	−1.8	+11.6 (+2.0)
Indonesia	GDP decrease of 3.7%	increase by 1.1% pts.	+5.9	+1.9 (+1.7)
Malaysia	increase by 2% pts.	increase by 0.4% pts.	+5.1	−6.1 (−5.8)
WORLD	slowing by 0.2% pts.	slowing by 5.0% pts.	+1.6	+2.5 (−0.8)

Sources: BP (1987), *Statistical Review of World Energy*, June; ADB (1987), *Key Indicators of Developing Member Countries of ADB*, July; IMF, International Financial Statistics; Arthur Andersen & Co. and Cambridge Energy Research Associates, (1987), *World Oil Trends, 1987–88;* British Petroleum Company, Corporate Planning Department; IMF (1987), *World Economic Outlook*, April; UN Dept. of International Economic & Social Affairs, Statistical Office

$28.00 in January to $9.60 by July for Arabian light crude, with a recovery to $14.50 by December) would have the following general effects, *ceteris paribus*: (1) an increase in the growth rate of GDP in energy-poor nations and a possible slowing or decrease in energy-rich nations, depending on their reliance on petroleum exports, (2) a decrease in the rate of inflation, (3) a moderate increase in the energy utilization index, indicating lower energy efficiency, and (4) an acceleration in the consumption of oil. The data in Table 23 tend to verify these hypothesized results with a few notable exceptions. Most noteworthy is the continuing improvement in energy efficiency in Japan, Hong Kong, Korea, Taiwan, and China despite the oil price drop of 1986.

What general conclusions can be drawn from these energy-related data with respect to the capacity to handle the risk of future energy-related shocks? Definitive conclusions concerning the macroeconomic effects of the crises of 1973 and 1979 are difficult to draw because of confounding variables and the less pronounced price increases of the second oil crisis. With respect to energy efficiency, most, but not all, of the major Pacific Rim nations manifested some ability to achieve essential efficiencies in energy use — a capacity that bodes well for a medium to longer-term future of tighter energy supplies.

A particularly cogent example of the generally increasing efficiency of energy use is captured by a measure of energy elasticity of GDP, defined as the percentage change in energy consumption divided by the percentage change in real GDP over a given time period. Because such a measure can vary markedly from year to year, a more robust analysis of significant shifts in efficiency can be derived from an examination of longer time periods. Table 24 summarizes national elasticity data for five-year periods following each oil crisis. In all cases, except Malaysia and Thailand, the countries of the Pacific Rim have achieved major advances on this dimension, although any elasticity measure greater than 1.0 (as in New Zealand) must be considered problematic. It is also noteworthy that only Japan, China, and the Philippines have elasticities lower than the world average.

Oil dependency remains a serious concern for several of the developing, energy-poor countries, such as Korea and Taiwan.[2] While the slippage in energy efficiency and acceleration in oil use in the Pacific Rim after the oil price crash of 1986 are undesirable, it should be stressed that oil gluts and price decreases are basically anomalous events in an industry with a shrinking resource base, and the inevitable future oil crises will reflect the continuing diminution in supply.

Table 24
Energy Elasticity of GDP*

Country	1973–8	1979–84
DEVELOPED, ENERGY-POOR		
Japan	0.24	0.20
New Zealand	38.42[a]	2.47
DEVELOPING, ENERGY-POOR		
Hong Kong	1.37	0.85
South Korea	0.88	0.81
Philippines	0.47	-2.29
Singapore	2.51	1.44
Taiwan	1.36	0.70
Thailand	0.74	1.05
DEVELOPED, ENERGY-RICH		
Australia	0.90	0.87
DEVELOPING, ENERGY-RICH		
PRC	1.67	0.33
Indonesia	1.74	0.98
Malaysia	1.17[b]	2.38
WORLD	0.82	0.41

*(% change in energy consumption) / (% change in GDP)
[a]1973–9
[b]1973–7

ENERGY-RELATED RISK REDUCTION ACTIVITIES IN THE PACIFIC RIM

Given the nature and magnitude of the risks associated with future energy supply in the Pacific Rim, it is instructive to examine policy initiatives by nations within the Basin that bear directly or indirectly on the issue of risk management.

Joy Dunkerley and Douglas Bohi point out that

> The energy price shocks of the last decade have demonstrated the importance of the energy sector to economic growth and stability in general. Moreover, it is commonly accepted that groups of countries acting cooperatively can achieve greater success in reducing the costs of energy supply disruptions than by acting independently. Thus, energy provides an example of a problem area which also serves as an incentive for cooperation.

The authors "examine the extent of energy cooperation already achieved in the Pacific Basin and the prospects for building on these initiatives in the future." Despite the extensive, regional, subregional, bilateral, and extraregional institutions already in place, the authors conclude that "further development in energy cooperation should appropriately take place in an evolutionary fashion, building on the present framework, which has been shown to be a logical response to the particular conditions existing in the area."

Professor *Vaclav Smil*, a leading expert in the field of energetics, presents a striking comparison of the post-1973 changes in the energy systems of two remarkably different nations, Japan and the People's Republic of China. As Smil observes, "shifts of surprising similarity . . . have demonstrated several essential commonalities guiding the development of energy systems in otherwise very disparate societies." He concludes that

> when prices rise enough, impressive conservation efforts and efficiency increases will follow. . . . The most encouraging finding in this respect is that the slack in the system is large enough even in the world's most energy efficient economy [Japan]. . . . Second, the right prices trigger substantial fuel substitutions. . . . The experience of Chinese and Japanese energetics during the fifteen years of the new, post-1973 energy era is thus clearly encouraging.

A major transformation has been wrought in the way that modern industrial societies utilize energy, and it is now possible to foresee, at least in some countries, the possibility of significantly increased economic activity with lower total energy consumption. These impressive developments in efficient energy utilization do not suggest that major growth in Pacific Rim energy consumption will not materialize. On the contrary, the rapidly industrializing nations of this area will still require significant accretions to their current energy use, and guaranteeing the required supply has become, and will continue to be, a central preoccupation of national economic planners.

One of the most urgent questions to be addressed is the form of government participation in, and direction of, the energy sector. Concerns over energy security have become so important that the question of government intervention is no longer an issue — the principal policy focus is on the nature of this activity and its economic efficiency.

One of the principal short-run concerns among national energy planners over the last decade and a half has been determining the appropriate response to rapidly changing prices of oil and natural gas. These price changes and the resulting cyclical global economic reaction have created major balance-of-payment and budgetary problems for many energy exporters as well as importers. One measure of the exposure of energy importers to external oil price perturbations is the relative role of petroleum in total imports. Table 25 indicates that while

Table 25
Petroleum Imports as a Percentage of All Imports (CIF) by Value

Country	1982	1988
Australia	13	4
Fiji	29	13
Hong Kong[a]	8	3[c]
Indonesia	n.a.	n.a.
Japan	39	14
Malaysia	5	n.a.
New Zealand[a]	18	9[d]
Philippines	22	11
PRC	n.a.	n.a.
Singapore[b]	34	14
South Korea	25	7
Taiwan[a]	24	11
Thailand	23	4

Sources: IMF, *International Financial Statistics;* ADB, *Key Indicators of Developing Member Countries of ADB*

[a]all mineral fuels

[b]not comparable to other countries because of Singapore's role as petroleum refiner

[c]1987

[d]1986

this role has declined significantly since the oil price peak of the early 1980s, petroleum continues to play a notable role in the total import bill of many Pacific Rim nations, and it will doubtless rise again with anticipated oil price increases in this decade (*New York Times,* 24 February 1990:A1).

One of the major strategic responses to these instabilities has been a growing interest in coal development and use. The subject of both coal and liquefied natural gas (LNG) development and trade raises several interesting questions concerning the role of fuel procurement policies in Japan, the world's foremost energy importer. Also evident are much more difficult questions concerning the uncertainty of energy-demand forecasting and the related issue of appropriate resource development policies in energy-exporting countries. Several authors, including Fesharaki and Schultz (1983), Morse (1984), and Nemetz and Vertinsky (1984), have remarked on the oversupply of fuels like coal and natural gas that allows Japan to extract significant price concessions from offshore suppliers. There is no indication that this situation will change appreciably in the foreseeable future, which implies potentially severe financial difficulties for some suppliers.

A similar situation exists with respect to metallurgical coal. The fundamental question remains whether the resource suppliers could have foreseen this development and adopted some form of self-protective measures. In at least one case there is strong evidence to suggest that foresight was possible but that the situation was ignored out of ignorance or for short-sighted political reasons. As *Harold Halvorson* states in his assessment of "The British Columbia Coal Industry," the problem was "overly optimistic forecasts of Japanese crude steel production and hence coking coal imports." A critical piece of evidence is displayed in Figure 15 where

> the Canadian/BC government forecasts lagged those being made in Japan. For example, the Japanese May 1981 forecast was less optimistic than the Victoria/Ottawa forecast made in July 1982, over a year later. Subsequently, when Japanese companies and government agencies were forecasting crude steel production levels in 1983 in the one hundred million tpy range, certain Canadian circles were dismissing such low forecasts as an attempt by the Japanese to effect lower coal prices. . . .
>
> It must be remembered when reviewing the forecasts shown in Figure 15 that even had the optimistic forecasts made in the 1980-82 period been realized, there was still too much coking-coal capacity built. It was possible as early 1980 to foresee a glut of coking coal on world markets.

As a result of these mistakes, Halvorson concludes that "the outlook for the BC coal industry is not optimistic. . . . Closure of BC capacity is a distinct possibility." Subsequent events in British Columbia have borne out this assessment (*Globe and Mail*, 15 January, 3 February 1986; Midland Doherty, 16 December 1985).

This unfortunate series of events is just symptomatic of a broader deficiency in the Canadian and, indeed, North American capacity to understand and formulate an appropriate response to the opportunities and risks inherent in expanded Pacific Basin trade and investment.

The most pronounced efforts at risk reduction in the Pacific Rim have been undertaken by Japan, a nation that depends on imports to provide over 80 per cent of its total energy and almost 100 per cent of its crude oil requirements. The Japanese strategy of offshore resource investment and multisourcing has not been without controversy. With respect to the claims that there has been a conscious effort to promote oversupply in such commodities as thermal and metallurgical coal and LNG, *David Anderson* concludes that

> the available evidence, which is admittedly circumstantial in nature, suggests that in the late 1970s and early 1980s, it was the JSM's [Japanese steel mills] interest to encourage excess supply [of coking coal] through such practices as overcontracting. However, it cannot be proven that they deliberately sought to

do so. Despite this qualifier, it must be stressed that such actions are entirely consistent with normal business behaviour. By doing so, they could pursue their twin objectives of enhancing security of supply and reducing costs in an efficient manner.

In spite of this conclusion, it is the author's view that "the events of the past twenty years are not likely to repeat themselves" for several reasons, including the development of coking-coal-saving technologies in steel production and the emerging role in steel capacity of such Pacific Rim countries as Korea, Taiwan, and China.

Accompanying the strategic Japanese initiative to seek a diversity of offshore fuels and suppliers has been a complementary attempt to displace oil by the increased use of nuclear power, with 26 per cent of Japan's electricity production provided by nuclear fuel in 1987 (Keizai Koho Center 1989:61). Nevertheless, Japan is not the only nation in the Pacific Rim intent on reducing its energy supply risk through alternative fuel options. *Kirk Smith* focuses his analysis on the major issues surrounding nuclear power and its relationship to economic development, especially in the Third World. The author concludes that

> except in the special conditions of Taiwan and South Korea, nuclear power has not found a major niche in the economic development of many poor nations. It is not dead, but it does not flourish. The places to watch during the next fifteen years are China and India, but it seems safe to say that growth will not be rapid. The extent to which concerns about climate change will affect nuclear power's growth rate in developing countries will largely depend on how much the developed countries are willing to pay to do something about it.

Two general types of conclusions concerning the future prospects of Pacific Rim energy use emerge from the analyses presented in this volume. The first focuses on the relative likelihood and attractiveness of alternative energy development and utilization strategies by both energy-rich and energy-poor nations within the Pacific Rim.

Group "A": Energy-"Poor," Developed Nations

Japan, with an approximately 84 per cent reliance on offshore energy supplies, presents an archetypal example of how to cope successfully with an extreme deficiency in a critical natural resource. It has adopted a multifaceted strategy that entails a diversification of fuel types and foreign supply sources while investing heavily in a nuclear option to provide some degree of insulation from external economic and political perturbations. It is noteworthy that while Japan has engaged in research on alternative sources of energy, such as geothermal, solar power, wind, ocean thermal, and hydrogen, much less commitment has been demonstrated to the development of these sources than in several other Pacific Rim countries, such as New Zealand, the Philippines, and Indonesia (Nemetz and Vertinsky 1984; Nemetz et al. 1984-5).

New Zealand, also faced with continuing dependence on external supplies of crude oil, has displayed several bold initiatives in the development and use of nonconventional fuels based on extensive domestic natural gas reserves. Foremost among these are the production and use of synthetic gasoline and compressed natural gas in the transportation sector as substitutes for crude oil imports.

Group "B": Energy-"Poor," Developing Nations

In many respects, it is this group of nations that faces the greatest challenge; yet some have already demonstrated a remarkable degree of success in the face of this adversity. Four of the nations within this category have become newly industrializing countries (NICs): Hong Kong, Korea, Taiwan, and Singapore — a tribute to the strength and resilience of their economic systems.

Singapore is a major entrepôt centre and has one of the largest global concentrations of oil-refining activity. Yet the economic health of this small island state is precariously tied to international financial flows and the increasing preference of some Pacific Basin nations such as Indonesia to assume the refining of their own or imported petroleum (Riek et al. 1985; Fesharaki 1986).

The vitality of the Korean and Taiwanese economies has to this point enabled them to overcome the potential constraints of offshore energy supply, although it is clear that the post-1973 price increases have presented particularly challenging problems for economic planning (Stewart and Nemetz 1982a, b). Their extensive nuclear power programs represent a concerted effort at risk reduction.

Of the countries within this category, it is perhaps the Philippines that faces the greatest challenge in meeting its energy requirements. Energy commodities amounted to 26 per cent of all imports in 1985 (although this fell to 11 per cent in 1988) (IMF-IFS, 1989:585; see also Table 25 in this chapter), and primary energy consumption patterns have been dominated by oil, 71.5 per cent of it imported in 1987 (ADB [1989], *Energy Indicators*:421). In that same year, domestic oil supplies contributed only 3.8 per cent of energy demand (ibid.:442). The serious economic implications of this dependence are apparent in the national balance of trade figures for the decade following the 1973 oil crisis. The main thrust of Philippine energy policy has been to substitute domestic energy sources, such as coal, hydropower, and geothermal resources, for foreign oil. It appears unlikely that the country will be able to meet domestic coal demand in the next five years, and the success or failure of the large-scale developments of geothermal and hydroelectric power will depend mainly on capital availability in foreign markets (Carley et al. 1985). The Philippines is in a unique position, however, in light of its special relationship with the United States. As long as the US chooses to retain its military bases in this country, it will feel compelled to sustain the Philippine economy if such a course of action is required.

Thailand has had, like the other nations within this category, a heavy reliance on imported oil. Not surprisingly, it has placed a large emphasis on energy alternatives by investing in the development of newly discovered natural gas fields, hydroelectricity, lignite, and a range of non-conventional sources such as bagasse, garbage, microhydro, and biogas. The greater utilization of domestic energy resources to back up imported crude and refined products will rely largely on the development of natural gas.

Group "C": Energy-"Rich," Developed Nations

Australia, the principal Pacific Rim nation in this category, has very large reserves of coal and uranium and significant quantities of natural gas. To a certain extent, Australia has the luxury of choice in determining the timing and scope of energy exports required to help finance continuing oil imports and economic development. It is currently one of the world's largest exporters of coal and has recently initiated development of natural gas reserves off the west coast for shipment in the form of LNG to Japan. Australia has historically, however, displayed considerable circumspection about the role of uranium as a potential export, citing concern over the issue of nuclear proliferation (Nemetz et al. 1984).

Group "D": Energy-"Rich," Less-Developed Countries

Although "rich" in energy resources, these nations face problems considerably more complex than industrialized countries like Australia. This is particularly the case for the People's Republic of China and Indonesia, which both have extraordinarily high "absorptive capacities" (Teese 1982), based in part on their very large populations at minimal income levels.

China is constrained by, among other variables, inadequate infrastructure, a relatively rigid economic and political system, and the legacy of political and economic disruption. Its future role in international energy trade remains uncertain. China has the potential for significant exports of oil and coal over the longer term, but issues of domestic demand, capital availability, technology, and infrastructure remain unsolved (Ho and Huenemann 1984; see also US CIA 1986).

Indonesia, with a population of 150 million, must grapple with the problem of a remarkably skewed population distribution spread over 13,677 islands. While over half the population is concentrated on Java, this island is energy deficient. The nation is highly dependent on oil and is attempting to diversify its domestic energy supplies. Fortunately, it has the natural resources to do so. The country is attempting to capitalize on income from its energy exports to encourage the production of textiles and other manufactures that will provide long-term employment for its plentiful labour resource. It is frequently the irony of oil wealth that the development of a resilient industrial structure designed to ultimately replace depleting energy reserves can be frustrated by an overvalued currency resulting from energy exports.

Malaysia's large natural gas reserves and high quality crude petroleum resources place it in a favourable position to develop export markets and generate revenue to encourage economic growth. Energy policies have stressed the reduction of domestic consumption of oil to accomplish a threefold objective: to lower the nation's import bill, to increase the availability of domestic resources for export, and to foster increased use of more extensive natural gas reserves (Riek et al. 1985).

The second major conclusion that may be drawn from this analysis concerns the role that Canada can play for each category of country:

(1) for energy-poor but developed countries such as Japan, Canada can directly fill some of the energy requirements. This energy export may be in raw or embodied form, but clearly the latter would be to Canada's greater benefit. In either case, such exports would help to finance the importation of Japanese goods essential for the Canadian economy;

(2) for energy-poor and less developed countries, Canada can facilitate the development and utilization of "appropriate" energy technology. Some of this work is already being conducted under the auspices of CIDA and IDRC; and

(3) for energy-rich, developing nations, Canada can aid in the development of domestic energy capability through the loan or transfer of advice, expertise, and equipment. Both the private and public

sectors of the Canadian energy industry have in fact been engaged in just such activity. It is important to note that in all three of these cases, both Canada and the recipient countries stand to reap economic and political benefits.

CONCLUSIONS

In many respects, the nations of the Pacific Rim have displayed not only a remarkable pattern of growth, but also an extraordinary degree of resilience in the face of a multitude of political, economic, military, and social shocks. This resilience is particularly auspicious in light of the risks that face the Basin in the coming decades. For the interna-

Table 26
Canada's Export Markets, 1988 (CDN $ millions)

Country	Value ($)		Percentage of total (%)	
Western Europe	$12,432		9.3	
United Kingdom		$3,448		2.572
Eastern Europe	$1,366		1.0	
Middle East	$1,129		0.8	
Other Africa	$1,001		0.7	
Other Asia	$16,244		12.1	
Hong Kong		$986		0.735
Malaysia		$192		0.143
Singapore		$275		0.205
PRC		$2,593		1.934
Indonesia		$299		0.223
Japan		$8,680		6.474
North Korea		$6		0.004
South Korea		$1,200		0.895
Philippines		$131		0.098
Taiwan		$967		0.721
Thailand		$259		0.193
Vietnam		$5		0.004
Oceania	$1,012		0.8	
Papua New Guinea		$11		0.008
Australia		$842		0.628
Fiji		$2		0.001
New Zealand		$138		0.103
British Oceania nes		$5		0.004
French Oceania		$4		0.003
United States Oceania		$10		0.007
South America	$1,392		1.0	
Central America & Antilles	$1,622		1.2	
North America	$97,875		73.0	
United States		$97,842		72.976
All Countries	$134,075		100.0	

Source: Statistics Canada 1988

Table 27
Canada's Domestic Exports, Excluding Gold, 1946–87 (CDN $ million)

Year	US	UK	Japan	Other EEC	Other OECD*	Other America*	Centrally Planned	Other Countries
1987	96,581	3,030	6,779	6,287	2,568			10,879
1985	93,794	2,457	5,598	4,488	2,170			10,565
1980	48,795	3,221	4,275	6,295	2,730			11,184
1975	21,059	1,889	2,140	2,323	2,140			4,321
*								
1975	21,074	1,795	2,130	2,347		1,583	1,049	2,571
1970	10,563	1,481	810	1,226		750	311	1,261
1965	4,840	1,174	316	626		433	418	717
1960	2,932	915	179	439		255	47	488
1955	2,548	768	91	261		216	12	363
1950	2,021	468	20	117		118	7	284
1946	884	594	1	189		202	91	312

Source: Statistics Canada 1983, 1987
*structure of data series changed at 1975

tional investor, a broadly based strategy of diversification can provide protection against many of the country-specific risks. What does remain, however, as a potentially serious threat to the Pacific Basin, as to all other major trading blocs, are the generic risks associated with rising protectionism, the vulnerability of the American dollar, international indebtedness, and the continuing instability in the price and availability of crude oil.

What role can Canada play in the Pacific Rim and what impact can the development of this vast and diverse region have on our country? Canada is at a historic turning point. While our traditional economic, political, and social bonds have been with Europe and the United States, we now have the opportunity to diversify these linkages by participating in the development and integration of the Pacific Basin. At least three factors are responsible for the emergence of this opportunity: the trend toward rapid economic growth in many Asian countries within the past decade and a half; new patterns in the organization of international economic activities that facilitate the coordination and integration of business ventures; and recent price instability and supply dislocations in petroleum — the principal energy source for modern industrialized economies. Canada's geographic location, coupled with its increasing economic and cultural ties to East Asia, suggest that this nation can have a profound effect upon, and will be profoundly affected by, Pacific Rim development in the coming decades.

Canada's overwhelming dependence on the American market has prompted several relatively unsuccessful efforts in the past to seek

Table 28
BC Origin and Total Canadian Exports, 1988

Country	BC Origin Exports (%)	Canadian Exports (%)
UK	4.61	2.57
Belgium	1.49	0.85
France	1.54	0.88
West Germany	2.86	1.28
Italy	2.01	0.74
Netherlands	1.01	1.04
Hong Kong	0.85	0.74
India	0.46	0.29
PRC	1.55	1.93
Indonesia	0.61	0.22
Japan	27.13	6.47
South Korea	2.80	0.90
Taiwan	2.02	0.72
Australia	1.84	0.63
New Zealand	0.20	0.10
Brazil	0.60	0.38
Mexico	0.25	0.36
US	42.68	72.98
Other	5.49	6.92
Total exports	100.00	100.00
Total value	$ 17.419 bill	$134.075 bill

DESTINATION OF EXPORTS FROM CANADA'S PACIFIC PORTS (1964–84) (%)

	1984	1979	1974	1969	1964
Western Europe	10.0	14.3	14.6	19.1	20.1
Eastern Europe	2.2	2.3	0.2	0.2	5.1
Middle East	1.7	0.3	0.7	0.2	0.1
Other Africa	1.6	1.0	0.6	0.8	1.5
Other Asia	41.5	36.3	41.7	31.0	29.0
China	5.7	4.2	4.8	5.3	8.4
Japan	25.9	26.7	30.6	21.9	16.8
Oceania	2.3	2.2	2.4	3.1	2.6
South America	2.2	1.6	1.8	1.3	2.6
Central America & Antilles	0.8	0.6	1.3	0.9	1.0
North America	37.7	41.5	36.8	43.5	37.9
Total[a]	100.0	100.1	100.1	100.1	99.9
Total value (billion CDN $)	$18.25	$12.72	$6.23	$2.29	$1.62

Sources: BC External Trade Reports; Statistics Canada

[a]differences from 100.0% due to rounding

more diversified markets for our products. (See Langdon 1983, ch. 5; and Tables 26 and 27, this chapter.) At a time of a potentially unique historical opportunity for Canada in the Pacific Basin, a highly competitive economic environment *inter alia* contributed to pressure for the recently completed bilateral free trade agreement with the United States. Despite the reliance of Canada and British Columbia on US markets, there has been a noticeable orientation towards the Pacific Rim with 12.4 and 38.3 per cent of exports respectively in 1988 destined for Asian countries (Statistics Canada, April 1989; see also Table 28, this chapter).

The conscious effort to seek Asian markets in the face of the almost irresistible imperative of Canadian-American linkage is clearly a strategy which entails risk. Yet, bilateral free trade bears risks of its own. Canada may face increased deindustrialization and an ultimate economic, social, and political union with its powerful southern neighbour. The 1985 MacDonald Royal Commission on the Economic Union and Development Prospects for Canada, after extensive and thoughtful consideration, concluded that a bilateral free trade agreement with the United States was in Canada's best interest. It might be wise to consider investing a comparable amount of intellectual resources in re-examining the option of Canada's role in Pacific Rim integration.

Where does one begin in such a daunting enquiry? It involves a significant commitment of human and material resources to study the unique problems and opportunities afforded by increased Pacific Basin linkages. But much more than that, it requires a fundamental shift in our attitudes towards time and risk in the negotiation of commercial and political ties. While the risks may be high and the payback period long, the return on this investment is potentially very large. In fact, the issues are even broader, since a preoccupation with short-term domestic political and commercial concerns could have a profound and potentially detrimental impact on Canada's economic, cultural, and political future.

NOTES

1 See, for example, Christopher 1983; Crocker et al. 1984; *Economist* 1983; Kuninori 1985; Minabe 1986; Nagato 1985; Ouchi 1981; Pascale and Athos 1981; Peters and Waterman 1982; Prestowitz 1988; Roberts 1973; Sethi et al. 1984; Taylor 1983; Uchino 1978; Vernon 1983; Vogel 1979; Yamamura and Yasuba 1987.

2 The most recent data available from British Petroleum Ltd. on the average compound rate of growth in oil use over the period 1985–9 is as follows: Korea 12.5%, Taiwan 12.1%, Thailand 12.0%, Singapore 11.8%, Philippines 10.8%, PRC 6.4%, Indonesia 5.9%, New Zealand 4.4%, Australia 3.5%, Japan 3.2%, Hong Kong 2.6%, and Malaysia 0.8%. Note that of these nations, only Malaysia's annual growth in oil use is lower than the world rate of 2.3%.

REFERENCES

Abernathy, William J., Kim Clark, and Alan M. Kantrow (1983). *Industrial Renaissance: Producing a Competitive Future for America*. New York: Basic Books

Aluminum Association Inc. (various years). *Aluminum Statistical Review*. Washington, DC

Arthur Andersen & Co. and Cambridge Economic Research Associates (1987). *World Oil Trends 1987–88*. Cambridge, MA

Asian Development Bank (various years). *Key Indicators of Developing Member Countries of ADB*. Manila, July

— (various years). *Energy Indicators of Developing Member Countries of ADB*. Manila, May

BC (various years). *External Trade Report*. Victoria

BP Gas (various years) *BP Review of World Gas*. London, August

BP (various years). *BP Statistical Review of World Energy*. London, June

Barlow, Colin (1978). *The Natural Rubber Industry: Its Development, Technology, and Economy in Malaysia*. Kuala Lumpur: Oxford University Press

Batsavage, Richard E., and John L. Davie (1978). "China's International Trade and Finance." In Joint Economic Committee, *Chinese Economy Post-Mao. Volume 1, Policy and Performance*. US Congress

Bluestone, Barry, and Bennett Harrison (1982). *The Deindustrialization of America*. New York: Basic Books

Brown, Lester R. et al. (1986). *State of the World 1986*. A Worldwatch Institute Report on Progress towards a Sustainable Society. New York: Norton

Bunge, Frederica M. ed. (1982a). *South Korea: A Country Study*. Foreign Area Studies, the American University. Washington DC: Government Printing Office

— (1982b). *Japan: A Country Study*. Area Handbook Series, Foreign Area Studies, the American University. Washington DC: Government Printing Office

— (1984). *Malaysia: A Country Study*. Area Handbook Series, Foreign Area Studies, the American University. Washington DC: Government Printing Office

Business Information Display Inc. (BID) (1983). *World Energy Industry, 4th Quarter, 1982*. Vol. 3, no. 1, September

Business Week (1986). Special Report: "The Hollow Corporation." 3 March

Carley, J. Scott, Peter N. Nemetz, Ilan Vertinsky, and Vinay Kanetkar (1985a). "Energy Policy in ASEAN: The Philippines." UBC Institute of Asian Research, Working Paper no. 25. Vancouver, July

Carley, J. Scott, Peter N. Nemetz, Ilan Vertinsky, and Alfred Stewart (1985b). "Energy Policy in ASEAN: Indonesia." UBC Institute of Asian Research, Working Paper no. 27. Vancouver, July

Chaffee, Frederick H. et al. (1969). *Area Handbook for the Republic of China.* Foreign Area Studies, the American University, Washington DC: Government Printing Office

Chen, Nai-Ruenn, and Jeffrey Lee (1984). *China's Economy and Foreign Trade 1981–85.* US Department of Commerce, International Trade Administration, September

China, Republic of (various years). *Statistical Yearbook of the Republic of China.* Directorate General of Budget, Accounting and Statistics, Executive Yuan, Taipei

— (1986). *Handy Economic Data Kit 1985.* China External Trade Development Council, Taipei

— (various issues). *Industry of Free China.* Taipei

Christopher, Robert C. (1983). *The Japanese Mind: The Goliath Explained.* New York: Linden Press

Cohen, Stephen S., and John Zysman (1987). *Manufacturing Matters: The Myth of the Post-Industrial Economy.* New York: Basic Books

— (1988). "Manufacturing Innovation and American Industrial Competitiveness." *Science* 239, 4 March: 1110–15

Commonwealth of Australia Department of Resources and Energy, Bureau of Resource Economics (1987). *Energy Demand and Supply: Australia 1960–61 to 1984–85.* Canberra: Australian Government Publishing Service, May

Crocker, Olga, Cyril Charney, and Johnny Sik Leung Chiu (1984). *Quality Circles: A Guide to Participation and Productivity.* New York: Methuen

Dertouzos, Michael L., Richard K. Lester, and Robert M. Solow (1989). *Made in America: Regaining the Productive Edge.* MIT Commission on Industrial Productivity. Cambridge, MA: MIT Press

Economist (1988). "Japanese Foreign Investment: On the Move, Again." 5 November: 83

Economist (1983). *Japan.* London

Economist Intelligence Unit (1987). *Hong Kong, Macau.* Country Profile Series. London

— (various issues). *Quarterly Energy Review, Far East and Australasia.* London

Fallows, James (1980). "American Industry, What Ails It, How to Save It." *Atlantic Monthly,* September: 35–50

Fesharaki, Fereidun (1986). "Singapore as an Oil Center." Resource Systems Institute, East-West Center, Honolulu, December

Financial Times (1985). *Financial Times Energy World.* Compiled and edited by Andrew Holmes and Christopher Cragg. London: Financial Times Business Information

Globe and Mail (1986). "Denison Writes off Quintette Investment." 16 January: B.1

—. "Quintette Seeks Way to Repay Debts in Wake of Price, Shipment Cuts." 3 February

—. "Report Urges Japan to Revamp Economic Structure." 2 December:B20

— (1989). "Don't Let Manufacturing Slide, Sony Chief Warns Canada, U.S." 5 May: B1

Grossling, Bernardo, F. (1981). *World Coal Resources*, 2d ed. London: Financial Times Business Information

Halberstam, David (1986). *The Reckoning*. New York: Morrow

Hitachi (1986). "Internationalization of the Japanese Palate." *Age of Tomorrow* 98, March: 5-9

Ho, Samuel P.S., and Ralph W. Huenemann (1984). *China's Open Door Policy: The Quest for Foreign Technology and Capital. A Study of China's Special Trade*. Vancouver: UBC Press

Holling, C.S. (1978). "Myths of Ecological Stability: Resilience and the Problem of Failure." *Journal of Business Administration* 9 (2): 97–109

Hong Kong (various issues). *Hong Kong Monthly Digest of Statistics*. Hong Kong

I.P. Sharp Associates. Economic Data Bases

Institute of Energy Economics (1983). *Energy Balances in Japan (1982)*. Tokyo

International Monetary Fund (various years). *Balance of Payments Statistics*. Washington, DC

—(various years). *Direction of Trade Statistics*. Washington, DC

— (various years). *International Financial Statistics*. Washington, DC

— (various years). *World Economic Outlook*. Washington, DC

Japan Economic Journal (1983). 17 November

Japan External Trade Organization (JETRO) (1982). *White Paper on International Trade*

Kanetkar, Vinay, Peter N. Nemetz, Sandra Schwartz, Ilan B. Vertinsky, Patricia Vertinsky, and William Ziemba (1983). "The Energy Future of Australia and New Zealand: A First Round of Modelling." In proceedings of the International AMSE Conference, *Modelling and Simulation*, vol. 5: 265–302, Nice, 12–14 September

Karatsu, Hajime (1985). "The Deindustrialization of America: A Tragedy for the World." KKC *Brief*, Keizai Koho Center, Japan Institute for Social and Economic Affairs, no. 31, October

Keizai Koho Center (Japan Institute for Social and Economic Affairs) (various years). *Japan: An International Comparison*. Tokyo

Kodama, Fumio (1986). "Technological Diversification of Japanese Industry." *Science*, 18 July: 291–96

Kuninori, Morio (1985). "U.S. Capital Stock Still Older than Japan's." *Economic Eye*, Quarterly Digest of Views from Japan, Keizai Koho Center, Japan Institute for Social and Economic Affairs, 6 (1): 29–32

Langdon, Frank (1983). *The Politics of Canadian-Japanese Economic Relations 1952–1983*. Vancouver: UBC Press

Lawrence, Robert Z. (1984). *Can America Compete?* Washington, DC: Brookings Institution

Lee, Chong-Sik (1982). "Historical Setting." In Frederica M. Bunge, ed., *South Korea: A Country Study*, Area Handbook Series, Foreign Area Studies, the American University. Washington, DC: Government Printing Office

Marlay, Robert C. (1984). "Trends in Industrial Use of Energy." *Science*, 14 December: 1277–83

McLauchlan, Gordon et al., eds. (1986). *The New Zealand Book of Events*. Reed: Methuen

Midland Doherty (1985). "Quintette Coal Limited." Institutional Research, G.S. Carter, Toronto, 16 December

Minabe, Shigeo (1986). "Japanese Competitiveness and Japanese Management." *Science*, 18 July: 301–64

Morgan, John D. (1986). "U.S. and the World Mineral Positions, 1985 to the Year 2000." *Mining Engineering*, April: 245–8

Morse, Ronald A. (1984). "Japan's Liquefied Natural Gas Dilemma: Oversupply and Lower Demand." Chapter 8 in R. Morse and C. Ebinger, eds., *U.S.-Japan Energy Cooperation and Competition*. Boulder: Westview

Nagato, Kazuhiko (1985). "The Japan-U.S. Saving-Rate Gap." *Economic Eye*, a Quarterly Digest of Views from Japan, Keizai Koho Center, Japan Institute for Social and Economic Affairs, 6(2):18–21

Nemetz, Peter N. (1988). "Risk and Resilience in the Pacific Rim: The Case of Energy." Working Paper, Faculty of Commerce, UBC

— (1990). "Primary Commodities and Strategies for Development in ASEAN." *ASEAN Economic Bulletin* 6(3):237–67

—, and Ilan B. Vertinsky (1984). "Japan and the International Market for LNG." *Columbia Journal of World Business* 19(1):70–76

—, and Ilan B. Vertinsky and P. Vertinsky (1984–5). "Japan's Energy Strategy at the Crossroads." *Pacific Affairs* 57(4):553–76

—, and Ilan B. Vertinsky, P. Vertinsky, and Vinay Kanetkar (1984). "Threat in Opportunity and Opportunity in Threat: Energy Prospects for Australia and New Zealand." *Journal of Energy and Development* 9(2):236–88

New York Times (1988). "U.S. Will Drop 4 Areas in Asia from Trade Aid." 30 January

New York Times (1989). "U.S. Assails South Korea on Currency." 6 May

New York Times (1990). "Doubts on Supply Spur Production of High Oil Prices." 24 February: A1

New Zealand Department of Statistics (1983). *New Zealand Official Yearbook 1983*. 88th Annual Edition. Wellington

Ouchi, William (1981). *Theory Z: How American Business Can Meet the Japanese Challenge*. Reading, MA: Addison-Wesley

Pascale, Richard Tanner, and Anthony G. Athos (1981). *The Art of Japanese Management: Applications for American Executives*. New York: Simon and Schuster

People's Republic of China State Statistical Bureau (various years). *Statistical Yearbook of China*. Beijing

Peters, Thomas J., and Robert H. Waterman, Jr. (1982). *In Search of Excellence: Lessons from America's Best-Run Companies*, Cambridge, MA: Harper and Row

Petroleum Publishing Co. (various years). *International Petroleum Encyclopedia*. Tulsa

Prestowitz, Clyde V., Jr. (1988). *Trading Places: How We Allowed Japan to Take the Lead*. New York: Basic Books

Reich, Robert (1983). *The Next American Frontier*. New York: Times Books

Riek, Christine, Peter N. Nemetz, Ilan B. Vertinsky, Martin Dresner, Vinay Kanetkar, and A.J. Hesford (1985a). "Energy Policy in ASEAN: Malaysia and Singapore." UBC Institute of Asian Research, Working Paper no. 26. Vancouver, July

Riek, Christine, Peter N. Nemetz, Ilan Vertinsky, Martin Dresner, and Alfred Stewart (1985b). "Energy Policy in ASEAN: Thailand." UBC Institute of Asian Research, Working Paper no. 28. Vancouver, July

Rinehart, Robert (1981). "Historical Setting." In Frederica M. Bunge, ed., *Thailand: A Country Study*, Area Handbook Series, Foreign Area Studies, the American University. Washington, DC: Government Printing Office

Roberts, John G. (1973). *Mitsui: Three Centuries of Japanese Business*. New York: Weatherhill

Ross, Joel E., and William C. Ross (1982). *Japanese Quality Circles and Productivity*. Reston, VA: Reston Publishing

Rundt's Risk Reports, various countries

Samuels, Richard J. (1983). "The Industrial Destructuring of the Japanese Aluminum Industry." *Pacific Affairs* 56(3):495–509

Seekins, Donald M. (1983). "Historical Setting." In Frederica M. Bunge, ed., *Indonesia: A Country Study*, Area Handbook Series, Foreign Area Studies, the American University. Washington, DC: Government Printing Office

Seekins, Donald M. (1984a). "Historical Setting." In Frederica M. Bunge, ed., *Philippines: A Country Study*, Area Handbook Series, Foreign Area Studies, the American University. Washington, DC: Government Printing Office

— (1984b). "Historical Setting." In Frederica M. Bunge, ed., *Malaysia: A Country Study*, Area Handbook Series, Foreign Area Studies, the American University. Washington DC: Government Printing Office

Sethi, S. Prakash, Nobuaki Namiki, and Carl L. Swanson (1984). *The False Promise of the Japanese Miracle: Illusions and Realities of the Japanese Management System*. Boston: Pitman

Shinn, Rinn-Sup (1981). "Historical Setting." In Frederica M. Bunge, ed., *China: A Country Study*, Area Handbook Series, Foreign Areas Studies, the American University. Washington, DC: Government Printing Office

— (1983). "Historical Setting." In Frederica M. Bunge, ed., *Japan: A Country*

Study, Area Handbook Series, Foreign Areas Studies, the American University. Washington, DC: Government Printing Office

Siddayao, Corazon M. (1982). "Demand for Energy and Economic Growth: Some Measurement and Conceptual Issues." Resource Systems Institute, East-West Center, Working Paper WP–82–13. Honolulu

Smil, Vaclav (1978). "China's Energetics: A System Analysis." In US Congress, Joint Economic Committee, *Chinese Economy Post-Mao, Volume 1, Policy and Performance*: 323–69

Statistics Canada (1983). *Historical Statistics of Canada*. 2d. ed. Ottawa

— (various years). *Exports by Countries*. 65–003

— Central Statistics Bureau (1989). "B.C. Origin and Total Canadian Exports 1988 Annual." April

Stewart, Alfred, and Peter N. Nemetz (1982a). "Patterns of Energy Supply and Demand in Taiwan." UBC Faculty of Commerce, Working Paper

— (1982b). "Patterns of Energy Use in Korea." UBC Faculty of Commerce, Working Paper

Sumita, Satoshi (1989). "Global Risk Management: The Importance of International Policy Coordination." *Speaking of Japan*, Keizai Koho Center, Japan Institute for Social and Economic Affairs, 10(106):20–24. Tokyo, October

Sycip, Gorres, Velayo & Co. (1983). *Energy Balance Forecasts in Developing Countries: The Case of the Philippines*. Institute of Developing Economies. Tokyo, January

Taylor, Jared (1983). *Shadows of the Rising Sun: A Critical View of the "Japanese Miracle."* New York: Morrow

Teese, David J. (1982). "A Behavioural Analysis of OPEC: An Economic and Political Synthesis." *Journal of Business Administration* 13(1&2): 127–59

Thurow, Lester C. (1985). *The Zero-Sum Solution: Building a World-Class American Economy*. New York: Simon and Schuster

Uchino, Tatruro (1978). *Japan's Postwar Economy: An Insider's View of Its History and Its Future.* Tokyo: Kodanska International. First English Edition 1983

United Nations (1983). *World Statistics in Brief*. New York

—. (various years). *Energy Statistics Yearbook*. New York

—. *International Trade Statistics*. New York

—. *National Accounts Statistics: Analysis of the Main Aggregates*. New York

—. *Statistical Yearbook*. New York

—. *World Trade Statistics*. New York

United Nations Department of International Economic and Social Affairs, Statistical Office (1979). *World Energy Supplies, 1973–1978*. New York

United Nations Economic and Social Commission for Asia and the Pacific (various years). *Statistical Yearbook for Asia and the Pacific*. Bangkok

—. *Foreign Trade Statistics of Asia and the Pacific*. Bangkok

United Nations UNCTAD (various years). *UNCTAD Commodity Yearbook*. New York

— (1988). *Handbook of International Trade and Development Statistics*. New York

United States Central Intelligence Agency (various years). *The World Factbook*. Washington, DC: Government Printing Office

— (1986). "China: Economic Performance in 1985." A Report Presented to the Subcommittee on Economic Resources, Competitiveness, and Security Economics of the Joint Economic Committee, 17 March

United States Department of Commerce, Bureau of the Census (various years). *Statistical Abstract of the United States*

—, International Trade Administration (1982). *China's Economy and Foreign Trade, 1979–81*. May

United States Department of the Interior, Bureau of Mines (1988). *Mineral Industries of the Far East and South Asia*. Washington, DC

United States Energy Information Administration (1985). *Annual Prospects for World Coal Trade 1985, with Projections to 1995*. Washington, DC: Department of Energy, May

United States General Accounting Office (1988). *Energy Security. An Overview of Changes in the World Oil Market*. Report to the Congress. GAO/RCED–88–170, August

United States Office of Technology Assessment (1981). *U.S. Industrial Competitiveness: A Comparison of Steel, Electronics, and Automobiles*. Washington, DC, July

— (1984). *Technologies to Sustain Tropical Forest Resources*. Washington, DC, March

Vernon, Raymond (1983). *Two Hungry Giants: The United States and Japan in the Quest for Oil and Gas*. Cambridge, MA: Harvard University Press

Vogel, Ezra F. (1979). *Japan as Number 1: Lessons for America*. New York: Harper Colophon

Vreeland, Nena et al. (1977). *Area Handbook for Singapore*. Foreign Area Studies, the American University. Washington, DC: Government Printing Office

Whitaker, Donald P. et al. (1974). *Area Handbook for Australia*. Foreign Area Studies, the American University. Washington, DC: Government Printing Office

Woodard, Kim (1980). *The International Energy Relations of China*. Stanford: Stanford University Press

World Bank (1983a). *China, Socialist Economic Development, Volume 1, The Economy, Statistical System, and Basic Data*. Washington, DC, August

— (1983b). *China, Socialist Economic Development, Volume 2, The Economic Sectors, Agriculture, Industry, Energy, Transport, and External Trade and Finance*. Washington, DC, August

— (1983c). *World Tables*. 3d ed. Vol. 1, *Economic Data*. Baltimore: Johns Hopkins University Press

— (1988). *World Tables*, 4th ed. *Economic Data*. Baltimore: Johns Hopkins University Press

— (various years). *World Development Report*. New York: Oxford University Press

World Resources Institute (1989). *World Resources 1988–89*. Washington, DC

World Resources Institute (1990). *World Resources 1990–91*. Washington, DC

World Resources Institute, the World Bank, and the United Nations Development Programme (1985). *Tropical Forests: A Call for Action*. 3 vols, October

Yamada, Mitsuhiko (1982). "Japan's Direct Overseas Investment and Its Impact on Domestic Industry." *Journal of Japanese Trade and Industry* 1(5): 18–23

Yamamura, Kozo, and Yasukichi Yasuba (1987). "Introduction." In Kozo Yamamura and Yasukichi Yasuba, eds., *The Political Economy of Japan, Volume 1, The Domestic Transformation*:1–29. Stanford: Stanford University Press

ACKNOWLEDGMENTS

The author would like to thank the following individuals for their advice and assistance in the preparation of this manuscript. The interpretation of the data remains the responsibility of the author:

Professor Anthony Arrott, SFU, Vancouver

Mr. Jeremy Carter, International Monetary Fund, Washington, DC

Ms Diana Chan, Librarian, Faculty of Commerce, UBC

Professor Chia Siow Yue, National University of Singapore

Mr. Chua Mui Huat, the Monetary Authority of Singapore

Mr. William Clive, UN Department of International Economic and Social Affairs, Statistical Office

Mr. Ian Davison, Corporate Planning Department, the British Petroleum Company, London

Ms Sarah Dennis, Deputy High Commissioner of New Zealand to Canada, Ottawa

Dr. David Fridley, East-West Center, Honolulu

Professor Samuel Ho, Department of Economics, UBC

Ambassador T. Koh, Ambassador of Singapore to the United States, Washington, DC

Dr. Jack Kulp, East-West Center, Honolulu

Professor Emeritus Frank Langdon, Department of Political Science, UBC

Ms Colleen Lee, Faculty of Commerce and Business Administration, UBC

Ms Sarah Lehman, New York, NY

Professor Terence McGee, Director, Institute of Asian Research, UBC

Professor Diane Mauzy, Department of Political Science, UBC

Professor Emeritus Stephen Milne, Department of Political Science, UBC
Ms Christine Riek, Vancouver, BC
Dr. Corazon M. Siddayao, the World Bank, Washington, DC
Professor Richard Stubbs, Department of Political Science, University of Toronto
Mr. Nagendra Subbakrishna, Vancouver, BC

CHAPTER TWO

Japanese Trade in the Pacific Rim: The Relationship between Trade and Investment

Yoko Sazanami

INTRODUCTION

The Pacific Rim is the most dynamic region in world trade today.[1] Not only is trade expanding rapidly, but also changes in national comparative advantage are occurring. Such changes have altered the commodity composition of both exports and imports in recent years. For example, the large energy price rise in the 1970s induced Japanese firms to adopt energy-saving devices in various stages of production processes and to shift to other production lines when they found their comparative advantage had been eroded. Presently, Japan exports more technology-intensive and fewer energy-intensive goods than it did a decade ago.

Although the changes in relative prices conceal the real changes that took place, the Japanese import market in the 1970s responded quite well to the rise in oil prices, liberalization of trade, and appreciation of the yen. When the commodity composition of imports is evaluated in 1970 constant prices, the share of raw materials declined between 1970 and 1983 while the share of manufactured goods increased (see Sazanami 1983; Bank of Japan 1984).

Many Asian developing countries also experienced changes in their commodity composition of trade during the 1970s. The Asian NICs succeeded in decreasing the export share of traditional exports such as clothing and other labour-intensive miscellaneous manufactures while increasing the share of more sophisticated exports such as electrical machinery. The exports from ASEAN-4 still consist primarily of raw materials and agriculture and food products, but these nations are trying to diversify their exports to resource-based manufactures, textiles, yarn and clothing, and even to some types of electric machinery.

Indeed, the Asian developing countries were able to expand their industrial base in the 1970s. As their economic performance proved better than countries in other regions, they attracted an influx of foreign capital. In addition, the industrialization and export promotion policies pursued by their governments were helpful in sustaining high economic growth and trade expansion.

Japan continued to provide a large outlet for the exports of the Asian developing countries and Oceania. The degree of dependence on the Japanese market increased considerably in the 1970s in the case of ASEAN-4 and Oceania but only moderately in the Asian NICs. The notable difference here was that ASEAN-4 continued to increase exports of raw materials and resource-based manufactures to Japan, while the Asian NICs shipped more sophisticated new products to the United States, the European Community, and the Middle East, but not much to Japan.

Hiemenz (1983) studied the export performance of Asian NICs and ASEAN countries in the 1970s and found that changes in the commodity composition of their exports clearly followed the standard neo-factor proportions paradigm. In other words, by 1979 Asian NICs exported more engineering products, and ASEAN-4 countries expanded their exports of the traditional trio of textiles, clothing, and miscellaneous manufactures while maintaining a comparative advantage in resource-based manufactures and foods. The new exports from Asian NICs penetrated American and European markets in the 1970s. However, they could not erode the Japanese market.

Hamilton and Kreinin (1980) concluded that differences in the trade performance of developing countries in selling manufactured goods to Japan and other industrial nations could be attributed to difficulties in penetrating Japan's domestic distribution system, tariff and nontariff barriers, and absence of minimum wage legislation, in addition to their own weak bargaining position.

It is quite true that Japan continued to provide the largest market for agricultural, food product, and raw material exports from the Asian NICs. And the rapid decline in importance of this commodity group in the exports of Asian NICs as well as the modest market penetration in new products explain the rather small gain in Japanese dependence of Asian NICs in the 1970s. However, it is difficult to attribute the modest market penetration of Asian NICs in the Japanese market to institutional reasons alone.

The penetration into the Japanese market occurred exactly in those fields where Japan lost its comparative advantage in the 1970s because of the oil price rise and wage increases reflecting the appreciation of the yen. These new market opportunities developed in such commodities as textiles, non-ferrous metals, wood, and wood products. However, the new product lines in which the Asian NICs gained their comparative advantage, such as electrical machinery and equipment, were fields where the Japanese gain in comparative advantage was the most substantial in the 1970s. Thus, the Asian NICs found it difficult to compete in the Japanese market. In addition, the tendency of Japanese firms to invest in resource development and resource processing in order to cope with the rise in energy prices helped to increase the imports of resource-based manufactures rather than sophisticated new products.

The purpose of this chapter is to assess the overall interdependence of trade and investment between Japan and other Pacific Rim countries in the 1972-82 period; to describe the trade patterns that emerged as a result of industrial development in the Asian NICs and ASEAN-4 in particular; and to point out that Japanese investment in resource development and resource processing after the oil crisis had distorted the application of the standard neo-factor proportions paradigm in the case of trade between Japan and these countries. In other words, the mobility of capital in developing resources and processing resource-based manufactures is making trade relationships between Japan and other Pacific Rim countries look rather different from what the neo-factor proportions paradigm would suggest.

THE GROWING ECONOMIC INTERDEPENDENCE BETWEEN JAPAN AND OTHER PACIFIC RIM COUNTRIES

As indicated in Table 29, Japan is the most important market for exports and source of supply for imports of other Pacific Rim countries. The countries that depend most heavily on the Japanese market as the outlet for their total exports are Indonesia (59.7 per cent), Australia (34 per cent), Malaysia (32.3 per cent), and the Philippines (30.2 per cent). Those countries endowed with rich natural resources have found the Japanese market particularly important and increased their export dependence on it in the late 1970s.

In 1981, Singapore and Hong Kong, both leading exporters of manufactured goods among the Asian developing countries, shipped only 9.2 per cent and 3 per cent of their total exports to Japan respectively. The other major exporter of manufactured goods, Korea, also found the

Table 29
Japanese Trade Interdependence with Pacific Rim Countries, 1977, 1981 (%)

	Exports to Japan as % of Total Japanese Imports		Exports to Japan as % of Total Exports of Exporting Nation		Imports From Japan as % of Total Japanese Exports		Imports From Japan as % of Total Imports of Importing Nation	
	1977	1981	1977	1981	1977	1981	1977	1981
ASIAN NICs								
Hong Kong	0.49	0.47	3.61	3.05	2.88	3.49	22.17	21.50
Korea	2.99	2.40	21.03	15.90	5.06	3.72	37.72	21.60
Singapore	0.96	1.37	8.33	9.20	2.13	2.91	16.39	16.05
ASEAN-4								
Indonesia	7.08	9.44	46.00	59.70	2.23	2.71	28.84	31.05
Malaysia	2.21	1.86	34.10	32.30	1.07	1.59	18.99	20.92
Philippines	1.27	1.22	28.46	30.20	1.36	1.26	25.73	24.21
Thailand	1.06	0.75	21.48	15.30	1.68	1.48	29.29	22.46
OCEANIA								
Australia	7.49	5.26	39.58	34.08	2.89	3.14	19.03	20.10
New Zealand	0.71	0.62	15.80	15.90	0.55	0.59	13.26	16.02

Source: UN (1983), *Yearbook of International Trade Statistics*

Japanese market less important than before. Sales to Japan declined from 21 per cent of all Korean exports in 1977 to 15.9 per cent in 1981.

With respect to Pacific Rim imports, Japan continues to be the major source of supply to the countries in the region. There was no observable difference in dependence on imports from Japan between countries like Australia and Indonesia, endowed with rich natural resources, and countries like Hong Kong and Korea that export mainly manufactured goods. Except for Singapore and Malaysia, countries in the region purchased between 20 and 30 per cent of their total imports from Japan.

Since the total amount of Japanese trade is substantially larger than that of her trading partners in the region, Japanese trade dependence on these countries is much less than their dependence on Japan. Nevertheless, the Pacific Rim region as a whole supplies about one-quarter of Japanese total imports and provides a market for 20 per cent of Japan's exports. As for the sources of supply for Japanese imports, resource-rich Indonesia and Australia are more important than the others.

If we measure trade interdependence by the proportion of bilateral trade in the total trade of all countries listed in Table 29, those that increased their trade interdependence with Japan towards the end of the 1970s were Indonesia and Singapore. Korea, which used to have

Table 30
Japanese Direct Investment in Pacific Rim Countries, 1973, 1977, 1983

	Amount in US $ Million[a]			Percentage of Japanese Total		
	1973	1977	1983	1973	1977	1983
ASIAN NICs						
Hong Kong	100	448	1825	1.47	2.30	3.43
Korea	207	690	1312	3.05	3.55	2.46
Singapore	90	305	1383	1.32	1.57	2.60
Taiwan	108	227	479	1.59	1.16	0.90
ASEAN-4						
Indonesia	473	2703	7268	6.98	13.92	13.67
Malaysia	76	356	764	1.12	1.83	1.43
Philippines	88	354	721	1.29	1.82	1.35
Thailand	129	228	521	1.90	1.17	0.98
OCEANIA						
Australia	307	818	2882	4.53	4.21	5.42
New Zealand	59	109	212	0.87	0.56	0.39
TOTAL	1637	6238	17367	24.12	32.09	32.63

Source: Ministry of Finance (various issues), "Zaisei Kinyu Tokei Geppo"
[a]Accumulated total as of March, respective years

the highest interdependence ratio with Japan, decreased its ratio toward the end of the 1970s. In other words, Korea was increasingly able to diversify its import supply.

The development of Japanese direct investment in Pacific Rim countries between 1973 and 1983 (Table 30) generally corresponded to the development of trade interdependence. Indonesia became the largest recipient of direct investment from Japan. The purpose of this investment was to exploit Indonesia's rich natural resources in the first half of the 1970s and to process these resources in the following period. Resource-rich Australia also continued to attract more Japanese direct investment in the later 1970s, but the rate of increase was rather modest compared to the preceding periods. Japanese direct investment in Asian NICs continued to grow, but there was relatively little investment in Korea compared to Singapore and Hong Kong. Hong Kong became the largest host country of Japanese direct investment among Asian NICs in 1983, followed by Singapore.

As of March 1983, the Pacific Rim had received about 32 per cent of total accumulated Japanese direct investment. Investment in Indonesia accounted for more than one-third of the total directed to the region. The heavy investment in exploiting Indonesia's rich natural resources and the subsequent investment in resource processing had promoted close economic interdependence between Indonesia and Japan.

JAPANESE DIRECT INVESTMENT IN RESOURCE DEVELOPMENT AND PROCESSING

Because the relative size of the Japanese economy in the Pacific Rim is so large, the development of Japanese trade exerts an overwhelming influence on trade flows in the region. Japanese export specialization in heavy industries like iron and steel and chemicals in the 1960s entailed a tremendous import demand for iron ore and petroleum. A huge Japanese import demand for resources and resource-processed manufactures created export opportunities for resource-rich countries, particularly those of the Pacific Rim. Their export specialization tended to be formed precisely in those fields where Japanese demand was the strongest.

For a country so poorly endowed with natural resources as Japan, the possibility of attaining high industrial growth by promoting expansion in heavy industries that are also resource-intensive depended on the availability of natural resource imports at low prices. Thus "resource development" has always been the most important motive for Japanese foreign investment. Even in the 1950s, when the outflow of capital was under strict government control, foreign investment projects in Alaskan pulp (1953), a steel plant in Brazil (1957), Arabian Oil (1958), and North Sumatra Oil (1960) started with strong government support. The outbreak of the Korean War and the subsequent rise in primary commodity prices was the factor that induced Japan to invest in resource development under government leadership. However, as primary commodity markets became supply abundant toward the late 1950s, Japan was able to import natural resources necessary for producing such resource-intensive goods as iron and steel and chemicals at relatively low prices during the period of high economic growth. It was not until the late 1960s that Japan again had to emphasize natural resource development projects.

By the end of the 1960s, Japan had become a major world importer of such natural resources as iron ore. Japan eventually found that the increase in imports would affect the world market price. Thus it became increasingly difficult for Japan to get a sufficient supply at low prices unless it undertook resource development that would increase world supply.

Several other factors help explain Japan's enthusiasm for investing abroad in the late 1960s. Firstly, the longstanding balance-of-payments deficit in Japan's basic account had turned to a surplus, and there was a rapid accumulation of foreign currency reserves. It was quite evident that Japanese currency was overvalued at that time, but government and the business community alike had a strong distaste for appreciating the yen. They tried to maintain the 350 yen to a dollar rate by accelerating capital outflow and by trying to keep the basic account in balance. Secondly, neighbouring Asian developing countries were turning to foreign capital imports to accelerate their growth. They stressed the importance of direct investment that brought together both capital and management skills necessary for promoting growth, and they welcomed Japanese direct investment in general.

The first boom in Japanese foreign direct investment came in the early 1970s when it grew by 52.7 per cent in 1972 and 51.6 per cent in 1973. The increase in 1972 reflected the large investment primarily in resource development. At the beginning of the 1970s, one-third of the total accumulated direct investment was in the resource industry. Starting in 1971, the Japanese government provided a tax concession to promote resource development by introducing a system that allowed 30 per cent of direct investment in petroleum, non-ferrous metal, iron ore, uranium, and coal development to be treated as reserve funds that are tax exempt for five years. In addition, financial support provided from the Export-Import Bank[2] and the Overseas Economic Cooperation Fund helped the resource development projects (see Sekiguchi 1982, ch. 2). Indeed, as much as 42.8 per cent of the direct investment undertaken in 1972 was related to resource development.

In 1973, the relative importance of resource development investment decreased, and the investment boom shifted to manufacturing. Japanese firms were eager to build foreign subsidiaries to overcome the rise in domestic wage costs after the appreciation of the yen and to avert the various trade barriers in developing countries intended to promote import substitution in manufacturing. The upsurge in Japanese direct investment continued until the end of 1973 when the sudden rise in oil prices caused a rapid deterioration in Japan's balance-of-payments.

In the period that followed the oil crisis, Japanese firms became very cautious about investing abroad. They were busy coping with domestic problems caused by the high energy price and its aftermath. However, the stagnation in direct investment was more obvious in manufacturing than in resource development. The oil crisis reminded Japan of the country's poor resource endowment, and there was a growth in investment in petroleum and LNG development projects, in Indonesia particularly. As a result of the sharp rise in domestic energy costs and appreciation of the yen, energy-intensive resource processing industries like aluminum smelting were rapidly losing their competitive strength. To cope with this situation, Japanese firms started to shift energy-intensive resource processing to foreign locations. This trend became more obvious in the late 1970s when Japanese firms adjusted well to the oil crisis and its aftermath and became fully prepared to invest abroad.

Traditionally, Japanese firms prefer to import resources and to undertake the smelting or fabrication process domestically. Such preferences reflect Japan's locational situation far from the industrial centres of the world. Government policies in the 1960s to promote domestic processing of imported raw materials helped assure employment opportunities at home and saved foreign currencies. At the same time they helped firms to build a self-sufficient production structure within Japan (see Sazanami 1980, ch. 6). However, these conditions were changing in the early 1970s as liberalization of trade and appreciation of the yen enabled cost savings through production in overseas subsidiaries. Neighbouring countries in the Pacific Rim, notably the Asian NICs, were building up an industrial base that could undertake processing for Japanese firms. The sharp rise in energy prices provided another opportunity for Japanese firms to undertake the processing of raw materials, particularly mineral resources, at foreign establishments.

The development of mineral resources requires huge amounts of capital, and Japanese capital contributed to resource development through investment in petroleum, non-ferrous metals, and iron ore from the late 1960s onward. The mineral ores extracted were supplied to Japan in most cases by long-term contracts made at the time of investment. The ore was generally smelted in Japan, but after the oil crisis, the rise in energy costs made smelting in energy-abundant, resource-rich foreign countries more profitable. The rise in energy prices also increased transportation costs, making it more economical to import processed products rather than raw materials in bulk. Another factor that increased Japanese investment in resource processing during this period was the industrialization policies of resource-rich developing countries that favoured the construction of fabrication and smelting facilities funded by foreign capital.

JAPANESE DIRECT INVESTMENT IN THE PACIFIC RIM

Japanese direct investment in Pacific Rim countries followed the general trend outlined in the previous section. Since Japanese firms had already built close economic ties through trade with this region, it is not surprising to find that they chose Pacific Rim countries to host their direct investment in the first investment boom in the early 1970s. As of March 1973, Japanese direct investment in the Pacific Rim amounted to US $1,788 million, representing 26.3 per cent of the total investment in these nations. Pacific Rim countries were the recipients of 31 per cent of total Japanese overseas investment for resource development and 46.7 per cent of total investment for manufacturing in the same year. In other words, Pacific Rim countries were receiving relatively more Japanese investment in manufacturing than in resource development in the early 1970s.

Ten years later, as of March 1983, Japanese direct investment in Pacific Rim countries reached US $17,713 million, representing 33 per cent of the total. Direct investment in resource development amounted to US $7,079 million, which accounts for over one-third of the direct investment in these countries and 62 per cent of Japanese total resource development investment. In other words, not only did the importance of Pacific Rim countries as hosts for Japanese direct investment increase during these years, but so also did the importance of resource development. Japanese investment in manufacturing industries remained important, but its share declined to 39.8 per cent of Japan's total world investment in March 1983.

There was an evident shift in the field of Japanese direct investment from manufacturing in the first investment boom in the early 1970s to resource development and processing after the oil crisis. In the former period, the major reason for investing in Asian developing countries was to mobilize their abundant labour supply and to avoid trade barriers intended to promote import substitution. But the prime motive of Japanese investment after the oil crisis was to assure resource supply and to overcome high energy prices by shifting their energy-intensive processes to foreign locations. The resource-rich Asian developing countries tried to attain resource-based industrialization by accommodating Japanese investment.

Differences in investment motives between the first direct investment boom in 1971-2 and after the 1973 oil crisis were well reflected in the regional distribution as well as the industrial composition of Japanese investment in the 1973-83 period. As shown in Table 31, the largest amount of Japanese direct investment went into resource-rich ASEAN-4, accounting for 54.3 per cent of total Japanese investment in the Pacific Rim between 1973 and 1983. And 58.9 per cent of the total direct investment to ASEAN-4 was in resource industries, Indonesia being the largest host country. Major projects in mineral resource development during this period included copper mines in Indonesia and Malaysia, iron ore in the Philippines, and petroleum and LNG in Indonesia.

The importance of investment in forestry and fisheries must not be overlooked, since they serve an important role in providing employment opportunities for the host country. The employment effects will

Table 31

Japanese Direct Investment in Manufacturing and Resource Industries in Pacific Rim Countries (in US $ millions)

Manufacturing	Food	Textiles	Wood & Pulp	Chemicals	Iron & Nonferrous Metal	Machinery	Electric Machinery	Transport Machinery	Other Manufacturing
DIRECT INVESTMENT 1973–7									
Asian NICs[c]									
$ mill.	7	109	14	65	43	44	106	70	45
(%)	(1.4)	(21.7)	(2.8)	(12.9)	(8.5)	(8.7)	(21.1)	(13.9)	(8.9)
ASEAN-4[d]									
$ mill.	53	306	64	85	135	9	33	24	139
(%)	(6.2)	(36.1)	(7.5)	(10.0)	(15.9)	(1.1)	(3.9)	(2.8)	(16.4)
Oceania									
$ mill.	14	2	43	90	33	6	9	42	3
(%)	(5.8)	(0.8)	(17.8)	(37.3)	(13.7)	(2.5)	(3.7)	(17.4)	(1.2)
DIRECT INVESTMENT 1977–81									
Asian NICs									
$ mill.	20	49	3	265	42	121	150	35	167
(%)	(2.3)	(5.7)	(0.3)	(31.0)	(4.9)	(14.1)	(17.5)	(4.0)	(19.5)
ASEAN-4									
$ mill.	24	149	27	235	706	26	53	90	47
(%)	(1.8)	(11.0)	(2.0)	(17.3)	(51.9)	(2.0)	(3.9)	(6.6)	(3.5)
Oceania									
$ mill.	8	1	14	2	184	15	9	172	26
(%)	(1.9)	(0.2)	(3.2)	(0.5)	(42.8)	(3.5)	(2.1)	(39.9)	(6.0)

Table 31 (continued)
Japanese Direct Investment in Manufacturing and Resource Industries in Pacific Rim Countries (in US $ millions)

Manufacturing	Food	Textiles	Wood & Pulp	Chemicals	Iron & Nonferrous Metal	Machinery	Electric Machinery	Transport Machinery	Other Manufacturing
DIRECT INVESTMENT 1981–3									
Asian NICs									
$ mill.	13	14	2	205	16	68	54	10	28
(%)	(3.2)	(3.5)	—	(52.0)	(4.0)	(17.2)	(13.7)	(2.5)	(7.1)
ASEAN-4									
$ mill.	9	57	19	41	473	15	18	64	61
(%)	(1.3)	(8.1)	(2.7)	(5.8)	(67.3)	(2.1)	(2.6)	(9.1)	(8.7)
Oceania									
$ mill.	13	1	28	0	84	8	0	21	40
(%)	(6.6)	(0.5)	(14.3)	(0)	(42.9)	(4.1)	(0)	(10.7)	(20.4)
ACCUMULATED TOTAL MARCH 1983									
Asian NICs									
$ mill.	45	297	20	548	130	247	354	143	279
(%)	(2.1)	(14.3)	(0.9)	(26.5)	(6.3)	(11.9)	(17.1)	(6.9)	(13.5)
ASEAN-4									
$ mill.	115	653	133	375	1350	54	123	190	272
(%)	(3.5)	(20.3)	(4.1)	(11.6)	(42.0)	(1.6)	(3.8)	(5.9)	(8.4)
Oceania									
$ mill.	57	6	122	99	338	30	21	242	70
(%)	(5.7)	(0.6)	(12.3)	(10.0)	(34.3)	(3.0)	(2.1)	(24.5)	(7.1)

Table 31 (continued)
Japanese Direct Investment in Manufacturing and Resource Industries in Pacific Rim Countries (in US $ millions)

	Total Manufacturing Industry	Total Resource Industry[a]	Total All Direct Investment	Mfg. as % of All DI[b]	Resource as % of all DI
DIRECT INVESTMENT 1973–7					
Asian NICs					
$ mill.	503	7	1046	48.1	0.7
(%)	(100)				
ASEAN-4[d]					
$ mill.	848	1853	2875	29.5	64.4
(%)	(100)				
Oceania					
$ mill.	241	209	909	26.5	23.9
(%)	(100)				
DIRECT INVESTMENT 1977–81					
Asian NICs					
$ mill.	854	52	1821	46.8	2.7
(%)	(100)				
ASEAN-4					
$ mill.	1360	947	2444	55.6	38.7
(%)	(100)				
Oceania					
$ mill.	431	549	1433	30.1	38.3
(%)	(100)				
DIRECT INVESTMENT 1981–3					
Asian NICs					
$ mill.	394	–6[c]	1256	31.3	0.4
(%)	(100)				
ASEAN-4					
$ mill.	703	2373	3189	22.0	74.4
(%)	(1100				
Oceania					
$ mill.	196	381	845	23.2	45.0
(%)	(100)				
ACCUMULATED TOTAL MARCH 1983					
Asian NICs					
$ mill.	2063	53	4520	45.6	1.1
(%)	(100)				
ASEAN-4					
$ mill.	3214	5526	9374	34.2	58.9
(%)	(100)				
Oceania					
$ mill.	985	1404	3370	29.2	41.6
(%)	(100)				

Source: Ministry of Finance (various issues), "Zaisei Kinyu Tokei Geppo"
[a]Resource Industries include Agriculture, Forestry, Fisheries, and Mining
[b]DI — Direct Investment
[c]Asian NICs: Hong Kong, Singapore, and Korea
[d]ASEAN-4: Indonesia, Malaysia, Philippines, and Thailand

be even greater if investments are also made in subsequent stages of resource processing. Some of the Japanese firms that invested in the marine industry also engaged in processing and cold storage. The investments in forestry are also related to production of pulp and paper, sawnwood, and plywood. But the largest amount of investment in resource processing in ASEAN-4 was directed to iron and nonferrous metal processing during 1973-83 period (see Table 31).

The tendency of Japanese investment in ASEAN-4 to focus more on iron and nonferrous metal processing than on light manufacturing became more pronounced towards the end of the 1970s. As shown in Table 31, more than one-third of Japanese investment in manufacturing industries in ASEAN-4 went into the textile industry during the period 1973-7. But in the 1977-81 period, textiles attracted only 11 per cent of the investment in manufacturing, and in the 1981-3 period, that proportion declined to 8.1 per cent. In contrast to this investment decline in textiles, the iron and nonferrous metal industry became the major recipient of Japanese investment by the mid-1970s, accounting for more than half of the direct investment in the manufacturing industry between 1977 and 1983. The purpose of the Japanese investment in resource processing was to shift the location of energy-intensive processes to resource-rich countries to meet the domestic demand of the host countries and to provide an export base. Increases in imports to Japan are causing serious domestic adjustment problems in areas such as wood and wood products. But this process is gradually changing the trade flows between Japan and ASEAN-4, as will be discussed in the following section.

The stagnant demand for textiles in Japan and the world was the primary cause for the small increase in Japanese direct investment in this sector in the Asian NICs after the oil crisis. Because the Japanese direct investment boom in manufacturing in the period prior to 1973 was caused partly by the rise in domestic wages reflecting the tight labour market situation, the firms lost their interest in investing in offshore labour-intensive manufactures when they found a more ample supply of domestic labour during the post-1973 business recession. The policy of the Asian NICs of diversifying their industrial structure from labour-intensive to more sophisticated lines of products attracted more Japanese investment in the chemical and machinery industries than in textiles. In addition, during the 1981-3 period, the relative importance of investment in manufacturing fell, and more investment was directed to service industries and construction in Asian NICs.

Japanese direct investment in resource-rich Oceania generally followed the pattern of ASEAN-4. Investment in the resource industry as a proportion of total investment increased, reflecting heavy mineral resource development of such commodities as uranium, coal, and aluminum. Following these general trends in resource development, investments in iron and nonferrous metal processing attracted more capital from Japan.

The importance of resource development and processing in Japanese investment after the oil crisis affected the Japanese trade relationship with other Pacific Rim countries in various ways. Japan tended to promote a trade relationship with resource-rich countries and also to increase the imports of resource-based products. Thus, resource-rich ASEAN-4 was not following the simple neo-factor proportions paradigm in exporting products to Japan.

JAPANESE-MANUFACTURED IMPORTS FROM ASIAN NICs, ASEAN-4 AND OCEANIA: ARE THEY FOLLOWING THE STANDARD NEO-FACTOR PROPORTIONS PARADIGM?

The commodity composition of Japanese imports from Asian developing countries remained almost unchanged in the 1970s and early 1980s. Raw materials plus agricultural and food products still account for over 90 per cent of imports from ASEAN-4. This proportion exceeds the comparable ratio for total Japanese-world trade which was about 75 per cent in 1981. Although ASEAN-4 increased their share of manufactured goods imported into Japan from 0.8 per cent in 1972 to 2.1 per cent in 1981, their share of textiles, yarn, fabrics, and clothing was still 3.7 per cent and 1.5 per cent respectively. The Japanese imports, in which ASEAN-4 had the largest share, were raw materials (16.3 per cent), agriculture and food products (7.2 per cent), and resource-based manufactures (4.4 per cent).

Considering the decline in the proportion of manufactured goods in total Japanese imports during this period, Asian NICs competed successfully with imports from the other regions. In 1981, 45 per cent of Japan's imports from Asian NICs were manufactured goods. But the major manufactured imports from Asian NICs continued to be clothing, textiles, yarn and fabrics, and resource-based manufactures. These three groups accounted for 89.8 per cent of total imports (see Table 32). Indeed, Asian NICs continue to hold a predominant share in Japanese imports of textiles, yarn and fabrics (26.1 per cent), and clothing (46.1 per cent).

One can see from Table 33 that there is a significant difference between the levels of market penetration reached by Asian NICs and ASEAN-4 in Japan. There is no clear indication that ASEAN-4 is expand-

Table 32
Commodity Composition of Japanese Imports, 1972, 1975, 1981 (%)

	From Asian NICs[a]			From ASEAN-4[a]			From World		
Commodities	1972	1975	1981	1972	1975	1981	1972	1975	1981
1 Total	100.0	100.0	100.0	100.0	100.0	100.0	100.0	100.0	100.0
2 Raw Materials[b]	34.6	23.7	31.0	76.7	70.5	86.2	51.8	61.5	63.0
3 Agriculture & Food Products[b]	17.5	20.0	13.0	14.1	23.8	7.6	18.5	17.9	12.7
4 Chemicals[b]	5.0	3.6	5.0	0.4	0.5	0.6	4.9	3.6	4.3
5 Textile, Yarn, & Fabrics[b]	13.3	12.0	7.4	0.3	0.5	0.4	1.7	1.3	1.2
6 Clothing[b]	8.4	13.5	13.9	0.0	0.1	0.2	2.9	0.9	1.3
7 Resource-based Manufactures[b]	6.8	6.2	9.3	1.2	0.8	0.8	2.0	2.7	2.2
8 Electric Machinery[b]	4.8	7.6	2.3	0.0	0.2	0.6	5.6	1.7	1.6
9 Nonelectric Machinery[b]	0.4	1.9	2.0	0.0	0.3	0.0	2.5	3.6	2.6
10 Transport Machinery[b]	0.3	0.3	2.4	0.0	0.0	0.0	2.9	1.3	1.9
11 Miscellaneous Manufactures[b]	6.4	5.1	3.7	0.1	0.2	0.2	0.6	1.3	1.2
12 Subtotal (4–11)	45.2	50.2	45.1	2.1	2.7	2.9	23.1	16.5	16.3

Source: UN Commodity Trade Statistics, various issues, statistical paper Series D

[a] Asian NICs are Korea, Hong Kong and Singapore; ASEAN–4 are Indonesia, Malaysia, Philippines and Thailand

[b] Raw materials, SITC (2–22) + 3; Agriculture & food products, SITC 0 + 1 + 22 + 4; Chemicals, SITC 5; Textiles, SITC 65; Clothing, SITC 84; Resource-based manufactures, SITC 61 + 62 + 63 + 64 + 66 + 67 + 68; Electric machinery, SITC 76 + 77; nonelectric machinery, SITC 71 + 72 + 73 + 74 + 75; Transport machinery, SITC 76 + 78; Miscellaneous manufactures, SITC 812 + 831 + 89

ing import shares in textiles, yarn and fabrics, or clothing more rapidly than other manufactures. In the case of ASEAN-4, resource-based manufactures and electrical machinery hold larger import shares in Japan than textiles, yarn and fabrics, or clothing. The commodities for which imports from ASEAN-4 exceeded those from Asian NICs in 1981 included agriculture and food products as well as raw materials.

Although it is generally difficult to make a precise evaluation of the influence of direct investment on trade flows, the shift in Japanese investment in ASEAN-4 from resource development to processing will eventually change Japanese imports from these countries. There is already a clear indication that technological changes are raising import coefficients (defined as imports used to produce one unit of output) of intermediate products in Japan. This implies that Japanese firms are using more imported intermediate products instead of domestic intermediate products fabricated from imported raw materi-

Table 33
Asian NICs and ASEAN-4 Share of Japanese Imports[a], 1972, 1975, 1981

Commodities	Percentage from Asian NICs[a]			Percentage from ASEAN-4[a]		
	1972	1975	1981	1972	1975	1981
1 Total	2.8	3.4	4.1	8.9	9.5	12.0
2 Raw materials	1.9	1.3	2.0	13.2	10.8	16.3
3 Agriculture & food products	2.6	3.8	4.3	6.7	12.6	7.2
4 Chemicals	2.9	3.4	4.8	0.6	1.5	1.8
5 Textile, yarn, & fabrics	22.8	30.3	26.1	0.5	3.2	3.7
6 Clothing	35.5	48.7	46.1	0.6	1.5	1.5
7 Resource-based manufactures	6.5	7.7	17.6	3.5	2.9	4.4
8 Electric machinery	6.6	14.7	6.0	0.0	1.3	4.6
9 Non-electrical machinery	0.2	1.9	3.1	0.0	0.8	0.2
10 Transport machinery	0.3	0.6	3.1	0.0	0.0	0.3
11 Miscellaneous manufactures	6.2	13.0	12.9	0.4	1.3	1.7
12 Manufactures subtotal (4–11)	5.5	10.2	11.5	0.8	1.6	2.1

[a]See Table 32 for source and notes
Imports from world total to 100

als (see Sazanami 1985:48-50). If direct Japanese investment in resource development can increase the supply of resource-based products in ASEAN-4, this investment can, in turn, accelerate the process of manufactured goods imported into Japan.

Presently, ASEAN-4 is trying to develop resource processing industries in such fields as aluminum (Indonesia), iron ore (Malaysia), and zinc and nickel (Indonesia). The increase in Japanese direct investment in the late 1970s went into these specific fields as indicated in Table 31. If the attempt to establish resource processing industries is successful, a shift from raw material to processed intermediate imports may lead to a substantial expansion in imports of manufactured goods. Currently, raw materials still account for over 80 per cent of total imports to Japan from these countries.

The lack of corporate data limits the assessment of how Japanese direct investment in resource processing is related to the shift in imports from raw materials to resource-based manufactures. In Table 34, we chose three industries to examine whether the shift in imports from raw materials to processed products is taking place: textiles, which received the largest amount of direct investment between 1973 and 1977 in Asian NICs; iron and steel; and nonferrous metals, which received over 40 per cent of direct investment between 1977 and 1983 in ASEAN-4 and Oceania.

In the case of textiles, a large increase in textile imports from Asian NICs proceeded *pari passu* with the shift from textile raw materials to textile products between 1973 and 1982. Now 98.5 per cent of Japan's total textile imports from Asian NICs are textile products. Textile imports from ASEAN-4 also increased during this period, but the amount in 1982 was less than one-tenth of Asian NICs, and the share of textile products remained almost unchanged. Oceania countries continued to be a major supplier of textile raw materials to Japan.

A shift in Japanese imports from iron ore and scrap to iron and steel products started in the mid 1970s in the case of Asian NICs. Now 96.5 per cent of iron and steel are in the form of products. Although ASEAN-4 still supplied a major portion of iron and steel imports to Japan in the form of iron ore and scrap, a gradual increase in the proportion of iron and steel products took place towards the end of the 1970s.

ASEAN-4 was the largest non-ferrous metal supplier to Japan in the

Table 34
Japanese Imports of Raw Materials versus Processed Products, 1973–82

6a. TEXTILE IMPORTS

	Total in US $ Millions			Textile Raw Materials[b]			Textile Products[b]		
Year	Asian NICs	ASEAN-4	Oceania	Asian NICs	ASEAN-4	Oceania	Asian NICs	ASEAN-4	Oceania
1973	$648.3	$67.8	$902.51	13.0%	20.6%	99.3%	87.0%	79.4%	0.7%
1974	718.2	73.3	461.7	11.6	20.2	99.2	88.4	79.8	0.8
1975	533.2	39.6	466.5	6.7	16.7	99.5	93.3	83.3	0.5
1976	824.1	57.3	606.7	3.2	35.1	99.6	96.8	64.9	0.4
1977	811.3	56.1	537.9	6.4	38.7	99.4	93.6	61.3	0.6
1978	1,273.1	75.0	562.8	6.6	26.7	99.2	93.4	73.3	0.8
1979	1,541.8	127.0	680.3	3.3	22.3	99.1	96.7	77.7	0.9
1980	1,099.8	109.4	698.9	3.1	23.1	99.3	96.9	76.9	0.7
1981	1,282.7	102.1	709.3	0.7	24.6	99.4	99.3	75.4	0.6
1982	1,256.8	115.9	720.6	1.5	24.4	99.4	98.5	75.6	0.6

6b. IRON AND STEEL IMPORTS

	Total in US $ Millions			Iron Ore and Scrap			Iron and Steel Products[b]		
Year	Asian NICs	ASEAN-4	Oceania	Asian NICs	ASEAN-4	Oceania	Asian NICs	ASEAN-4	Oceania
1973	16.9	32.9	874.9	47.6%	100.0%	96.3%	52.4%	0 %	4.7%
1974	36.2	31.5	1162.4	58.5	95.3	93.0	41.5	4.7	7.0
1975	22.4	26.7	1117.8	41.4	98.3	98.0	58.6	1.7	2.0
1976	32.9	24.2	1177.0	37.9	70.5	96.6	62.1	29.5	3.4
1977	29.4	84.1	1237.4	26.9	88.0	96.9	73.1	12.0	3.1
1978	51.0	145.5	1145.8	22.4	90.1	98.7	77.6	9.9	1.3
1979	184.0	176.4	1327.0	8.1	88.6	95.8	91.9	11.4	4.2
1980	304.8	198.0	1501.1	6.0	82.6	97.5	94.0	17.4	2.5
1981	406.0	205.3	1503.7	4.0	82.4	97.9	96.0	17.6	2.1
1982	460.5	210.0	1604.3	3.5	81.7	97.2	96.5	18.3	2.8

Table 34 (continued)
Japanese Imports of Raw Materials versus Processed Products, 1973–82

6c. NON-FERROUS METALS IMPORTS

	Total in US $ Millions			Metal Ore			Non-ferrous Metal Products		
Year	Asian NICs	ASEAN-4	Oceania	Asian NICs	ASEAN-4	Oceania	Asian NICs	ASEAN-4	Oceania
1973	26.3	509.1	391.1	57.0%	68.0%	70.9%	43.0%	32.0%	29.1%
1974	32.0	847.7	567.7	64.7	71.9	73.1	35.3	28.1	26.9
1975	25.0	523.9	487.4	79.6	71.8	66.4	30.4	28.2	33.6
1976	32.1	654.3	599.2	65.5	64.4	71.7	34.5	35.6	28.3
1977	37.2	726.2	622.8	67.8	59.0	65.5	32.2	41.0	54.5
1978	32.2	846.4	519.7	53.8	57.3	55.4	46.2	42.7	44.6
1979	48.6	1191.0	653.9	38.9	61.9	64.3	61.1	38.1	35.7
1980	56.5	1679.2	770.1	38.1	67.9	70.3	61.9	33.1	29.7
1981	32.4	1284.7	789.1	33.2	65.9	53.7	66.8	34.1	46.3
1982	33.1	1088.6	803.0	13.0	66.3	52.7	87.0	33.7	48.3

Source: Kanzei Kyokai (various issues), ''Gaikoku Boeki Gaikyo''

[a]ASIAN NICs: Hong Kong, Korea, and Singapore
ASEAN-4: Indonesia, Malaysia, Philippines, and Thailand

[b]Textile raw materials include silk, wool, animal hair, raw cotton, jute, and waste materials from textile fabrics. Textile products include thread of synthetic fibres, cotton, woolen and synthetic fabrics, tulle, lace, made up articles of textile materials, floor coverings, undergarments, and knitted articles. Iron and steel includes pig iron, iron and steel bars, rods, universal plates and sheets, tubes and pipes. Non-ferrous metal ores include copper, nickel, zinc, lead, bauxite, chrome, manganese, tungsten, and molybdenum ores. Non-ferrous metal products include silver and platinum, and the following and their alloys: copper, nickel, aluminum, zinc, lead, tin, and cobalt.

Special table note: For any year and any country grouping (e.g., Asian NICs, ASEAN-4, Oceania) the sum of raw material and processed product entries equals 100%. For example, (6a) Textile Raw Materials & Textile Products = 100%; (6b) Iron Ore and Scrap & Iron and Steel Products = 100%; (6c) Metal Ore & Non-Ferrous metal products = 100%.

Pacific Rim. In 1982, 66 per cent of these imports still consisted of metal ore. Asian NICs and Oceania supplied 13 per cent and 53 per cent respectively of their products in the form of metal ore.

In all three industries, Asian NICs experienced a shift in the exports of raw materials to processed products. Now almost 90 per cent of Japanese imports from Asian NICs are processed products. ASEAN-4 is following the pattern of imports from Asian NICs where the proportion of processed products is increasing in the case of iron and steel and nonferrous metals but not textiles. For Oceania, nonferrous metals was the only industry where a shift from imports of ore to products was observed.

From the experience of these three industries, one may conclude that ASEAN-4 is following the general industrialization paradigm in shifting their supplies from raw materials to processed products in the Japanese market, as did the Asian NICs. But ASEAN-4 is not following the Asian NICs in exporting to Japan the traditional trio of products suggested by the standard neo-factor proportions paradigm, namely textiles, clothing, and miscellaneous manufactures.

In part, the reasons for ASEAN-4 not following Asian NICs in their trade relationship with Japan can be ascribed to the resource abundance of ASEAN-4 and to the role of resource development and processing investment from Japan. If Japanese investments in resource processing in iron and steel and nonferrous metals in ASEAN-4 continue to expand as they did in the late 1970s, imports from ASEAN-4 are expected to grow exactly in those fields where investments increased, namely resource-based manufactures rather than textiles.

NOTES

1 In this chapter, Pacific Rim countries are defined as Japan, ASEAN-4 (Indonesia, Malaysia, Philippines, and Thailand), Asian NICs (Hong Kong, Korea, Singapore, and Taiwan), and Oceania (Australia and New Zealand). Singapore is included in Asian NICs instead of ASEAN because its exports are mainly manufactured goods like other NICs.

2 See the Export-Import Bank of Japan (1984) for details of the export promotion policies of Asian Developing Countries.

REFERENCES

Bank of Japan (1984). *Recent Trends in Imports. Chosa Geppo*, April

Crawford, J., and Saburo Okita, eds. (1978). *Raw Materials and Pacific Economic Integration*. London: Croom Helm

Export Import Bank of Japan, The (1984). "Report on Research Institute of Overseas Investment." Vol. 10, no. 6, June

Hamilton, C., and Mordechai E. Kreinin (1980). "The Structural Pattern of LDCs' Trade in Manufactures with Individual and Groups of DCs." Weltwirtshaftlich Archive

Heimenz, U. (1983). "Export Growth in Developing Asian Countries: Past Trends and Policy Issues." Weltwirtshaftlich Archive, Haft 4, Band 119

Sazanami, Y. (1980). *International Trade and the Japanese Economy* (in Japanese). Tokyo: Toyokeizai Shinposha

—. (1983). "Japanese Trade after the Oil Crisis: A Structural Approach." *Journal of Japanese Trade and Industry*, May/June

—. (1985). "Japanese Trade Liberalization: An Assessment of Implications for Southeast Asian Countries." In W.F. Gossling, ed. *Western Pacific Trade*. Input-Output Publishing Co.

Sekiguchi, S. (1979). *Japanese Direct Foreign Investment*. London: Macmillan

—, ed. (1982). *Pacific Rim and Japanese Direct Investment* (in Japanese). Tokyo: Nihon Keizai Shimbun-sha

CHAPTER THREE

Japanese Foreign Direct Investment in the 1980s: An Exercise in Financial Power

Tracy Redies

INTRODUCTION

In the 1980s Japanese foreign direct investment (FDI) has undergone a very significant metamorphosis in terms of magnitude, motivation, and geographic distribution. Annual net Japanese FDI has risen from US $250 million in fiscal 1970 to US $2.1 billion in fiscal 1980 and to US $33.8 billion in fiscal 1988. The accumulated value of Japanese FDI by the end of 1988 was US $110.8 billion, representing a sixfold increase over the 1980 level. This enormous increase in Japanese investment activity has been funded by large cash surpluses arising out of the persistent macroeconomic imbalances which have characterized Japan's economy since 1973. In fact, these cash surpluses have been so large that despite its rapid growth, net FDI in fiscal 1988 still accounted for only 27.5 per cent of total Japanese net long-term foreign investment. (Foreign portfolio investments in bonds and securities accounted for the balance.)

The availability of funds, advantageous exchange rates, the dictates of trade balances, and the increasing sophistication of Japanese corporate objectives have been key determinants in the delineation of new investment strategies. During the last few years, there has been a clear trend away from the reactive, defensive FDI practices of the past and towards investment approaches that are often offensive in nature; that is, profit-motivated and influence-expanding.

Changing investment motivations have brought with them a concomitant geographical redirection of Japanese FDI. Whereas such investment used to be directed to resource-rich or low labour cost areas, the recent focus has been on the developed economies of North America and Europe. The technology exported in association with FDI has changed in like manner; from low-level sectors, such as basic textiles, to the advanced systems of modern automobile and steel production.

In the past, Japanese foreign investments were predominantly driven by considerations that were directly linked to relatively specific national objectives. For example, they were made to ensure the availability of resources imported into Japan or to facilitate trade from Japan. However, as Japanese corporate investment in foreign assets has become more sophisticated and self-motivated, so the ties to such types of national objectives have diminished. This movement away from Japan-oriented considerations as the justification for FDI is a natural consequence of the growing interest in "internationalism." In turn, the trend from national to international perspective is a normal and inevitable consequence of the success achieved by the large Japanese manufacturing, commercial, and financial organizations. Companies that rank among the largest in the world in their respective fields *cannot* look to continued expansion within the narrow confines of the Japanese domestic market. These companies *must* look to the broader international field for outlets for their products; and access to these markets via exporting can only be considered a short-term expedient. Organizations that wish to penetrate world markets on a large scale must become international in policy and practice. In no case has this been more evident, or more recognized, than with the major Japanese financial companies. These companies (which include the world's largest banks and security firms) have been at the forefront of the new form of Japanese FDI—investment designed to establish international presence and maximize growth opportunities for the companies involved.

GROWTH OF JAPANESE FOREIGN DIRECT INVESTMENT

Japan became the world's leading creditor nation in 1984 and by the end of 1988 held net overseas assets of US $291.8 billion; of this, US $110.8 billion, or 38 per cent, was in the form of foreign direct investment.[1] This large accumulation of FDI assets has been accomplished in the short span of less than forty years; however, roughly 50 per cent of the current holdings have been amassed since 1984. Accompanying this tremendous increase in Japanese FDI have been significant changes in the rationale, methodology, and geographic targets of the investment. The following brief synopsis of Japanese FDI activities to 1985 has been provided to underline the extent of change since then. The analysis examines the postwar practice of Japanese FDI in terms of the changing level, target locations, and motivations of the investment. Albeit at different levels and sophistication, Japanese FDI remained reasonably consistent throughout this period, with investment undertaken principally for defensive reasons and, up until the end of the 1970s, concentrated heavily in the Asia-Pacific region.

The Magnitude of Japanese FDI

Table 35 shows the cumulative total and industry concentration of Japanese FDI between 1951 and 1987. These figures are based on the total applications for FDI approved by the Ministry of Finance in accordance with the Foreign Exchange and Trade Control Law (1949 and 1980). Since the Ministry of Finance (MOF) figures tend to include all reported or licensed investments, including those which do not proceed and investments which are later divested, these data are, in themselves, an overstatement. However, a number of authorities (OECD Economic Survey 1987/8) believe that this overestimation is offset by the exclusions from the MOF data of direct investments financed through local borrowing, technology transfers, and reinvestment of retained earnings by Japanese subsidiaries abroad.

Up until 1984, cumulative Japanese FDI was only US $73 billion, representing an average annual growth rate of 26 per cent from 1960. Despite the impressive growth of Japanese FDI during this period, the absolute value of cumulative foreign investment in 1984 was only 53 per cent of the 1987 cumulative total of FDI. Indeed, until the mid-1970s, Japanese FDI remained under US $10 billion.

A number of factors contributed to the relatively low absolute level of Japanese FDI until the 1970s. First, all Japanese foreign investments were expropriated at the end of World War II, and FDI was forbidden until 1951. Even after 1951, foreign direct investment, functioning under the tight control of the Foreign Exchange and Trade Control Act of 1949, remained quite modest until the start of the 1970s. These regulatory restrictions were implemented to conserve Japan's foreign exchange earnings, which remained in short supply as a result of persistent trade balance deficits until the late 1960s. In addition, the rapid expansion of the Japanese economy throughout the 1960s and early 1970s provided ample investment opportunities within Japan. Supported by a variety of government industrial policy measures, including protective tariffs and low-interest financing, investments in

Table 35

Japanese Direct Foreign Investment, Classified by Industry on a Reported Basis, 1951–87, Cumulative Totals for Specified Year (US $ millions)

	1951–9	1960	1965	1970	1972	1977	1980	1983	1984	1985	1987	Compounded annual rate of growth of EDI 1959–87 (%)
INDUSTRY												
Manufacturing												
Foodstuffs	6	7	27	61	99	314	587	806	973	1,091	1,546	21.9
Textile	16	27	63	190	416	1,127	1,637	1,795	1,998	2,083	2,353	19.5
Pulp & lumber products	49	50	74	212	296	575	758	899	1,005	1,120	1,531	13.1
Chemicals	0	1	8	60	141	1,044	2,626	3,176	3,759	3,982	5,247	35.8
Iron & ferrous metals	8	10	61	138	240	952	2,619	3,608	4,472	5,190	6,304	26.9
General machinery	10	11	27	67	128	452	894	1,265	1,786	1,971	3,284	23.0
Electrical machinery	0	1	13	71	172	687	1,579	2,322	3,338	3,747	7,155	37.3
Transport machinery	13	16	58	103	142	453	979	1,822	2,936	3,373	5,675	24.2
Others	3	10	21	61	117	460	894	1,258	1,626	1,841	5,923	31.1
Subtotal	105	133	352	963	1,751	6,064	12,573	16,951	21,893	24,398	39,018	23.5
PRIMARY INDUSTRIES												
Agriculture-forestry	2	3	15	58	83	260	609	723	754	780		24.7[a]
Fisheries	2	4	9	27	49	148	301	358	418	442		22.1[a]
Mining	42	86	307	1,127	2,273	4,859	7,071	10,291	11,272	11,756	12,936	22.7
Subtotal	46	93	331	1,212	2,405	5,267	7,981	11,372	12,444	12,978	12,936	23.2[a]

Table 35 (continued)

Japanese Direct Foreign Investment, Classified by Industry on a Reported Basis, 1951–87, Cumulative Totals for Specified Year (US $ millions)

	1951–9	1960	1965	1970	1972	1977	1980	1983	1984	1985	1987	Compounded annual rate of growth of EDI 1959–87 (%)
TERTIARY INDUSTRIES												
Construction			17	38	47	163	396	536	686	798	1,134	21.0[b]
Commerce	28	40	107	403	756	2,611	5,409	8,482	11,195	12,677	16,807	25.7
Finance-insurance	8	11	69	322	541	1,518	2,426	3,802	8,774	10,859	28,772	34.0
Services									4,005	4,686	9,026	31.1[c]
Transportation									4,249	5,900	9,970	32.9[c]
Real estate							962		2,103	2,533	11,958	52.2[d]
Others	9	12	84	659	1,273	3,782	6,750	11,988	8,144	8,819	9,713	28.3
Subtotal	45	63	277	1,422	2,617	8,074	15,943	24,808	39,156	46,272	87,380	31.0
TOTAL	196	289	960	3,597	6,773	19,405	36,497	53,131	73,493	83,648	139,334	26.4

[a]Compounded annual rate of growth during 1959–83

[b]Compounded annual rate of growth during 1965–87

[c]Compounded annual rate of growth during 1984–7

[d]Compounded annual rate of growth during 1981–7

government targeted industries like petrochemicals and iron and steel tended to be highly profitable. Given the general lack of investment resources available, the abundance of domestic investment opportunities made FDI unattractive to most Japanese investors. As a result, until the early 1970s, financial resources generated from private sector (corporations and households) savings were entirely absorbed by private sector investments at home. These factors restricted Japanese FDI to less than $70 million per year between 1951 and 1965, and the cumulative total FDI by the end of 1965 was only US $960 million.

After 1965, when increasingly larger investments in offshore resource developments were made to secure feedstocks for the country's burgeoning industrial economy, the levels of Japanese FDI expanded rapidly, averaging about $725 million per year to 1973. The increased requirements for imported raw materials also coincided with Japan's current account turning to surplus, thus reducing the need for restrictions on capital outflows. In this more liberal atmosphere, the government actively encouraged FDI by providing specific incentives for investments in foreign resource developments. Among these incentives were the provision of low-interest loans from the Japanese Export-Import Bank, tax inducements, and overseas investment insurance schemes. Within this favourable environment, foreign direct investment flourished, reaching a cumulative total of US $10.3 billion by 1973. In 1972 and 1973 alone, Japanese FDI increased by US $2.3 billion and US $3.5 billion respectively, with the combined total for these two years representing 56 per cent of the cumulative FDI to 1973.

The precipitate expansion of Japanese FDI in 1972-3 was interrupted by the oil price and supply crisis of late 1973 and the ensuing world recession it induced. Faced with the largest current account deficit since 1961, the government instituted a series of foreign exchange controls to discourage outflows of domestic capital. These short-term measures quickly brought the current account balance into a surplus position by 1976, and FDI recovered to average between US $4 and US $5 billion per year between 1976 and 1980. By 1980, Japanese FDI totalled over US $36 billion. Although the pace of growth slowed in the early 1980s (to about 18 per cent per year between 1980 and 1984), annual FDI flows increased to slightly over US $10 billion by 1984.

Several factors promoted this acceleration of Japanese FDI during this period. These included the continuing appreciation of the yen against the US dollar, decreasing factor cost differentials and rising trade frictions between Japan and its industrialized trading partners, and increased incentives for FDI in many developed countries. Finally, by 1984 the overall Japanese economy was characterized by high levels of surplus capital. This condition resulted from continued high savings rates in the household sector and a decline in private sector investment requirements. The decline in private sector investments began after 1973 as the Japanese economy shifted away from its former emphasis on heavy industry. As a result of these factors and the strong commitment of the public sector towards fiscal balance, the Japanese economy was awash with excess capital by 1984. This excess capital provided both the motivations and the means for the explosion of Japanese offshore investment after 1984.

Industry Concentration and Geographic Targets

As Table 35 shows, the industry concentration of Japanese FDI changed radically over the thirty-four-year period under discussion. This shift in focus reflected the changing motivations for Japanese FDI over the period, a subject which will be addressed later in this chapter.

Until 1973, Japanese FDI was largely concentrated in primary sector investments, particularly in the extractive mining field. As late as 1984, mining investments represented the single highest level of Japanese FDI, followed closely by investments in commerce-related areas. However, by the second half of the 1970s, tertiary and manufacturing investments represented 42 and 31 per cent of total Japanese FDI respectively.

Manufacturing investments abroad began to increase substantially in the 1970s as first labour-intensive and then resource-intensive industries moved offshore to preserve their international comparative advantage. Offshore investments undertaken by the petrochemical industry, in particular, grew by an astonishing 1762 per cent between 1973 and 1981. Other manufacturing industries that rapidly increased their offshore investment between 1973 and 1980 were iron and ferrous materials (up 991 per cent), electrical machinery (up 818 per cent), and transport machinery (up 589 per cent). Since 1977, tertiary investments in the areas of finance, insurance, and commerce have gained increasing ground. By 1984, tertiary investments represented 55 per cent of total Japanese FDI, followed by manufacturing investments at 29 per cent and primary investments at 16 per cent.

Table 36 demonstrates the changing geographical distribution of Japanese offshore investment. North America, Japan's most important export destination, realized the largest share of Japanese investment in the 1960s and early 1970s, accounting for 24 per cent of total cumulative investment in 1974. These investments were made primarily in the commercial sector to support the trade-related activities of Japanese manufacturers. Asia followed closely with 23 per

Table 36
Japanese Foreign Direct Investment, by Region on a Cumulative Basis, 1951-87, (US $ millions)

Region	1951-65	1970	1971	1973	1975	1977	1979	Compounded Annual Growth Rate 1971-9 (%)
N. America	241	912	1,142	2,462	3,917	5,401	8,202	27.9
Central & S. America	281	567	707	1,811	2,881	3,757	5,580	29.5
Asia	188	753	988	2,388	4,219	6,328	8,643	31.1
Europe	25	639	724	1,996	2,518	3,075	3,893	23.4
Oceania	7	281	391	640	930	1,257	2,078	23.2
Africa	11	92	114	253	501	913	1,306	35.6
Middle East	196	334	370	716	976	1,479	2,101	24.2
Total	949	3,578	4,436	10,266	15,942	22,210	31,803	27.9

Region	1980	1981	1982	1983	1984	1985	1986	1987	Compounded Annual Growth Rate 1980-7 (%)
N. America	9,798	12,320	15,225	17,926	21,470	26,965	37,406	42,322	23.2
Central & S. America	6,168	7,349	8,852	10,730	13,020	15,636	20,373		22.0[a]
Asia	9,830	13,168	14,552	16,399	18,027	19,462	21,789	26,657	15.3
Europe	4,471	5,269	6,145	7,135	9,072	11,002	14,471	21,047	24.8
Oceania	2,525	2,949	3,370	3,561	3,718	4,243	5,235		12.9[a]
Africa	1,445	2,018	2,507	2,871	3,197	3,369	3,678		16.8[a]
Middle East	2,259	2,355	2,479	2,654	2,927	2,972	3,016		4.9[a]
Total	36,496	45,428	53,130	61,276	71,431	83,649	105,968		19.4[a]

[a]1980-6

cent of the investment, while the remaining FDI was largely divided between Central and South America (18 per cent) and Europe (19 per cent).

However, by 1979, Asia had replaced North America as the single most important destination of Japanese FDI. This shift was principally the result of large resource-related investments in Indonesia and the relocation of labour-intensive, low-technology industries to nearby Southeast Asia. Nevertheless, both Asia and North America increased their overall share of Japanese FDI during this period. In 1979, Asia accounted for 27 per cent of total Japanese FDI, which grew at an average rate of 28 per cent per year between 1971 and 1979. Over the same period, Japanese FDI in North America increased by 25 per cent per year and accounted for 26 per cent of total Japanese FDI by 1979. Central and South America retained a constant 18 per cent share of the total, but Europe lost ground with only 12 per cent of total Japanese FDI at the end of 1979.

In the early 1980s, two trends emerged. One was the reemergence of North America as the largest recipient of Japanese FDI, and the other was the general shift in focus of Japanese investment towards developed, as opposed to developing, regions. By 1984, North America had received 30 per cent of total cumulative Japanese FDI; by contrast, the share of cumulative Japanese investment in Asia had dropped to 25 per cent. A large proportion of the incremental investment earmarked for North America was in the commercial and financial sectors; however, manufacturing investments also increased sharply. By 1984, North America accounted for 29.4 per cent of total Japanese manufacturing investment compared to 19.3 per cent in 1980. On the other hand, Japanese manufacturing investment in Asia declined from 36.4 per cent of Japan's total offshore manufacturing investment in 1980 to 32 per cent in 1984 (JETRO 1986). During the early 1980s, Japanese investment in Europe grew at a faster rate than any other region; although, in 1984, Europe still represented only 13 per cent of total Japanese FDI.

Motivations for Japanese FDI

During the period 1951 to 1984 Japanese FDI was primarily undertaken for defensive reasons, being consistently employed to protect the national and corporate interests of the country. These interests included ensuring a stable, reasonably priced supply of raw materials for Japanese industry, protecting the comparative advantage of Japanese companies both at home and abroad, and circumventing trade barriers to Japanese exports.

In the early 1950s, the dominating influence which drove FDI was the perceived need to secure reliable, reasonably priced primary resources for Japan's emerging industries. As Sazanami notes (this volume), this government-sponsored (and financially supported) policy led to investments in Alaska Pulp (1953), the Nippon Usiminas steel project in Brazil (1957), the Arabian Oil project (1959), and the North Sumatra Oil development (1960). Towards the end of the 1950s ample supplies of primary commodities were readily available through normal purchasing practices, and resource-FDI became less crucial.

However, in the latter half of the 1960s, Japan's rapid industrialization resulted in a tremendous expansion in the country's need for primary resources. Under these circumstances, security of supply and price stability became major corporate and national concerns.

Crude steel production rose from 23.2 million metric tons (Mmt) in 1960 to 119.3 Mmt in 1973; associated coking-coal imports increased from 14.6 Mmt to 52.5 Mmt over the same interval; and the corresponding growth in iron ore imports was from 38.8 Mmt in 1965 to 134.7 Mmt in 1973 (*Japan's Iron and Steel Industry* 1976). Japanese concern over their dependency on overseas resources led to renewed use of FDI as a means of securing overseas resources. Commodities targeted for resource related FDI included coking coal in Australia (Moura and Goonyella); iron ore in Australia (Savage River and Mt. Newman); copper in the Philippines (Toledo) and Papua–New Guinea (Bougainville); and petroleum in the Middle East (offshore in the Neutral Zone) and Indonesia (N. Sumatra and offshore Eastern Kalimantan) (MITI 1970).

A further impetus for Japanese FDI growth during the 1960s was the rising cost of domestic production. Textiles and other labour-intensive industries responded to rising domestic labour costs in the late 1950s and early 1960s by relocating operations in neighbouring Southeast Asia. This process continued throughout the 1960s and early 1970s as competitiveness (both at home and abroad) was eroded by the rapid escalation of domestic labour and land prices and environmental restrictions. Wages, for example, rose by 20 per cent in 1972 alone, and industrial land prices increased by 66 per cent between 1965 and 1972. At the same time, pollution problems (such as the Minimata mercury poisoning incident) underscored the need for more stringent and expensive environmental protection regulations.

Accompanying these "push" factors was the Japanese government's decision to liberalize imports from developing countries after August of 1971. This move provided further incentive for Japanese manufacturers of labour-intensive, low-technology products to relocate in developing countries and export at least part of the production back to Japan. According to Yoshihara (1979:6), increased imports under the revised tariff scheme amounted to US $760 million in 1972 and US $806 million in 1973.

Southeast Asia was a major recipient of this early offshore manufacturing investment because of its geographic proximity to the Japanese market and the incentives that many Southeast Asian nations introduced to encourage foreign capital and technology investments. These policies included the establishment of export processing zones that permitted the duty-free import of inputs; unrestricted repatriation of foreign earnings; and the provision of tax incentives for foreign investors. South Korea, for example, allowed 100 per cent foreign ownership of companies and provided tax reductions of up to 50 per cent for three years. By 1974, the number of Japanese investment projects in South Korea (581) exceeded those in Taiwan (426), Singapore (121), and Hong Kong (97) (Yoshihara 1978:18).

The 1973 oil crisis underscored Japan's dependence on imported natural resources. Consequently, the FDI emphasis switched from manufacturing investments in Southeast Asia to reduce labour costs to investments that were primarily related to resource sourcing and processing. The post-1973 escalation of energy prices, rising internal costs of production, and the halving of economic growth rates after 1973 forced Japan to reevaluate its concentration on heavy, resource-processing industries. Such concentration had been sustainable in an era of easy access to the required resource inputs under stable price conditions. However, these conditions had begun to change in the late 1960s, and the change accelerated with the dramatic oil price hikes of 1973-4. As noted by Abegglen (1985: 244), Japanese industries were faced with two choices: to "source semi-finished or finished products from offshore, or move offshore to control the sourcing by investing in facilities in foreign countries." Many industries decided on the latter course, resulting in large-scale offshore investments in petrochemicals, aluminum smelting, steel production, and shipbuilding. With the dual purpose of securing oil supplies and relocating petrochemical production abroad, the Japanese petrochemical industry invested heavily in the Middle East. These investments were strongly supported by parallel loans from the Japanese government. In 1973 alone, the Japanese government extended US $3 billion in loans to Middle East countries, representing a fivefold increase over 1972 (Ozawa 1979: 144). Government aid and corporate investment were openly welcomed by the Middle East host countries, and in 1974, Japan was placed on OPEC's list of "friendly nations." These investments were not without their difficulties; the early 1970s investment by Mitsui Bussan in the world's largest petrochemical development southwest of Tehran, for example, faced construction delays and finally indefinite postponement after the fall of the Shah in 1979. After suffering crippling losses, Mitsui has since decided to pull out of the project altogether (*Japan Economic Journal*, 8 April 1989).

Indonesia was also a large recipient of Japanese investment, primarily in the fields of LNG production and aluminum processing. Beginning in 1974, Japanese investors provided US $800 million for the development of the Asahan electric power and aluminum project. These investments represented a modified version of the Build-Operate-Transfer (BOT) approach. The initial Japanese equity in the aluminum refinery was 90 per cent but it was planned to transfer 25 per cent of the equity to the Indonesian government after ten years of operation. In the case of the 430,000 kilowatt electric power station, the government was to assume full control after thirty years.

The Asahan project and others like it were lauded by the Japanese investors and the Indonesian government as major contributions to the industrialization objectives of Indonesia. These objectives were undoubtedly advanced by such projects, but, in general, the Japanese FDI strategy in Indonesia (and other developing countries) was only coincidentally related to local national development objectives. Sazanami (this volume) favourably contrasts Japanese resource-processing investments in Indonesia during the late 1970s with the investments of the early 1970s, which were designed to "exploit Indonesia's rich natural resources." In reality, the increased "processing" of the late 1970s was either enforced by technical considerations (for example, natural gas had to be converted to liquefied natural gas to facilitate transportation to Japan) or was a consequence of Japan's program of relocating energy-intensive operations (such as aluminum smelting) from Japan to energy-rich countries. Hence, the trend towards increased offshore processing was not motivated by Japanese altruism towards recipient country development objectives, but rather by normal "defensive" considerations of energy supply and changing comparative advantage. Indeed, Japanese policies of concentrating investment in developments that were primarily capital-intensive and resource-related have been criticized for failing to meet the employment needs of Indonesia's large population (Kuntjoro-Jakti 1983: 45). As a footnote to the Asahan example, the Indonesian government now has 41 per cent ownership of the smelter, which has a total price tag of US $2.1 billion, and is using the tight market situation for aluminum in an attempt to lever a bigger equity stake out of the Japanese participants (*Economist*, 5 November 1988).

Unquestionably, Japan's resource-related investments undertaken after 1973 were primarily motivated by defensive considerations. Such considerations were also the reason for many of the manufacturing investments made in the United States and Europe during the late 1970s. Earlier Japanese investments in the United States and Europe, during the 1960s and early 1970s, were mainly in the fields of commerce, finance, insurance, and transportation, and they were made to support export activities. After 1975, Japanese FDI was increasingly used to circumvent trade barriers imposed by nations that were highly critical of Japan's rising trade surpluses. In response to import restraints between 1977 and 1980, Japanese manufacturers rapidly expanded their United States production of colour television sets. Similar investments were made by the Japanese auto industry in American and European production facilities during the early 1980s.

In the United States, investments undertaken prior to 1984 by Honda, Nissan, and Toyota amounted to about US $1.7 billion, with a resultant capacity of about 650,000 units per year.

Summary of Japanese FDI: 1951-84

Throughout this thirty-four-year period, Japanese FDI remained as a defensive tool, intended to protect and nurture Japan-centred activities. In other words, the ownership of foreign assets was seldom undertaken as a profit-making or influence-expanding activity in its own right. It was almost always a means to assist or protect bilateral trade in which Japan was, or had been, one of the participants. Thus, the principal motivations for FDI were to:

— secure essential raw material feedstocks for the burgeoning Japanese industry;
— protect export markets threatened by trade barriers;
— relocate industries that had lost comparative advantage because of increased input factor costs in Japan; and,
— provide commercial and financial services in support of Japan's booming international trade.

The classical motivations of securing vital resources, circumventing trade barriers, and protecting activities and markets threatened by the loss of comparative advantage have been discussed in some detail above. However, it was in the tertiary sector that the greatest expansion of FDI occurred. Japanese international trade volumes (exports plus imports) grew from US $47.1 billion in 1972 to US $113.4 billion in 1975, US $271.3 billion in 1980, and to US$305.9 billion in 1984 (*Statistical Survey of Japan's Economy*, Ministry of Foreign Affairs, various years). FDI in the commerce and finance/insurance categories grew apace with trade, from US $1.3 billion in 1972 to US $7.8 billion in 1980 and US $21.2 billion in 1984. The acceleration in finance-related FDI between 1980 and 1984 was especially pronounced. Foreign direct investment by Japanese banks helped to maintain established, relationships with their Japanese customers who became involved with offshore investments or trade. It also provided the contacts and experience that were to be used in the post-1985 surge of aggressive FDI by Japanese financial institutions.

JAPANESE FDI, AFTER 1985: FINANCIAL POWER

In 1985 a number of macroeconomic factors combined to change the nature of Japanese FDI. Continued strength in personal savings, surplus private and government sector balances, and a widening current account surplus combined with low interest rates, enormous increases in the collateral value of Japanese land holdings, and an appreciated yen to cause an explosion of foreign direct investment. Total annual long-term capital outflows rose from US $27.5 billion in 1982 to US $81.8 billion in 1985, US $132.1 billion in 1986, and US $136.5 billion in 1987. A high proportion of these cash flows was devoted to foreign portfolio investment (FPI): that is, the purchase of bonds and noncontrolling positions in foreign corporate stocks. However, there was also a significant increase in FDI, which grew from US $5.8 billion in 1985 to US $14.3 billion in 1986, US $18.4 billion in 1987, and US $33.8 billion in 1988.

The classical defensive motivations have been clearly present in this trend towards rapidly increased FDI. Japan's trade surpluses are a large, and growing, source of friction between Japan and its trading partners; the appreciated yen has eroded the competitiveness of many industries located in Japan; and the Free Trade Agreement between Canada and the US and the impending 1992 unification of the European Community market herald the potential for even stronger obstacles for Japanese imports in the future.

However, since 1985, it has become increasingly evident that the large Japanese companies are now using their financial strength to make overseas investments that are primarily designed to increase profits and improve strategic positioning in world markets. These new investment tactics are an integral part of a movement towards full international status by the major Japanese corporations, and they have led to a revised distribution of Japanese FDI, with the bulk of new investments now being made in the developed economies. The United States share of cumulative FDI was 37.9 per cent in 1987, up from 30.1 per cent in 1980. Cumulative direct investment in Europe increased from 12.7 per cent of the total in 1980 to 15.1 per cent in 1987, while the South/Central American share stayed relatively stable at 18.1 per cent, largely as a result of finance investments in attractive tax havens, such as the Cayman Isles and Barbados. Asia, once the favourite target for Japanese FDI, saw its share fall from 25.2 per cent in 1980 to 19.1 per cent in 1987. All other jurisdictions experienced a reduction in their share of cumulative investment from 1980 to 1987.

Among the reasons for the increased level of investment in the United States were:

- the continuing strength of the American economy;
- the decisions of the Japanese automobile manufacturers, both alone and in partnership with US companies, to expand their production facilities within North America;

— the huge surplus in trade with the US and the growth of American protectionist sentiment;
— the relatively low prices of American real estate and the spiralling interest of major Japanese investors in this market; and,
— the relative weakness of the fragmented American banking and finance system and the opportunities that existed for well-financed Japanese banks and financial institutions to move into this sector.

The increased importance of the finance/insurance component of Japanese FDI since 1984 is signified by its growth from US $8.7 billion in 1984 to US $28.8 billion in 1987, almost 21 per cent of the total accumulated Japanese FDI to that date. This investment is flowing from a huge base of financial power. At the end of March 1986, Japan's financial companies, in aggregate, held about US $6.3 trillion in assets (Viner 1988), and this figure is undoubtedly larger in 1989. The ten largest banks in Japan are also the largest in the world in terms of assets and capitalization, and the Japanese are now the world's leading international bankers. Nomura, Daiwa, Nikko, and Yamaichi are the largest securities firms in the world. Nomura itself has a stock market capitalization that is three times that of the combined capitalization of the top four American companies. The twenty-three largest Japanese life insurance companies had assets of over US $440 billion at the end of 1986 (Viner 1988).

Given the enormous financial resources of the Japanese banks, insurance companies, and securities firms, it was only to be expected that they would seek to exercise their power in the international markets. Nomura, for example, plans to obtain 50 per cent of its pre-tax profits from international operations by 1999 (Viner 1988). These plans began to acquire real substance from 1985 onwards. All of the major financial institutions embarked on a policy of acquiring existing financial operations (merchant banks, leasing companies, factors, securities firms, real estate specialists, bond dealers, and the like), largely in the United States and England. These investments provided a number of benefits. First, they gave the Japanese companies access to the inventory of international and local finance skills and knowledge reposited in the acquired companies. Second, the Japanese financial companies were able to give immediate, local support to their clients from Japan who were also investing in North America or Europe. And third, in some cases, the investment offered a platform, or nucleus, from which the financial strength of the Japanese parent could be used to facilitate expansion. An example of this third type of benefit is provided by the acquisition of the J. Henry Schroder Bank and Trust by the Industrial Bank of Japan (IJB). The acquired company (later called the IJB Schroder Bank and Trust Company) then used the financial power of its new parent to purchase Aubrey G. Lanston & Co., an independent primary bond dealer in the US, for US $234 million (Viner 1988).

Other Japanese financial investments included the previously mentioned Fuji Bank acquisition of the leasing and factoring services of the Walter E. Heller International Company (initially, US $425 million but finally US $1.15 billion), and the purchases by the Sumitomo Bank, Nippon Life Insurance, and Yasuda Mutual Life Insurance of minority (12.5 to 25 per cent) interests in Goldman Sachs, Shearson Lehman, and Paine Webber respectively. The aggregate cost of the investments in these three large Wall Street companies amounted to US $1.38 billion (Viner 1988). In California, Japanese companies (Sanwa Bank, Bank of Tokyo, Mitsubishi Bank, Sumitomo Bank, and Tokai Bank) now own five of the eleven major banks and control more than 25 per cent of the US $363 billion total banking assets in the state (*Japan Times*, 22 May 1989).

The flood of finance-related investment into the United States and Europe is of particular interest because it appears to presage a general thrust towards global systems of business activity by the large Japanese financial institutions. Further, it demonstrates how financial power can be used to facilitate the drive to internationalism by acquiring existing financial operations, absorbing the associated skills and expertise, then expanding from these bases to provide appropriate platforms from which the immense strength of the Japanese financial companies can be best exploited.

However, the financial companies are not alone in the aggressive program of FDI that has characterized the post-1985 period. Among the most visible investors have been the automobile manufacturers, who, in succession, have rapidly expanded their production facilities in North America and Europe. By 1992, the aggregate capacity of Japanese automobile plants in North America will be approximately 2.3 million units per year (around 14 per cent of the projected total capacity), and will approach 800,000 units per year in Europe by the mid-1990s (*Business Week*, 14 August 1989). Clearly, the potential for trade barriers has been a motivation for this investment. Nonetheless, it is also evident that the Japanese manufacturers have broader targets than the circumvention of tariffs. These investments have given Toyota et al. a well-entrenched "beach-head" within the lucrative American and European car markets. Given the established competitiveness of the Japanese manufacturers[2] and the anticipated excess capacity that will exist in the 1990s, it seems apparent that the Japanese investments will seriously affect American automobile producers. In fact, it has been estimated (ibid.) that for each three cars produced by the new Japanese-owned plants in North America, one import and two Detroit-built units will be displaced.

From the Japanese perspective, these investments represent a phase in the evolution towards full multinational status. The ultimate objective is to make optimal use of the labour, capital, and technology resources available to the parent company and its subsidiaries by producing automobiles with the best combination of plant and market locations. Honda is moving aggressively towards this goal, and to that end, has consolidated its US, Canadian, and Mexican operations into one North American company. Nissan is attempting something similar for its European operations and has established a regional headquarters in Rotterdam.

Apart from the automobile sector, the investment activities of Dainippon Ink & Chemicals (the largest printing supplies company in Japan) are a prime example of a Japanese company's efforts to establish a truly international presence. This company's investments in the United States during 1986 and 1987 are especially noteworthy because they involved hostile takeovers. Despite opposition from the target companies, Dainippon acquired the graphic arts materials group of Sun Chemicals Corp. (for US $550 million) and Reichhold Chemicals (for US $540 million). These acquisitions were entirely motivated by strategic considerations associated with Dainippon's drive towards an international network of companies and facilities intended to establish a dominant position in the company's product field.

No discussion of recent Japanese FDI could ignore the massive acquisition investments of Sony. Following its US $2 billion purchase of CBS records, the company has now paid US $3.4 billion for Columbia Pictures Entertainment (*Financial Post*, 28 September 1989) and US $200 million for Guber-Peters Entertainment Company (*Globe and Mail*, 29 September 1989). It is clear that Sony intends to become a major *global* electronic entertainment company, delivering both the hardware and the associated entertainment (software). The purchase of the film-producing company Guber-Peters is also rumoured to be a means of providing Sony with a new president (Peter Guber) for Columbia Pictures. Sony's activities in this area are graphically illustrative of the use of financial power to buy a dominant position in a global market.

The very high real estate prices in Japan, relative to those in the United States and other countries, provide Japanese investors with enormous collateral, which can be used to secure low-interest loans from Japanese financial houses to fund foreign real estate purchases. Low prices and the availability of higher depreciation rates provide much better returns on foreign real estate investments than the 1 to 2 per cent that might be realized on similar investments in Japan. As a result, Japanese investment in foreign real estate has exploded since 1985. The United States has been the favourite target of companies such as Shuwa Corp., Mitsui Fudosan, and Sumitomo Life Insurance, who are buying American properties at an unprecedented rate; US $5.5 billion in 1986 (an increase of 366 per cent above 1985) and about US $12.8 billion in 1987 (*Asian Business,* December 1988). Japanese companies have replaced the British as the leading foreign investors in American real estate. On a somewhat smaller scale, but just as aggressively, Japanese investors are buying properties in Europe and other countries. For example, according to the *Japan Economic Journal* (25 March 1989), about 80 per cent of total Japanese FDI in Australia during 1988 was directed toward real estate purchases and tourist resort development. Clearly, these investments have been totally motivated by profit.

Finally, no discussion of Japanese FDI activities after 1985 would be complete without some reference to "zaitek." The word is an amalgam of the Japanese word "zai," money, and "tek," from the English word "technology." In Japanese usage it refers to the rampant, and sometimes speculative, activities of nonfinancial institutions in the securities and foreign exchange markets. Issues (bonds, convertibles, and warrants) have been placed in the Euromarkets at low interest rates (in some instances, exchange profits even resulted in *negative* interest rates) and the proceeds invested in stocks, bonds, and futures. A survey by the *Japan Economic Journal* suggested that in 1986 about one-third of publicly listed, *non-financial* companies profited from zaitek (Viner 1988). The most successful "zaiteker" was Toyota, which was reported to have made about US $850 million. On the other hand, in September 1987, Tateho Chemicals Industries announced losses of 28 billion yen, compared to a net worth of 16.9 billion yen.

The cult of zaitek, while not directly related to FDI, was, and remains, associated with foreign investment and reflects, in the clearest possible terms, *the growing interest of Japanese companies in profit as an end in itself*. In the case of Toyota, the cash pools being handled have become so large (over US $12 billion) that the company is often referred to as the "Toyota Bank."

JAPANESE FDI IN THE FUTURE

The trends of Japanese FDI that have been in evidence since 1985 appear likely to continue, but on an expanded scale of magnitude and sophistication. Quite apart from the macroeconomic considerations involved, the sheer size of the major Japanese companies requires that they look to foreign markets for their future expansion. The Japanese market is simply not big enough for these giants of finance (banks, securities, insurance), commerce (trading companies), and manufacturing to exercise their growth potential properly.

The principal target sectors for Japanese offshore investment and expansion are likely to be in the areas of financial services, advanced technology manufacturing and processing, logistics and distribution services, entertainment media, telecommunications, and information processing. The magnitude, motivations, and possible strategies of, and the related obstacles to, future Japanese FDI are discussed below.

Magnitude of Future Japanese FDI

There is little evidence to suggest that the rate of Japanese FDI will moderate during the next few years. The macroeconomic factors which have driven such investment in recent years are likely to remain strong, and the growing inventory of foreign assets, and the income to be derived therefrom, will add to the capacity and flexibility of the Japanese investors. The Japanese economy continues to demonstrate inherent strength based on the fundamentals of high rates of reinvestment, continuous improvements in productivity, and realistic assessments about which business sectors have ongoing viability. Expanded investments in automation will mitigate labour shortages, which, together with improved productivity, will keep unit labour-cost increases within manageable bounds. There are no tangible signs of inflationary pressures (although a temporarily weaker yen could cause some inflation of import prices), but a controlled increase in real wages can be expected. Along with government efforts to promote a domestic demand-driven economy, this greater disposable income should increase consumer spending. However, the new 3 per cent consumption tax enacted in 1988 and the need to save an increasingly larger proportion of disposable income for home purchases due to spiralling housing costs may moderate the impact of this trend. Notwithstanding American pressures to the contrary, the level of Japanese household savings can be expected to remain high. Since it is anticipated that residential housing investment will stay at current levels or decline slightly the existing household sector surplus (that is, the positive difference between private sector, non-corporate savings and expenditures) is likely to persist.

The corporate sector is enjoying record profits, and the average net worth to total capital ratios of Japanese companies are much healthier than in the past, exceeding 30 per cent for the first time at the end of fiscal 1988 (NRI *Quarterly Review* 19, no.3, August 1989). Continued investment in research and development, new businesses, and productivity improvements is likely. However, the high liquidity of Japanese companies suggests that corporate spending will not result in excessive corporate sector deficits (that is, corporate capital expenditures in excess of retained earnings). On balance, the overall household plus corporate sector surpluses of recent years (that is, 4 to 5 per cent of GNP) should continue.

Following the very large deficits of the 1975 to 1984 era, the government appears to be committed to a policy of fiscal conservatism. Increasing expenditures for health and social services will probably be offset by improved efficiency in the country's notoriously inept tax collection systems. It seems unlikely that government deficits will fully absorb the private sector surpluses within the near or intermediate term. As such the domestic economy should continue to generate large surpluses of capital which, in turn, will be available for foreign investment.

In the area of international transactions, the Japanese current account surplus remains persistently high, and lower values of the yen (151 yen to the US dollar in June 1989, compared to 120 yen to the dollar in November 1988) are apt to exacerbate this problem. These projected surpluses will mandate the continuation of large, balancing outflows of capital investment. Such outflows will be financed by the Japanese domestic savings surpluses. Among the factors that will encourage and facilitate the use of these surpluses for foreign investment are:

— Japanese banks have been compelled, by Ministry of Finance (MOF) administrative guidance, which was initiated by pressures from Western financial institutions, to prune their low-quality assets and increase their capital to asset ratios. As a result, they will be even more interested in acquiring profitable foreign subsidiaries.

— While real estate prices in Japan may stabilize, they are unlikely to decline to any great extent. Thus, the enormous collateral value of Japanese real estate assets and the comparatively low cost of real estate in Western countries (especially North America) will result in continued, and probably accelerated, acquisitions of foreign real estate.

— In March 1986 the limit placed by the Japanese Ministry of Finance on the proportion of insurance company and trust bank portfolios that could be held in foreign securities and real estate was raised to 25 per cent. At the end of 1986, the actual share of such investments held by the twenty-three life insurance companies (the country's biggest investors) stood at only 11 per cent of total assets. The large-scale ventures into foreign real estate made since 1986 have undoubtedly increased this percentage, but until the limit is reached, further acceleration of such investments can be anticipated.

Thus, in summary, Japanese long-term foreign investment will probably be maintained at current levels, or higher, for the near to medium term at least. The foreign direct investment portion of this total investment can be expected to increase.

Motivations and Strategies for Japanese FDI

The established stimuli of comparative advantage, the need to maintain access to foreign resources, and the circumvention of trade barriers will continue to motivate Japanese FDI. However, the trend towards emphasis on return will become increasingly important in establishing the investment policies of Japanese companies. As these companies expand the sophistication of their drive towards "internationalism," the definition of return will assume broader connotations.

Foreign direct investments to maintain comparative advantage will occur in two forms. In certain advanced technology areas, policies of acquisition and joint ventures will be used in the industrialized economies to compensate for reductions in the competitiveness of Japan-based manufacturing, to allay concerns about Japanese imports, and to further strategic plans of corporate internationalism. The steel industry is a case in point; foreign direct investments (for example, Nippon Kokan's takeover of National Steel) alleviate trade barrier problems and also position the Japanese companies for a probable future restructuring of steel-making methods and distribution systems. At the lower end of the technology scale, comparative advantage FDI is more likely to involve the relocation of production from existing offshore subsidiaries, currently located in advanced Newly Industrialized Economies (NIEs), such as South Korea and Taiwan, to lower cost areas, such as Indonesia, Thailand, and Malaysia. Apart from a few exceptions such as chopstick manufacturing, low-technology, labour-intensive manufacturing has been largely eliminated in Japan.

Japanese FDI related to resource development and import to Japan has declined substantially in comparative importance from the heydays of the late 1960s and early 1970s. In 1987, FDI in mining accounted for only 8.4 per cent of total cumulative Japanese FDI compared to 33.6 per cent in 1972. This general trend will persist, although the major trading companies, with their extensive distribution networks and resource-related expertise, will continue to seek opportunities. In many instances, these opportunities will involve the movement of resources to markets other than Japan.

Despite the decline in the relative importance of *natural* resources, Japanese companies continue to be interested in acquiring technology and expertise resources from abroad. The investments of Hitachi, NEC, and Kobe Steel in research laboratories on, or adjacent to, American university campuses appear to be a new version of the resource develop-import approach. Pharmaceutical companies are also expected to embark on aggressive programs of overseas acquisitions to compensate for lagging research progress within their own organizations and to respond to the changing pharmaceutical needs of Japan's aging population (*Tokyo Business Today*, June 1989).

The existence, or threat, of trade barriers will remain as an important motivation for Japanese FDI. Since the two largest markets are North America and Europe, it follows that these regions will continue to be the principal recipients of trade-motivated Japanese FDI. Automobiles, consumer electronics, and steel are fields where Japanese companies have already established production facilities behind the trade barriers. It seems likely that these positions will be used as nuclei from which the Japanese companies will expand their positions in the respective markets.

Impediments to market access are also likely to encourage Japanese FDI in office automation and telecommunications. Both of these areas have been targeted by Japanese industry as prime growth industries, and each sector involves global market products that will encounter strong competition and the real possibility of market protection.

Geographically, the impending 1992 restructuring of the European market and language and cost advantages are making the United Kingdom a favoured European target for Japanese FDI. West Germany, with its high standards of labour quality (and very high trade deficit with Japan — US $8.15 billion in 1986), is also an attractive domicile for advanced technology investments. In North America, the United States will continue as the investment location of choice; but the Free Trade Agreement, lower energy costs, and labour cost advantages in some sectors could make Canada an interesting alternative.

Although the conventional factors described above will continue to motivate future Japanese FDI, even greater importance will be attached to the new driving forces of profit and strategic positioning. In these areas the foreign investment practices of the Japanese financial companies offer a model of what can be expected. The large Japanese manufacturing companies will continue to expand their presence in the principal market areas of Europe and North America; but, more and more, the motivations will be global in scope rather than specific to local market targets. Joint ventures and, increasingly, mergers and acquisitions will be used to attain rapid growth, take over established markets, and gain the skills and experience needed for the transition to international company status. As a part of this evolution, companies will try to introduce some form of controlled devolution of decision-making authority to regional headquarters. Honda's regional headquarters for the North American market has already been mentioned. Nissan and Toyota are also establishing production in the UK in readiness for the new, post-1992 European market. Apart from the automobile industry, it is in the growth industry areas of electronics and telecommunications that the greatest efforts are being, and will continue to be, made. Sony, which sells 70 per cent of its output in foreign markets, is a leader in this process. It has appointed the Swiss-born chairman of Sony Europe and the president of Sony America to its main board of directors (*Financial Post*, 9 October 1989). NEC, Hitachi, Matsushita, and other advanced technology companies are also trying to move in the same direction. Japanese companies have always allowed a good deal of decision-making freedom by their overseas branch and subsidiary company managers. However, these managers have nearly always been Japanese employees dispatched, on a temporary basis, from the corporate head office. The progression from this practice to a true multinational management system utilizing non-Japanese decision-makers will, necessarily, be slow. Thus, acquisition will be an increasingly attractive option. This practice, although contrary to traditional Japanese business values, is already a growing trend. A recent survey of 463 firms indicated that only about 10 per cent had no interest in mergers and acquisitions. Overseas acquisitions increased from 44 in 1984 to 228 in 1987 and 199 in the first six months of 1988. Almost 58 per cent of the 1988 acquisitions involved American companies. The anticipated acquisition approach will provide in-place foreign management as well as plant and markets and will facilitate extended programs of two-way acclimatization and adjustment between the practices of Tokyo head offices and the newly emerging multinational management structures. Although the management decentralization associated with the trend towards international operations will be difficult, there is already one Japanese company that has demonstrated its ability to adjust its organizational structure to the requirements of the international marketplace. Uniden, a medium-sized producer of telecommunications equipment, has manufactured all of its products outside of Japan since 1979. Further, it has moved its production facilities from its original plants in Taiwan and Hong Kong to new facilities in the Philippines and China as the former countries lost competitiveness. From 1989 onwards, it plans to sell 30 per cent of its products in Japan and the rest in other countries. It will have four regional "headquarters": Tokyo, Hong Kong, Fort Worth, and Brussels. Each of the headquarters outside Japan will run operations in its own region, with Tokyo acting as the coordinator. Of the total of six thousand employees, only four hundred will be in Tokyo (*Economist*, 24 September 1988). Although this is a relatively small company and it has taken ten years to effect the devolution of authority, it does illustrate that Japanese companies can be flexible — even with regard to management structure and practice.

The anticipated growth in foreign acquisitions will be greatly assisted by the established and growing power of the Japanese financial companies in foreign markets. Thus, the projected scenario is one in which large Japanese companies will use their financial power and, especially, the financial power of their associated group (keiretsu) financial institutions to buy market position, technology, and skilled, Western-style management. In this sense, the banks and other financial institutions have been, and will continue to be, the spearhead of Japanese corporate internationalism.

In the area of real estate, Japanese FDI, notwithstanding the potential for growing opposition in some countries, can be expected to increase. It is anticipated that the Ministry of Finance will authorize trust banks and life insurance companies to invest corporate pension funds directly into foreign real estate, rather than through shareholdings in subsidiary companies (Viner 1988). Clearly, these investments are totally motivated by profit and will be driven by the comparative overall returns available.

Obstacles to Japanese FDI

Japanese FDI is, at least in part, a response to demands from the recipient countries that their consumer needs be satisfied by home-based production rather than by Japanese imports. The efforts to convince Japanese companies that they should invest in North America or Europe have been intense. Illustrative of this intensity are the twenty-eight American states, two territories (Puerto Rico and Guam), and four port authorities that have established offices in Japan with the primary purpose of attracting Japanese investment to their home state or territory (*Tokyo Business Today*, April 1987). Other countries are also actively soliciting Japanese investment and the jobs it brings.

However, not every country thinks that Japanese FDI is unambiguously beneficial. Early in 1989 the Australian Foreign Investment Review Board rejected a Japanese-sponsored development project in

Sydney as being "contrary to the national interest"(*Japan Economic Journal*, 25 March 1989). In the United States, the generally non-union proclivities and the tendency of the Japanese automobile manufacturers to use their own parts suppliers have diminished the perceived value of Japanese automobile-manufacturing investments. A number of American politicians have proposed limits to foreign investment and there has been an increase in the general inclination towards protectionism, in all its forms. It is evident in the Super 301 provision of the US Omnibus Trade Act, passed in 1989, and the growth of the "Revisionist" theory, which claims that there are irreconcilable differences between Western and Japanese business practices and that the only way to have "fair" trade with the Japanese is through bilateral negotiation of reciprocity (*Business Week*, 7 August 1989). There is also opposition to increased Japanese investment in Europe, although in many cases this opposition reflects individual country protectionism rather than Common Market policy. For example, Renato Ruggiero, the Italian minister for foreign trade, has said that Toyota's use of the UK as a manufacturing base for supplying the EEC is "equivalent to having Italy invite Suntory to produce whiskey for export to Scotland" (*Tokyo Business Today*, April 1989). A further example of this type of resistance is provided by the French insistence that automobiles produced in Nissan's UK plant must have less than 20 per cent Japanese component content; otherwise France will consider them to be Japanese cars and therefore subject to the associated entry barriers. The visibility of Japanese foreign investments and the differences in culture and corporate approaches mean that Japanese companies will have to display considerable sensitivity to local needs and customs if this kind of opposition is to be contained.

Aside from external obstacles, increasing Japanese foreign investments and the move toward multi-country operations will pose severe difficulties for the traditional, hierarchical relationships between subsidiary companies and their Japan-based parents. The devolution of meaningful management control will be a difficult adjustment for most Japanese companies. The extent and efficacy to which they can adapt to Western-style management needs while still retaining the strengths of the Japanese system will be a key determinant of their success in the multinational world.

CONCLUSION

For over three decades Japanese foreign direct investment was largely utilized as a means of protecting the cost and availability of critical imported natural resources, maintaining access to export markets, and compensating for the inevitable loss of sectoral comparative advantage that accompanied the country's economic evolution. From the mid-1980s onwards, the macroeconomic characteristics of the Japanese economy, current account surpluses, and massive appreciations in the value of the yen have created a huge pool of capital in excess of domestic needs. This surplus capital has enabled large Japanese companies seeking international market "elbow room" for their products and services to unleash a flood of foreign direct investment. These investments are different from their defensive predecessors. They are targeted at establishing a substantial international presence. The leading investor companies intend to establish manufacturing facilities for their products or delivery centres for their services that are optimally located to serve the major global markets in the most efficient and profitable way attainable. As with their export strategies of the past, the major Japanese companies will seek dominance or, at least, significant influence in their fields of activity.

The large Japanese banks and other financial institutions have been at the vanguard of this new form of expansionary investment. By establishing a strong presence in the major financial centres of the world, they have positioned themselves to serve and advise their Japan-based clients who are also involved in direct foreign investment. In many instances, it appears that the financial companies have played either an initiating or, at least, a strong advisory role in formulating investment targets and strategies. The extensive use of acquisitions by the financial institutions and the knowledge and expertise obtained through these purchases have provided other Japanese companies with useful models of how to implement their own internationalization strategies. At the same time, the acquisitions have equipped the financial companies with the professional and financial services necessary for their clients to implement such strategies. The clear message of the post-1985 period is that financial power can, and will, be used by cash-rich Japanese companies to buy market position, technology, and management skills in the principal market areas of the world. The purchases by Dainippon of Sun Chemicals and Reichhold, Sony of CBS Records and Columbia Pictures, and Bridgestone of Firestone are explicit demonstrations of the use of Japanese financial power as a key element in a strategy of global expansion.

Analysis of the factors which have facilitated the recent explosion of Japanese FDI suggest no persuasive reasons why (in the near and medium term, at least) the investment pace should abate. In fact, as Japanese companies become more comfortable with the acquisition and mergers approach, the magnitude and sophistication of their investments may increase. The greatest potential obstacles to continued growth of Japanese FDI are adverse public opinion in the recipient countries (and the political response that such opinion could engender) and the changes in management style and practice that internationalism will require.

The rapid increase in Japanese FDI will have significant impact on the future patterns of international production and trade. Japanese-owned production facilities in North America and Europe will reduce imports into these regions and provide goods that can be exported to meet expanding consumer demand in Japan. Japanese companies may well provide the additional financial and technological resources needed for the Western economies to achieve their full potential. However, in assessing this impact, it is important to keep Japanese FDI in proper perspective. While it is true that Japan is, in terms of net investment, now the world's leading creditor nation, Japan is by no means the largest practitioner of direct foreign investment. In 1988, when the United States became a net FDI debtor nation for the first time since 1914, cumulative American FDI amounted to US $327 billion, compared to the cumulative total of foreign direct investment in the United States of US $329 billion (*Economist*, 26 August 1989). Since these figures are stated in nominal terms, they tend to overestimate the value of the more recent surge of investments in North America; thus, the net investment balance in terms of current *value* would probably be in North America's favour. Notwithstanding this distortion, cumulative American FDI in 1988 was double the cumulative Japanese FDI. Furthermore, Japanese investment in the United States during 1988 amounted to US $14.2 billion compared to British investment of US $21.5 billion. On a cumulative basis, Japan trailed Britain by an even bigger margin, with US $53.4 billion invested in the United States compared to US $101.9 billion by the British. Finally, it may be noted that the level of Japanese production abroad is low compared to that of the United States; in 1986, overseas production amounted to about 3.8 per cent of the Japanese total, compared to 17.3 per cent for the United States (*Tokyo Business Today*, April 1987). Thus, Japanese FDI has a long way to go before Japan's international presence in any way threatens the current preeminence of the American multinationals. As Seizaburo Sato, adviser to former Prime Minister Nakasone, is reported to have said, "The twentieth century was the American century. The twenty-first century will be the American century" (*Economist*, 13 August 1989).

Still, the Japanese *have* embarked on a program of internationalizing their major corporations. Given the financial power at their disposal, the demonstrated skills and tenacity of Japanese industry and commerce, and the rapid progress of the last couple of years, it seems likely that several large Japanese companies could attain multinational status within the next few years. The adoption of global production and distribution strategies by these companies could have an impact on the entire fabric of Japan's trade relations with other countries. The output of the foreign plants could replace Japan-sourced imports and supply goods for export to Japan. In the latter case, Japanese ownership should ensure that design and quality are suitable for the Japanese consumers and that the goods are properly distributed within the Japanese market. Thus, Japanese foreign direct investment has the potential to be one of the most important factors in reducing the frictions between Japan and its trading partners. Leon Hollerman (1988) has noted that Japanese FDI could cause Japan's trade balance to turn to deficit, while its service account moves to significant surplus. This switch would deflate existing criticisms of Japan's direct exports. At the same time, it could put the new global Japanese companies in an ideal position for access to world markets from their foreign manufacturing bases. The current restructuring of economic ideology in many communist countries offers enormous opportunities for increased international trade in plant, equipment, and technology. Given the economic circumstances of the potential importers, much of this trade will entail long-term financing; a circumstance which could be tailor made for a Japan that has large current account surpluses generated by the service sector. This monetary power, married to the advanced technology and dispersed production facilities of Japanese manufacturing companies and the global networks of the Japanese financial community, would place Japan in a preeminent position to capitalize on the needs of the newly democratizing economies. Viner (1988) encapsulated the essence of this situation when he stated that capital will become "a crucial strategic asset." And the Japanese, sustained by the returns of their foreign investment programs, appear well positioned to be the capital masters of the next decade.

NOTES

1 The remaining US $181 billion was in the form of foreign portfolio investments such as bonds and securities.

2 Based on the consolidated accounts of the two companies, the average Toyota employee produces over four times the sales value produced by a GM employee (*Tokyo Business Today*, August 1989).

REFERENCES

Books

Abbeglen, James C., and George Salk Jr. (1985). *Kaisha: The Japanese Corporation*. Tokyo: Tuttle

Hollerman, Leon (1988). *Japan's Economic Strategy in Brazil: Challenge for the United States*. Lexington, MA: Lexington Books

Katano, Hikoji, Atsushi Murakami, and Kiyoshi Ikemoto, eds. (1978). *Japan's Direct Investment to Asian Countries*, Kobe: Research Institute for Economics and Business Administration, Kobe University

Lincoln, Edward (1988). *Japan: Facing Economic Maturity*, Washington, DC: The Brookings Institute

Ozawa, Terutomo (1979). *Multinationalism, Japanese Style*. Princeton: Princeton University Press

Sekiguchi, Sueo (1983). *ASEAN-Japan Relations-Investment*.Singapore: Institute of Southeast Asian Studies

Uno, Kimio (1987). *Japanese Industrial Performance*. Amsterdam: Elsevier

Viner, Aron (1988). *The Financial Samurai: The Emerging Power of Japanese Money*. London: Kogan Page

Yoshihara, Kunio (1978). *Japanese Investment in Southeast Asia*. Honolulu: University of Hawaii Press

Yoshihara, Kunio (1983). *The Sogo Shosha*. Oxford: Oxford University Press

Articles

"Australia Begins Resisting Japanese Land Buyers" (1989). *Japan Economic Journal*. Tokyo, 25 March

"Challenge and Dilemma for Corporate Japan: The EC Gears for 1992" (1989). *TOKYO Business Today*. Tokyo, April

"Japanese Direct Investment in US Gains Momentum" (1988). *Keidanren Review No.113*. Tokyo, October

"Japanese Manufacturers Go Local" (1988). *TOKYO Business Today*. Tokyo, July

Murphy, Terence (1989). "The War between the States." *TOKYO Business Today*. Tokyo, April

Oda, Takeshi (1986). "Overseas Investment." *Japan Economic Almanac*

"On the Move Again" (1988). *Economist*, 5 November

Ota, Toshiki (1988). "The Costly Takeover of Firestone." *TOKYO Business Today*. Tokyo, June

"Rapid Increase in Japanese Overseas M&A" (1989). *TOKYO Business Today*. Tokyo, January

"Rusty Guns Threaten Toyota's Grip on Top Slot" (1989). *TOKYO Business Today*. Tokyo, August
"Shaking up Detroit" (1989). *Business Week*, 14 August
Takahashi, Masami (1988). "Overseas Investment." *Japan Economic Almanac*
Takahashi, Yuichi (1986). "Japanese Companies' Overseas Ventures: Automobile Industry Leads Investment in Developed Nations." *Japan Economic Almanac*
"The Overwhelming Japanese" (1989). *World Property*. London: RICS, May

Papers

JETRO, (1986). White Paper on World and Japanese Direct Foreign Investment. Tokyo
MITI (1970). White Paper on Japan's Natural Resources. Tokyo

Newspaper articles

"Auto Parts Maker Has U.S. Plans" (1989). *Japan Times*, 20 May
Done, Kevin (1989). "Car Wars after Yen Shock." *Financial Times*, London, 12 May
Hudson, Richard L. (1989). "Competition from Japan Begins in the Backyard." *Asian Wall Street Journal*, 26 February
"Japanese Are Biggest Foreign U.S. Investors" (1989). *Financial Times*, 28 June
"Japanese Internationalization: Banking on the Golden State" (1989). *Japan Times*, 22 May
Lewington, Jennifer (1989). "Foreigners Invest $65 billion in U.S." *Globe and Mail*, 3 July
McCooey, Christopher (1989). "Japanese Direct Investment in Europe: Why Is the U.K. So Attractive?" *Japan Times*, 15 May
Murphy, Terence (1987). "The War between the States." *TOKYO Business Today*, April
"Now the World Is Japan's Co-Prosperity Sphere" (1988). *Economist*, London, 13 August
"Re-thinking Japan" (1989). *Business Week*, 7 August
Shirozu, Norihiko (1989). "Toyota Weighing Options on Making Cars in Europe." *Asian Wall Street Journal*, 27–8 January
"TSE's Big Four Securities Companies Post Record High Operating Revenues" (1989). *Japan Times*, 20 May
"World's Top 50 List dominated by Japanese Financial Houses" (1987). *Mainichi Daily News*, 23 June
"Xenophobia Rules" (1989). *Economist*, London, 26 August

Reports and Yearbooks

Ministry of Finance (1965–88). *Japan Statistical Yearbook*. Tokyo

MITI (1977 edition). *Japan's Overseas Investments*

Japan's Iron and Steel Industry, 1976 Edition (1976). Tokyo: Kawata Publicity, October

JETRO (1989). *Nippon Business Facts and Figures*. Tokyo

NRI Quarterly Review 19 no.3, (1989). Tokyo: Nomura Research Institute, August

OECD Economic Survey of Japan (1987/8). Paris

Statistical Survey of Japan's Economy (various years). Tokyo: Economic Affairs Bureau, Ministry of Foreign Affairs

Chapter Four

ASEAN in Pacific Basin Trade: Export Composition and Performance, 1970–86

Rod Tyers and Prue Phillips*

The ASEAN countries are important members of the rapidly growing and increasingly interdependent Pacific Basin economy. Economists have given much attention to the potential for mutual gains through trade liberalization within this region, gains that are seen as feasible because of the geographic proximity of many members, especially in the Western Pacific, the present discriminatory pattern of their trade barriers, and the wide diversity of their resource endowments (Hickman et al. 1977; Crawford 1981; Anderson 1983; Ojala and Rae 1983). The principal trading partners of the ASEAN countries are in the Pacific Basin, and the potential for expansion of their economies is dependent upon changes in the patterns of trade and comparative advantage that are taking place there at present.

The first objective of this chapter is to examine the changes in the patterns of trade and comparative advantage between the ASEAN countries and their major trading partners since 1970; the second is to evaluate critically, in this context, both the performance of ASEAN and their competitors in exporting to other Pacific Basin countries and the performance of Pacific Basin country groups in exporting to ASEAN.[1]

Aggregate income in the ASEAN economies is of comparable magnitude to that in Australia and Canada (US $196 billion in ASEAN in 1986, compared with US $185 billion in Australia and US $324 billion in Canada), despite the great discrepancy in their populations (295 million, compared with 16 million and 26 million, respectively, in 1986). The value of merchandise trade is relatively more important to the ASEAN economies, however—about one-third of aggregate GNP, compared with less than one-eighth in Australia and about one-quarter in Canada.[2] In addition, the rates of growth of real income and total merchandise trade in ASEAN have been very much higher. Average real ASEAN GNP growth exceeded 6 per cent a year during the 1970s, while in Australia annual real economic growth averaged less than 3 per cent. The average rate of growth of ASEAN merchandise exports exceeded 9 per cent a year in real terms, while the corresponding rates for Australia and Canada were about 4 per cent. In the early 1980s, however, changes in wages policy in Singapore, political instability in the Philippines, and a generally adverse shift in the terms of trade saw the growth in trade and income slow throughout ASEAN. From 1980 to 1986, the average rates of income and trade growth in ASEAN (3 and 5 per cent, respectively) were similar to those achieved by Australia and Canada.[3]

The trends analysed in this chapter are dominated by major shifts in the distribution of factor endowments (particularly physical and human capital) between countries in the Pacific Basin and their associated impacts on specialization in exports. Most prominently, Japan's export composition has moved away from labour-intensive goods to goods intensive in technology and human capital. Following Japan are the Asian newly industrializing countries (the Republic of Korea, Taiwan, and Hong Kong, hereafter referred to as NICs), whose comparative advantage in labour-intensive goods remains strong despite a significant shift into exports intensive in human capital.[4] For ASEAN as a whole, the shift is away from agricultural resource-based goods toward labour-intensive goods. We expect this transformation to be relatively gradual in the case of ASEAN, however, considering their relatively large endowments of natural resources per capita and the potential for competition with the newly export-oriented manufacturing sector of China.

In the following section, the directions and intensities of the merchandise trade of the ASEAN countries with their major trading partners are examined. We then review some relevant developments in the theory of comparative advantage and discuss the observed changes in the directions and composition of ASEAN and Pacific Basin trade in this context. With that background, we then discuss the performance of Pacific Basin country groups and the European Economic Community (EC) in exporting to ASEAN and the corresponding export performance of ASEAN.

CHANGES IN THE GENERAL PATTERN OF ASEAN AND PACIFIC BASIN TRADE

Since the early 1970s the economies of Asian NICs and some other middle-income, less-developed countries (LDCs), including the members of ASEAN, have grown more rapidly than those of the industrialized countries of the OECD. It is not surprising, therefore, that there has been a corresponding rise in these countries' world trade shares. The commodity boom of the mid-1970s was a watershed, particularly for the OECD countries and the petroleum-importing LDCs, whose terms of trade deteriorated after 1973. In the first three years of that decade, world trade grew at 24 per cent a year in nominal terms; later, it slowed to 18 per cent a year.

The slowdown in ASEAN export growth after 1973 was much less marked than that for the world as a whole, in part because the petroleum price increases during the decade were favourable to Indonesia and Malaysia and the ASEAN group is a small net exporter of petroleum.[5] Over the decade, ASEAN exports rose from 2 per cent to 4 per cent of world trade. The corresponding decline in Australia's export growth after 1973 was considerably greater, however, and Australia's share in world exports declined from 1.7 per cent to 1.4 per cent (Tyers and Phillips 1982: Table 1).

The 1970s commodity boom had an adverse effect on the average terms of trade throughout the Pacific Basin, and the share of Pacific Basin countries in world trade (both imports and exports) fell from about one-quarter to about one-fifth. In nominal terms, the total trade of the Pacific Basin countries increased tenfold between 1965 and 1980. Meanwhile, the share of exports directed to other Pacific Basin countries increased from 54 per cent to 60 per cent. The corresponding share of imports held steady at about 60 per cent.[6] A more detailed picture of ASEAN trade with Pacific and non-Pacific trading partners is provided by Table 37. Adding across columns shows that ASEAN increased its intra-Pacific share of total trade between 1970 and 1986 — exports grew from 65 per cent to 75 per cent and imports from 62 per cent to 71 per cent. Furthermore, there has been a significant increase in intra-ASEAN trade. On the import side, this has been largely at the expense of Japan and the EC, while on the export side it is primarily the result of a decline in the share destined for non-Pacific countries.[7]

The natural-resource-rich Pacific Basin countries (Australia, New Zealand, and Canada) have also increased the share of their imports from other Pacific Basin countries. In the case of Canada the increase is primarily the result of the redirection of exports to the United States and away from the EC. The exports of Australia and New Zealand have also been redirected away from the EC, but their export growth has been to East Asia and ASEAN (as well as outside the Pacific Basin, principally to the Middle East). The imports of Australia and New Zealand have become significantly "Asianized," with almost half com-

Table 37
Changes in Trade Shares, 1970–86 (%)[a]

Share of in Trade of		ASEAN[b]		ANZ[c]		Canada		KTHK[d]		China		Japan		US		EC-12		Rest of World	
		1970	1986	1970	1986	1970	1986	1970	1986	1970	1986	1970	1986	1970	1986	1970	1986	1970	1986
ASEAN[b]	X	15	17	2	2	1	0.8	6	9	1	2	23	23	28	21	16	13	19	12
	M	7	16	5	3	1	1	5	8	3	4	26	22	16	16	19	14	19	15
ANZ[c]	X	5	5	6	6	3	1	2	8	2	4	24	23	14	10	28	15	16	27
	M	2	5	6	6	4	2	2	7	0.7	1	12	22	23	21	36	24	14	12
Canada	X	0.5	0.6	1	0.7	—	—	0.4	2	1	0.9	5	5	65	77	17	7	10	8
	M	0.4	0.7	1	0.6	—	—	1	4	0.1	0.5	4	7	71	68	12	12	10	8
KTHK[d]	X	5	4	2	2	3	3	5	6	0.1	2	12	11	42	44	17	13	13	13
	M	6	7	2	3	0.9	2	4	7	7	12	34	29	21	16	14	11	11	14
China	X	12	8	2	1	1	1	26	34	—	—	14	18	0	17	19	13	25	8
	M	3	4	8	4	8	2	0.6	23	—	—	34	30	0	9	27	20	19	8
Japan	X	9	6	4	3	3	3	11	12	3	5	—	—	31	39	12	15	27	18
	M	8	14	9	6	5	4	3	9	1	5	—	—	29	22	9	10	36	29
US	X	3	4	3	3	21	20	4	7	0	2	11	11	—	—	29	24	31	29
	M	3	4	2	1	28	17	5	12	0	1	15	22	—	—	24	21	24	22
EC-12	X	1	1	2	0.9	1	1	0.7	1	0.4	0.8	1	1	8	9	53	57	32	27
	M	0.7	1	2	0.7	2	0.8	0.7	2	0.3	0.5	2	4	11	7	50	57	32	26
Rest of world	X	1	2	1	0.6	1	1	2	2	0.4	0.5	5	7	11	16	42	39	35	32
	M	0.7	2	1	1	2	1	1	3	0.5	0.5	5	8	15	12	43	42	33	31

Source: ANU International Economic data bank, based on United Nations Trade Statistics

[a]X and M refer, respectively, to shares of total exports and imports
[b]Brunei, Indonesia, Malaysia, Philippines, Singapore, Thailand
[c]Australia and New Zealand
[d]Republic of Korea, Taiwan, and Hong Kong

ing from other Western Pacific countries in 1986. Again, the redirection is principally at the expense of the EC.

The Asian NICs, on the other hand, have maintained a comparatively stable distribution of exports since 1970, with some redirection away from the EC and towards China. This redirection is very much more pronounced on the import side, with a substantial share of the much-expanded exports of China being directed to Hong Kong for further processing. Japan's trade, too, has been increasingly with East and Southeast Asian countries, particularly on the import side. In 1970, three-quarters of Japan's imports came from the United States, the EC, and non-Pacific countries. By 1986 this share had fallen to 60 per cent, while that from the Asian NICs, ASEAN, and China rose from 12 to 28 per cent. The pattern is similar on the export side, though the United States remains the dominant destination for Japanese exports.

The distribution of United States exports has remained comparatively stable since 1970, with some minor redirection from the EC to the Asian NICs and China. On the import side, the redirection has been more significant, with substantial increases in the shares of imports coming from Japan, the Asian NICs, and ASEAN and a decline in Canada's share. This latter tendency might be expected to stabilize with the implementation of the recent North American trade agreement, however.

The ASEAN shares of the imports of other ASEAN countries, the Asian NICs, the natural-resource-rich countries, Japan, and the United States have all increased (see the first two columns of Table 37). The largest proportional gain is in the share of the imports of the natural-resource-rich countries, particularly those of Australia, where the gain was from 2 per cent to 5 per cent (Tyers and Phillips, 1984a). Not surprisingly, the shares of the Asian NICs in the imports of their trading partners have also expanded, as have those of China, albeit from a low base at the beginning of the 1970s. The slower-growing natural-resource-rich countries, on the other hand, have lost shares in the total imports of all the country groups listed in the table, except the natural-resource-poor Asian NICs. This trend is most striking in the imports of Japan and the United States, which were strongly affected by the petroleum price increases of the 1970s, and in China's imports, which changed in composition away from natural-resource-based goods towards technology-intensive and human-capital-intensive goods as China's trade began expanding in the late 1970s (see Findlay et al. 1985).

Changes in Trade Intensities

The relative importance of a particular bilateral trading relationship can be gauged using the intensity-of-trade index.[8] This index is defined as the share of one country's trade with another country (or region) divided by the other country's (or region's) share of world trade. It has been applied to Pacific Basin trade (for 1979) by Anderson (1983). By taking a trade-weighted average over all intra-Pacific trading partnerships, Anderson derived a value of 1.84 for the average intensity for all the Pacific Basin market economies (excluding Latin America). Thus, on average, trading partners in the Pacific Basin are roughly twice as important to Pacific Basin exporters as are their counterparts in the rest of the world. In Table 38, the changes that occurred in Pacific Basin trade intensities between 1970 and 1986 are highlighted.

As Anderson indicates, the high levels of trade intensity exhibited between Pacific Basin countries are the result not so much of complementarity of the commodity mixes of imports and exports in each bilateral relationship as of "special country bias." That is, these high intensities are explained by low resistances to trade in these particular bilateral relationships (low costs of transportation, communication, and other factors associated with trade) relative to those obtaining for trading relationships with the rest of the world (Drysdale and Garnaut 1982). This is particularly evident from a comparison between the respective trade intensities of Australia and Canada with Western Pacific countries. Their similar factor endowment patterns, and hence their similar potential complementarity with the natural-resource-poor countries of East Asia, are not reflected in the distribution of their exports and imports. Clearly, resistances to trade between Canada and the Western Pacific are substantially higher than they are for Western Pacific trade with Australasia.[9]

More specifically, patterns of resistance to trade and gradual changes in comparative advantage have ensured that the general pattern of trade intensities exhibited in the table has been stable throughout the period. The intensities of ASEAN export flows to important trading partners have also been stable, with only slight increases in intensities to Australasia and Japan and decreases to the United States. On the import side, the United States became a more important trading partner, while the intensities of trade with China and Japan decreased.

The major changes in the overall pattern of intensities are in the bilateral trading patterns of China and the Asian NICs. It is in these countries that changes in comparative advantage and in trade composition have been most evident. China's imports have shifted from natural-resource-based goods, such as food, for which Australia and Canada were important sources of supply, to capital goods from the United States, Japan, and the Asian NICs. Accordingly, intensities

Table 38
Changes in Intensities of Trade[a]

From	To	ASEAN[b]	ANZ[c]	Canada	KTHK[d]	China	Japan	US	EC-12	Rest of world
ASEAN[b]	1970	6.1	1.3	0.2	2.7	1.3	3.6	1.4	0.4	0.7
	1980	5.1	2.2	0.1	2.0	1.1	4.1	1.3	0.3	0.5
	1986	5.5	1.7	0.2	2.0	1.2	3.9	1.1	0.4	0.5
ANZ[c]	1970	2.1	3.1	0.5	1.1	4.3	3.7	1.0	0.7	0.7
	1980	2.4	4.8	0.7	1.6	4.2	3.1	0.7	0.4	1.0
	1986	1.7	4.2	0.3	1.9	2.7	3.9	0.5	0.4	1.1
Canada	1970	0.2	0.7	—	0.2	1.5	0.7	4.8	0.4	0.3
	1980	0.3	0.8	—	0.4	1.3	0.8	4.8	0.3	0.4
	1986	0.2	0.5	—	0.4	0.6	0.8	4.0	0.2	0.3
KTHK[d]	1970	2.2	1.3	0.7	2.5	0.2	2.0	3.3	0.4	0.4
	1980	2.1	1.9	0.8	1.8	0.7	1.6	2.5	0.5	0.7
	1986	1.5	1.5	0.9	1.3	1.5	2.0	2.4	0.4	0.5
China	1970	4.7	1.2	0.2	12.3	—	2.2	0.0	0.5	0.9
	1980	3.0	1.2	0.3	7.6	—	3.4	0.5	0.4	0.5
	1986	2.6	0.8	0.3	7.4	—	3.0	0.9	0.3	0.3
Japan	1970	3.3	1.8	0.6	5.0	5.0	—	2.3	0.3	0.9
	1980	2.9	2.3	0.6	3.3	4.2	—	1.8	0.3	1.0
	1986	1.8	2.0	0.6	2.6	2.8	—	2.0	0.4	0.7
US	1970	0.9	1.1	4.0	1.2	0.0	1.5	—	0.6	1.0
	1980	1.1	1.5	4.5	1.4	1.8	1.2	—	0.6	1.1
	1986	1.1	1.7	4.1	1.2	0.8	1.6	—	0.5	1.0
EC-12	1970	0.4	0.8	0.3	0.3	0.7	0.2	0.6	1.3	1.1
	1980	0.3	0.6	0.2	0.2	0.4	0.1	0.4	1.4	1.2
	1986	0.3	0.6	0.3	0.3	0.5	0.3	0.5	1.5	1.2
Rest of world	1970	0.4	0.5	0.3	1.1	0.7	0.8	0.9	1.0	1.3
	1980	0.7	0.5	0.4	0.6	0.4	1.2	1.2	1.0	1.1
	1986	0.6	0.4	0.3	0.5	0.4	1.2	0.9	1.0	1.3

Source: ANU International Economic data bank, based on United Nations Trade Statistics

[a]The intensity-of-trade index is the share of one country group's exports going to another country group divided by the latter's share of world imports (net of the first group's imports). It exceeds unity where the trade specializations are complementary or where resistances to trade are lower than average.
[b]Brunei, Indonesia, Malaysia, Philippines, Singapore, Thailand
[c]Australia and New Zealand
[d]Republic of Korea, Taiwan, and Hong Kong

with Australasia and Canada have declined, while those with the United States have increased. The Asian NICs, on the other hand, have imported with increasing intensity from Australasia and Canada, reflecting increased domestic specialization in manufacturing, the resulting need for raw material imports, and the comparatively low cost of trade with these Pacific neighbours.

On the export side, ASEAN has become a less important destination for China's exports, and Japan and the United States have grown in importance. Throughout, China's exports to Hong Kong have been dominant, yielding the highest intensities in the table. The Asian NICs have also exported less intensively to ASEAN. Their export intensities with Japan and the United States remain high, but that to the United States is declining as the NICs diversify their exports elsewhere in the Pacific Basin and the rest of the world.

CHANGES IN COMPARATIVE ADVANTAGE

Theoretical Developments and Empirical Studies

Since the 1960s the theory of comparative cost as a means of explaining the location of production has developed considerably. The shortcomings of the Heckscher-Ohlin model (the Leontief paradox, for example, asserts that the model does not accurately predict the pattern of exports of the United States) have long been recognized as stemming in part from the aggregation of factors of production to the levels of "capital" and "labour."[10] Extensions to separate out human (as distinct from physical) capital were made in the 1960s in attempts to explain the Leontief paradox; papers by Kenen (1965) and Keesing (1966) are representative of a considerable body of literature on the independent significance of human capital in the United States, including the relatively recent work of Branson and Monoyios (1977) and Stern and Maskus (1981). This literature has been further extended to cover developing countries in an empirical study by Balassa (1977), in which he regressed the pattern of export specialization against measures of both physical and human capital endowment and found that human capital was a significant explanator in more than half of a sample of thirty-six countries.

Another series of developments in the theory, again primarily in the United States literature, supports the further disaggregation of capital to separate out technology. Contributors to this literature have emphasized the research and development component of value added as a measure of technology intensity; they include Gruber, Mehta, and Vernon (1967), Hufbauer (1970), Branson and Junz (1971), Morall (1972), and Goodman and Ceyhun (1976). The incorporation of technology as a factor of production has contributed to dynamic extensions based on product life-cycle theory (Vernon 1966; Wells 1968).

A further stream of theoretical developments has emphasized the role of natural resources as a factor of production. Jones (1971) was the first to extend the Heckscher-Ohlin model to incorporate specific factors such as natural resources, and his model was subsequently generalized by Krueger (1977) and applied in explaining the pattern of ASEAN and Western Pacific trade by Garnaut and Anderson (1980) and Anderson and Smith (1981). This branch of the theory defines three factors (capital, labour, and natural resources) and two classes of goods (natural-resource-based goods and manufactures). The work of Garnaut, Anderson, and Smith has found that this extension to the theory explains well the changes in the patterns of export specialization in the natural-resource-rich Pacific countries, such as Australia and Canada, relative to those in the natural-resource-poor countries, which include Japan and the Asian NICs.

The disaggregation of factors of production to include natural resources, human capital, and technology considerably weakens the most general form of the Heckscher-Ohlin theorem — it can only be said that "on average" countries will have lower autarky prices for goods intensive in the factors with which they are well endowed and that lower autarky prices will lead to exports under free trade (Dixit 1981). The generalizations that remain possible still justify empirical testing, however. Furthermore, the empirical studies based on the disaggregated models mentioned above have had important implications for policy (Krueger 1978).

A recent study by Krause (1982) goes even further in disaggregating the factors of production that are important in United States exports to ASEAN. Krause's factors are natural resources, labour, technology, and human capital. The present analysis follows the approach of Krause in that all merchandise is considered to be the result of production processes involving multiple factors and that each item can be classified according to its dominant factor — that used most intensively and/or that which determines the location of production.

The Approach Adopted

To allow a more detailed examination of the structure of ASEAN exports and those of the natural-resource-rich countries, both of which are dominated by natural-resource-based goods, the factors of production are further disaggregated to separate out agricultural from mineral resources. Note that physical capital is excluded. It is assumed to be relatively mobile and therefore not so important in determining the location of production. As Krause asserts, its exclusion, combined with the inclusion of natural resources, helps to remove some problems with factor intensity reversals — mining and crop production, for example, can both be either labour-intensive or capital-intensive, but their location of production is determined by access to natural resources.

The 189 commodities of the three-digit level of the Standard International Trade Classification (SITC) have therefore been divided into five groups according to their intensities in the five factors — agricultural resources, mineral resources, labour, technology, and human capital. First, agricultural resource-based goods were identified as those for which the location of production depends primarily upon cultivable land. From the remainder, mineral-based goods were similarly identified as those produced in close proximity to mineral and energy-bearing deposits. To identify the labour-intensive goods among the manufactures which remained, we drew upon the work of Garnaut and Anderson (1980), who ranked manufactures at the three-digit level of the SITC in order of increasing value added per worker. Those with particularly low value added per worker were classified as labour-intensive. Finally, to separate the technology and human-capital-intensive categories we drew from the results of Krause (1982), who examined research and development expenditures in the United States, classifying goods with high research and development content as technology-intensive. The resulting classification is listed in Table 39.

In the following analysis, the trade of the ASEAN countries with their principal trading partners is divided into these five factor groups. First, the shares of their total trade in each group are examined and trends in export specialization analysed. In subsequent sections, bilateral trade in each commodity group is examined in more detail. The measure of export specialization adopted is the "revealed" comparative advantage index introduced by Balassa (1965) — the share of each commodity group in an economy's total exports divided by that commodity group's share of world exports. Provided that the economy's export specialization has not been distorted by government policies (which generally distort a country's import mix more than its export mix), index values greater than unity indicate a comparative advantage over the rest of the world.[11]

Results

Table 40 breaks down the total imports and exports of the ASEAN countries and their principal trading partners into the five commodity groups according to factor intensity. The petroleum price increases of the 1970s significantly increased the share of ASEAN exports in the

Table 39
Classification of Merchandise into Factor Groups[a]

Commodity	SITC, revised	Commodity	SITC, revised
AGRICULTURAL-RESOURCE-INTENSIVE GOODS		TECHNOLOGY-INTENSIVE GOODS	
Food and live animals	0	Chemical elements, compounds	51
Beverages and tobacco	1	Coal, petroleum, related chemicals	52
Hides, skins, furs undressed	21	Fertilizers, manufactured	56
Oil seeds, nuts, kernels	22	Explosives, pyrotechnical products	57
Crude and synthetic rubber	23	Plastic materials	58
Wood, lumber, and cork	24	Chemicals nes	59
Pulp and waste paper	25	Machinery, non-electric	71
Textile fibres	26	Electric power machinery switchgear	722
Other crude animal and vegetable matter nes	29	Electric distributing machinery	723
Animal, vegetable oil, fat	4	Electro-medical, X-ray equipment	726
Leather, dressed fur	61	Aircraft	734
Other wood, cork manufactures	63	Instruments, apparatus	861
MINERAL-RESOURCE-INTENSIVE GOODS		Photo, cinema supplies	862
Crude fertilizer, minerals nes	27	Developed cinema film	863
Metalliferrous ores, scrap	28	HUMAN-CAPITAL-INTENSIVE GOODS	
Minerals, fuels	3	Dyes, tanning, colour products	53
Nonmetal mineral manufactures	661–3	Perfume, cleaning products	55
Pearls, precious and semi-precious stones	667	Rubber manufactures nes	62
Pig iron	671	Paper, paperboard manufactures	64
Nonferrous metals	68	Steel	672–9
UNSKILLED-LABOUR-INTENSIVE GOODS		Other metal manufactures	692–4, 698–9
Medicinal products	54	Telecommunications equipment	724
Textile yarn, fabric	65	Domestic electric equipment	725
Glass	664–6	Railway vehicles	731
Base metal household equipment	695–7	Road motor vehicles	732
Electrical machinery nes	729	Road vehicles, nonmotor	733
Ships and boats	735	Watches and clocks	864
Plumbing, heating, lighting equipment	81	Sound recorders, producers	891
Furniture	82	Printed matter	892
Travel goods, handbags	83	Works of art	896
Clothing	84	Gold, silverware, jewellery	897
Footwear	85		
Articles of plastic nes	893		
Toys, sporting goods	894		
Office supplies nes	895		
Other manufactured goods	899		
Special transactions	931		
War, firearms, ammunition	951		

[a]This classification is based on the work of Krause (1981) and Garnaut and Anderson (1980). Further explanation is provided in the appendix to Tyers and Phillips (1984a). Minor modifications to the classification since the first edition of this chapter include the transfer of medicinal products, base metal household products, and electrical machinery from technology-intensive to labour-intensive. These modifications follow the examination by Ariff and Hill (1986) of the factor composition of ASEAN exports.

Table 40

Resource Endowment Proxies, Factor Group Shares of Total Trade and "Revealed" Comparative Advantage: ASEAN and Principal Trading Partners (%)[a]

		ASEAN		ANZ[b]		Canada		KTKH[c]		China		Japan		US		EC-12		Rest of World	
		1970	1986	1970	1986	1970	1986	1970	1986	1970	1986	1970	1986	1970	1986	1970	1986	1970	1986
FACTOR GROUP SHARES OF TOTAL TRADE																			
Agricultural	X	60	29	61	49	23	19	16	7	50	23	6	2	21	18	15	14	30	18
	M	22	13	10	8	12	9	29	16	28	11	34	26	23	10	26	18	20	14
Mineral res.	X	30	31	23	35	27	19	3	3	6	16	2	2	10	7	10	10	38	39
	M	15	18	10	8	10	8	11	16	14	5	45	43	18	16	23	18	13	14
Unskilled labour	X	5	20	2	2	2	3	60	46	29	45	24	7	6	5	14	12	8	9
	M	13	21	13	13	9	8	16	16	3	11	3	7	12	13	10	12	12	12
Technology	X	2	13	7	9	16	18	11	20	7	8	25	40	44	53	33	36	12	20
	M	26	31	40	44	33	34	26	36	25	46	15	18	16	27	23	30	30	36
Human capital	X	3	7	7	5	32	41	10	24	8	8	43	49	19	17	28	28	12	14
	M	24	17	27	27	36	41	18	16	30	27	3	6	31	34	18	22	25	24
REVEALED COMPARATIVE ADVANTAGE																			
Agricultural		2.74	1.92	2.76	3.22	1.06	1.30	0.75	0.47	2.33	1.51	0.27	0.10	0.97	1.18	0.68	0.94	1.37	1.18
Mineral res.		1.59	1.85	1.25	2.03	1.45	1.13	0.18	0.15	0.33	0.97	0.13	0.11	0.53	0.44	0.55	0.59	2.01	2.27
Unskilled labour		0.33	1.25	0.14	0.19	0.20	0.21	5.33	3.96	2.50	3.75	2.14	0.62	0.50	0.44	1.22	1.05	0.69	0.78
Technology		0.09	0.49	0.26	0.31	0.62	0.57	0.42	0.64	0.28	0.25	0.99	1.32	1.69	1.64	1.27	1.15	0.49	0.62
Human capital		0.14	0.29	0.31	0.20	1.43	1.71	0.44	0.98	0.35	0.33	1.90	1.99	0.86	0.68	1.28	1.11	0.53	0.59

Source: ANU International Economic data bank, based on United Nations Trade Statistics

[a]This table is derived following the earlier work of Anderson (1983). "Revealed" comparative advantage is defined as the ratio of the share of a commodity group in total exports for a country or group of countries to that commodity group's share of world exports.

[b]Australia, New Zealand

[c]Republic of Korea, Taiwan and Hong Kong

[d]The commodity classification on which the factor groups are based is derived from that used by Krause (1982)

mineral-resource-intensive category. As would be expected from their large endowments of natural resources (relative to their East Asian neighbours), they sustained high levels of revealed comparative advantage in natural-resource-based goods. At the same time, their comparative advantage in agricultural-resource-intensive goods declined and that in labour- and skill-intensive goods increased over the decade. This is predicted by the theory, considering that the ASEAN countries grew rapidly (and therefore had high rates of growth of physical and human capital per worker) during that decade relative to the rest of the world. The increased significance of labour-intensive exports also follows the production life-cycle theories. ASEAN comparative advantage in labour-intensive manufactures would be expected to increase with accelerating wage growth in the countries with which its exports of labour-intensive goods compete, such as Japan and the Asian NICs.[12]

The very low population densities of Australia, Canada, and New Zealand would be expected to lead to specialization by these natural-resource-rich countries in the export of agricultural- and mineral-resource-intensive goods, which would persist despite their relatively high average per capita incomes (and therefore generally large endowments of capital per worker). As Garnaut and Anderson (1980) indicate, the degree of specialization would be expected to increase with the relatively rapid economic growth of the neighbouring natural-resource-poor East Asian countries. These expectations are borne out by Table 40.

The shares of agricultural- and mineral-resource-intensive goods in the exports of the natural-resource-rich countries remained high throughout the 1970s. Their "revealed" comparative advantage in agricultural-resource-intensive goods began high and increased. In other respects, Australasia differs from Canada. The latter is a comparatively important exporter of human-capital-intensive goods (largely as a result of intra-industry trade across the long border with the United States). Canada's specialization in the exportation of these goods increased at the expense of its mineral-intensive exports.

It is also clear from Table 40 that there has been a striking decline in the relative importance of labour-intensive exports from Japan. This finding is to be expected in view of Japan's very high levels of physical and human capital per worker and their relatively rapid growth. Correspondingly, Japan has developed a significant comparative advantage in technology- and human-capital-intensive goods, with the latter having been strong and increasing into the 1980s. A similar but more subdued pattern is observable for the Asian NICs. Although they sustained a very strong comparative advantage in labour-intensive manufactures, these fell by 14 per cent as a share of their exports, but the share of human-capital-intensive goods in their exports more than doubled (to a level exceeding that for the United States).

As real wages continue to grow in the Asian NICs, their degree of export specialization in labour-intensive goods can be expected to decline further. Although this trend should see an expansion in the role of labour-intensive manufactures in ASEAN exports, the gap left by the Asian NICs is more likely to be filled by China. Labour- intensive manufactures have had an increasing share of China's rapidly growing merchandise exports. According to Findlay et al. (1985), there is considerable potential for further expansion of China's exports, particularly textiles, clothing, and footwear.

The pattern of United States exports remained relatively stable during the 1970s. Most notably, the United States sustained a very strong comparative advantage in technology-intensive goods throughout the decade. This is consistent with the results of Gruber, Mehta, and Vernon (1967) and subsequent authors, who found that research and development expenditures in the United States were greater than those in other countries.

Returning briefly to the measures of comparative advantage for ASEAN and the natural-resource-rich countries of the Pacific Basin, another striking result is the similarity between them. Considering this, it is not surprising that only a small share of the total exports of natural-resource-rich countries are currently directed to ASEAN and vice versa. The changes over the decade that are of interest in this regard are, first, the decline in the revealed comparative advantage of ASEAN countries in agriculture-based goods — matched by a corresponding increase, particularly in Australia; and, second, the decline in ASEAN's comparative disadvantage in labour-intensive goods relative to the world as a whole — an increase in ASEAN's comparative advantage over the industrialized countries of the Pacific Basin.

PERFORMANCE IN EXPORTING TO ASEAN

Factor Composition and Country Shares

Both the commodity composition of ASEAN imports and the shares in these imports of each of their principal trading partners can be seen in Table 41. The commodity composition rows of the table are marked by a significant decrease in the share of agricultural products and increases in the shares of products intensive in minerals, labour, and technology. The increase in the share of labour-intensive products, coming particularly from the United States, is probably overstated. It

Table 41
ASEAN Imports from the Pacific Basin and the EC: Commodity Composition and Exporter Shares[a]

	Merchandise-Intensive in[b] (percentage)											
	Agricultural Resources		Mineral Resources		Labour		Technology		Human Capital		All Merchandise	
	1970	1986	1970	1986	1970	1986	1970	1986	1970	1986	1970	1986
FROM ASEAN												
Composition	34	22	50	33	5	20	3	17	8	8	100	100
Share of total imports	11	28	23	28	3	16	1	9	2	7	7	16
FROM ANZ[c]												
Composition	47	48	13	22	10	5	12	15	18	10	100	100
Share of total imports	11	12	4	4	4	1	2	2	4	2	5	3
FROM CANADA												
Composition	18	25	20	15	3	6	18	39	42	14	100	100
Share of total imports	1	2	1	1	.2	.3	1	1	2	1	1	1
FROM KTHK[d]												
Composition	15	9	6	5	39	42	15	26	25	18	100	100
Share of total imports	3	6	2	2	13	17	3	7	5	9	5	8
FROM CHINA												
Composition	45	30	2	41	36	15	6	7	11	7	100	100
Share of total imports	6	9	.4	8	7	3	1	1	1	2	3	4
FROM JAPAN												
Composition	5	3	4	3	19	19	30	39	41	37	100	100
Share of total imports	6	5	8	4	37	20	21	28	44	48	26	22
FROM US												
Composition	26	12	5	3	10	32	41	46	19	9	100	100
Share of total imports	20	15	5	2	12	25	26	24	13	8	16	16
FROM EC-12												
Composition	11	8	4	5	11	19	43	48	31	21	100	100
Share of total imports	10	8	6	4	14	12	31	21	24	16	19	14
FROM THE WORLD												
Composition	22	13	15	19	14	21	26	31	24	17	100	100
Share of total imports	100	100	100	100	100	100	100	100	100	100	100	100

Source: ANU International Economic data bank, based on United Nations Trade Statistics

[a]This table gives the composition of ASEAN imports from Pacific country groups, from the EC, and from the world across the five commodity groups used in Table 40. The shares in the composition rows of the table add across, summing to 100 except where rounding causes small errors. The shares of each country group in total ASEAN imports are also listed. These sum vertically over country groups. The "rest of the world" group is omitted, however, so that the given import shares sum to less than the 100 listed on the bottom line.

[b]See footnote d to Table 40

[c]See footnote b to Table 40

[d]See footnote c to Table 40

stems from the classification of some electrical equipment and office supplies (which include computers) as labour-intensive (see Table 39). ASEAN and the Asian NICs export extensively in these categories, but such exports are labour-intensive components which are not separable at the three-digit level of the SITC. The problem is therefore one of aggregation bias, rather than of factor intensity reversal. In any case, the dominant part of ASEAN imports from the United States (about half) continues to be in the technology-intensive category.

The composition of ASEAN imports from its largest trading partner, Japan, has increasingly comprised products intensive in technology and human capital. Labour-intensive goods appear to have held their share of ASEAN imports from Japan, though the bias mentioned above is also present in these results. The unskilled labour content of Japan's exports to ASEAN has therefore declined consistent with the trends in comparative advantage discussed earlier. ASEAN imports from the Asian NICs are similarly consistent in their content with the overall pattern of comparative advantage of the Asian NICs relative to ASEAN. An exception to this general pattern, however, is the small volume of direct imports from China. These are dominated by natural-resource-intensive products despite China's specialization in labour-intensive manufactures. This bias is the result of the very limited direct trade between China and Indonesia or Malaysia. Where Chinese labour-intensive products are imported by these countries, the declared port of origin has probably been Hong Kong.

The rows of Table 41 marked "share of total imports" indicate the performance of each trading partner in exporting to ASEAN within each commodity group. It is these shares which we decompose in the next section in order to refine our assessment of export performance. The dominant commodity group in ASEAN imports is technology-intensive products. The rivalry for shares of these imports is between the EC, the United States, and Japan, with Japan gaining at the expense of the EC and the United States share holding steady. The second most important group of imports are human-capital-intensive. Here again Japan is the principal gainer, this time at the expense of both the United States and the EC. In fact, the share of the EC in ASEAN imports declined by one-third between 1970 and 1986, and the bulk of this substantial decline was in technology- and human-capital-intensive goods. By 1986 EC exports to ASEAN comprised primarily technology-intensive goods. It therefore came into competition more with the United States than with Japan. The decline in the significance of the EC as a source of ASEAN imports is not surprising, however, considering the lower trade resistances that accompany the relative proximity of the United States and Japan to the ASEAN countries.

Australasian and Canadian exports to ASEAN became more intensive in mineral resources and less intensive in human capital (those of Canada became significantly more intensive in technology). At the same time, these countries' already small shares of ASEAN imports fell slightly, the greatest proportional loss being in the human-capital-intensive group. Table 5 shows that the doubling of intra-ASEAN trade over the decade was primarily owing to a fourfold increase in the share of intra-ASEAN trade in ASEAN imports of agriculture-based goods, especially food. Intra-ASEAN trade in manufactures has also expanded relative to total manufactured imports, increasing its share fivefold to 1986. These gains were at the expense of the EC and other non-Pacific Basin exporters rather than of the Pacific Basin food exporters, Australia, Canada, and the United States.

Constant Market Share Analysis of Exports to ASEAN

Constant market share (CMS) analysis has been a popular method of analysing a country's export performance over time. It takes a base-year set of export shares (across commodities and country destinations) and evaluates the country's export growth over some subsequent interval in terms of these shares and a residual "competitiveness" effect. If the commodity shares are distributed in favour of commodities in which international trade has grown relatively rapidly, the commodity composition of exports has contributed to overall export growth. Similarly, if the destinations of the exports are distributed in favour of countries whose total imports have grown relatively, it is said to have contributed positively to overall export growth. When these two effects are removed, the residual is the average extent to which individual commodity exports have expanded or contracted. In its simplest form, the method attributes this residual export growth or contraction to changes in the relative prices of the country's exports. This interpretation encounters a number of difficulties, which are reviewed by Leamer and Stern (1970) and Richardson (1971). In what follows, the analysis is restricted to the decomposition of export growth. A more complete presentation of the methodology used is given by Tyers and Phillips (1984b).

One criticism of CMS analysis is that the market shares on which the decomposition is based tend to change during the interval of analysis and that the choice of which set of shares to use is arbitrary (Richardson 1971). To minimize this problem, the period of analysis has been divided into five short intervals, 1970–3, 1973–6, 1976–80, 1980–3, and

1983–6, and a new CMS analysis is conducted on each interval. A second criticism is that inappropriate standards are chosen against which to evaluate export performance. In this case, the performance of exporters to ASEAN is evaluated by comparing it with changes in ASEAN imports from the world as a whole.

A final criticism of the method is that too commonly it must be based on the value rather than the volume of trade. This is important because even if it is accepted that market shares are dependent only on relative trading prices, an increase in a country's value share does not necessarily mean that the relative price of the country's exports has declined. A decline is implied only if the elasticity of substitution at the point of destination between the country's exports and those of its competitors is greater than unity — that is, if the country's exports are not greatly differentiated from those of its competitors. The authors have found no solution to this problem. Trade values are used, and the results should therefore be interpreted with caution.

The CMS analysis of exports to ASEAN decomposes total export growth into components that are the result of commodity composition and market distribution (the distribution of exports over countries of destination, in this case the five ASEAN countries) and a residual component presumed to be the result of competitiveness. The results are summarized in Table 6, which presents only the "competitiveness" residuals across all traded merchandise for each of seven countries and country groups of origin. In the body of the table are listed the results from CMS analysis across only those commodities within each factor group, down to the SITC three-digit level.

Consider first the performance of Australasian exports to ASEAN. The competitiveness residuals listed in Table 42 indicate the average per cent change by which the growth in the value of these exports to ASEAN has differed from the standard country group (in this case the totality of other exporters to ASEAN) after biases arising from commodity composition and market distribution have been removed. The first entries in the final column of the table indicate that Australasian export growth to ASEAN matched that of all competitors in 1970–3 but subsequently lost ground. Applying these per cent changes sequentially and controlling for commodity composition and market distribution, Australasian exports to ASEAN were 45 per cent smaller in 1986 than they would have been if they had kept pace with those of competitors since 1970.

This loss of ground was entirely the result of poor performance by manufactured exports to ASEAN. The top entries of the first five columns of the table demonstrate this finding clearly. While the gain in exports of agricultural goods, similarly accumulated over the five

Table 42
ASEAN Imports from the Pacific Basin and the EC:
"Competitiveness" Residuals from Constant Market Share Analysis[a]

	Merchandise-Intensive in[b] (percentage)					
	Agricultural Resources	Mineral Resources	Labour	Technology	Human Capital	All Merchandise
FROM ANZ[c]						
1970–3	26	33	-76	-5	36	0
1973–6	3	10	-53	-42	-50	-24
1976–80	-11	75	-15	16	-60	-9
1980–3	-18	-24	-21	-40	-21	-22
1983–6	9	15	-40	-5	-10	2
FROM CANADA						
1970–3	68	-42	-28	-18	-76	-45
1973–6	7	-22	80	113	80	60
1976–80	-13	212	-2	-37	-53	-7
1980–3	33	-28	21	8	-1	-3
1983–6	10	14	-36	22	-20	6
FROM KTHK[d]						
1970–3	67	30	64	29	4	41
1973–6	-28	22	59	18	-13	18
1976–80	148	-78	21	44	149	39
1980–3	17	40	2	16	10	9
1983–6	-12	0	18	23	-2	13
FROM CHINA						
1970–3	88	177	16	25	102	48
1973–6	-68	484	-6	-2	-21	-26
1976–80	-12	287	-13	133	2	29
1980–3	10	-59	-4	-22	-13	-22
1983–6	31	184	-6	-121	0	35
FROM JAPAN						
1970–3	-16	-55	-41	-9	11	-6
1973–6	-39	54	10	-5	1	1
1976–80	25	-55	-34	4	21	-1
1980–3	-13	-11	-3	-2	3	0
1983–6	4	-4	-28	25	-7	5
FROM US						
1970–3	28	-1	10	19	-17	2
1973–6	-12	-96	-5	9	20	8
1976–80	35	32	-39	-7	-52	6
1980–3	-2	18	13	5	-4	-3
1983–6	-21	-16	1	-13	-10	-12
FROM EC-12						
1970–3	-30	-30	5	-26	-24	-22
1973–6	-3	-54	-39	-12	1	-22
1976–80	-21	59	1	-22	-48	-27
1980–3	7	-44	44	1	-8	-2
1983–6	0	16	-14	-7	8	-4

[a]This table lists the residual terms from the constant market share analysis. These terms indicate the percentage by which the value of trade expanded in the intervals shown, after the effects of commodity composition and market distribution have been removed. The terms, therefore, indicate the average degree to which trade in individual commodities would have expanded had the commodity composition and the distribution across destination (ASEAN) countries conformed to that of imports by ASEAN from the world as a whole

[b]See footnote d to Table 40

[c]See footnote b to Table 40

[d]See footnote c to Table 40

intervals, was 3 per cent and that in mineral goods was 83 per cent, manufacturing exports fell behind by between 64 and 95 per cent. These massive losses of competitiveness stem in part from the commodity booms of the 1970s. By raising the real exchange rates of Australia and New Zealand and diverting domestic resources from manufacturing to mining and agriculture, manufacturing costs were increased in foreign currency terms, ensuring that this sector would no longer compete on price (the "Dutch disease" effect as described in detail by Gregory 1976; Corden 1982; and Corden and Neary 1982).

The real exchange rate component of the above effect is evident from the indices plotted in Figure 9. It is also evident that there has been substantial divergence since 1970 among the paths taken by the real exchange rates of Pacific Rim and European countries. At the upper extreme, there has been substantial net appreciation (and hence, presumably, loss of competitiveness) in Japan while, at the lower extreme, there has been net depreciation (and therefore improved competitiveness) in the Asian NICs. Significantly, however, the average real exchange rate for the ASEAN group has charted a middle course. Generally, they have maintained nominal rates against the United States dollar and contained domestic inflation. The concentration of their exports in the natural-resource-based commodity groups has led to some real rate fluctuations of the type which impaired Australia's competitiveness. But these effects have been more modest for the ASEAN countries as a group.

By contrast with Australasia, whose share of all ASEAN imports fell between 1970 and 1986, the Asian NICs expanded their share by almost half. Their strong export performance in the manufacturing sector was the source of this expansion. By 1980 manufactures constituted four-fifths of their total exports, and manufactured exports to ASEAN were distributed evenly across the three factor groups. Agriculture-based exports (mainly income-elastic processed foods and leather goods) remained important at 14 per cent, however. The food exports were destined mainly for Indonesia, where they lost ground as Indonesia expanded its rice imports in the mid-1970s — a high market distribution effect occurs with the low competitiveness residual for 1973–6. The value of these exports expanded sixfold between 1976 and 1980, however, as national income rose in Indonesia and rice imports declined.

China's share of ASEAN imports held steady, but the composition of this trade has changed substantially. Early in the decade it was dominated by agriculture-based goods and labour-intensive manufactures, but after 1973 China's exports of these commodity groups to ASEAN proved uncompetitive. In the case of labour-intensive manufactures,

Figure 9 Real Exchange Rate Indices Relative to the US $ (1970 =100)

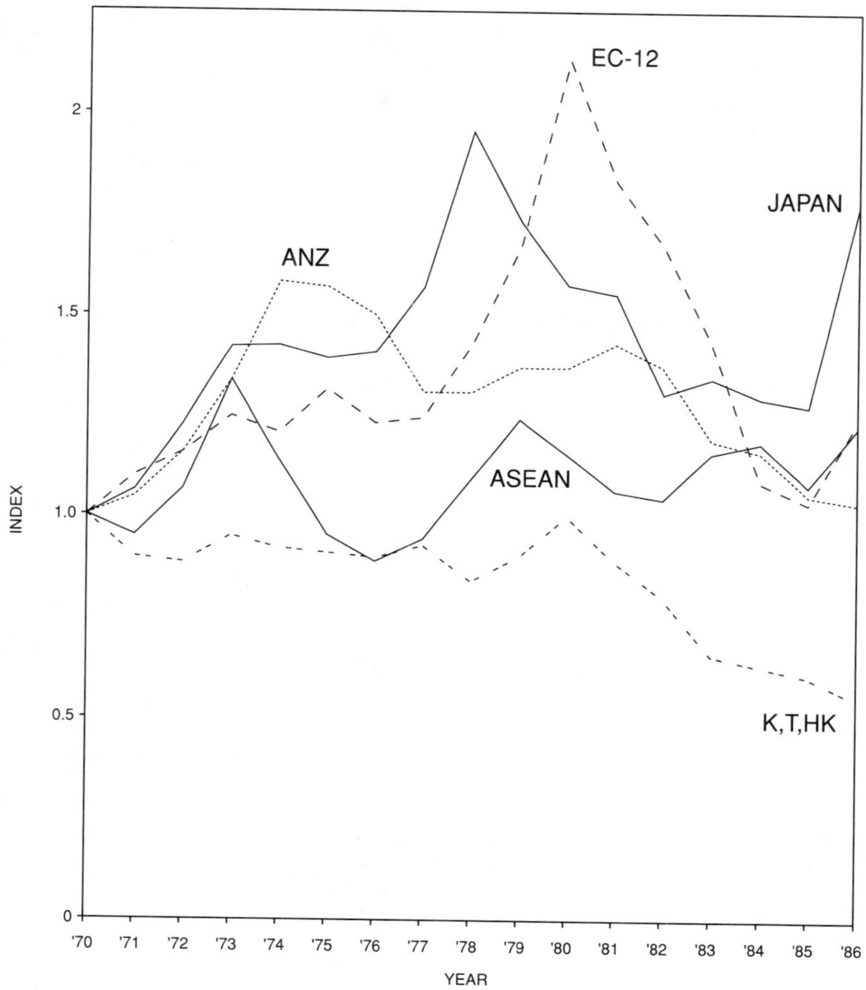

this change may be the result either of discriminatory commercial policies in ASEAN or of a preference for the higher quality textiles, clothing, and footwear that the Asian NICs were able to supply late in the decade. Whatever the reason, this loss of share in no way restrained China's total exports of labour-intensive goods (Findlay et al. 1985). As the share of labour-intensive goods in China's exports to ASEAN declined, their place was taken by mineral-based goods – mostly petroleum exports to the Philippines and Thailand – which the CMS analysis shows were highly competitive through 1986.

Imports from the ASEAN countries' largest trading partner, Japan, consisted mostly of manufactures intensive in technology and human capital. During the decade, Japan's share of ASEAN labour-intensive imports declined owing to its loss of competitiveness. Japan's share of overall ASEAN imports expanded until 1973 but declined thereafter because the trade comprised commodities – especially petroleum products – in which ASEAN imports were relatively slow-growing. After 1976, however, the analysis attributes the slight decline in Japan's overall share to competitiveness rather than to commodity composition or market distribution. On the other hand, Japan's share of ASEAN human-capital-intensive imports, the dominant component of this trade, increased steadily through 1983. This gain was the result of competitiveness, but the analysis indicates that subsequently Japan's exports to ASEAN became uncompetitive as the yen appreciated (Figure 1). The aggregate market share fell only slightly across the entire period because Japan was exporting the right technology- and human-capital-intensive products to the most rapidly growing ASEAN markets, principally Indonesia and Singapore.

The other Pacific trade giant, the United States, maintained its share of total ASEAN imports through 1986. The composition of United States exports to ASEAN was characterized throughout by the dominance of the technology-intensive factor group. While the United States' share of ASEAN imports of these commodities held steady, its share of ASEAN imports of agriculture-based and human-capital-intensive goods declined. Although competitiveness was the deciding factor before 1976, the losses of share in technology-intensive imports would have been larger had it not been for positive commodity composition and market distribution effects. The most important destinations for these exports were Malaysia and Singapore, while the countries in which the United States registered positive competitiveness residuals were the Philippines and Thailand.

After 1976, technology-intensive exports to Indonesia from the United States were greatly outpaced by those from Japan, whose technology-intensive exports to Indonesia tripled in this period, making Indonesia Japan's most important ASEAN market for these goods. This result lends some support to Krause's (1982) argument that United States regulations affecting the non-price aspects of competition, which are important in the marketing of technology-intensive goods with a large unit value, have hindered its competitiveness compared with that of Japan.[13] All groups of United States manufactured exports were uncompetitive in the late 1970s, despite the depreciation of the US dollar against the Japanese yen during this period by 30 per cent.[14] In the early 1980s the United States continued to lose ground in technology-intensive and human-capital-intensive exports as the dollar revalued substantially against the yen and the European currencies.

ASEAN EXPORT PERFORMANCE

Factor Composition and Shares of Imports

The commodity composition of exports from the ASEAN countries and the shares of these exports in the imports of each of their principal trading partners are listed in Table 43. By 1980 the destination where ASEAN exports had the largest share of total imports was ASEAN itself. As noted above, the commodity composition of intra-ASEAN trade changed little during the 1970s, but there was an almost fourfold increase in the share of intra-ASEAN trade in total ASEAN imports of agriculture-based goods, principally food. This increase in the significance of intra-ASEAN food trade was at the expense of non-Pacific Basin exporters, not of the major food exporters of the Pacific Basin — Australasia, Canada and the United States (see Table 41).

The share of intra-ASEAN trade in ASEAN imports of manufactures remained small, but it showed substantial growth during the 1970s. Since February 1977 the ASEAN countries have been implementing Preferential Trade Arrangements. Until recently, the most important components of these arrangements were item-by-item reductions in tariffs, but these appear to have had little impact on intra-ASEAN trade (Tan 1982). The product-by-product approach was dropped at the twelth ASEAN Economic Ministers' Meeting in January 1982. Since then, a 20 to 25 per cent margin of preference has been given automatically to items with import values of less than US $1 million; more recently this limit has been extended to US $10 million, foreshadowing a greater impact on intra-ASEAN trade in the 1980s. There is a danger in taking the recorded increase in intra-ASEAN trade too seriously, however—it may be the result, for example, of the reporting of trade between the four larger ASEAN countries and the non-ASEAN countries as trade with Singapore, where either the goods are directly transshipped or minor value is added before reexportation. To the extent that gains in intra-ASEAN trade have in fact occurred, they are probably attributable to the formation of ASEAN associations of businessmen, bankers, and professionals (Naya 1980; Hiemenz and Naya 1983).

The performance of ASEAN in exporting to the natural-resource-rich

Table 43
ASEAN Exports to the Pacific Basin and the EC:
Commodity Composition and Shares of Total Imports by Destination Countries[a]

	Merchandise-Intensive in[b] (percentage)											
	Agricultural Resources		Mineral Resources		Labour		Technology		Human Capital		All Merchandise	
	1970	1986	1970	1986	1970	1986	1970	1986	1970	1986	1970	1986
TO ASEAN												
Composition	59	21	30	32	3	20	3	18	5	9	100	100
Share of total imports	34	29	25	31	3	17	2	11	3	9	7	16
TO ANZ[c]												
Composition	35	24	46	34	13	19	4	14	3	9	100	100
Share of total imports	9	16	12	23	2	5	.3	2	.3	2	2	5
TO CANADA												
Composition	69	38	22	1	7	38	.4	13	1	10	100	100
Share of total imports	2	3	1	.1	.3	2	0	.3	0	.2	.4	.7
TO KTHK[d]												
Composition	75	32	14	34	6	17	1	10	4	7	100	100
Share of total imports	14	13	7	14	2	5	.3	2.4	1	3	6	7
TO CHINA												
Composition	99	44	.1	20	.3	6	.2	21	.0	9	100	100
Share of total imports	10	15	.0	16	.2	1	.0	2	.0	1	3	4
TO JAPAN												
Composition	52	21	46	68	1	5	.2	4	.1	1	100	100
Share of total imports	11	10	8	21	1	7	.1	4	.3	3	8	14
TO US												
Composition	66	19	26	16	6	34	1	23	1	8	100	100
Share of total imports	8	7	4	4	1	7	.2	4	.1	9	3	4
TO EC-12												
Composition	78	49	17	5	4	26	.4	10	.8	10	100	100
Share of total imports	3	3	.6	.3	.2	2	.0	.5	.0	.5	.7	1.1
TO THE WORLD												
Composition	61	29	30	31	5	20	2	13	3	7	100	100

Source: ANU International Economic Databank, based on United Trade Statistics

[a]This table gives the composition of ASEAN exports to Pacific Basic country groups and to the EC across the five commodity groups. The shares in the composition rows sum across the table to 100 per cent, except where rounding causes small errors. The shares of ASEAN exports in the imports of each Pacific Basin country group are also listed. These are the shares of each country group's total imports

[b]See footnote d to Table 40

[c]See footnote b to Table 40

[d]See footnote c to Table 40

countries, Australasia and Canada, is dominated by growth in the ASEAN share of Australia's total imports. Even by 1986, only 0.8 per cent of ASEAN exports — principally non-food agricultural commodities, such as rubber — were destined for Canada, and these made up only 0.7 per cent of Canada's total merchandise imports. On the other hand, the share of ASEAN exports in Australia's imports expanded from 2 per cent in 1970 to 5 per cent by 1986. The factor composition of Australia's imports changed relatively little during the 1970s. Higher petroleum prices led to an expansion in the share of mineral-based goods in the total value of Australia's imports, accompanied by small declines in the shares of agriculture-based and technology-intensive goods.

ASEAN exports to Australia are principally petroleum, petroleum products,and agriculture-based goods, although manufactures have grown increasingly important in the 1980s. This high petroleum content, combined with low trade resistance between the ASEAN countries and Australia, led the way in a significant expansion in ASEAN's share of Australia's total imports in the 1970s. It does not fully explain the expansion, however, since the ASEAN share of Australia's imports in all five commodity groups increased. The largest proportional increase in the ASEAN share was in labour-intensive manufactures (from 0.2 per cent to 5 per cent). This increase accords with the findings from the market penetration analysis of Hamilton (1983): that the Australian producers' domestic trade share of the labour-intensive product group of textiles, clothing, and footwear fell over the decade by more than it did in Japan, Canada, and the United States and that, of all the countries studied, Australia showed the largest increase during the decade in the share of ASEAN in total home demand for these goods.

The commodity compositions of exports to Australasia by their other principal trading partners show similar patterns in their total exports (see Table 40). Again, the changes in the pattern of Australia's imports are similar in direction but greater in magnitude than those for the group as a whole. The most striking changes in the share composition of Australia's total imports during the 1970s were the rising shares of Japan, the Asian NICs, and the ASEAN countries and the falling shares of the EC and the United States. The rise in Japan's share was led by a virtual doubling of its share of Australia's human-capital-intensive imports, while that of the Asian NICs is the result of a doubling of their share of Australia's imports of labour-intensive manufactures. The battle for shares in Australia's imports of technology- and human-capital-intensive goods is still between the United States, Japan, and the EC, with the United States remaining strongest in technology-intensive goods and the EC losing share to Japan in human-capital-intensive goods.

There was an increase in the share of ASEAN exports destined for the Asian NICs (6 to 9 per cent, see Table 37) and in the share of these exports in the total imports of the Asian NICs during the decade. As the petroleum price increases of the 1970s raised the value share of mineral-based goods in the imports of the Asian NICs, the share of petroleum in ASEAN exports to these countries also grew. Consequently, the expansion in the ASEAN share of their total imports extended uniformly across all commodity groups. China, on the other hand, has remained a relatively insignificant destination for ASEAN exports; they constituted only 1 per cent more of China's total imports in 1986 than they did in 1970, mostly because of an increase in the ASEAN share of China's imports of manufactured goods.

In their exports to Japan and the United States, the ASEAN countries appear to have performed well. These destinations combined take more than 40 per cent of ASEAN exports (see Table 37), and the ASEAN share of the imports of both Japan and the United States almost doubled between 1970 and 1986. Although their share increased in both markets across all five commodity groups, a principal factor in the gains was the expansion of petroleum exports from Indonesia and Malaysia. In the case of the United States, however, another important factor was a tenfold increase in ASEAN's share of total imports of technology-intensive goods—primarily electronic components. These exports have expanded as a consequence of direct investment, primarily by Japanese and American firms, in the ASEAN countries. In general, technology is not the location-determining factor in the production of these components. Local subsidiaries carry out the labour-intensive stage in the production of electronic goods that are ultimately exported for consumption or further assembly in the United States (Yamazawa et al. 1983).

These gains to the ASEAN countries came chiefly at the expense of Australasia and Canada, whose share of Japanese imports fell from 14 per cent to 10 per cent and whose share of United States imports fell from 30 per cent to 18 per cent, and of the EC, whose share of Japanese imports held steady while its share of United States imports fell from 24 per cent to 21 per cent (see Table 37). The corresponding losses of share by Australasia and Canada came primarily in their exports of mineral-based goods—their petroleum content was low relative to that of ASEAN mineral-based exports. When the relative prices of petroleum products increased, the value share of these exports declined. This is not surprising considering that mineral-based products still constitute almost half of Japan's total imports and one-sixth of the total imports of the United States. The loss of share by the EC, on the other hand, is the result of declines in its shares of Japanese and United States imports of manufactures. In Japanese imports, these declines in the EC share were in labour- and technology-intensive goods, and the corresponding gainers were China and the Asian NICs. In imports by the United States, the losses fell principally in the labour- and human-capital-intensive commodity groups. In this case the corresponding gainers, in addition to ASEAN, were again the Asian NICs.

Constant Market Share Analysis of ASEAN Exports

The results are summarized in Table 44. Although the analysis has been carried out for all five commodity groups and all five ASEAN countries, only the all-ASEAN results are presented here.[15]

As the results in Table 43 lead us to expect, the share of ASEAN exports in the imports of its principal trading partners expanded in almost all periods, the one exception being ASEAN exports to Japan in the years 1973–6, when the share of petroleum in Japan's total imports grew rapidly. Since ASEAN exports at the time also contained petroleum, the commodity composition effect for total exports to Japan is high for that period. The loss of ASEAN market share was caused by a loss in the minerals category, showing that Indonesia and Malaysia were slow to increase the volume of their petroleum exports in response to the 1973 price increase.

The gains after 1973 in the ASEAN share of the imports of major trading partners are explained by competitiveness rather than commodity composition or market distribution, as the results in Table 44 indicate. The only exception is the trade with Canada, which is so small (less than 1 per cent of Canadian imports) that the competitiveness residuals may reflect changes in firm-level trading arrangements. This general pattern is as might be expected, given the rapid economic growth of the ASEAN group and their comparatively stable macroeconomic environment (Figure 9).

A surprising result is the consistency of positive competitiveness residuals in ASEAN exports to the Asian NICs. Two-thirds of this trade is still in natural-resource-based goods, such as timber, rubber, and sugar, and it is in these commodity groups that ASEAN competitiveness was strongest and most consistent. Here the forces of comparative advantage and low resistances to trade appear to have outweighed the increasing gap between the average real exchange rates of ASEAN and the Asian NICs as a group.

Exports to the most important destination, Japan, have held their

Table 44
ASEAN Exports to the Pacific Basin and the EC:
"Competitiveness" Residuals from Constant Market Share Analysis[a]

	Merchandise-Intensive in[b] (percentage)					
	Agricultural Resources	Mineral Resources	Labour	Technology	Human Capital	All Merchandise
TO ANZ[c]						
1970–3	12	240	360	122	121	-98
1973–6	23	221	39	–45	65	32
1976–80	-39	194	–85	23	–114	6
1980–3	–4	–36	–5	–17	–6	–26
1983–6	1	6	–22	56	16	7
TO CANADA						
1970–3	–15	–1	–158	–1773	372	11
1973–6	27	–133	–2	–10	194	19
1976–80	–57	–92	23	–133	–333	–116
1980–3	25	171	51	–22	44	26
1983–6	–7	–28	7	–8	32	9
TO KTHK[d]						
1970–3	21	60	102	–84	38	30
1973–6	5	92	–88	–5	–118	2
1976–80	35	45	22	84	159	49
1980–3	8	45	–13	–7	–11	11
1983–6	23	19	17	36	42	22
TO CHINA						
1970–3	125	6841	—	–254	3374	141
1973–6	–15	355	–96	–199	–60	–6
1976–80	132	–180	435	7515	77143	267
1980–3	9	55	–116	–18	–78	–27
1983–6	46	1116	60	426	740	156
TO JAPAN						
1970–3	6	119	1361	847	448	69
1973–6	3	–76	–92	213	52	–40
1976–80	–7	–6	–85	225	–37	0
1980–3	3	–7	–1	0	–25	–6
1983–6	8	1	–11	15	58	–4
TO US						
1970–3	–33	15	128	190	137	21
1973–6	–21	198	–47	–44	–2	21
1976–80	–56	–45	13	19	–19	–44
1980–3	17	–21	58	36	36	13
1983–6	–7	2	3	–11	24	2
TO EC-12						
1970–3	13	12	169	275	522	31
1973–6	2	15	152	56	59	–21
1976–80	–19	–68	–12	52	–98	–18
1980–3	–10	–10	–37	–22	0	–16
1983–6	–6	–8	–10	13	22	6

[a]These terms indicate the average degree to which trade in individual commodities would have expanded had the commodity composition and the distribution across countries within destination groups conformed to that of imports by each destination country group from the world as a whole. Negative numbers exceeding 100 per cent indicate reversals in the direction of trade. They result when the standard growth (world to destination) exceeds that of the focus trade flow by more than 100 per cent

[b]See footnote d to Table 40

[c]See footnote b to Table 40

[d]See footnote c to Table 40

own in terms of competitiveness. The gain in overall market share indicated in Table 43 is primarily the result of commodity composition. Some high competitiveness residuals are recorded in the technology and human-capital-intensive categories, though the expansion which results is from a low base. As mentioned earlier, this trade is driven increasingly by foreign direct investment in ASEAN by Japanese multinationals.

Both in exports to Japan and to the United States, quite spectacular expansions in import shares of labour-intensive manufactures have been achieved, once again from low bases (Table 43). In the trade to Japan the expansion came from competitiveness early on. Since 1973, however, market share in this group has been lost to other developing countries, particularly the Asian NICs. In ASEAN exports of this commodity group to the United States, however, competitiveness has been more consistent throughout the period. The real exchange rate increases of 1973–6 (Figure 9) inhibited export growth in that period and, most recently, growth in the imports of textiles and clothing from ASEAN countries by the United States is retarded by MFA quotas. Nevertheless, the strong overall performance of the ASEAN countries as exporters of both natural-resource-based and manufactured goods is borne out by the CMS analysis as being primarily the result of competitiveness rather than of commodity composition or market distribution.

SUMMARY AND CONCLUSION

As interdependence through merchandise trade has increased among Pacific Basin countries, the ASEAN countries have increased the shares of their trade with other Pacific Basin countries, especially with other members of the ASEAN group, with the Asian NICs, and with China. The rapid overall export growth of the ASEAN group has ensured that it looms larger in the imports of all its major trading partners in the 1980s than it did in 1970. Its significance has expanded with particular rapidity in Australasia and Japan, however. On the import side, the dominance of Japan persists, while shares of the Asian NICs have expanded at the expense of the EC. Except as a destination for the exports of Japan, the EC declined greatly as a trading partner for Pacific Basin countries in general and for ASEAN in particular.

The changes in the pattern of ASEAN imports were characterized by the increased importance of intra-ASEAN trade and a diminished share originating in the EC. Japan, the dominant exporter to ASEAN, expanded its shares of ASEAN imports intensive in technology and human capital to offset declines in its shares of labour-intensive imports. The Asian NICs, combined with intra-ASEAN trade, have provided substitutes for the labour-intensive exports of Japan. The role of intra-ASEAN trade may, however, be overstated by the data, given the importance of entrepôt trade, particularly with Indonesia and Malaysia, in Singapore's total trade.

The share of Australasia in ASEAN imports fell, the principal loss being in human-capital-intensive goods. All of Australia's manufactured exports suffered a considerable loss of competitiveness after 1973, partly because of the "Dutch disease" effect of the commodity boom on the cost of production and Australia's exchange rate between 1973 and the early 1980s. Finally, despite rapid growth in China's total exports, its share of ASEAN imports has remained small. China's export expansion appears to have been concentrated to date in the markets of the Asian NICs (particularly Hong Kong), Japan, and the United States.

The results from constant market share analysis go beyond changes in the commodity group shares and indicate where aggregate gains are the result of differences in commodity composition or market distribution rather than competitiveness. As for the export performance of the trading partners of ASEAN, the general pattern of the competitiveness residuals corresponds with that of the gains in aggregate shares of ASEAN imports. Exceptions late in the 1970s are the manufactured exports to ASEAN of the United States, the good performance of which depended mostly upon specialization within the technology-and human-capital-intensive commodity groups and the distribution of these exports among ASEAN countries. The good performance of ASEAN exports during the decade similarly corresponds with high competitiveness residuals for all destinations except the EC, whose imports are of declining importance for ASEAN.

Of special significance for the trading partners of ASEAN are the trends in trade specialization that have occurred since the 1970s. ASEAN exports came to be dominated in the 1970s by petroleum and other mineral products. Although these continue to make up nearly one-third of total exports, the composition of what remains has shifted markedly from agriculture-based goods towards manufactures, which were 40 per cent of exports in 1986. Future trends in the overall pattern of ASEAN export specialization will depend upon the degree to which growth in domestic demand diminishes the petroleum surplus and upon movements in the world prices of petroleum products. Nevertheless, as the capital endowments of the ASEAN countries continue to rise, these countries should specialize increasingly in manufactured exports. Relative to their principal trading partners, the ASEAN countries have a growing comparative advantage in labour-intensive goods. Relative to China, however, their comparative advantage remains in natural-resource-based goods. In the world market for labour-intensive manufactures, China may be a formidable competitor (Findlay et al. 1985; Tyers et al. 1987). The degree to which ASEAN manufactured exports are labour-intensive will depend, therefore, on the pattern and growth of China's exports.

As for the pattern of ASEAN import specialization, mineral-based imports also increased in share. Again, however, there were major changes in the pattern of ASEAN non-mineral imports. The share of agriculture-based goods has fallen substantially and that of manufactures has risen. The latter increase has been mainly in labour-intensive goods, including components, and final technology-intensive products, while the share of human-capital-intensive goods, such as motor vehicles, has declined. Although future trends in overall import specialization will depend upon movements in petroleum prices as incomes and capital endowments grow in ASEAN countries, the trend away from agriculture-based goods can be expected to continue. Among exporters to this rapidly expanding market, these trends will favour Japan, the United States, and the Asian NICs over exporters with relatively large endowments of agricultural resources, such as Australia and Canada.

Finally, while the emphasis of this chapter has been on the fundamental forces affecting the international distribution of factor endowments and the changes in the pattern of international trade that occur in response to these forces, the continuation of the observed trends into the 1990s will depend substantially upon government policies. The low intra-Pacific resistances to trade which have been primarily responsible for the preeminence of Pacific Basin destinations in the exports of ASEAN and other Pacific countries are partly the result of close political ties and the exchanges of direct investments which accompany them. Still greater significance would accrue to Pacific Basin trading partnerships should further steps be agreed upon to integrate the Pacific economy (Crawford 1981; Anderson et al. 1984). More important still, however, are unilateral policies that distort the pattern of trade directly. World trade in agricultural goods is increasingly influenced by high levels of protection in Europe and East Asia. Subsidized exports are adversely affecting the market shares and the terms of trade facing some ASEAN countries and the traditional food exporters of the Pacific Basin (Tyers and Anderson 1986). This trend should encourage the shift in ASEAN export specialization away from agriculture-based goods and into manufactures.

The expansion of ASEAN manufactured exports will also depend on policies adopted in ASEAN countries and their principal trading partners. Within ASEAN, governments have attracted investment by using generally stabilizing macroeconomic policies, by improving the skill levels of their labour forces, and by actively inhibiting labour monopolies. These policies are generally entrenched and should continue to foster growth. Outside ASEAN, however, export prospects for manufactures depend not only on the recent policy changes in China and its entry into world markets for labour-intensive manufactures but also on the access of Pacific developing countries to markets in industrial countries. Slow economic growth in Europe and the United States, combined with increased exchange rate uncertainty, have increased political pressures for protection (Salvatore 1985). The effects of this "new protectionism" have thus far been largely sidestepped by the Asian NICs, however (Hughes and Waelbroeck 1981). While the resurgence of protectionist sentiment in the industrialized world may retard the growth of the shares of ASEAN and other developing countries in world manufactures trade, its determinants are fundamentally different from those of agricultural protection, which has increased steadily in most industrialized countries as agriculture's shares of income and employment have declined to relative insignificance. World trade in manufactures is much more important as a determinant of global economic growth. Accordingly, the larger industrialized countries cannot afford to inhibit too greatly the changes in structure within manufacturing sectors and in the international division of labour that have underlain the trade patterns analysed in this chapter.

NOTES

*The original edition of this chapter was based on research conducted as part of the ASEAN Australia Economic Relations Joint Research Project. Updates to 1986 were supplied by the ANU International Economic Databank courtesy of the Australia-Japan Research Centre. The authors are indebted for helpful discussions and comments to Kym Anderson, David Lim, and Hal Hill.

1 In this chapter, the Pacific Basin is defined as including the Western Pacific market economies and the United States and Canada.
2 Canada's long border with the United States results in a significant amount of intra-industry trade, stimulated primarily by the relatively low cost of internal transportation. In this respect, Canada must be considered a special case.
3 The statistics in this paragraph are drawn from World Bank 1982, Appendix Table 2 and 8, and World Bank 1988, Appendix Tables 1, 2, 3, and 11.
4 All merchandise is classified on the basis of its intensity in the primary factors of production that most determine where production takes place. These primary factors include natural resources, labour, human capital, and technology.
5 In 1970 ASEAN was a net exporter of petroleum and petroleum products worth US $0.4 billion. By 1980, the value of these net exports had risen to US $5.5 billion.
6 See Ojala and Rae (1983), Table 3. Ojala and Rae also note that agricultural trade represents about one-sixth of Pacific Basin imports and exports. That portion of

agricultural exports directed to other Pacific Basin countries grew between 1965 and 1980 from 48 per cent to 55 per cent, while the corresponding share of imports rose from 70 per cent to 77 per cent.

7 Some of the recorded increase in intra-ASEAN trade is the result of poor recording of entrepôt trade between Malaysia and Indonesia and non-ASEAN countries via Singapore.

8 The intensity-of-trade index was used first by Kojima (1964) and then by Drysdale (1969). It has more recently been applied to measure Pacific Basin interdependence by Anderson (1983) and Ojala and Rae (1983). It is defined for country i's exports to country j as the share of i's exports going to j relative to the share of j's imports in world imports net of i's imports.

9 Australasia is the sum of Australia and New Zealand.

10 Even at this level of factor aggregation, the model does have considerable predictive power; see, for example, Hamilton and Svensson (1982).

11 The accuracy of the revealed comparative advantage index has been criticized in a recent article by Bowen (1983). It has intuitive appeal, however, as an index of specialization across exports.

12 Throughout this paper, the ASEAN group of countries is considered as a single entity. Clearly, natural resource endowments vary considerably among ASEAN countries, and the patterns of trade specialization observed for ASEAN as a whole do not necessarily reflect those of individual ASEAN countries. Singapore is a case in point; it has more in common with the other Asian NICs than with its ASEAN partners. While Singapore's pattern of trade specialization relative to the other ASEAN countries reflects its scarcity of natural resources, its exports are more natural-resource-based than those of the Asian NICs, primarily because of entrepôt trade and petroleum processing—points to be discussed further in later sections.

13 The competition between the United States and Japan for shares of ASEAN technology-intensive and human-capital-intensive imports is discussed in detail by Krause (1982). He indicates that the United States has performed comparatively well in its exports to ASEAN of relatively small-unit-value, homogeneous, and therefore price-sensitive items such as electronic components. In its exports of larger technology-intensive goods, the demand for which is less price-sensitive, the United States has performed less well — especially in Indonesia and the Philippines, where commercial policies are perceived by Krause as weakly administered. He indicates that this may be in part the result of changes in United States law and government practices overseas, such as the Foreign Corrupt Practises Act, the taxation of American citizens abroad, and the introduction of human rights criteria into Exim Bank Lending.

14 The US dollar eventually floated upwards against the yen following the surge in the real interest rate in the United States that began in 1978, but this rise in the dollar did not begin until after 1980 (Figure 9).

15 For a comprehensive set of CMS results, see Tyers and Phillips (1984b).

REFERENCES

Anderson, K. (1983). "Intensity of Trade between Pacific Basin Economies." *Economic Papers* 2:58–67

Anderson, K., and B. Smith (1981). "Changing Economic Relations between the Asian ADCs and Resource Exporting Advanced Countries of the Pacific Basin." In W. Hong and L.B. Krause, eds., *Trade and Growth of the Advanced Developing Countries in the Pacific Basin*. Seoul: Korea Development Institute

Anderson, K., P. Drysdale, C. Findlay, P. Phillips, B. Smith, and R. Tyers

(1984). "Pacific Economic Growth and the Prospects for Australian Trade." Discussion Paper no. 85/02, Economic Planning Advisory Council, Government of Australia, Canberra, November

Ariff, M., and H. Hill (1986). "Industrial Policies and Performance in ASEAN's Big Four." In H. Mutoh et al., eds., *Industrial Policies for Pacific Economic Growth* (PAFTAD)

Balassa, B. (1965). "Trade Liberalization and Revealed Comparative Advantage." *Manchester School of Economics and Social Studies* 33:99–1214

Balassa, B. (1977). "A 'Stages' Approach to Comparative Advantage." In I. Adelman, *Economic Growth and Resources*, Proceedings of the Fifth Congress of the International Economic Association, Tokyo, 4:121–56. London: Macmillan

Bowen, H.P. (1983). "On the Theoretical Interpretation of Indexes of Trade Intensity and Revealed Comparative Advantage." *Weltwirtschaftliches Archiv*, Band 119, Heft 3:464–74

Branson, W.H. and H. Junz (1971). "Trends in U.S. Comparative Advantage." *Brookings Papers on Economic Activity* 2:285–346

Branson, W.H. and N. Monoyios (1977). "Factor Inputs in US Trade." *Journal of International Economics* 7:111–31

Corden, W.M. (1982). "Booming Sector and Dutch Disease Economics." *Working Papers in Economics and Econometrics* no. 79, Australian National University, Canberra, November

Corden, W.M., and P.J. Neary (1982). "Booming Sector and Deindustrialization in a Small Open Economy." *Economic Journal* 92 (368):825–48

Crawford, Sir John, ed., assisted by G. Seow (1981). *Pacific Economic Cooperation: Suggestions for Action*. Heinemann Asia, for the Pacific Community Seminar

Dixit, A. (1981). "The Export of Capital Theory." *Journal of International Economics* 11:279–94

Drysdale, P. (1969). "Japan, Australia and New Zealand: The Prospects for Western Pacific Integration." *Economic Record* 45 (3):321–42

Drysdale, P., and R.G. Garnaut (1982). "Trade Intensities and the Analysis of Bilateral Trade Flows in a Many-Country World." *Hitotsubashi Journal of Economics* 22 (2):62–84

Findlay, C., P.R. Phillips, and R. Tyers (1985). "China's Merchandise Trade: Composition and Export Growth in the 1980s." *ASEAN- Australia Economic Papers*, no. 19, Australian National University, Canberra, May

Garnaut, R.G., and K. Anderson (1980). "ASEAN Export Specialization and the Evolution of Comparative Advantage in the Western Pacific Region." In R. Garnaut, ed., *ASEAN in a Changing Pacific and World Economy*. Canberra: Australian National University Press

Goodman, B., and R. Ceyhun (1976). "U.S. Export Performance in Manufacturing Industries: An Empirical Investigation." *Weltwirtschaftliches Archiv*, Band 112, Heft 3

Gregory, R.G. (1976). "Some Implications of the Growth of the Mining Sector." *Australian Journal of Agricultural Economics* 20:71–91

Gruber, W., D. Mehta, and R. Vernon (1967). "The R&D Factor in International Trade and Investment of United States Industries." *Journal of Political Economy* 75:20–37

Hamilton, C. (1983). "Australian Manufacturing Industry during the 1970s: An International Comparison and Implications for the ASEAN Countries." Seminar Paper no. 255, Institute for International Economic Studies, University of Stockholm

Hamilton, C., and L.E.O. Svensson (1982). "Testing Theories of Trade among Many Countries." Seminar Paper no. 209, Institute for International Economic Studies, University of Stockholm

Hickman, B.G., Y. Kuroda, and L.J. Lau (1977). "The Pacific Basin in World Trade." Working Papers nos. 190, 191, and 192, National Bureau of Economic Research, San Francisco

Hiemenz, I.V., and S. Naya (1983). "Changing Trade Patterns and Policy Issues: Prospects for East and Southeast Asian Developing Countries." Paper presented at East-West Center Conference on Patterns of Growth and Structural Change in Asia's NICs and Near-NICs in the Context of Economic Interdependence, Honolulu, 3-8 April

Hufbauer, G.C. (1970). "The Impact of National Characteristics and Technology on the Commodity Composition of Trade in Manufactured Goods." In R. Vernon, ed., *The Technology Factor in International Trade*. New York: Columbia University Press

Hughes, H., and J. Waelbroeck (1981). "Can Developing Country Exports Keep Growing in the 1980s?" *The World Economy* 4 (2):127–47

Johnson, H.G. (1968). *Comparative Cost and Commercial Policy Theory for a Developing World Economy*. Stockholm: Almqvist and Wiksell

Jones, R.W. (1971). "A Three Factor Model in Theory, Trade and History." In J. Bhagwati et al., eds., *Trade, Balance of Payments and Growth*. Amsterdam: North Holland

Keesing, D.B. (1966). "Labour Skills and Comparative Advantage." *American Economic Review* 56:249–58

Kenen, P. (1965). "Nature, Capital and Trade." *Journal of Political Economy* 73:437–60

Kojima, K. (1964). "The Pattern of International Trade among Many Countries." *Hitotsubashi Journal of Economics* 5 (1):16–36

Krause, L.B. (1982). *U.S. Economic Policy toward the Association of Southeast Asian Nations: Meeting the Japanese Challenge*. Washington, DC: The Brookings Institution

Krueger, A.O. (1977). "Growth, Distortions and Patterns of Trade among Many Countries." *Princeton Studies in International Finance*, no. 40, Princeton University, February

— (1978). "Alternative Trade Strategies and Employment in LDCs." *American Economic Review* 68 (2):270–74

Leamer, E.E., and R.M. Stern (1970). *Quantitative International Economics*. Boston: Praeger

Morall, J.F. (1972). *Human Capital, Technology and the Role of the U.S. in International Trade*. Gainsville: University of Florida Press

National Science Foundation (1980). *Research and Development in Industry 1978*. Washington, DC

Naya, S. (1980). "ASEAN Trade Development and Cooperation: Preferential Trading Arrangements and Trade Liberalization." Report of the UNCTAD, UNDP, and UNESCAP Project RAS/77/015/A/40. New York: United Nations

Ojala, E.M., and A.N. Rae (1983). "Trade and Dependence in the Pacific Basin." Discussion Paper no. 2, Centre for Agricultural Policy Studies, Department of Agricultural Economics and Farm Management, Massey University, New Zealand

Richardson, J.D. (1971). "Constant Market Shares Analysis of Export Growth." *Journal of International Economics* 1 (2):227–39

Salvatore, D. (1985). "The New Protectionism and the Threat to World Welfare: Editor's Introduction." *Journal of Policy Modelling* 7 (1):1–22

Stern, R.M., and K.E. Maskus (1981). "Determinants of the Structure of U.S. Foreign Trade, 1958–1976." *Journal of International Economics* 11:207–24

Tan, G. (1982). "Trade Liberalization in ASEAN: An Empirical Study of Preferential Trading Arrangements." Research Notes and Discussions Paper no. 32, Institute of Southeast Asian Studies, Singapore

Tyers, R., and K. Anderson (1986). "Agricultural Policies of Industrialised Countries and Their Effects on Traditional Food Exporters." *Economic Record* 62 (179):385–99

Tyers, R., and P.R. Phillips (1984a). "Australia, ASEAN and Pacific Basin Merchandise Trade: Factor Composition and Performance in the 1970s." *ASEAN-Australia Economic Papers* no. 13, Australian National University, December

— (1984b). "ASEAN Merchandise Trade with the Pacific Basin: Factor Composition and Performance." *Pacific Economic Papers*, no. 116, Australia-Japan Research Centre, Australian National University, December

—, and C. Findlay (1987). "ASEAN and China Exports of Labour-intensive Manufactures: Performance and Prospects." *ASEAN Economic Bulletin* 3 (3):339–67

Vernon, R. (1966). "International Investment and International Trade in the Product Cycle." *Quarterly Journal of Economics* 80 (2):190–207

van Dijk, P., and H. Verbruggen (1981). "A Constant Market Shares Analysis of ASEAN Manufactured Exports to the EEC." Paper presented to the Conference on ASEAN-EEC Relations, Institute of Southeast Asian Studies, Singapore, 6-8 August

Wells, L.T., Jr. (1968). "A Product Life Cycle for International Trade?" *Journal of Marketing* 32:1–6

World Bank (1982). *World Development Report 1982*. New York: Oxford University Press

Yamazawa, I., K. Taniguchi, and A. Hirata (1983). "Trade and Industrial Adjustment in Pacific Asian Economies." *Developing Economies* 21 (4):281–312

CHAPTER FIVE

Investing in Rural Industry for Employment and Balanced Growth: The Case of Thailand

Theodore Panayotou

INTRODUCTION

Since the early 1980s, Thailand, like other developing countries in the Pacific Rim, has found itself at the crossroads in its development strategy. Agriculture, which receives the lion's share of development assistance, faces absorptive capacity constraints at home and depressed prices abroad. Industrial exports, which enjoy generous promotional privileges, face increasing protectionism from developed countries at a time when foreign exchange earnings are needed to service a rising foreign debt and to contain a growing balance of trade deficit. Equally disturbing is the growing employment deficit at home. Agriculture is increasingly becoming labour-saving as it shifts from the extensive to the intensive margin, and urban-based industry is becoming increasingly capital-intensive because of factor-price distortions and promotional incentives at a time when the labour force is growing faster than ever before because of the historically high population growth rate of the 1960s.

The development policy challenge is to identify new investments with high employment generation, unconstrained market demand, and low capital requirements to bridge the employment gap while minimizing the adverse effect on the budget deficit and balance of payments.

The present study makes the case for investment in the development of labour-intensive rural industry to support and supplement agricultural development, which faces absorptive capacity constraints, and to compete with the capital intensive urban-based industry, which has been overpromoted with little regard to employment, market demand and balanced growth. It is not an argument for abandonment of agriculture, which is the backbone of the Thai economy, but a call for rationalization of the development effort in the light of emerging constraints and the scarcity of investment funds. The growth of agriculture at its historically high rate of 4 to 5 per cent would be ensured more by reform of restrictive price policies than by additional development funding. Agriculture is receiving as much funding as it can possibly absorb while it releases labour to the capital-intensive, urban-based industry beyond the latter's absorptive capacity. Because of administrative constraints at the Ministry of Agriculture and the political supremacy of Bangkok industrial elites, little can be done either to enhance agriculture's absorptive capacity or to reduce industry's capital intensity. However, at the margin, development funds can be directed to rural industry, which has been neglected despite its potential contribution to employment and growth and its strong linkages with agriculture. The conclusions reached are of relevance not only to Thailand but also to other developing countries in the region, such as the Philippines, Indonesia, and Malaysia, which have been following similar development strategies.

After a brief overview of the Thai economy, this study reviews the investment funding and absorptive capacity of agriculture as well as its development constraints and sources of future growth. Then it estimates the employment gap by projecting and comparing the growth of the labour force to the expansion of agricultural and non-agricultural employment and relates employment to growth in the context of the national development objectives. Finally, it assesses the potential contribution of rural industry to additional employment and more equitable growth.

THE THAI ECONOMY AND THE DOMINANCE OF AGRICULTURE

In a study of this breadth and time frame it is not possible to reduce the analysis to a set of testable (and tested) hypotheses or a limited number of fully documented propositions. It is, therefore, helpful to clear as much ground as possible right from the start by distilling a set of generally accepted (if not indisputable) stylized facts about the Thai economy that do not require detailed documentation but are essential to the argument that follows. Some eighteen relevant facts have been identified:

(1) Over the past two decades, the Thai economy has been growing at an impressive rate (7 to 8 per cent per annum in real terms), one of the highest in the world.

(2) Thailand is one of the very few developing countries that is a major net food exporter. Thai food and foodstuff exports include rice, maize, sugar, cassava, pineapple, fish, and livestock products.

(3) Agriculture has dominated, and continues to dominate the Thai economy in terms of Gross Domestic Product, employment, and exports. However, agriculture's relative contribution to the economy has been diminishing steadily, while its absolute contribution continues to rise.

(4) Manufacturing, which has been growing faster than agriculture (9.9 per cent compared to 4.5 per cent during 1970-81), is about to surpass agriculture in terms of contribution to GDP, while it lags far behind agriculture in terms of employment (9.2 per cent compared to 64 per cent in 1987).

(5) Labour productivity in agriculture is very low, since agriculture employs over 60 per cent of the labour force but produces less than 20 per cent of GDP. However, agriculture is indirectly "responsible" for about 50 per cent of all manufacturing trade and services in the sense of backward and forward linkages with these sectors.

(6) Most of the past agricultural growth has been attained through expansion into new lands (mainly in reserved forests) rather than through productivity improvements.

(7) Agricultural yields have been stagnant, at best. Productivity increases in some areas have been barely sufficient to offset declines in other areas. Fertilizer application in Thailand is among the lowest in the world and so are crop yields.

(8) Thai farmers are known to be very responsive to economic incentives except for a sociocultural preference for producing rice for their own consumption.

(9) It is generally recognized that the limits to the land frontier are being approached and that future agricultural growth will have to come from productivity improvements (higher yields per unit of land).

(10) It is also generally recognized that the rapid expansion into watershed areas and marginal lands has brought about second-generation problems (erosion, floods, droughts) that pose a

threat to the resource base and hence to the sustainability of Thai agriculture.

(11) Partly for historical reasons and partly because of the availability of an open-access land frontier for expansion, neither land tenancy nor landlessness have been serious problems in Thailand. For the same reasons, insecurity of ownership has been, and continues to be, a serious problem affecting more than 50 per cent of the agricultural land. With the frontier land approaching exhaustion and the increasing commercialization of agriculture, both tenancy and landlessness have been increasing in recent years and are expected to accelerate with the intensification of agriculture.

(12) Poverty has been substantially reduced over the past two decades. However, a not insignificant 20 per cent of the population, over ten million people, continue to live in "absolute" poverty despite the impressive growth of the past twenty to twenty-five years.

(13) Regional, sectoral, and rural-urban inequalities have generally been widening, with much of the country's wealth being concentrated in Bangkok and the outlying central region.

(14) There is a large and rising flow of seasonal and permanent migration from rural areas to urban centres, especially Bangkok, which is about fifty times larger than the next largest city in the country. In recent years, Bangkok has undergone a dramatic growth, with consequent overcrowding and serious problems that make further expansion undesirable.

(15) While Thailand has succeeded in reducing the population growth rate from over 3 per cent in the late 1960s to under 2 per cent in the early 1980s, the number of new entrants into the labour force is still rising because of the earlier rapid population growth.

(16) While there is little unemployment in the Western sense (of people actively but unsuccessfully searching for jobs) and the labour market is known to function fairly efficiently, there is substantial underemployment and seasonal unemployment as well as pockets of labour shortage during the planting and harvesting peaks of the agricultural season.

(17) Thailand has chronic balance of trade and payments deficits that would have been substantially larger, and perhaps unmanageable, without agriculture's steadily rising balance of trade surplus.

(18) The net effect of government policies amounts to a taxation of agriculture and other rural activities and a subsidization of large-scale urban-based industry. Government investment expendi-

tures in agriculture and related activities have been heavily biased in favour of large-scale irrigation infrastructure in the central region of Thailand. There is currently a shift towards small irrigation projects in northeast Thailand and a more diversified allocation of the agricultural development budget.

In conclusion, agriculture has played a dominant role in the Thai economy, and despite the gradual decline in its contribution to GDP, it will continue into the foreseeable future to be a major employer of the Thai labour force and a net contributor to foreign exchange earnings in addition to being the supplier of food to fifty million people.

INVESTMENTS IN AGRICULTURE: FUNDING AND ABSORPTIVE CAPACITY

Given the continuing importance of agriculture to the Thai economy, it is necessary to ensure that agriculture receives sufficient attention and funding to continue growing despite the approaching exhaustion of frontier land. Doing so will require investments in irrigation, research, and extension as well as in land development and land improvement to raise agricultural productivity.

Table 45 shows planned development expenditures by sector during the past four and the current fifth Five-Year Development Plans covering the twenty-six-year period from 1961 to 1986. The development expenditures in agriculture are seen to have increased from under 5 billion baht[1] during the First Plan (1961-6) to over 122 billion baht during the Fifth Plan (1982-6). This is a tremendous increase by any measure, whether in absolute or relative terms, whether by comparison to the rate of inflation (which averaged 6 per cent per annum over the period) or to the growth rate of the agricultural sector or by comparison to other sectors. As a recipient of development expenditures, agriculture is second only to education.

Over time, the share of agriculture in planned development expenditures has increased from 13.5 per cent during the First and Third Plans to 15.5 per cent during the Fourth and Fifth.[2] In absolute terms, the most spectacular increase in agricultural development expenditures was the recent increase from 39 billion baht during the Fourth Plan (1977-81) to 123 billion baht during the Fifth Plan (1982-6), a 215 percent increase in a time of one-digit inflation. These figures do not include funds (4 billion baht during the Third Plan and 12 billion during the Fourth Plan) that have not been specified as agricultural but were, in fact, used for agriculture. Moreover, the Fifth Plan, unlike earlier plans, has earmarked 24 billion baht for rural development, a significant part of which is allocated for agricultural activities in back-

Table 45

Planned Development Expenditures during Thailand's First, Second, Third, Fourth, and Fifth National Economic and Social Development Plans (million baht)[a]

Sector	First Plan (1961–6)	Second Plan (1967–71)	Third Plan (1972–6)	Fourth Plan (1977–81)	Fifth Plan (1982–6)
Agriculture & co-operatives	4,622	10,645	13,965	39,100	122,630
Industry, mining, & commerce	2,563	1,277	2,350	3,605	20,070
Transportation & communication	10,230	17,393	19,745	37,175	117,520
Energy	4,329	6,084	7,875	15,950	102,360
SUBTOTAL	21,744	35,398	43,395	95,830	362,580
Public welfare & community development	1,154	1,659	2,700	8,630	22.560
Public facilities	4,344	6,099	14,930	33,335	94,110
Public health	3,178	2,290	6,340	19,380	56,280
Education	2,491	6,387	32,910	95,285	237,610
Others	1,560	3,876	—	—	2,210
Rural development	—	—	—	—	23,990
TOTAL	34,471	55,712	100,275	252,450	799,340

Source: National Economic and Social Development Board, Division of Economic and Fiscal Planning, "Unpublished Data Sheets"

[a]From all sources: central government, local government, foreign loans, and foreign grants

ward areas: namely, projects on food production for nutrition, upland rice production, soil improvement, northeast saline soil development, agricultural credit for rural poor, water resource development, and so forth.

On an annual basis and in relation to other economic sectors, the growth of expenditures in agriculture has been remarkable. As shown in Table 46, the share of agriculture in the total government budget allocated to economic services rose from under 10 per cent in the late 1960s and early 1970s to over 40 per cent in the late 1970s and early 1980s. In absolute amounts, the government expenditures in agriculture rose from less than 1 billion baht (or 2 per cent of total expenditures) in the early 1970s to over 16 billion baht in 1986.

The public funds for development expenditures come from a number of sources. As shown in Table 47, of a total development budget of 800 billion baht for the Fifth Plan, 67 per cent was from the national budget, 17 per cent from foreign loans, and 2 per cent from foreign grants, with the balance coming from self-financed government agencies (8 per cent) and local government (5 per cent). Agriculture relies more heavily on the national budget (73 per cent) and on foreign loans (22 per cent) than all other sectors combined (65 per cent and 16 per cent respectively), which might be one of the reasons why the Thai government is reluctant to borrow more for agriculture (although the loan component for energy exceeds 50 per cent). The foreign grant component in agriculture (4 per cent) is also larger than in other sectors (under 2 per cent), but the contribution of self-financed government agencies is negligible and that of local governments nonexistent.

Thus, agriculture, far from being neglected, has attracted, and continues to attract, increasing attention and funds from both the government and foreign donors. Productivity-augmenting activities such as irrigation, soil improvement, and research and extension receive the lion's share of the agricultural development budget. Agriculture receives as much funding for research as do all other sectors combined (industry, energy, transportation, health, education, defence, utilities), a share which is twice as high as agriculture's contribution to GDP. Yet, this is not a sufficient reason for not investing additional funds in agriculture in general, and agricultural research in particular, if the expected return from such investments exceeds the opportunity cost, which is the foregone return from alternative investments.

Unfortunately, even at the current level of funding of agriculture, the government is facing serious absorptive capacity constraints in designing, implementing, and evaluating projects. During the 1960s and the early 1970s the funding for agriculture kept pace with the

Table 46

Total Budget Expenditures for Economic Services and the Share of the Ministry of Agriculture and Co-operatives (million baht)

Year	Total Budget Expenditures	Allocated to Economic Services		Allocated to Ministry of Agriculture and Co-operatives		
		Amount	as % of Total	Amount	as % of Economic Services	as % of Total Expenditures
1967	19,239.2	5,791.0	30.1	490.6	8.5	2.6
1968	21,249.3	6,247.3	29.4	583.7	9.3	2.7
1969	23,929.4	6,843.8	28.6	637.9	9.3	2.7
1970	27,324.7	7,869.5	28.8	643.3	8.2	2.3
1971	28,598.5	7,664.4	26.8	671.5	9.8	2.2
1972	28,987.2	6,580.2	22.7	647.7	9.8	2.2
1973	30,603.2	6,793.9	22.2	2,384.9	35.1	7.8
1974	39,081.3	7,503.6	19.2	2,847.8	0.4	7.3
1975	50,457.9	12,715.4	25.2	4,258.4	33.5	8.4
1976	62,670.4	12,722.1	20.3	5,451.9	42.9	8.7
1977	68,790.1	14,583.5	21.2	6,805.2	46.7	9.9
1978	80,786.9	16,076.6	19.9	7,008.8	43.6	8.7
1979	92,152.3	17,785.4	19.3	7,691.8	43.2	8.3
1980	114,743.3	24,096.1	21.0	9,431.6	39.1	8.2
1981	140,102.2	31,943.3	22.8	11,926.1	37.3	8.5
1982	161,063.7	32,857.0	20.4	13,587.0	41.4	8.4
1983	177,326.7	33,869.4	19.1	15,131.3	44.7	8.5
1984	181,262.0	n.a.	n.a.	15,885.2	n.a.	8.8
1985	199,548.0	n.a.	n.a.	16,878.1	n.a.	8.5
1986	203,984.0	n.a.	n.a.	16,142.2	n.a.	7.9

Source: Bureau of Budget and Bank of Thailand, Monthly Bulletin

Table 47

Planned Development Expenditures for Thailand's Fifth Plan Period (1982–6) (classified by source of funds in million baht)

	National Budget	Self-Financed Government Agencies	Local Government	Foreign Loans	Foreign Grants	Total
Agriculture & co-operatives	89,940	2,500	n.a.	27,070	5,120	122,630
Industry & mining	4,800	3,980	n.a.	6,770	260	15,810
Commerce	3,730	530	n.a.	n.a.	n.a.	4,260
Transportation & communication	68,750	21,430	n.a.	27,210	130	117,520
Energy	10,660	34,360	n.a.	56,580	760	102,360
SUBTOTAL FOR ECONOMIC SERVICES	175,880	62,800	n.a.	117,630	6,270	362,580
Public welfare & community	20,250	110	n.a.	n.a.	2,200	22,560
Public facilities	29,310	2,790	50,640	11,370	n.a.	94,110
Public health	52,760	n.a.	n.a.	1,760	1,760	56,280
Education	232,700	n.a.	n.a.	2,710	2,200	237,610
SUBTOTAL FOR SOCIAL SCIENCE	335,020	2,900	50,640	15,840	6,610	410,560
Rural development	22,100	n.a.	n.a.	1,890	n.a.	23,990
Other	n.a.	n.a.	n.a.	n.a.	2,210	2,210
Total development budget	533,000	65,700	50,640	135,360	14,640	799,340

Source: NESDB, Division of Economic and Fiscal Planning, unpublished data

n.a. Figures not available

absorptive capacity of the Ministry of Agriculture. However, as the funding accelerated during the 1970s and the 1980s, the ministry has found it increasingly difficult to design and implement a sufficient number of projects to absorb the entire development budget allocated to agriculture. As seen in Table 48, during the first two development plans (1961-71), the actual development expenditures in agriculture amounted to 91 per cent of the planned development expenditures for the sector. While the economy as a whole continues to absorb over 85 per cent of the planned expenditures, agriculture's absorptive capacity (defined as the ratio of actual to planned development expenditures) fell from 91 per cent to 80 per cent during the Third Plan (1972-6) and to 64 per cent during the Fourth Plan (1977-81). That is, of the 39 billion baht planned for agricultural development during 1977-81, only 25 billion (or 64 per cent) were expended by the end of 1981.

With the dramatic increase of the planned agricultural development expenditures during the Fifth Plan (1982-6) from 39 to 122 billion baht, it was likely that the absorptive capacity of agriculture would fall below 50 per cent. The government was, therefore, legitimately reluctant to borrow additional funds for agricultural development when the share of agriculture in foreign loans (22 per cent) is already above that for the economy as a whole (17 per cent) and the Ministry of Agriculture is unable to absorb the existing development funds.

The absorptive capacity limits of the Ministry of Agriculture are partly the result of the rapidity with which the annual development budget of the ministry has expanded (from less than 1 billion baht to about 25 billion baht within two decades) and partly the result of institutional, administrative, and personnel constraints. For example, the Office of the Permanent Secretary of Agriculture, which is responsible for the implementation of donor-assisted agriculture projects is understaffed by at least 30 per cent; that is, 30 per cent of the authorized positions remain vacant.

Despite the absorptive capacity constraints of the public sector, which had limited the actual development expenditures in agriculture to 64 per cent of the planned level, during the Fourth Development Plan, the capital formation in agriculture proceeded at a faster rate than during earlier plans because of the contribution of the private sector, which accounts for about 70 per cent of all capital formation in agriculture.[3] The gross investment of the private and public sector combined averaged 6.5 billion baht and the capital stock in agriculture reached 87 billion baht in 1981, the last year of the plan (see Table 49). The average annual growth of the agricultural capital stock during the Fourth Plan was 5.6 per cent, which is 60 per cent higher than the growth rate during the Third Plan (3.5 per cent).

Table 48

Discrepancy between Actual and Planned Development Expenditures in Thailand as an Indicator of Absorptive Capacity Limits

Plan	Agriculture			Industry, Commerce, Mining			Economy as a Whole		
Plan Period	Planned (P)	Actual (A)	P/A	Planned (P)	Actual (A)	P/A	Planned (P)	Actual (A)	P/A
First Plan (1961–6)	4,622	4,203	0.91	2,563	2,572	1.00	34,471	27,617	0.80
Second Plan (1967–71)	10,645	9,735	0.91	1,277	868	0.68	55,712	65,937	1.18
Third Plan (1972–6)	13,695	10,961	0.80	2,380	2,419	1.03	100,275	91,548	0.91
Fourth Plan (1977–81)	39,100	25,032	0.64	3,605	5,552	1.54	252,450	219,007	0.87
Fifth Plan (1982–6)	122,630	—	—	20,070	—	—	699,340	—	—

Source: National Economic and Social Development Board, Division of Economic and Fiscal Planning, "Unpublished Data Sheets"
Figures not yet available

Table 49
Capital Formation in Thailand's Agricultural Sector (at 1972 prices in million baht)

Year	Private Sector Gross Investment	Private Sector Stock of Capital	Public Sector Gross Investment	Public Sector Stock of Capital	Total Gross Investment	Total Stock of Capital
1961	588	29,348	340	16,249	928	45,597
1962	712	29,033	453	16,134	1,165	45,166
1963	953	28,969	578	16,147	1,531	45,118
1964	1,218	29,173	625	16,207	1,843	45,381
1965	1,242	29,395	704	16,344	1,946	45,733
1966	1,546	29,912	818	16,591	2,364	46,503
1967	2,371	31,236	969	16,980	2,340	48,218
1968	2,455	32,597	1,076	17,462	3,531	50,059
1969	2,204	33,660	1,142	17,993	3,346	51,653
1970	2,153	34,635	1,817	19,181	3,970	53,816
1971	2,405	35,828	1,463	19,972	3,868	55,800
1972	1,979	36,553	1,125	20,398	3,104	56,951
1973	2,627	37,900	889	20,573	3,516	58,473
1974	3,547	40,121	615	20,468	4,162	60,569
1975	3,538	42,225	1,175	20,926	4,714	63,162
1976	3,651	44,428	1,775	21,968	5,426	66,396
1977	4,396	47,288	1,789	22,988	6,185	70,257
1978	4,704	50,318	1,807	24,091	6,611	74,409
1979	5,403	53,960	1,910	25,158	7,313	79,118
1980	5,200	57,272	2,089	26,367	7,289	83,639
1981	4,566	59,834	2,068	28,711	6,634	87,347

Source: General Economic Research Section, Department of Economic Research, Bank of Thailand, "Unpublished Data Sheets"

The capital stock embodies all (net) investments in Thai agriculture whether private or public, domestic or foreign. Private foreign investment in agriculture is usually very limited, except in plantations, which are not common in Thailand. Yet, in recent years, Thai agriculture began to receive non-negligible amounts of private capital inflow. For example, during 1980-2, Thailand received 413 million baht of foreign private investment in agriculture compared to 21 million during the preceding three-year period. While this is less than 1 per cent of the total private capital inflow into Thailand, it is, nevertheless, indicative of the maturity of Thai agriculture and its healthy and highly diversified sources of funds. Availability of capital does not appear to be a severe constraint on agricultural growth and productivity improvement in Thailand; misallocation or maldistribution of resources, including capital, is. The allocation of the development budget including foreign assistance has been skewed in favour of the better off areas. Until recently, little has been expended on irrigation and research for rainfed areas, and little productivity improvement has been achieved outside the central region and the irrigated areas of the north.

AGRICULTURAL GROWTH: CONSTRAINTS AND PROSPECTS

If there is no scarcity of development funds for agriculture, what can explain the stagnation of agricultural yields in Thailand? First, the aggregate yields are somewhat misleading because they are averages of areas such as the central plain, where yields have been rising, and areas such as the northeast, where yields have been falling. Second, the effect of development investment in irrigation and technology has been more to expand the dry season cultivation (in the central plain) rather than to increase yields. Third, the existence of an easily accessible land frontier (in the form of "reserved" forests) for the expansion of the cultivated areas has eased the need for intensification, which would have been inevitable with the growth of population and export demand. As Table 50 shows, as much as 90 per cent of the past growth in agricultural production has been accomplished through expansion of the cultivated area rather than through yield increase.

Fourth, fertilizer prices have been among the highest and fertilizer use among the lowest in Asia because of misguided government intervention, the oligopolistic structure of the central fertilizer market, and the uneconomic compound fertilizers used. Fifth, the irrigated area is limited to the central plain and parts of the north, irrigation structures are poorly maintained, and irrigation water, which is provided free of charge, is wastefully used, limiting the effectively irrigated area. Sixth, insecurity of ownership, which affects over 50 per cent of the agricultural land (World Bank 1982: 30), deprives the owners of both the means (for example, credit) and the incentive to undertake the investments and purchase the inputs necessary for agricultural intensification. Seventh, as a consequence of relentless encroachment of watersheds and high-slope lands, there have been increasing problems of floods, droughts, and soil erosion, which have depressing effect on yields in certain areas.

Last, but equally important, Thailand "has long pursued agricultural price policies and, more recently, industrial trade policies which sharply distort producer incentives against agriculture and in favor of capital intensive.... manufacturing" (World Bank 1983:16). The World Bank has estimated the direct income impact on farmers of rice taxation to be between 8,400 and 14,500 million baht annually and of rubber taxation 3,300 million baht, and it has concluded that "these direct income effects of the pricing policies alone take out about as

Table 50

Growth Rates of Production, Planted Area, and Yield of Major Crops, Thailand, 1975/6–1987/8 (%)

Year	Wet season rice			Dry season rice			Maize			Cassava**		
	Prod.	Area	Yield	Prod.	Area	Yield	Prod.	Area	Yield	Prod.	Area	Yield
1975/6	13.2	11.3	1.7	28.6	14.0	12.8	14.5	5.8	8.0	29.8	23.8	4.8
1976/7	-3.4	-4.5	1.5	15.3	16.0	-0.6	6.6	-2.1	-4.6	25.2	17.7	6.3
1977/8	-9.8	5.1	-14.1	13.9	8.9	4.5	-37.3	-6.2	-33.0	22.0	37.2	-11.0
1979/80*	23.3	9.2	12.6	42.7	42.7	0.0	66.5	14.7	44.4	21.6	5.2	15.6
1980/1	5.2	0.1	5.0	78.5	53.4	15.2	4.7	-6.0	11.7	49.0	37.2	8.6
1981/2	0.2	-0.9	2.9	2.8	10.9	-7.2	15.0	9.3	5.1	7.3	9.5	-2.0
1982/3	-6.2	-0.4	-5.7	4.4	10.8	-5.9	-12.9	7.1	-18.8	0.2	-2.7	2.9
1983/4	14.69	3.46	7.4	23.86	13.07	9.65	18.33	0.56	-1.36	5.25	2.67	-19.77
1984/5	1.96	-0.35	1.64	0.92	-1.48	0.85	18.48	7.61	7.17	-3.62	5.13	-6.52
1985/6	3.8	2.63	0.65	-11.26	-9.74	-1.68	16.76	9	5.92	-20.81	-16.06	-9.52
1986/7	-6.16	-2.52	0.32	-12.51	-8.96	-3.93	-12.67	-1.48	-7.77	28.18	13.84	12.69
1987/8	-9.24	-6.96	-6.71	35.7	25.8	9.24	-35.46	-10.28	-13.69	14.08	12.01	1.06
Total	23.85	9.76	6.4	172.1	124.8	33.3	52.44	38.01	-4.23	152	118.1	9.68
Average	2	0.81	0.5	14.4	10.4	2.8	4.37	3.2	-0.4	12.7	9.8	0.8

Source: Office of Agricultural Economics, "Agricultural Statistics of Thailand," MOAC, Bangkok (various issues)

*1979/80 corresponds to 1980, 1980/1 to 1981, 1981/2 to 1982, and 1982/3 to 1983

**1979/80 corresponds to 1979, 1980/1 to 1980, 1981/2 to 1981, and 1982/3 to 1982

much or more from the rural areas as the combined rural development expenditures for agriculture and non-farm activities" (ibid.: 16).

The industrial trade policies also tax agriculture (and rural industry) by increasing the prices of production inputs and consumer goods purchased from urban areas. Undoubtedly, a combination of low crop prices, high input prices, and high consumer prices (that is, adverse terms of trade for agriculture) are potent disincentives for agricultural growth, unless it is attainable through inexpensive expansion of the cultivated area. Indeed, most (90 per cent) of the agricultural growth of the past twenty years has been attained through expansion of area rather than increase in productivity (see Table 50).

Thus, it is not lack of investment in irrigation and agricultural research and extension that has held yields low in Thailand — indeed, lower than any comparable Asian country — but institutional failures (insecurity of land ownership, open-access forest land, unpriced irrigation water), market imperfections (fragmented capital markets, an uncompetitive fertilizer market at the import/wholesale level), and, above all, misguided government policies (export taxes, quotas, and industrial trade policies). Investment in irrigation and research has not been a binding constraint and additional investment funds in these areas would do little to increase yields unless institutional and policy constraints are removed and the absorptive capacity of the Ministry of Agriculture is enhanced to accommodate additional projects.

What promises to be more effective in the area of irrigation and research is an increase in the effectiveness of existing funds through reallocation away from large irrigation structures to research for rainfed agriculture and water control in the northeast. Such a shift was initiated within the Fifth Plan, but more could be done in this direction. Unfortunately, the Ministry of Agriculture faces its most severe staff constraints in its northeast regional office. Moreover, institutional constraints, market imperfections, and policy distortions tend to affect more seriously the more remote and backward areas, which are, in addition, disadvantaged by transportation costs, information gaps, and agroclimatic conditions.

If the frontier for further expansion of agricultural land is being exhausted and if additional development assistance for agriculture is unlikely to produce dramatic increases in yields within our time horizon (1985-90), what are the likely sources of agricultural growth? This is a key question because of the significance of agriculture to the Thai economy as a source of employment, income, foreign exchange, and growth linkages to other sectors.

The very factors that have constrained agricultural growth in the past are also the most promising sources of growth in the future. The approaching exhaustion of easily accessible new land is certain to put pressure on farmers to use existing land more efficiently and more intensively, utilizing existing seed-fertilizer-water technologies.

Since Thailand has been among the slowest adopters of the new technology in Asia, there is still considerable potential for increasing yields with existing technology and infrastructure, given appropriate incentives. According to the World Bank (1978), "in the case of irrigated agriculture there is a substantial backlog of known technology and improved practices which could raise yields" (96).

Large gains in yields are also to be expected from increased fertilizer use following a reduction in the cost and increase in the effectiveness of fertilizer, to be accomplished through: the promotion of competition among importers/wholesalers of fertilizers, the availability and promotion of low-cost (unsubsidized) single-nutrient fertilizer, effective quality control, and improved water control. According to the World Bank (1982), "one of the most urgently needed means to improve productivity in Thailand is to reduce the farm cost of fertilizer application by substantially increasing the availability of single-nutrient fertilizer and thus doubling the incremental value/cost ratio for many crops" (vol. 4, Annex 6: 18). Based on farmer-field trials the bank has found that the use of cheaper (unsubsidized) sources of nitrogen, such as urea, instead of the mixed fertilizers like ammonium phosphate currently in use would more than double the value/cost ratio for rice, maize, sorghum, cassava, kenaf, and cotton. With value/cost ratios between 2.5 and 5 (compared to current ratios of about 1.5 or lower), a dramatic increase in fertilizer use and yield can be expected.

If, in addition to lowering the cost of fertilizer and improving its quality, the government allows the prices of crops to rise to their competitive market levels, the value/cost ratio of using fertilizer and other yield-augmenting inputs will increase further. For example, elimination of rice export taxes in 1981 would have increased the value/cost of fertilizer by 60 per cent, inducing additional fertilizer use. As we have seen earlier, the tax burden on the rice sector alone exceeds 8 billion baht. Domestic and trade restrictions, which include price control, export taxes, export premiums, and quotas, reduce farm prices and production incentives especially for rice, rubber, and feedstuff. Again, according to the World Bank (1982), "relaxation of trade restrictions is likely to be the most efficient way of attaining Government's objective of increasing production" (2:27).

Other sources of agricultural growth that are now in operation and will continue to gather momentum well into the 1990s include: (1) improved maintenance and management of existing irrigation sys-

Table 51
Projected Annual Growth Rate of Thai Agriculture by Subsector, 1981–6, 1986–90 (%)[a]

GDP in Constant Prices	1960–71	1970–5	1975–80	Fifth Plan 1982–6	World Bank Mission Projections 1981–6	Actual[e] 1981–6	1986–90
Crop	4.7	5.2	3.3	4.7	4.2	3.1	4.3
Livestock	3.5	7.6	5.5	4.2	5.0	3.1	5.2
Fisheries	20.7	4.7[b]	-3.1[c]	5.4	3.7	2.9	4.4
Forestry	4.1	2.9	0.3	0.3	0.3	-0.2	0.2
Agriculture[d]	5.5	5.1	0.5	4.5	4.1	4.1	4.3

Source: World Bank (1982), 2:56

[a]Semi-log trend regressions: 1960–70 is at 1962 constant prices and 1970–90 is at 1972 constant prices

[b]1970–7

[c]1977–80

[d]Agriculture includes ''agricultural services'' and simple agricultural processing products in addition to crops, live rock, fisheries, and forestry

[e]Actual 1981–6 figures: Office of the National Economic and Social Development Board, Office of the Prime Minister

tems and improved water control in rainfed areas; (2) a higher percentage of cultivated area under secure ownership; (3) modest reduction in idle land and increased cropping intensity; (4) increased use of improved seeds of available varieties and pest and disease control; (5) reduction of damaged crop area and improvement in the resource base of agriculture through a combination of measures, such as soil improvement, land development, replanting of watersheds, and creation of alternative employment opportunities for forest squatters; (6) some success of current efforts to produce improved crop varieties and more intensive cropping systems for rainfed areas; and (7) continued funding of agriculture at the current level (in real terms) and an increasing shift of emphasis (and funding) to rainfed areas.

Assuming a minimum performance of the most likely of these growth sources, it is safe to conclude that agriculture will continue to grow at its historical rate throughout the next decade without additional development assistance (see Table 51). In the light of absorptive capacity constraints of the Ministry of Agriculture, additional development assistance is unlikely to increase agricultural growth beyond the projected rates.

GROWTH AND EMPLOYMENT

We have thus far established a number of facts and made some projections about Thai agriculture: (1) agriculture has played and continues to play a dominant, though gradually declining, role in the Thai economy; (2) agriculture in general and productivity-augmenting investments (irrigation and research and extension) in particular receive strong support and growing funding from the government, foreign development agencies, and the private sector; (3) the absorptive capacity of the Ministry of Agriculture in general and of the project-implementing departments in particular is being taxed by existing project commitments to the point that additional development assistance for agriculture is unlikely to be put to effective use; and (4) the all-important growth of the agricultural sector throughout the early 1990s is ensured more by policy reforms than by additional development assistance.

Two issues remain to be tackled. First, if additional direct assistance to agriculture faces absorptive capacity constraints, is there scope for effective development assistance in other sectors of the economy that by their virtue of strong linkages with agriculture can enhance the growth potential of agriculture beyond its projected rate? Second, is agricultural growth as sufficient as it is necessary for the attainment of the national objectives of respectable growth, reduction of inequality, and enhancement of political and social stability? According to the Fifth National Economic and Social Development Plan (1981-6):

> national development must create national stability and economic justice. . . . This is vital for the maintenance of future political stability and national survival. . . . [The Fifth Plan] stresses "the adjustment of economic structure" rather than "economic growth." . . . [and] "equality" in national economic and social development effort by aiming to disperse income and economic activities to provincial areas. . . . rather than simply allowing the benefits of national development to remain in certain areas or in the hands of certain groups of people as in the past. (NESDB 1981: 2-3).

The Thai planners are convinced (and the available evidence seems to support their conviction) that "past development efforts have benefited only certain parts of the country." Development benefits were not evenly dispersed, and a large part of the country and population did not benefit from past development efforts and are still living in absolute poverty. It is estimated that there are ten million people in the rural areas who are in this category (ibid.:1-2). When the benefits from development do not trickle down sufficiently, when land reform and other efforts at asset redistribution are too slow, ineffective, or politically unpalatable, and when income transfers are inoperative, employment emerges as the single most promising means of access to development benefits. Productive and gainful employment is not only rewarding to the individual, but it also generates social benefits in the form of full utilization of the country's human resources, multiplier effects from increased income, reduced social tensions, and enhanced political stability.

Agriculture and related activities have been for centuries the main sources of employment for the rural population. The availablity of open access land and other common property resources, such as fisheries and forests, has ensured gainful employment and adequate food supplies for a relatively small and slow-growing population. The old Thai saying "in the water there is fish and in the field there is rice and who wants to trade trades" is an expression of contentment with the prevailing availability and distribution of resources and opportunities.

Since the land frontier is being exhausted and open-access natural resources depleted and since agriculture is becoming more intensive and market-oriented, employment opportunities in primary production are declining. On the other hand, the increased agricultural output generates related activities such as marketing, storage, transport, processing, and distribution as well as demand for additional agricultural inputs, which may be supplied by labour-intensive, secondary (agro-industry), and tertiary (services) sectors. Whether, on balance, more or less employment opportunities are available is an empirical question, to which we turn in the next section. Here, it suffices to say that even if it can be shown that the labour absorption by agriculture and related activities will not diminish in the foreseeable future, there may still be an employment problem if indeed there is underemployment and seasonal unemployment or if the labour force is growing faster than it has in the past.

Thus, the thrust of the remainder of the study is twofold. First, it examines the dimensions of the employment problem over the next decade and establishes the need for additional employment creation outside (but not unrelated to) agriculture in line with the national objective of equity and political stability. Second, it shows that rural industry and rural employment are complementary to and have strong linkages with agriculture to be considered as indirect investments toward sustainable agricultural growth.

THE EMERGING EMPLOYMENT GAP

In this section we attempt to project the supply and demand for labour in order to determine the dimensions of the employment problem into the early 1990s and the extent to which additional labour creation will be needed.

Thailand has succeeded in reducing its population growth rate from over 3 per cent in the late 1960s to under 2 per cent in the early 1980s, a 43 per cent reduction in the growth rate in less than fifteen years. In 1983, the population growth rate was 1.8 per cent per annum, and it was expected to decline to 1.5 per cent by 1986, the last year of the Fifth Plan. This reduction, being the net result of concurrent reductions in birth and death rates, brought about a change in the age structure of the population; between 1970 and 1980 the percentage of the population of a working age (15-64) rose by 7.7 per cent for males and by 6.6 per cent for females. During the Fifth Plan (1981-6), it was projected that the population of preschool children (0-4) would decrease by 1 per cent, that school-age children (5-25) would increase by 1.4 per cent, and that the working-age population (26-64) would increase by 3.2 per cent (see NESDB 1981: 177).

This change in the age structure of the population means larger numbers of new entrants into the labour force than in the past. In the early 1970s, the growth of the labour force was slower than that of the population (because of the low population growth rate in the 1950s). Since the mid-1970s the growth rate of the labour force has exceeded that of the population because of the high population growth rate in the 1960s compared to the present rate (see Figure 10). Today, the labour force grows at an average annual rate above 3 per cent, and it is projected to grow at this rate through 1990; that is, the labour force is growing today at a faster rate than in any other time in Thailand's past or foreseeable future. In absolute numbers, the labour force is projected to have grown by over 6 million during the 1980s compared to 5 million during the 1970s and 3.4 million during the 1960s. The total labour force in 1987 exceeded 26 million, and it is expected to reach 30 million by 1990. Not only are the new entrants more numerous, they are also more educated and skilled.

The question is whether the Thai economy in its current slowly changing structure would generate sufficient numbers of additional jobs to employ the new entrants of the early 1990s. Given the projected rate of agricultural growth of 4 to 5 per cent and the gradual structural change of the sector, will agriculture generate increased employment in proportion to the projected growth of the labour force of 3 per cent per annum? Will the non-agricultural sector grow fast enough to absorb the balance?

During the past two decades, agricultural employment averaged a growth rate of less than 2 per cent with a tendency to fall over time. Based on past trends, agricultural employment was expected to grow at the rate of 1.2 per cent during the 1980s and below 1 per cent during the 1990s. Based on a baseline of 15 million persons employed in agriculture in 1980, we project agricultural employment at 17.1 million

Figure 10 Growth Rate of Population and the Labour Force in Thailand

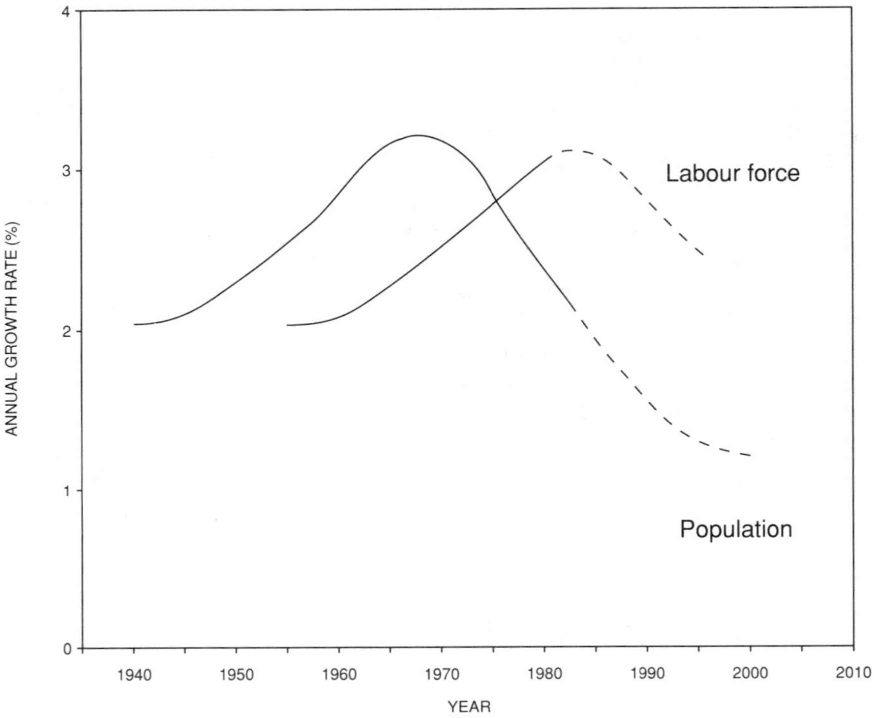

in 1990. However, to the extent that the structural change in agriculture during the 1980s was expected to be faster than during the 1970s, these figures overestimate the growth in agricultural employment.

As we have seen in the preceding section, unlike the 1970s, when 90 per cent of the agricultural growth came from expansion into new land, during the 1980s at least 50 per cent of the growth had to come from intensification, that is, from increased use of improved seed and appropriate fertilizers, improved efficiency of water use, increased cropping intensity, land improvements, and so forth. Some of these activities require additional labour input (application of fertilizers and pesticides,

Table 52
Labour/Output, Labour/Land, and Output/Land Ratios of the Agricultural and Nonagricultural Sectors in Thailand, 1971–80

	Labour/GDP		Labour/Land		GDP/Land	
	1971–3	1977–80	1971–3	1977–80	1971–3	1977–80
WHOLE KINGDOM						
Agriculture	0.234	0.219	0.135	0.142	578	648
Nonagric.	0.037	0.030	—	—	—	—
NORTH						
Agriculture	0.254	0.240	0.177	0.161	684	673
Nonagric.	0.071	0.044	—	—	—	—
NORTHEAST						
Agriculture	0.405	0.394	0.128	0.152	315	386
Nonagric.	0.076	0.042	—	—	—	—
CENTRE						
Agriculture	0.127	0.112	0.106	0.102	838	916
Nonagric.	0.034	0.030	—	—	—	—
SOUTH						
Agriculture	0.169	0.149	0.136	0.145	802	970
Nonagric.	0.058	0.042	—	—	—	—
BANGKOK/THONBURI						
Nonagric.	0.021	0.012	—	—	—	—

Source: Calculated based on the GDP figures reported in Rijk and Meer/ADB (1984), the employment figures reported in World Bank (1983), and the land figures reported in World Bank (1982)

weeding, land preparation, double cropping) while others, such as mechanization of tilling and threshing, are displacing labour.

Although they are often thought of as labour-saving, the high-yielding varieties and improved cultivation practices are not necessarily so, and they could, in fact, be labour-using. It all depends on the type of technology and the relative prices of capital, labour, and other inputs. Whether crop intensification in Thailand, on balance, would increase or reduce the demand for labour is an empirical question.

Because of lack of detailed data, a rather crude approach is used to obtain a measure of the employment effect of the expected growth and intensification of Thai agriculture during the 1980s and early 1990s. First, Thai agriculture has become increasingly intensified (albeit at a slow pace) at least since the early 1970s. A comparison of the agricultural labour/output[4] ratio between the early and the late 1970s gives some idea whether agriculture is becoming more or less labour-intensive over time. As Table 52 shows, the labour/output ratio has declined from 0.234 in the early 1970s to 0.219 in the late 1970s, a 6.5

per cent decrease in labour per unit of output produced as the output per unit of land increased by 12 per cent. But how can we be certain that the fall in the labour/output ratio is related to intensification rather than extensification since much more of the latter than the former has been taking place?

In Thailand, virtually all intensification took place in the central region and the north, while most of the expansion into new areas took place in the northeast. If intensification is more labour-intensive than extensification, the central region should have higher (than the northeast) and rising labour/land ratios. Table 52 indicates that the reverse is true. The labour/land ratio of the central region is the lowest in the country, 0.112 and falling, while that of the northeast has risen considerably since the early 1970s, from 0.128 to 0.152. The north has the highest labour/land ratio because of a more labour-based intensification (in the Chiangmai Valley) as well as because of expansion into new areas requiring clearing and manual harvesting which are labour-intensive activities. However, even in the north the labour/land ratio is falling.

Consistent with the hypothesis that intensification as practised in Thailand is, on balance, labour-saving, is the fact that the central region has the lowest labour/output ratio, 0.112, down from 0.127 in the early 1970s (an 11 per cent fall). In contrast, the northeast has the highest ratio of 0.394, down only 2.7 per cent from its 1971-3 level of 0.405. The north and the south are intermediate cases, as one would expect. Unfortunately, there are no figures on capital by region; but few would doubt that the capital/output and capital/labour ratios are highest in the central region (especially if irrigation systems and other social infrastructure provided free of charge are included) and lowest in the northeast. However, even in the central region, agriculture remains more labour-intensive than the non-agricultural sector. Yet, under present market conditions, agricultural intensification in Thailand is likely to be more labour-saving than labour-using, following the central region pattern, which is to some degree a precursor of the intensification in the rest of the country, subject, of course, to variations in the agroclimatic conditions and relative prices.

It is, therefore, not unreasonable to expect the rate of growth of agricultural employment to fall further as a result of the approaching limits to the land frontier and the mounting pressures and opportunities for intensification. Conservatively, we project the agricultural employment growth rate to be around 1 per cent per annum, which is considerably higher than the rate experienced in the central region; in fact, agricultural employment in this region fell in absolute terms between 1977 and 1980. Based on this modified rate, agriculture employment is expected to reach 16.7 million in 1990; at any rate, it is unlikely to exceed 17 million by 1990.

However, agriculture's contribution to employment is not limited to agriculture. Agricultural growth has powerful forward, backward, and consumer demand linkages (to transport, processing, production inputs, consumer goods, and so forth), which create additional employment in non-agricultural sectors.

While we do not have access to complete input-output tables or social accounting matrices to measure all the backward and forward linkages from a 4 to 5 per cent rate of agricultural growth and technical change, we may project non-agricultural employment following recent trends, taking into account what we know about structural change during the 1980s. Over the past decades non-agricultural employment grew by 5 to 6 per cent because of the rapid economic growth of 7 to 8 per cent. With planned economic growth of 6.6 per cent during the Fifth Plan and a falling employment/GDP ratio for both the agricultural and the non-agricultural sectors (see Table 52), non-agricultural employment is not expected to grow faster than 5 per cent per annum. According to the Asian Development Bank, a scenario of annual growth rates of non-agricultural employment of 5 per cent over the 1980s and of 4 per cent over the 1990s "is ambitious and its realisation will depend on foreign demand for Thai industrial and agricultural products and on whether sufficiently high economic growth rates can be achieved to generate new employment for the 1980s at that rate" (Rijk and Meer/ADB 1984: 144).

Using a baseline figure of 7 million persons for 1980[5] and an annual growth rate of 5 per cent, we project non-agricultural employment at 9 million in 1985 and 12 million in 1990. (ADB's projections for 1990 range between 11.7 and 12.9 million.)

Summing up our projections of agricultural and non-agricultural employment, we arrive at a total employment figure of 24.7 to 25 million by 1985 and 28.7 to 29 million by 1990. Recall that the labour force has been projected to reach 30 million in 1990. These projections imply a shortfall of employment by one million at best and 1.3 million at worst, or a 3 to 5 per cent "unemployment" rate. This is hardly a worrisome figure; many developed countries are accustomed to unemployment figures twice as high. A number of reasons, however, make this figure worrisome for Thailand.

First, Thailand has had little experience with unemployment; historically, unemployment figures in Thailand rarely, if ever, exceeded 2 per cent in the urban areas and 1 per cent in the rural areas. Second, Thailand, like other developing countries, has no income transfer mechanisms such as unemployment and social insurance to deal with the problem. Third, and more importantly, the official statistics are unlikely to register such a "high" (by Thai standards) unemployment figure, since, in the absence of unemployment compensation, few people can afford to remain unemployed for prolonged periods of time. Open unemployment is likely to increase only moderately, perhaps to 2 per cent as predicted by the Fifth Plan. The rest would be translated into disguised unemployment and underemployment in agriculture and the informal sectors, especially in Bangkok, as has been the case in the past. Fourth, any additional underemployment during the 1980s would have been added to the existing high rates of underemployment and seasonal unemployment, especially in the northeast.

In total, the employment problem in Thailand has at least three dimensions of which only one, open unemployment, fits the conventional Western definition of unemployment (persons searching but unable to find work). Open unemployment was expected to average no more than 2.5 per cent of the labour force or 0.50 to 0.75 million[6] persons throughout the 1980s. At least one-third of the openly unemployed would be in the twenty to twenty-nine age group, many of them with secondary or higher education residing in Bangkok or the provincial urban centres.

Seasonal "unemployment," defined as the difference between employment during the peak (wet) and the slack (dry) agricultural seasons, has ranged between 22 and 35 per cent of the labour force, or three and six million persons, during 1975-81 (according to the Labor Force Survey), and it is expected to continue at least at this level. Seasonal unemployment consists mainly of unpaid family members (mainly young or female) waiting for the agricultural season, not all of whom would take up employment during the slack season, if such existed. However, the fact that seasonal unemployment is highest in the northeast, where employment opportunities during the slack season are most scarce, while it is lowest in the central region, where employment opportunities are relatively abundant, suggests that a large proportion of those waiting for the agricultural season would be willing to take up employment if it existed. It is difficult to estimate this proportion, but if one was to assume that two-thirds of the males and half of the females among the seasonally unemployed would be willing to work, over three million additional jobs would have been necessary during the dry season of 1981. Seasonal unemployment increased from 3.1 million in 1975 to 5.6 million in 1981, that is, at a rate several times larger than the growth rate of the labour force. The intensification of agriculture beyond the central region is expected to slow down the growth of seasonal unemployment, but it cannot reverse it because rainfed agriculture will continue to dominate the economy of the northeast and the north in the years to come.

While it is not known under what conditions (wage rates, work type, and location) the seasonally underemployed would accept additional work, they do remain idle because the prevailing wage rate is below their reservation price, which brings us to the third and most serious dimension of the employment problem: underemployment. Underemployment may be defined in one of three (complementary) ways: persons working in occupations not matching their qualifications; persons working less than a certain number of hours per week; and persons earning less than a certain minimum level of income. The Labor Force Survey defines as "underemployed" an unpaid family member who works less than twenty hours a week and wants to work more or an employed person who works less than thirty-five hours a week; underemployed in terms of income is an urban dweller earning less than the minimum wage, a rural household earning less than the minimum wage, or a rural household earning less than 250 baht per head (see Hongladarom and Charsombut 1984). Underemployment in terms of hours worked has been relatively low, 3 to 5 per cent of the labour force during 1977-81; it is most severe in the northeast among male adults, mainly farmers with low educational levels. Underemployment in terms of mismatch between occupation and education has been generally less than 1 per cent and is found mainly in Bangkok among males twenty to twenty-nine years of age with vocational or university education. Most important was underemployment in terms of income, which ranged between 14 and 34 per cent of the labour force during 1977-81 (see Table 53). It was important in the rural areas, particularly of the northeast and the north; it affected equally both sexes and was most severe among farmers thirty to fifty-nine years of age and of low educational level. In 1981 there were as many as 3.2 million people in rural areas and 1.0 million in urban areas earning less than 3,000 baht (US $130) per year compared to a per capita GDP of 17,630 baht (see Hongladarom and Charsombut 1984: 25).

Related to the employment situation is the stagnation of real wages for unskilled labour and the widening of rural-urban income differentials. If indeed the labour market is not tight, that is, if there is considerable underemployment (as well as other forms of underutilization of labour), we would observe stagnation of real wages for that part of the labour force that experiences the highest rates of underemployment: unskilled workers. Indeed, as shown in Table 54, between 1965 and 1977 the agricultural real wages remained virtually unchanged in the northeast and the north but increased somewhat in the central

Table 53
Rate of Underemployment in Municipal and Nonmunicipal Areas in Thailand (%)

Year	Type	Municipal areas		Nonmunicipal areas	
		Dry Season	Rainy Season	Dry Season	Rainy Season
1977	hour work	1.4	1.4	5.4	4.1
	income	15.5	14.5	26.2	34.2
	mismatch	0.1	0.2	[a]	[a]
1979	hour work	2.2	1.8	3.3	2.4
	income	15.3	14.5	20.7	28.3
	mismatch	0.4	0.3	[a]	[a]
1981	hour work	2.3	1.5	3.5	1.8
	income	27.9	28.8	13.3	15.1
	mismatch	0.6	0.7	[a]	[a]

Source: National Statistical Office, Report of the Labour Force Survey, Whole Kingdom (round 1 and 2), 1977, 1979, 1981, and 1982 (quoted from Hongladarom and Charsombat)

[a]Less than 0.1

region. Similarly, between 1977 and 1980 there was no sustainable rise in real wages anywhere in the country, except perhaps in the nonmunicipal areas of Bangkok-Thonburi, as shown in Table 55. (Tables 54 and 55 are not comparable because of differences in the sample population and in the base year of the deflator; moreover, the figures in Table 55, unlike Table 54, are adjusted to a standard eight-hour day.)

Another observation from Table 54 is that wages in the rural northeast are only two-thirds of the wages in the rural central area and in the urban northeast. This is an indication of the persistent wage differentials among regions and between rural and urban areas. Wages also vary between seasons. The World Bank (1977) reports that in the central region the nominal wage rate in the 1976-7 crop year rose

Table 54
Agricultural Wage Trends in Thailand by Region, 1965–77 (baht/day)

Year	North	Northeast	Central	CPI (Central)
1965–7	8 (8)[a]	8 (8)	10 (10)	100
1972	9–10 (7.6–8.4)	9–10 (7.6–8.4)	12–13 (10.1–10.9)	119
1976–7	20 (10.4)	16 (8.2)	27 (14.1)	192

Source: World Bank 1977: 38

[a]Figures in parentheses are real wages computed by using the CPI for the central region (1965–7 = 100)

Table 55
Average Daily Nominal and Real Wages[a] for Male Private Employees (Hourly, Daily and Other Paid), Age 20–59, with Lower Elementary Education, Thailand, July-September, 1977–80 (baht/day)

	Non-Municipal				Municipal			
	1977	1978	1979	1980	1977	1978	1979	1980
North	29.5 (27.4)	28.0 (24.1)	33.3 (26.1)	40.0 (25.6)	36.1 (33.6)	44.9 (38.7)	43.9 (34.4)	52.3 (33.5)
Northeast	23.6 (22.1)	28.4 (25.4)	28.9 (22.6)	38.1 (24.4)	36.5 (33.9)	45.2 (38.9)	43.2 (33.9)	48.8 (31.3)
South	38.0 (35.4)	43.2 (37.2)	50.4 (39.5)	54.6 (35.0)	36.5 (33.9)	40.7 (35.1)	40.5 (31.7)	50.3 (32.3)
Centre	36.0 (33.5)	38.5 (33.2)	47.7 (37.4)	53.7 (34.4)	42.7 (39.6)	44.1 (38.0)	52.7 (41.3)	61.1 (39.2)
Bangkok-Thonburi	36.5 (33.9)	42.9 (37.0)	48.3 (37.3)	62.9 (40.3)	49.6 (46.1)	48.3 (41.6)	58.4 (45.8)	67.5 (43.2)

Source: World Bank 1983: 108. The real wages (in parentheses) were computed using the consumer price index for the whole country. Obtained from the Department of Business Economics, Ministry of Commerce

[a]Adjusted to a standard eight-hour day. Figures in parentheses are the corresponding real wages (using CPI 1976 = 100)

from 20 baht in the slack season to 30 baht in the peak agricultural season. In the northeast, where even in the peak season there is a relative abundance of labour, the nominal wage rate rose from 15 baht in the slack season to 17 baht in the peak season. In the north, with features of both the central region and the northeast, the nominal wage rose from 15 baht in the slack season to 20 baht in the peak season.

The seasonal variations in wage and employment indicate that wages are responsive to changes in the demand for labour and that labour supply is not infinitely elastic. On the other hand, the larger seasonal variation in labour supply with a small variation in wage rates in the northeast indicate a more elastic labour supply in this region than elsewhere in Thailand.

While the seasonal variations in wages indicate a labour market that is functioning well, the persistence of regional variations in wages seems to indicate just the opposite: a segmented labour market that contradicts one of our stylized facts, according to which labour in Thailand is mobile and the labour market efficient. However, the persistence of regional wage differentials can be explained by the lack of scope for permanent migration and the high cost of temporary migration. For better paid activities, such as sugar cane and paddy harvesting, there is considerable rural-rural migration, but it is never sufficient to equalize wages because the economic and psychic cost of movement of farmers is likely to be higher than that of purely wage labourers, who are a rarity in rural Thailand.

There is also evidence which indicates that even in the nonagricultural sectors, the real wage rates of unskilled workers have stagnated as they did in the agricultural sector (a fact which supports the hypothesis that the labour market in Thailand operates efficiently). According to the World Bank (1977), during 1962-76 non-agricultural wages (particularly manufacturing) remained stagnant or increased slightly in nominal terms and declined in real terms. More recently, wages in manufacturing, construction, and other formal, non-agricultural sectors have been influenced by minimum wage legislation and, to some extent, by trade unions, and therefore they cannot be used as indicators of the tightness of the labour market.

From the above discussion, four seemingly contradictory findings emerge: the economy grew rapidly, the labour market operates efficiently, unskilled real wages stagnated, and regional wage differentials persist. The apparent contradiction disappears when one considers the rapid increase in population and the decrease in land availability, which means that increasing numbers of poor families have been willing to supply labour at the same supply price. This is not the same as an infinitely elastic supply of labour; it is rather a case of the labour market loosening up over time as supply rises while demand fails to keep pace. Double-cropping in the central region and parts of the north succeeded in tightening the market and raising real wages, but such opportunities have not been available to the northeast, nor has the wage differential been high enough to warrant the necessary movement costs. In other words, the migration costs are too high to expect equalization of wages across the board.

It is not only the real wages of the unskilled workers that remained stagnant, but also the returns to marginal farmers and the non-wage urban sector, which constitute the sources of unskilled labour. This situation is expected to continue and intensify during the 1980s because of the higher growth rate of the labour force and lower availability of land for expansion and self-employment at the extensive margin. The implications are clear; poverty will persist and income distribution will deteriorate while economic growth continues at historically high rates. But there is more to this than just the welfare of the ten million "poor" of the northeast and parts of the north. In the absence of more rewarding employment opportunities, the clearing of watersheds for land and the migration to Bangkok for work will intensify. The end result is easy to predict: further degradation of agriculture's resource base and growth potential and further congestion of Bangkok and deterioration of social infrastructure with consequent political, social, and economic instability.

What should the right response be? Are there any alternative labour-demand and income-augmenting policies? Since agricultural investments face tight absorptive capacity constraints and urban industry (which basically means Bangkok-based industry) generates little employment and attracts much undesirable migration into Bangkok, there is only one alternative left: investment in nonagricultural rural activity, that is, rural industry in a broad sense to include food-processing, transportation, commerce, and other rural services. Other alternatives, such as employment generation through public projects or income enhancement through transfer payments, have already been proven either ineffective or inoperative.

INVESTMENT IN RURAL INDUSTRY: POTENTIAL FOR GROWTH AND EMPLOYMENT

The conclusion that rural industry might hold the key to additional employment, growth, and equity raises more questions than can be possibly answered in the context of this study. What types of rural industry? What are the binding constraints to rural industry, and what can the government do about them? What specific investments or interventions are likely to work, at what cost and within what time frame? How much employment would be generated per dollar spent, and how would growth and income distribution be affected? What is the expected impact on agriculture?

It is beyond the scope of this study to attempt to answer all these questions. Instead, it focuses on the last three, that is, the employment generation potential of the rural industry, its likely effects on growth and equity, and its potential linkages to agriculture.

Rural industry, used here in a broad sense, is a generic term for all non-agricultural activities taking place outside the greater Bangkok metropolitan area and the outlying provinces of Nontaburi, Pathumtani, and Samutprakan. In a narrower sense, rural industry refers only to rural manufacturing, such as food-processing, textiles, and cottage industries. Rural industry does not mean public job-creation projects (which have been tried with little success) or large-scale government projects, such as the Eastern Seaboard Industrial Project, which are capital intensive and cannot be expected to provide much rural employment.

It should also be stated categorically at the outset that the promotion of rural industry is not presented as an alternative to agricultural growth, which is a *sine qua non* for virtually any other economic activity in rural Thailand; it is, rather, a necessary complement to the projected agricultural growth in recognition of (1) the inadequacy of agricultural employment (direct and indirect) to absorb a labour force growing at unprecedented rates; (2) the absorptive capacity limits to public investments in agriculture beyond current levels; and (3) the potential linkages between rural industry and agricultural growth.

A last qualification concerns the meaning of "promotion" of rural industry. Here it does not mean subsidization, but rather improvement in the allocation of resources and creation of an environment conducive to competitive operation of rural industry through intervention in areas where there are market failures or policy distortions (for example, credit, infrastructure, extension of technology, training, market information) that prevent the realization of existing growth potential. Even when the objective is distributional, a rural industrial strategy should be pursued only if it is the most cost-effective avenue for achieving a given reduction in poverty or improvement in income distribution. We do not advocate import substitution, but rather rural industries for which there is either local demand (arising from the projected agricultural and income growth) or export demand (for example, textiles, handicrafts) and rural industries that have comparative advantage by virtue of the locally available materials (food and fibre), relatively inexpensive labour, and little foreign exchange requirements. Whether there is a potential for further expansion of such industries or establishment of new ones is an empirical question to be answered by another study. However, there are a priori reasons and some evidence suggesting that opportunities for further expansion of rural industry do exist.

According to the World Bank (1983), the government's industrial trade and investment promotion policies have sharply distorted incentives against rural areas and in favour of capital-intensive, large-scale enterprises via rigid cut-off points on the size of industrial plants eligible for subsidies and other incentives. These policies must have seriously hampered the growth of rural non-farm activities and employment. Agricultural price policies, such as the rice and rubber taxation, have further distorted the incentives against both agriculture and rural industry.

In contrast, very little is being returned to the rural areas in terms of development assistance, loans, and promotional policies. A summary of the government policies in favour of the rural areas is given in Table 56. From this table and the earlier discussion of development expenditures, a number of observations may be made. First, "the major trans-

Table 56
Summary of Government Policies in Favour of Rural Areas, Thailand

	Subsidy Element (million baht)
Commercial bank loans to agriculture	
Interest differential of 2–5 per cent on about B 10 billion	200–500
Commercial bank loans to agribusiness	
Voluntary lending exceeds quota	none
BAAC loans to agriculture	
Interest subsidy of 5–10 per cent on about B 10 billion	500–1,000
Loss of capital from overdues: 10–20 per cent of loans outstanding per year	1,000–2,000
IFCT loans to food and tobacco	
Interest subsidy of 5–10 per cent on B 400 million	20–40
SIFO loans outside Bangkok	
Interest subsidy of 5–10 per cent on about B 80 million	4–8
Special regional incentives	
Reduce capital costs by only about 10 per cent relative to urban areas	negligible
Rural Employment Generation Program (1980)	3,500
Agricultural development expenditures	
on irrigation	7,165
on extension	917
on research	515
Total of quantified effects	13,821–15,645

Source: World Bank 1983: 15

fers in favor of the rural areas are specific agricultural investment programs in irrigation, extension and research (roughly B 8.5 billion)" (World Bank 1983: 14), which are largely spent in the central region. Second, rural employment creation through public projects received another 3.5 billion baht. Third, rural industry received virtually no attention; special regional incentives are negligible and Small Industry Finance Office (SIFO) loans to rural industry are next to nothing. The World Bank estimates that the tax effects of the industrial and trade policies "exceed the income transfers implied in special rural industrialization efforts many-fold" (1983:17) and concludes that these policies discriminate against labour-intensive industries with depressing effects on wages.

A similar view of Thai industrial policies is expressed by Narongchai Akrasanee of the Industrial Finance Corporation of Thailand (IFCT):

> [The] industrial policy of the government so far has not had favorable impact on the development of either village or town industries. For industry in general, the industrial incentive system and the availability of basic infrastructure in fact have the effect of being biased in favor of Bangkok [and nearby provinces] location and thus against location in provincial towns. The government so far has few activities which are of a real help to [small] town industry. . . . The private sector and the donor countries and agencies have played a very small role in the promotion of village and town industries. (Akrasanee et al. 1983: 176).

If rural areas are being discriminated against by government policies, the first-best course of action for restoring the rural area's true comparative advantage would be a sweeping reform of government policies and correction of market imperfections and distortions. Such a first-best alternative, however, is unlikely to be adopted in full or to any significant degree in the foreseeable future because of political reasons and administrative constraints. Agricultural price policies stand a better chance of being reformed appreciably within the coming years. (A beginning has already been made with fertilizer prices, maize quotas, and rice premiums). The industrial promotion and trade policies persisted throughout the 1980s because of the vested interest of the politically powerful Bangkok establishment.

Given the dimensions and the urgency of the employment and poverty problems and the untapped potential of rural industry, a pragmatic second-best policy would be development assistance to labour-intensive rural industry to restore its comparative advantage vis-à-vis the highly protected and promoted Bangkok-based capital-intensive industry. Such assistance, combined with the ongoing investments and policy reforms in agriculture, is likely to increase the proportion of input and consumer demand supplied by labour-intensive rural activities, to generate additional demand, and to exploit any unutilized export potential (for example, textiles and handicrafts). That is, for any given rate of agricultural growth, more rural industry output and employment would be generated if rural industry were put on a more equal footing with Bangkok-based industry. Even more important would be the catalytic and dynamic effects of such a strategy; modest development assistance could demonstrate the potential of rural industry in the absence of discriminating policies, thereby facilitating the reform of current industrial policies.

How much additional employment would the promotion of rural industry generate? The answer depends on the extent of the promoted industries as well as on the general economic conditions, particularly the growth of agriculture. Wattanavitukul et al. (1980) reports an employment elasticity for (rural) industry with respect to GDP of 0.98 compared to only 0.3 for agriculture. Rural industries are usually small and more labour-intensive than Bangkok-based industries for a good reason: labour is cheap and capital expensive. Any assistance to rural industry, especially with credit, and the consequent expansion would alter the relative prices of capital and labour and the labour intensity of the industry.

The prevailing factor intensity in a given industry is partly related to technological reasons and partly to economic ones (for example, relative prices). Economic factors may reflect distortions. In urban areas there are relatively high wages because of unions and minimum wage legislation and low-cost capital because of subsidized interest and investment promotion. In the rural areas wage rates are low because of seasonal unemployment and underemployment, imperfect mobility, no minimum wage or unions, high-cost capital, informal credit, and so forth.

To the extent that the labour intensity of rural industry is caused by price distortions, correcting them or lowering of the cost of capital (through credit) to the rural industry would reduce rural industry's contribution to employment through substitution. On the other hand, the rural industry would expand, generating more employment as a result of its increased profitability. The net effect on employment would depend on the relative size of the elasticity of substitution between labour and capital, the production elasticity of labour (or employment elasticity), the elasticity of output with respect to the price of capital, and economies of scale. Empirical work is needed to obtain estimates for these important parameters before the net effect of alternative policies on employment can be precisely assessed. On balance, however, rural employment can reasonably be expected to increase appreciably.

Table 57 shows the present regional distribution of industrial activity; the central region, essentially the greater Bangkok area, accounts for 81 per cent of the total value added compared to 4.8-7.6 per cent for each of the other three regions, where two-thirds of the Thai population live. This distribution is partly the result of comparative advantage and partly the result of a policy bias against rural industry and in favour of Bangkok. With modest but catalytic development assistance to rural industry and with gradual reform of industrial trade and investment promotion policies, it should be possible to stimulate rural industry or disperse some of the existing activity to regional centres and provincial towns and to increase its labour-intensity. The rising transportation cost is an added factor working in favour of production

Table 57
Statistics of Regional Industries in Thailand

	Year	Central	South	North	Northeast	Total
Population (million persons)	1976	14.1	5.3	9.0	14.8	43.2
	1982	16.3	6.0	9.8	16.7	48.8
GDP from manufacturing	1976	54.8	1.9	3.3	3.0	63.0
	1980	118.1	4.9	5.4	6.1	134.5
Distribution of manufacturing	1976	87.0	3.0	5.2	4.8	100.0
	1980	87.8	3.6	4.0	4.6	100.0
	1985[a]	90.3	2.0	3.2	4.5	100.0
Growth rates of manufacturing value added (%)	1976–80	21.2	26.7	13.1	19.4	20.9
Share of manufacturing value added in regional GDP (%)	1976	25.7	5.0	6.1	6.1	18.7
	1980	27.1	6.0	5.9	6.4	19.6
	1985[a]	—	—	—	—	22.1
	1987[a]	—	—	—	—	23.9
Distribution of products by region (%)						
Office of The Board of Investment	1960–82	84.7	7.1	5.6	2.6	100.0
IFCT	1960–81	76.8	7.2	7.9	8.1	100.0
SIFO	1964–81	63.9	7.2	12.5	16.4	100.0
No. of factories (%)	1973	14,654	4,258	6,202	10,743	36,057
		41.2	11.8	17.2	29.8	100.0
	BKK	8,293	—	—	—	—
(%)		23.0	—	—	—	—
	1979	27,718	6,797	10,885	22,336	67,736
(%)		40.9	10.0	16.1	33.0	100.0
	BKK	14,337	—	—	—	—
(%)		21.2				
Ranking of industries (based on no. of factories)						
Rank 1		Processed foods	Wood products	Tobacco	Processed foods	
Rank 2		Textiles	Rubber & rubber products	Processed foods		
Rank 3		Chemical products & wood	Processed foods	Wood products	Textiles & non-metallic mineral products	

Source: NESDB (quoted from Akrasance 1983)
[a]NESDB, GDP by province, 1985

near the source of raw materials and the market since 90 per cent of consumers live outside Bangkok.

To be successful, the promotion of rural industries should be built on the basic features of the rural areas: the availability of raw materials, the seasonality of labour supply, and the dispersion of the market. The emphasis should be on restoring the comparative advantage of the rural areas (rather than subsidizing any particular line of production) vis-à-vis Bangkok by improving infrastructure, making credit available at competitive cost, providing technical assistance and market information, and assisting in skill development. What industries are likely to have a comparative advantage? Two obvious candidates are agri-based industries, which are favoured by raw material availability and transport cost, and cottage industries, which are small and do not require expensive machinery and, therefore, can be operated on a seasonal basis. Finally, export-oriented, labour-intensive industries, such as textiles and handicrafts, might have a comparative advantage if they were based near town centres and linked to a reformed export promotion policy that is not biased in favour of Bangkok. (For more details, see Akrasanee 1983.)

The rural industry's contribution to the national objectives of equity and stability lies in its potential to increase the demand for labour in the rural areas, particularly the northeast and the north. A stronger demand for labour is expected to have two related effects: increased rural employment, especially during the slack season, and upward pressure on unskilled and semi-skilled wages.

Additional rural employment at higher wages is certain to improve rural incomes both in absolute terms and vis-à-vis Bangkok and central region incomes. Both equity and alleviation of poverty would be served, since the landless and the small farmers are likely to benefit more than other socioeconomic groups from a rural employment strategy. Equally important is the effect on socioeconomic and political stability. Availability of year-round rural employment at above-subsistence wages is certain to stem the destabilizing flow of landless and marginal farmers into watershed areas, marginal lands, and the Bangkok slums. The long-term sustainability of Thai agriculture is intimately linked to the condition of the watersheds, which has been deteriorating in recent years at an alarming rate (Panayotou 1983). This situation raises the issue of linkages between rural industry and agriculture.

The important linkages from agriculture to rural industry and employment in Thailand have been well documented (World Bank 1983). However, little attention has been paid to the equally important linkages from rural industry and employment to agriculture: (1) the increased demand for agricultural products as inputs (raw materials) for industry; (2) the increased demand for agricultural products for consumption resulting from the increased incomes (for example, more employment at higher wages) of rural poor with high income elasticity of demand for food; (3) increased supply of agricultural inputs such as implements, containers, transport, and repair and service of agricultural machinery; (4) generation of cash income, the subsistence farmer's most scarce resource, for the purchase of inputs such as fertilizer, seed, and pesticides needed for agricultural intensification; (5) reduction of risk aversion resulting from the increase in income and the diversification of its sources leading to adoption of modern agricultural technologies and increased input use; and (6) improvement of agriculture's resource base (water and soil) by attracting squatters out of the watersheds and marginal lands and thereby reducing the incidence and severity of floods and droughts, soil erosion, and sedimentation of irrigation systems.

How strong these linkages are is an empirical question requiring further study. However, we can identify the factors on which the strength of these linkages would depend: (1) the employment coefficient of rural industry; (2) the food and fibre input of rural industry; (3) the income elasticity of those who gain additional employment; (4) the magnitude and distribution of income generated; (5) the farmer's attitude towards risk at different income levels and the yield variability of new technologies; and (6) the mobility and responsiveness of marginal farmers to economic incentives outside agriculture. The available evidence on these parameters suggests that the linkages from rural industry and employment to agriculture are likely to be anything but trivial.

With strong linkages running both ways, a mutually supporting and reinforcing relationship between rural industry and agriculture is possible. The current level of funding of agriculture, appropriately complemented with a modest development assistance for rural industry and a gradual reform of government policies to put rural Thailand on equal footing with the centre, provides hope that the national objectives of sustainable growth, improved income distribution, and stable government and society can be attained.

CONCLUSION

The purpose of this study has been to identify the most appropriate investment strategy for Thailand. To do so, a large number of parameters have been considered: (1) the dominance of agriculture in the Thai economy and its gradual structural change; (2) the current level of funding for agriculture compared to its absorptive capacity; (3) the growth prospects of agriculture in the absence of additional public investment beyond current levels; (4) the dimensions of the employment problem in the light of projected growth rates of the labour force and of agricultural and industrial employment; (5) the bias of agricultural and industrial policies against the rural areas and the likelihood of policy reform; and (6) the potential of rural industry for growth and employment generation and linkages with agriculture.

The findings suggest that agriculture is generously funded beyond its absorptive capacity and that it has excellent growth prospects despite the approaching limits to land expansion, provided that current efforts at agricultural policy reform continue. An intensified agriculture, however, is expected to generate little additional employment for the rapidly growing labour force. For political reasons, the Bangkok-based industry will probably continue to receive generous promotional privileges and protection, thus maintaining its capital intensity in the face of relatively abundant low-cost labour. Of the remaining options, rural industry, which has received little assistance thus far and which has been heavily discriminated against by government policies, holds the greatest promise for additional rural growth and employment generation in line with the national objectives of growth with equity.

Rural industry, being intrinsically labour-intensive, would generate more employment per dollar invested than either agriculture or industry, thereby narrowing the employment gap without significantly increasing the budget deficit or the foreign debt. In fact, if the promoted rural industries are carefully selected to have a low import component and a high export value, the balance of trade/payments might improve as a result. Judiciously administered, a modest level of development assistance to rural industry not only promises to generate additional growth and employment but also is likely to have catalytic effects on industrial policy reform. It is encouraging that the Thai government has included rural industry and employment among its priority areas for the Sixth National Economic and Social Development Plan, which is now in progress.

NOTES

1 During the Second Plan, agriculture's share in planned total development expenditures was 19 per cent, but its share in actual total expenditure fell below 15 per cent.

2 Data for the Fifth Plan are not available.

3 As will be seen later, the contribution of the private sector to capital formation in agriculture is adversely affected by capital market distortions and government

policies that discriminate against agriculture.

4 The labour-output ratio is the amount of labour in persons per one thousand constant baht (1972 prices) worth of output.

5 A compromise figure between 6.581 million (World Bank 1983: 174) and 7.709 million (Rijk and Meer/ADB 1984, Annex L).

6 Based on the Labor Force Surveys, open unemployment rose from 85,000 in 1972 to 457,000 in the wet season of 1982 (Hongladarom and Charsombat 1984: 19).

REFERENCES

Akrasanee, N. (1983). "The Role of Government in Off-Farm Income and Employment Promotion." In Akrasanee et al., eds., *Rural Off-Farm Employment in Thailand*. Bangkok: USAID/IFCT

Hongladarom, Chira, and Pradit Charsombat (1984). "Current Employment Situation with Specific Reference to Rural Employment." Paper prepared for a seminar on Employment Problem and Rural Credit in Thailand at Dusit Thani Hotel, 31 March

NESDB (1981). The Fifth National Economic and Social Development Plan (1982–6). National Economic and Social Development Board, Office of the Prime Minister. Bangkok

Panayotou, Theodore (1983). "Renewable Resource Management for Agricultural and Rural Development in Southeast Asia: Research and Policy Issue." Paper presented at the Fifth Biennial Meeting of the Agricultural Economics Society of Southeast Asia (AESSEA), Bangkok, 16-19 November

Rijk, A.G., and C.L.J. Van Der Meer (1984). "Thailand Agricultural Assessment Study." Asian Development Bank, January

Wattanavitukul, S., et al. (1980). "Labor Absorption in Thai Agriculture: An Exploratory Study." Faculty of Economics, Thammasat University, Bangkok, November

World Bank (1977). "Thailand: Special Report on Employment." 6 October

— (1978). "Thailand: Towards a Development Strategy of Full Participation, A Basic Economic Report." September

— (1982). "Thailand Programme and Policy Priorities for an Agriculture in Transition." Vols. 1-4, 3 December

— (1983). "Thailand, Rural Growth and Employment"

CHAPTER SIX

Japan in the Pacific Policy Environment for Strategic Planning

Gavin Boyd

The regional pattern of domestic and international economic involvement by governments in East Asia and North America is expanding with the broadening of industrial policies, shifts toward managed trade and strategic trade policies, the increasing use of trade-related fiscal, monetary, and financial interventions, and the development of methods of regulating foreign direct investment. Contributing to the expansion of this economic involvement are rising levels of interdependence, which, because of associated vulnerabilities, are activating interest groups and domestic as well as international policy communities. These changes are happening in the context of serious strains in the international trade and monetary systems and of slow recovery from the general recession.

The most comprehensive functional measures, with the strongest elements of neo-mercantilism, are those implemented by Japan. These are put into effect with active cooperation by Japanese firms, and while they influence the activities of those firms, they also influence the behaviour of other enterprises in East Asia and North America. Japanese enterprises have a stable, orderly, and supportive domestic policy environment. Because of their strong country ties, moreover, the expansion of their overseas operations tends to result in extensions rather than losses of Japanese economic sovereignty. American policies affecting Pacific business activity are narrower in scope, less integrated, and less functional, but they are more liberal.

US enterprises are not closely associated with these policies, which are mainly neutral regarding corporate overseas operations, and the home country ties of these firms tend to weaken.

The economic policies of the developing East Asian states are mostly interventionist, inspired by Japan's achievements in administrative guidance of export-oriented industrialization. These policies are significant for the trading activities of local firms, for the overseas operations of emerging East Asian multinationals, and for other Pacific enterprises exporting to or producing in the developing East Asian countries. Most of the measures adopted are intended to accelerate growth by protecting domestic firms as well as aiding enterprises that serve foreign markets.

Japanese firms have established extensive trade and production links with the more advanced developing East Asian states, known as the Newly Industrializing Countries (NICs) — South Korea, Taiwan, and Singapore.[1] Strong economic bonds have also been forged by Japanese enterprises with resource-rich Southeast Asian countries like Indonesia, Malaysia, Thailand, and the Philippines. With Singapore and the small state of Brunei, these countries constitute the Association of Southeast Asian Nations (ASEAN), a regional organization that fosters modest political economic cooperation among its members.

The principal trend in Pacific trade and industrial activity is a new wave of Japanese direct investment that is strengthening ties with the developing East Asian states, partly at the expense of American and West European shares in regional commerce and production. For several of those states, Japan is the main trading partner and the main source of foreign direct investment. The new wave of outward Japanese direct investment has been facilitated by the appreciation of the yen, and it has been given impetus by protectionist threats in the United States and Western Europe. These developments have increased the long-term significance of evolving complementarities between Japan and the larger ASEAN members as well as the NICs, in addition to encouraging Japanese direct investment in the United States and the European Community.

POLICY MIXES

The economic measures through which Pacific states influence business activity are shaped by national policy styles in which leadership, institutional, and cultural factors interact. Consensual styles contrast with those that are pluralistic, and the more functional ones contrast with those which are reactive and biased by political exchange concerns. Problems of governance can have major effects, for example, because of pluralistic stagnation, a fragmentation of power, inadequate leadership expertise, demand overload, and information overload. These factors can be especially significant in affecting policy orientations and the scope or range of policy choices. The breadth of choice is extensive in Japan because of a well-established emphasis on administrative guidance of industry and commerce and a tradition of close government-business cooperation (Zysman 1983: ch. 5; McCraw 1986; Patrick and Tachi 1986).

A national mix of economic measures, as in Japan, can guide the activities of firms for rapid, orderly development of the political economy, with wide-ranging consultations ensuring correction of any flaws in the process of administrative guidance (Schmiegelow 1985). In contrast, a liberal policy mix, allowing wide autonomy for firm behaviour can, in effect, leave the way open for problems of market failure, while allowing firms to move into international operations in ways that reduce the effectiveness of national economic policies, even though those firms will tend to have increasing influence on the evolution of economic structures in both home and host countries. Industrial restructuring necessitated by losses of comparative advantage can be difficult to achieve in a liberal policy context, but it can be managed effectively if a government-business partnership is well established (ibid.).

A liberal policy mix tends to be implemented with political exchange biases that dilute the liberal orientation. National firms have an incentive to influence those biases but also to reduce their vulnerability to such biases by locating operations abroad. Impetus to that outward investment is often given by fiscal expansionism, driven by the pressures of political competition, which causes enterprises to move production activities into countries less prone to inflation and less heavily taxed to service public debts. If monetary restriction is used to counter inflation, the reduction of domestic demand and the higher cost of credit can make the outward movement of operations more desirable. Alternatively, a loose monetary policy will motivate outward investment to escape the upward pressure of inflation on production costs.[2]

A neo-mercantilist policy mix tends to be fiscally restrictive, to restrain internal demand and prevent inflation. Currency appreciation caused by trade surpluses is normally countered by financial controls that ensure low-cost loans for industry. National firms respond to industrial and investment measures that provide incentives to cooperate with the administration. Ambitions for increased shares of global markets, however, can motivate efforts to develop operations outside the scope of home government intervention, especially to collaborate with foreign multinationals for technology-sharing and collaborative marketing (Doz 1986; Casson et al. 1986; Dunning 1985).

National size and status are important determinants of the feasibility of alternative policy options. The range of choice is considerable for the United States, since it is the largest industrialized democracy and has a relatively low dependence on foreign trade and a dominant position in the international monetary system. Political concerns over business cycle effects, in conjunction with needs for adjustment measures, can cause a government to request fiscal expansion by a major trading partner, as has been evident in American interactions with Japan and West Germany. Where differences in bargaining power facilitate leverage, the target state's capacity to secure cooperation from firms in dampening the effects of any expansion can be especially important. The external pressure, of course, may strengthen government-business links in the target state and enable it to implement a more active industrial policy for greater international competitiveness.[3]

The Pacific setting is dominated by forms of competitive and cooperative interaction between Japanese neo-mercantilism and American liberalism. The main business activity — high-volume, arm's-length commerce between Japan and the United States — is changing with the new wave of Japanese investment in the US. Japanese managements appears to be confident that their large resources, managerial capacities, and technological advances, as well as their supportive home environment, will enable them to preserve competitive advantages while operating in the United States. In conjunction with large-scale Japanese lending, which helps cover the borrowing needs of the US government, this direct investment in the United States raises levels of interdependence, requiring American restraint in the use of leverage to reduce the current trade imbalance (Patrick and Tachi 1986). For Japan, however, it is becoming increasingly necessary to balance this interdependence by promoting greater diversification in foreign economic relations, especially through broadening commercial and industrial links with high-growth East Asian trading partners.

JAPANESE POLICIES

Japan's economic policies have neo-mercantilist objectives that are served by fiscal and monetary restraint, informal protectionist trade measures, and industrial guidance activities aimed at enhancing the competitiveness of national firms. These firms can plan domestic and international operations on the basis of identification with this pervasive governmental economic involvement, which is a source of security, assistance, and strategic orientation. Transaction costs and risks tend to be lowered, there is extensive information-sharing, and bargaining with host governments is aided by their awareness that the Japanese economic presence can provide multiple benefits but that these may be reduced if new Japanese ventures are discouraged (Dunning 1985). American and West European firms, as well as those in the developing East Asian countries, have to reckon with the broad scope and external reach of Japanese policies as well as with the market power and political influence of Japanese enterprises whose activities are associated with those policies.

Cultural factors that help to exclude foreign influence allow Japanese economic measures to shape the home policy environment with a high degree of autonomy. The policies implemented are functional and in the national interest, and they derive from broadly shared concerns, based on economic nationalism, which are given direction by highly professional bureaucratic expertise. Japanese management has extensive involvement in the consultative activities through which each policy consensus is achieved, and it has potent incentives to cooperate with policies as they are put into effect. Foreign firms in Japan have very limited opportunities to contribute to policy; they have to operate within the pervasive pattern of administrative economic involvement. From the national point of view, this is justifiable because highly competitive performance in the international economy, based on domestic strength, is necessary to overcome Japan's serious resource deficiencies and maintain an acceptable pace of growth.

Fiscal policy restrains Japanese consumer demand, with declining budget deficits. Credit for this policy is due to the Ministry of Finance, apparently the main source of opposition to American demands for larger deficit-spending. The financial system is being liberalized and internationalized in response to opportunities for outward investment and also to meet American requests that have reflected expectations that interest rates would rise, thus eliminating low-cost loans that have assisted Japanese industries. American leverage, however, has *also* been exerted to induce reductions of Japanese interest rates to stimulate consumer demand, despite other US efforts to cause appreciation of the yen against the dollar so that American exports will be more competitive (McCraw 1986: ch. 9). Budget allocations for industrial policy and export promotion have been kept modest, in line with general fiscal restraint, thus obliging Japanese firms to assume greater responsibility for financing their domestic and international operations. Industrial policy is now devoting increasing attention to the encouragement of small- and medium-sized firms that have potential for technological advancement and, therefore, superior export performance.

Japanese technology policy seeks to promote rapid commercial utilization of production-related scientific advances by enlisting the cooperation of numerous firms in collaborative research and development projects. This policy is aided by strong emphasis on science and engineering in the education system and by the degree to which many Japanese enterprises have used their resources to build up their own research and development capabilities. A tacit official concern is to ensure that despite the increasing direct investment in the United States, Japanese firms will continue to undertake most of their research and development in the home environment. A major problem has been insufficient basic research in Japanese academic institutions, the effects of which have been aggravated by inadequate links between these institutions and the more practical research undertaken by firms. Current policies are promoting more fundamental research at universities and enabling enterprises to draw more directly on that work (Patrick 1986).

Direct investment policy, while responding to perceived needs to produce in and reduce exports to the United States, is continuing to implement a well-established design for the movement of heavy, chemical, and energy-intensive industries into resource-rich developing East Asian countries and for the development of extractive and manufacturing operations in those countries (Dunning 1985: ch. 5). Administrative influence on these overseas activities is, on the whole, ensured by the economic nationalism that sustains the home country ties of Japanese management abroad and that pervades their distinctive management culture. Inward direct investment is accepted on a modest scale, mainly for the benefits of anticipated technology transfers. This inflow is modest, and totalled only US $6.6 billion in 1985, half of which was from the United States. Japanese direct investment abroad reached a cumulative total of US $83.6 billion in 1985, of which nearly one-third was in the United States (Japan Institute for Social and Economic Affairs 1987; McCraw 1986: ch. 4).

Trade policy now provides only small-scale assistance for export promotion, since many national firms are well established in foreign markets. Nevertheless, customary informal limitations on imports have been maintained. The significance of these is difficult to estimate because of the importance of personalized links among Japanese firms, the influence of economic nationalism on consumer taste, and the traditionally high rate of domestic saving. Administrative measures, adopted under US pressure, have gradually reduced some of the official restrictions on imports, but vigorous exporting, especially by the large Japanese general trading companies, has tended to increase the nation's trade surplus. Business groups in the United States and other major trading partners have not been able to build commercial organizations comparable to the Japanese general trading companies (Kojima and Ozawa 1984).

Japan's trade policy has a strategic quality because of the extent to which it helps firms undercut foreign competitors and establish strong positions in overseas markets through deep penetration, while preparing the way for manufacturing in those markets. The cultural and institutional factors that aid export development are resistant to change because of the strength of economic nationalism augmented by successful neo-mercantilism, but pressures from trading partners are posing urgent issues for the Japanese economy. Those partners are being challenged to resort increasingly to managed trade and to burden-shifting measures that could be costly for Japan. The most fundamental issue for Japanese decision-makers, however, is whether to use administrative guidance to facilitate the development of intra-industry commerce with major advanced trading partners or to continue fostering the growth of a highly integrated national political economy for intensely competitive involvement in world trade. Increased intra-industry commerce could lead to more symmetrical interdependence, especially with the United States, and, if well managed, to wider diffusion of the international gains from commerce. For the present, Japanese bureaucrats and management appear to be committed to the second option on the basis of their established neo-mercantilist policy (Packard 1987/8). Yet the current direction of industrial policy, adjusting to the emergence of joint ventures between Japanese and foreign firms and to the movement of Japanese enterprises into the United States, could gradually adapt to an expansion of intra-industry commerce, while guiding, through consultations, the evolution of specialized foreign involvement in the nation's economic structures.

For American and other firms in the Pacific, the main consequence of the present Japanese policy mix is that the scope for incoming direct investment is likely to remain fairly restricted for the immediate future. There will probably be a tightening of the informal bonds linking Japanese national firms with each other and with their economic ministries because of general increases in economic nationalism. This nationalism is caused by what is seen as the abrasive behaviour of trading partners who are indifferent to the nation's heavy dependence of energy and raw material imports. Incentives for foreign firms to export to and undertake direct investment in Japan, however, will continue to be strong because of the appreciation of the yen and because a moderate shift toward more consumption-oriented policies may be under way. This could serve the domestic political interests of the ruling Liberal Democratic Party while meeting American requests aimed at increasing Japanese consumer demand.[4]

A secondary but increasingly important consequence of the current Japanese policy mix is a strengthening of economic bonds with the developing East Asian states as the large outflow of Japanese direct investment continues. Overall, this investment is tending to reduce the American share of trade with and production in most of those developing states, despite their interest in diversifying their foreign economic relations. For Japanese enterprises, the establishment of production bases and extractive ventures in those states, as well as the promotion of exports to them, is assuming greater importance for the support of global trade promotion activities and for more effective adaptation to strains in trade and investment dealings with the United States. Japan's exports to South Korea, Taiwan, and the ASEAN countries represent more than 30 per cent of its exports to the US and are somewhat larger than its exports to the European Community. If exports to China and Hong Kong are added, the total is more than half the volume going to the US. For the ASEAN countries as a group, Japan is the most important trading partner (representing 24 per cent of total trade) and the main source of foreign direct investment (16 per cent of the total, compared with about 14 per cent for the US) (US Chamber of Commerce 1987). Advantages derived from the large-scale informal networks among Japanese firms, and their capacities to form massive diversified consortia, are facilitating expansion of the Japanese economic presence.

POLICY INTERACTIONS

Japan's economic policies, broad in scope and with a considerable external reach, interact with those of the United States, the Northeast Asian NICs, and the ASEAN members. While the resulting regional policy environment influences the activities of firms, their trade and production ventures shape national economic structures and interdependencies in ways that often reduce economic sovereignty and diminish the effectiveness of economic policy instruments. The principal trends in this pattern concern Japan-US policy interactions and the behaviour of each country's firms, which respond in different ways to contrasting domestic and external incentives.

In the policy interactions with the United States, Japan is disadvantaged by weaker bargaining power because of dependence on access to the US market. Nevertheless, Japan has considerable adaptive capacity because it has a high degree of internal unity and a more functional macro-management capability. Trade-related discussions have been initiated mostly by the United States, which has demanded moderation of the continuing Japanese export drive and an expansionary Japanese fiscal policy as well as reduction of Japan's informal tariff barriers. The requests for export restraint are accepted by the Japanese as a lesser evil than the increased protectionism threatened by the US administration, which is made credible by strong legislative pressure. Modest fiscal expansion has been agreed to reluctantly, despite concerns that the government's substantial deficits will increase and that production costs in Japanese firms will tend to rise. Gradual reduction of import barriers has also been recognized as a necessity, especially to allow increased purchases of foreign agricultural products at prices well below those of Japan's heavily protected farms (Bergsten and Cline 1987).

The Japanese strategy of incremental accommodation is made feasible in part by the pluralism of the American policy process. In addition, over time, the US government's increasing need for foreign lending to cover its budget deficits is making the interdependence between the two states less unequal, while the growth of Japanese direct investment in the United States is helping to reduce the trade imbalance. There are risks of discriminatory changes in American policies that could adversely affect Japanese enterprises in the US, but American official borrowing is tending to become more dependent on Japanese lending because of stagnation in the West European economies. The investment outflows from Japan assist that nation's trade policy to some degree by exerting downward pressure on the yen, thus reducing the costs of yielding to US demands for increased access to the Japanese market (Patrick and Tachi 1986).

The principal uncertainties in the relationship are the health of the American economy and the future of the dollar. Both are being affected more and more seriously by the unsustainable American budget and trade deficits and, in addition, by the destabilizing effects of volatility in poorly regulated stock markets. Moreover, the outward movement of American firms, producing abroad for the home market and for sales to foreign countries, while reducing vulnerability to home country regulation and exposure to home country taxation, is having a significant influence on the state of the US economy. Japan can assist reduction of the US trade deficit, but roughly two-thirds of that deficit occurs in American trade with the rest of the world, and the current effects of dollar depreciation suggest that Japan may soon have difficulty in covering its own trade deficit with the oil-exporting countries, especially in the Middle East. These are countries on which the United States is much less dependent for oil and with which it has a substantial trade surplus. Japan's overall trade balance is being reduced by cheaper American exports, but Japanese monetary cooperation is needed by the United States to keep the dollar at an acceptable level. Any major contraction of Japanese lending to the American government would tend to force increases in interest rates, causing upward pressure on the dollar but diminishing general confidence in the US economy and threatening to cause a recession (Pugel and Hawkins 1986: part 2).

Japanese policies also interact significantly with those of the ASEAN countries and the Northeast Asian NICs, tending to perpetuate asymmetries in these relationships. The options that can be seen for Japan are to build partnerships for growth with those states or to draw them into more unequal interdependencies in which they will be virtually obliged to direct their strategies for export-led growth more toward other states. ASEAN and Northeast Asian NIC governments have expressed concern about Japanese inclinations toward the second option, but individually they have little capacity to bargain. Indeed, these nations have to fear that Japanese policy toward them will become more demanding in order to cope more effectively with the tasks of managing relations with the United States. The administrations in ASEAN and the NICs are being challenged to strengthen their domestic structures for improved macro-management and the implementation of more vigorous export-oriented growth strategies, yet they see needs for greater inflows of foreign direct investment to compensate for reductions in earnings from exports to the United States.

Because of the strength of Japan's bargaining power in dealings with the ASEAN members and the Northeastern NICs, there is evidently a danger that its policies towards them will be very much influenced by the interests of Japanese firms and that they will be guided less by the long-term political considerations that would be relevant in more equal relationships. There is also a danger that over time the growth of asymmetries in the interdependencies with those developing countries will provoke antagonisms. South Korea and Taiwan, having moved to advanced levels of export-oriented industrialization, have to direct most of their export promotion efforts at the United States because of the limited opportunities to market their products in Japan. The larger ASEAN states, endeavouring to increase their exports of manufactures and move toward more advanced industrialization, also have to look more toward the US market (US

Chamber of Commerce 1987; UNECAP 1983; Kraus and Lutkenhorst 1986). For these states, and for South Korea and Taiwan, Japan is becoming the most important source of technology, but a large proportion of the substantial inflow of direct investment from Japan is going into manufacturing ventures aimed at their own markets and the United States. Japanese managements endeavour to avoid stirring local resentment and have shown a willingness to accept minority positions in joint ventures with firms in host countries, but restricted entry to the Japanese market is an increasingly serious problem for the developing East Asian states that are seeking to earn more revenue from the export of manufactures.

More active political cooperation among the ASEAN states, it must be stressed, could enable them to undertake collective bargaining, which could lead to more equal and more productive interactions on trade and investment with Japan. Because of their lack of political cohesion, it is evidently difficult for the ASEAN members to evolve a common policy and a common strategy for the negotiation of a comprehensive economic collaboration agreement that would promise genuine partnership with their large Pacific neighbour. Under the strains of coping with losses of earnings from exports to the US and with the frustrations in trade with Japan, the ASEAN members may adopt increasingly divergent approaches to their external economic problems instead of attempting to strengthen unity within their organization. Hence, Japanese policy may not be challenged to shift toward a more integrative approach in dealings with these states.

More active and more constructive American involvement could alter the terms of interactions between Japan and the developing East Asian states, with beneficial effects for each side. The liberal orientation of US policy is based on confidence that international market forces tend to maximize efficiency and welfare. In the global economy, however, there are no controls on oligopoly power corresponding to antitrust restraints in the United States, and the trade-restricting effects of transaction costs are much greater than they are in the US or in any other single national market. A considerable growth of Japanese oligopoly power in several of the ASEAN countries, and possibly also in South Korea and Taiwan, may well result from the strengthening of asymmetric economic bonds between Japan and those countries. Japanese policy-makers and managements may not intend this result, but the weak bargaining positions of those developing East Asian states and the gradual reduction of the American share of trade and production in this area may make it inevitable. Meanwhile, American firms, some in joint ventures with Japanese companies, may share in the acquisition of oligopoly power even while their overall role declines.

This prospect is an insufficiently recognized challenge for the ASEAN members and the Northeast Asian NICs, and it calls for efforts by concerned groups to promote serious discussion of fundamental issues of interdependence between the United States, the developing East Asian nations, and Japan. These are issues which tend to be obscured by the emphasis on regional trade liberalization that dominates American Pacific economic diplomacy. The interests of US firms are involved in the East Asian area because, on present indications, most of the oligopoly power gained there will be Japanese. This observation concerns large American international enterprises, but there are significant numbers of small- and medium-sized US firms that will be indirectly affected. These firms are deterred from involvement in Pacific trade by high transaction costs, while their counterparts in Japan benefit from the services of the large Japanese general trading companies. High transaction costs also deter entry into regional trade by many firms in the developing East Asian countries — as well as by firms in Canada, Australia, and New Zealand.

Policy interactions between the United States, Japan, and the developing East Asian nations could focus productively on the problems of transaction costs, starting with the recognition of the need for the development of regional marketing infrastructures and of the utility of the services provided by the Japanese general trading companies. Collaboration for the launching of innovative service enterprises could become possible. These, in turn, could help to resolve the difficult problem of oligopoly power, in conjunction with regulatory collaboration at the governmental level.

PROSPECTS

Japan is endeavouring to cope with problems of interdependence while avoiding losses of economic sovereignty and the lessened effectiveness of policy instruments that tend to result from increases in interdependence. To cope with change in the asymmetries of the primary area of interdependence — the relationship with the United States — there is evidently a tendency in Japan to impose compensating change in the more unequal secondary interdependencies with developing East Asian states while strengthening domestic structures for more intensely competitive involvement in the global economy. General awareness of the problems posed in relations with the US is probably stimulating vigorous managerial entrepreneurship for such involvement and at the same time causing managements to assign greater importance to their active links with their home economic bureaucracy, especially the Ministry of International Trade and Industry.

A crisis in US-Japan relations has been predicted because frustrations on the American side, aggravated by perceived delays in Japanese accommodation, are expected to cause an escalating sequence of hostile interactions in which strong resentments will narrow perceptions of mutual interest and available choices. Pervasive economic nationalism in the large Japanese policy communities, together with culturally based restraints on leadership in those communities, may well prevent the adoption of sufficiently conciliatory initiatives. In the US, strong protectionist demands from Congress may oblige the administration to adopt drastic trade restrictions under pressure to achieve short-term results. Japanese investors could then reduce lending to the United States, thus contributing to increases in American interest rates and to further American stock market volatility. With increasing stresses in the US economy, more retaliatory trade restrictions against Japan could follow, especially because of intensified Congressional pressures (Packard 1987/8).

For Japanese managements and policy-makers it is clearly important to accelerate the transition from exporting to manufacturing within the US economy so that the trade imbalance will be substantially reduced before Congressional leverage on the US administration becomes much greater. This could entail less production and employment in Japan, but not if there were major increases in exports to other areas, which could become possible if wide-ranging economic cooperation began with the ASEAN countries and the Northeast Asian NICs. For American firms serving primarily their home market, increased Japanese competition would rapidly become a major challenge and could be expected to arouse interest in building stronger American trade and industry associations for mutual assistance and more effective lobbying. More harmonious absorption of the Japanese manufacturing presence, however, would be possible if American business organizations were to build up very active relationships with Japanese peak economic associations for collaborative planning. This possibility deserves emphasis because it could open the way for complementary inputs into policy processes on each side.

Since ASEAN firms, and those in South Korea and Taiwan, must reckon with intensified Japanese and American competition in their own and regional markets, they have reasons for seeking stronger ties with their own administrations to encourage the adoption of more supportive policies. These are likely to be forthcoming, especially in South Korea and Taiwan, because of administrative recognition of the need to strengthen domestic government-business links for competitive involvement in a more difficult regional economic environment. Despite the potential conflict at times with efforts to strengthen domestic economic structures, more permissive policies toward foreign direct investment may well be adopted in the ASEAN states that are less advanced in their strategies for export-oriented industrialization. These states — Indonesia, Thailand, and the Philippines — are more vulnerable to the currently unfavourable trends in primary product markets and to American protectionism directed at Third World exports of low technology manufactures.

Difficulties in the promotion of exports to the United States, and also to Japan, may well cause the ASEAN members to increase the presently slow pace of trade liberalization within their organization. This could stimulate trade-induced growth, facilitate the development of collective bargaining strength, and attract more foreign direct investment. Japan's interest in strengthening economic ties with the member states would become very active, and depending on the evolution of its relations with ASEAN members, this interest could have considerable influence on the course of intra-ASEAN trade liberalization and on ASEAN's external economic relations. Over time, the Japanese economic presence in ASEAN will tend to become stronger even if there is little progress toward market integration within that association. The longer such integration is delayed, the greater will be the probability that it will evolve along lines compatible with Japanese interests and that this will be reflected in what would tend to become a common ASEAN foreign economic policy.

If there is deepening economic integration within ASEAN despite the differences in levels of development that have hindered such a process, it will have significant implications for the growth of Pacific regional economic cooperation. Because of its strengthened connections with ASEAN, Japan would be much better placed than at present to play a major role in negotiating the terms of collaboration in that larger setting. That would be reflected in the evolving policy environment of the region and the expanding activities of Japanese firms. Those activities, meanwhile, would have a widening range of effects on national economic structures and the growth of interdependencies between those structures throughout the region. Enlightened long-range Japanese planning could ensure that this expanded regional involvement would be a process of integrative cooperation, seeking partnerships in growth, which would aid regional community formation instead of expressing a narrowly neo-mercantilist orientation which would have seriously alienating effects.

NOTES

1 Hong Kong is often listed with this group, but it is a British colony and will come under Chinese Communist control in 1997.

2 See references to fiscal and monetary policies in Patrick and Tachi (1986) and discussion of the larger context in IIE (1987).

3 On cultural factors operating in the Japanese context, see Dore (1986) and Aoki (1987).

4 See report of new consumption-oriented policy shift in the *New York Times*, 23 December 1987: 24.

REFERENCES

Aoki, Masahiko (1987). "Incentives to Share Knowledge and Risk: An Aspect of Japanese Industrial Organization." In Stefan Hedlund, ed., *Incentives and Economic Systems*: 57–78. New York: New York University Press

Bergstrom, C. Fred, and William R. Cline (1987). *The United States-Japan Economic Problem*. Rev. ed. Washington, DC: Institute for International Economics

Casson, Mark et al. (1986). *Multinationals and World Trade*. London: Allen and Unwin

Dore, Ronald (1986). *Flexible Rigidities*. Stanford: Standford University Press

Doz, Yves (1986). *Strategic Management in Multinational Companies*. Elmsford, NY: Pergamon Press

Dunning, John H., ed. (1985). *Multinational Enterprises, Economic Structure, and International Competitiveness*. New York: Wiley

Institute for International Economics (IIE) (1987). *Resolving the Global Economic Crisis*. Special Report 6. Washington, DC

Japan Institute for Social and Economic Affairs (1987). *Japan 1987*. Tokyo

Kojima, Kiyoshi, and Terutomo Ozawa (1984). *Japan's General Trading Companies*. Paris: OECD

Kraus, Willy, and Wilfried Lutkenhorst (1986). *The Economic Development of the Pacific Basin*. New York: St. Martin's Press

McCraw, Thomas K., ed. (1986). *America versus Japan*. Boston: Harvard Business School Press

Packard, George R. (1987/8). "The Coming US-Japan Crisis." *Foreign Affairs* 66(2):348–67

Patrick, Hugh, ed. (1986). *Japan's High Technology Industries*. Seattle: University of Washington Press

Patrick, Hugh T., and Ryuichiro Tachi, eds. (1986). *Japan and the United States Today*. New York: Center on Japanese Economy and Business, Columbia University

Pugel, Thomas A., and Robert G. Hawkins, eds. (1986). *Fragile Interdependence*. Lexington, MA: D.C. Heath

Schmiegelow, Michele (1985). "Cutting across Doctrines: Positive Adjustment in Japan." *International Organization* 32(2):261–96

US Chamber of Commerce (1987). *The ASEAN-U.S. Economic Relationship: Overcoming Barriers to Business Cooperation*. Washington, DC

United Nations Economic Commission for Asia and the Pacific (UNECAP) (1983). *ASEAN and Pacific Economic Cooperation*. Bangkok

Zysman, John (1983). *Governments, Markets and Growth*. Ithaca: Cornell University Press

CHAPTER SEVEN

Trade Policy in the Asia-Pacific Region: A United-States-Japan Comparison

Alan M. Rugman and Alain Verbeke

INTRODUCTION

The methods by which nations can shape industrial policy have been at the forefront of recent work on Asia-Pacific relations. The economic success of Japan in the postwar period has led many other nations to attempt to emulate its perceived policy of state support for industry and trade. Even in the United States, influential voices have articulated the need for a new view of international economic policy; one in which the United States uses its size to turn the terms of trade in its favour by the use of import protection and export subsidies.

In this chapter we develop a new conceptual framework to contrast Japanese and American attempts to formulate and implement such trade-oriented industrial policies. We demonstrate that the Japanese have been successful in reshaping their comparative advantage by the use of effective administrative structures at the national level. We find evidence of a policy structure that enhances the successful implementation of Japanese industrial strategies, since centralized policy choices are possible. In the United States, however, we have observed the recent escalation of decentralized administered protection, rather than the implementation of efficient national trade policies. The nature and extent of this new type of US-administered protection is considered and the failure of US structure and trade strategy is contrasted with the Japanese experience.

Examples and case histories are used, such as American attempts to protect the steel, textile, agricultural, and semiconductor industries and the Japanese policies to promote exports of autos, consumer electronics, and related high technology products. The existence of transaction costs in the execution of US trade policy in these areas is noted and contrasted with the methods by which Japan has dealt with the costs of policy administration. Implications are drawn out for both trade policy and the strategic planning of corporations. Finally, the interaction of such business-government relations is examined and lessons are drawn for the formulation of trade policy in other countries of the Asia-Pacific region.

THE ASSESSMENT OF INTERNATIONAL TRADE STRATEGIES

The new theoretical framework developed in this paper allows us to compare American and Japanese trade policies and to contrast their distinctive characteristics. Figure 11 is a conceptual assessment of the international trade strategies of governments according to their free trade or non-free trade orientation and the perceived degree of their success. The horizontal axis deals with the nature of trade strategy and the vertical axis with the "perceived" outcomes of these strategies.

A free trade strategy means that government policy is to have the international flows in goods and services determined by the economic principles of comparative advantage. In this situation, the nation's "natural" country specific advantages (CSAs) will influence trade patterns. The CSAs capture the factor endowments of a nation, basically the variables in its aggregate production function (Rugman 1981).

With a non-free trade orientation, the government shapes comparative advantage in its favour, or at least it attempts to do so. It can do this by shifting its terms of trade (if it is a large country like Japan or the United States). In this case, unnatural market imperfections are created in favour of national firms, which give them a competitive edge vis-à-vis foreign rivals (Rugman and Verbeke 1987a). To some extent, every country in the world grants certain trading advantages to domestic firms. Methods include special export-financing arrangements, tax rebates, preferential government procurement, and so on.

In Figure 11 it is the degree of government support that matters. The main question is whether government has a central policy to guide and direct international trade or to let the market system determine trade flows. Turning to the vertical axis, the issue of policy effectiveness is a complex one. The concept of effectiveness used here is the perception of trade policy success, which is a normative assessment. This approach can be contrasted to the narrower concept of economic efficiency whereby, from a global perspective, a free trade environment is always the most efficient (first best). Also, in terms of

Figure 11 Assessing International Trade Strategies

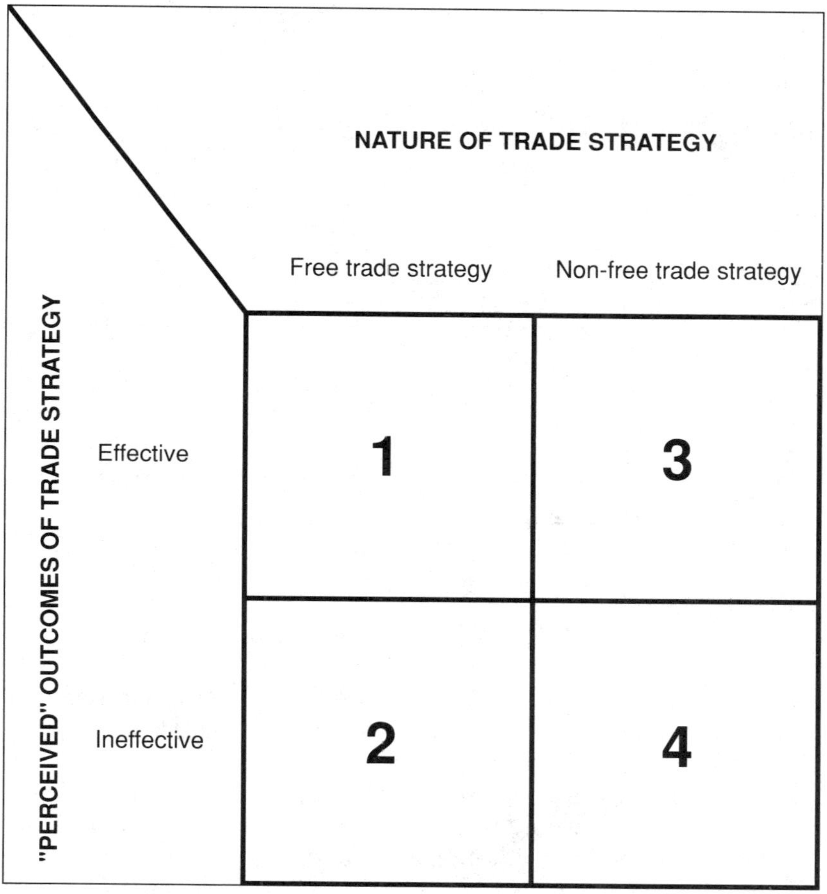

economic efficiency from a national perspective, it may be efficient to pursue a non-free trade strategy in particular cases, such as the monopoly tariff case; the externalities and market imperfections case; the infant industry protection case; the profit-shifting case; and the "compensating for unnatural market imperfections" case. However, in the next section it will be argued that even from a national perspective, such non-free trade strategies will only be efficient if specific conditions are fulfilled.

Table 58
American and Japanese Trade Balances
(with all nations) (US $ billions)

	US	Japan
1975	2.2	–2.0
1980	–36.2	–10.9
1981	–39.6	8.6
1982	–42.6	6.9
1983	–69.4	20.6
1984	–123.3	33.5
1985	–143.8	39.6

Source: McCraw 1986: 31

Table 59
American Trade Deficit with Japan (US $ billions)

1975	–1.6
1980	–10.4
1981	–15.8
1982	–17.0
1983	–21.1
1984	–37.0
1985	–40.7

Source: McCraw 1986: 33

THE US TRADE DEFICIT

The trade balance of a country is often used to assess the effectiveness of a nation's trade policy (McCraw 1986). If the American and Japanese trade balances (with all nations) and their bilateral balances are used as a proxy for the success of the trade strategies of the United States and Japan, it would then appear that Japan has developed an enormous competitive advantage vis-à-vis the United States, as shown in Tables 58 and 59.

McCraw (1986) and his colleagues at the Harvard Business School have argued that Tables 58 and 59 suggest that the United States, which consistently had a trade surplus before 1971 but accumulated high trade deficits in the recent past, now has an ineffective trade strategy. In contrast, the Japanese surpluses indicate a highly effective trade strategy that has allowed Japanese firms to develop into global competitors and to penetrate foreign markets through exports

The US trade balance is actually influenced by many factors, including tax policies, government spending, social and industrial policies, and macroeconomic factors, all of which constitute the elements in a nation's set of CSAs. Moreover, the strength of the firm specific advantages (FSAs) of the companies located in the nation and their choices of entry mode in foreign countries also have a profound influence on the trade balance, as does industry structure in general.

Internalization theory suggests that unnatural market imperfections in other nations, such as tariff and nontariff barriers, will increase the relative benefits associated with foreign direct investment as compared with exports (Rugman 1981). While such effects may influence a nation's trade balance, they can hardly be considered to represent "bad" trade policy. International trade policy strategies alone do not constitute the main determining factor in explaining how trade deficits or surpluses evolve over time, although they may directly influence the export performance of domestic firms and/or the volume of imports from other countries.

Moreover, a nation's trade balance is only one element in its balance of payments. A trade deficit can be compensated for by a surplus on the capital account because of large short- or long-term investment opportunities. Then the trade deficit should not be regarded as the result of an inappropriate trade policy; instead it may reflect macroeconomic factors, such as changes in currency valuations and real interest rates. Hence, if a non-free trade strategy is implemented as a response to the perceived ineffectiveness of a free trade strategy signalled by a trade deficit, the result may well be greater economic inefficiency not only from a global point of view, but also from a national one.

Indeed, it has been demonstrated by Lawrence and Litan (1987) that the US trade deficits merely result from the macroeconomic imbalance between American spending and production, which itself is caused by the government deficit ranging between US $150 billion and US $200 billion. Moreover, the Japanese "portion" of the trade deficit has not increased substantially between 1981 and 1985, so Japanese non-free trade strategies in favour of domestic firms cannot be held responsible for the rising import volume of the United States.

CLASSIFICATION OF NON-FREE TRADE STRATEGIES

Figure 12 is used to suggest that two broad types of non-free trade strategies exist, depending upon their "FSA-developing" or "sheltering" orientation. An FSA-developing non-free trade strategy has as its prime long-run purpose to strengthen the FSAs of the firms involved and to maintain or improve their competitive position vis-à-vis foreign rivals on the basis of their economic efficiency. In contrast, a sheltering strategy does not aim at stimulating the development of strong

Figure 12 A Classification of Non-Free Trade Strategies

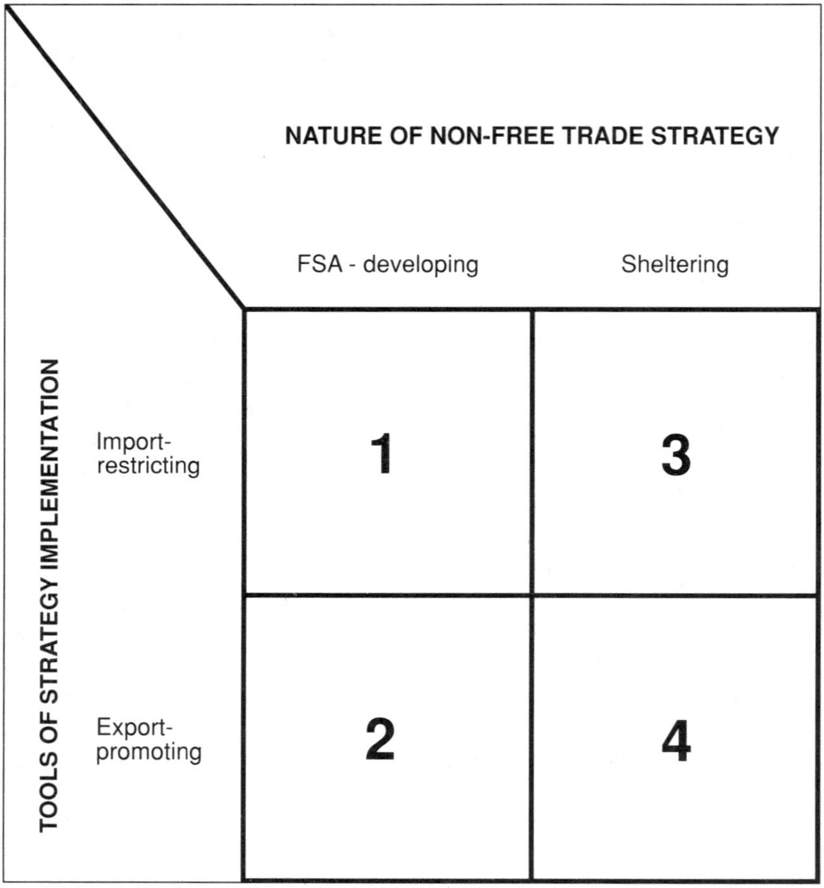

FSAs; protection against foreign rivals is granted. This is done first where shelter in itself is the ultimate objective (perhaps as a response to lobbying pressures) and, second, when the satisfaction of social goals (such as maintaining inefficient employment levels in declining industries) is of major importance.

Two types of "tools" can be used to implement either of these non-free trade strategies: import-restricting tools and export-promoting ones. Both types may be complementary components of a nation's trade strategy. Moreover, short-term import-restricting measures may well have long-term export-promoting consequences if domestic firms are able to develop strong FSAs in the absence of foreign competition in the domestic market. This leads to the issue of whether non-free trade strategies are efficient from the national point of view.

Sheltering strategies are always inefficient in the long run. They result from the pursuit of non-economic objectives and the influence exerted by specific pressure groups on government, reflecting the sensitivity of government decision-makers to the demands of clientele groups. High sensitivity to such groups can be explained by the utility-maximizing considerations of politicians and bureaucrats (Rugman and Verbeke 1987b).

In contrast, FSA-developing strategies may be efficient if the long-term benefits of government intervention are higher than their short-term costs. Such strategies are often difficult to implement successfully. In the infant industry case, a fast-growing internal market and active competition between domestic firms are some of the requirements for achieving economic efficiency (Brander 1987; and Doz 1986).

In the profit-shifting case (Brander and Spencer 1985; Brander 1986, 1987), subsidies and other advantages may be granted by government to domestic firms to generate strategic effects (such as deterring entry by potential foreign competitors) or dynamic scale economies (learning curve effects). International competition is required to stimulate cost efficiency and innovative behaviour on the part of the domestic firms.

Efficient FSA-developing strategies are characterized by selectivity in the choice of firms and industries to which advantages will be granted. Moreover, a policy structure must exist, suitable to implement government strategies, without being dominated by the narrow interests of pressure groups. These two elements are especially important in the case of compensating for unnatural market imperfections. Here, a government that may be in favour of free trade can adopt a non-free trade strategy because of unnatural market imperfections, such as trade barriers or export subsidies, imposed by foreign nations. As a result, domestic industries face unfair competition from the treasuries of foreign governments. Through countervailing actions, such as trade remedy laws, this unfair competition can be restricted (Hufbauer and Erb 1985).

The efficient implementation of such trade remedy laws then requires a policy structure able to discriminate between domestic firms seeking government intervention on the basis of economic efficiency grounds and those merely interested in acquiring shelter. If

Figure 13 Potential Effectiveness of Non-Free Trade Strategies

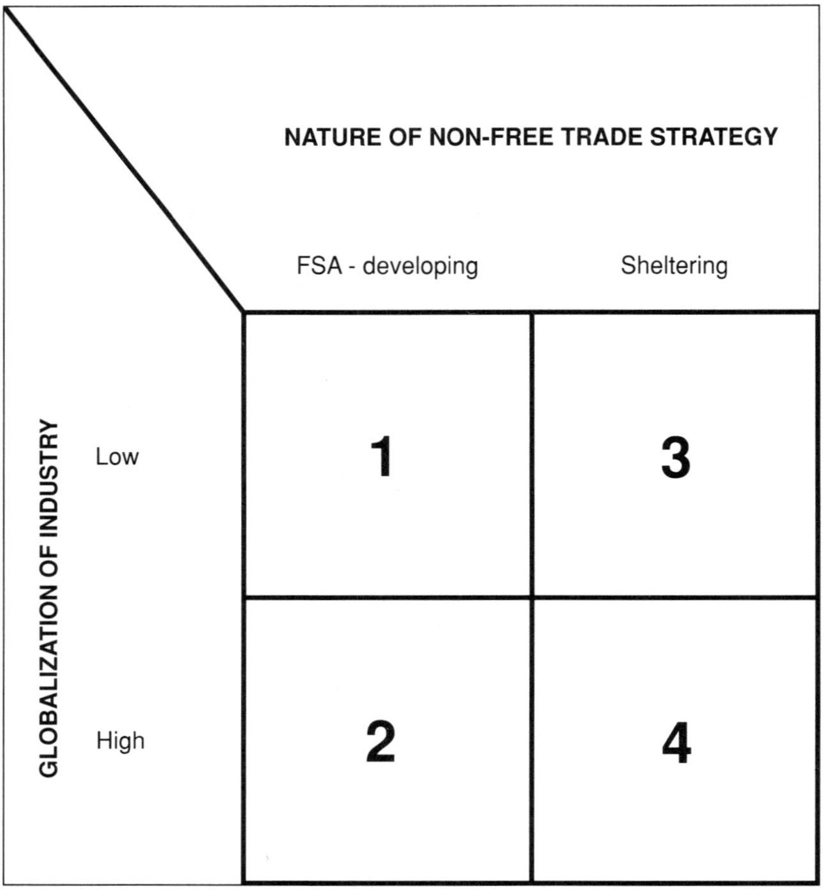

advantages are granted to domestic firms, the chances of achieving long-run economic efficiency may be increased by imposing performance requirements (such as productivity improvements) and by making government intervention self-liquidating.

Figure 13 is useful in predicting the potential (in)effectiveness of FSA-developing and sheltering strategies, based upon the degree of globalization of the affected industries. It is hypothesized that an FSA-developing strategy may potentially have positive long-run trade balance effects, irrespective of the level of globalization of industries. A lower level of global competition will obviously increase potential effectiveness, since domestic firms will not be confronted with global competitors in the international environment after having developed strong FSAs. In contrast, a sheltering strategy, which is always inefficient, can only be "effective" in the long run, as measured by the trade balance, in the absence of global competition.

There are six main reasons why such a strategy is bound to fail in the long run in the presence of global competition. First, if the main competitive advantage of a firm is not based on overall cost competitiveness, product differentiation, or focus (Porter 1980) but on protection, the development of additional inefficiency in resource allocation and production can be expected, in the spirit of Leibenstein (1976), as the firm will be (partly) sheltered from pressures exerted by market forces. In the long run, the chances of competing successfully in the international environment with global competitors are reduced. This situation can lead to negative trade balance effects in contrast to the case in which government measures would help the firm to develop its FSAs.

Second, if government only grants shelter to firms on the condition that they will comply with social objectives such as maintaining high (inefficient) employment levels and production capacities or increasing income levels in underdeveloped regions, then a new source of microeconomic inefficiency will be created, again with negative long-run trade balance effects.

Third, if inefficiency in resource allocation and production becomes too high as compared with foreign competitors, the shelter provided by governmental protection mechanisms may still be insufficient to guarantee the survival of the firm in the long run, especially if a large part of its production is exported. In this case, exit may become inevitable.

Fourth, the advantages granted by government may depend upon precarious political circumstances, such as foreign policy options. The termination of those advantages could then jeopardize the firm's survival and lead to exit, especially if these advantages constituted the firm's main source of strength vis-à-vis foreign competition.

Fifth, imposing trade barriers on foreign competitors may result in retaliation by foreign governments with negative trade balance outcomes.

Sixth, if the products of sheltered industries (for example, steel) are themselves used in downstream global industries (for example, automobiles), then the international competitiveness and trade balance performance of the processing industry may be negatively affected.

This is especially true if shelter is provided through trade barriers against cheap foreign imports.

US TRADE POLICY

In this section, the recent evolution of American and Japanese trade policies will be contrasted using the theoretical framework developed above. The United States has traditionally pursued a free trade strategy. Trade policy implementation was delegated to a technical track by Congress in 1934 in order to shift the responsibility for trade policy measures to a forum in which no interest bias would exist in favour of protectionism. In this sense, Congress insulated itself from its own tendency to subvert national free trade goals to which most members of Congress agreed (Destler 1986; Finger et al. 1982). The 1934 Reciprocal Trade Act allowed the executive branch of government to negotiate reciprocal tariff reductions up to 50 per cent of existing levels with other nations.

After World War II, the American free trade strategy became even more predominant. Two major principles of trade strategy were formulated. The first one suggested that international political interests should dominate trade issues. The second one implied that free trade would, in the long run, generate the most effective economic results for the United States (Quadrant 1 of Figure 11).

There were a number of "exceptions" to this strategy. First, all presidents since Eisenhower have protected industries with high lobbying power, such as textiles, steel, and footwear. In these cases, sheltering strategies were implemented using import-restricting tools. Secondly, limited export-promoting incentives were provided to American firms, such as American Export-Import Bank financing and tax advantages. These partly compensated for sometimes much larger incentives granted by other nations to their firms. In these cases, FSA-developing strategies were used.

Within the executive branch, however, the possibilities of implementing sheltering strategies were limited, since protectionist views in one department (such as Commerce or Labor) would be confronted with the free trade preferences of other departments (usually Treasury and State). The leading role performed by the United States in the past seven GATT rounds demonstrates, however, that an overall executive branch preference existed for free trade and for the elimination of international trade barriers.

Today, trade policy is again the prerogative of Congress. The perception by Congress that free trade strategies resulted in major negative effects for a number of American industries affected by international rivalry (a perceived shift from Quadrant 1 to Quadrant 2 in Figure 11) led to the quasi-protectionist Trade Acts of 1974, 1979, and 1984 (an intended shift to Quadrant 3 in Figure 11).

The 1974 act introduced a number of specific non-free trade elements in US trade law. First, it increased the power of the International Trade Commission vis-à-vis the president, who has traditionally been in favour of free trade because of broader international diplomatic and political objectives. Second, Congress limited the power of the president to reduce nontariff barriers, since each such agreement required a majority vote of Congress.

The Trade Act of 1979 and the Trade and Tariff Act of 1984 were designed to change the implementation of US trade policy substantially. In both cases the intent of Congress was to move towards Quadrant 3 of Figure 11 and to allow American producers to be protected against alleged illegal dumping and foreign export subsidies. Hence, it was argued that unnatural market imperfections introduced by foreign nations should be "corrected" through the use of an American non-free trade strategy in severely affected sectors. The 1979 Trade Act shifted power to administer dumping and countervailing duty cases from the liberal Treasury Department to the Commerce Department. The act also contained restrictions limiting the power of the executive branch in trade policy implementation. The 1984 act also encouraged the president to engage in retaliation against unfair foreign competition, and the International Trade Commission was asked by Congress to use broader criteria when determining the eligibility of an industry for import relief.

These three consecutive changes in US trade policy shifted part of the power to implement trade policy from the executive branch to private industry and labour organizations, and it became much easier to demand the implementation of protectionist measures. However, some observers, such as Yoffie (1986:44), would suggest that the intended shift towards Quadrant 3 is nothing more than a "secondary" strategy, since free trade goals would still guide trade policy in many areas. Such a view can be documented by the fact that Presidents Ford, Carter, and Reagan have rejected the same percentage of "escape clause" and other general petitions as former presidents, although the number of industries filing petitions for import relief went up from forty in 1977 to almost two hundred in 1984.

In reality, a major shift is presently going on from a free trade strategy towards a non-free trade strategy. Today any US firm or industry can file a petition against alleged unfair foreign imports and try to obtain countervailing actions. Moreover, the criteria for determining what constitutes a countervailing foreign subsidy have been broadened as a result of the softwood lumber case of October 1986 (Rugman and Porteous 1988). As a result, it will become much easier for American firms with weak FSAs to raise the transaction costs for their foreign competitors through the use of US administered protection.

Figure 12 identifies the characteristics of the current US non-free trade strategy. The present protectionist strategy of the United States, as reflected in the institutional framework available to US producers to petition against alleged "unfair" imports, is not a "secondary" strategy at all. This would only be implemented in cases of unfair foreign competition when the "primary" free trade strategy led to undesirable outcomes for the nation.

If the present non-free trade strategy were really a secondary strategy, its orientation would be FSA-developing. In that case, alleged foreign subsidies and dumping practices would be compared with "advantages" given to US producers. Moreover, it would require selectivity in granting protection; the US government would discriminate between industries and firms that will remain or become internationally competitive in the long run and those that have no future in a more global envionment. In this case, the temporary imposition of a CSA (such as protection against unfair imports) would build upon the FSAs of the firms involved or allow them to develop strong FSAs (Quadrants 1 and 2 of Figure 12). In the case of a sheltering strategy, however, regulations imposed by government in favour of domestic firms may merely compensate for the absence of strong FSAs.

The non-free trade strategy as developed by the United States has a sheltering orientation without any effort at serious selectivity. This was discussed in Rugman and Verbeke (1987c), where two countervailing actions against Canadian imports were studied (the Fresh Atlantic Groundfish case and the Softwood Lumber case). Morever, little has been done to provide special assistance to facilitate American exports; the United States has provided few tax advantages, little preferential export-financing, and only a small number of export subsidies for non-agricultural and non-defence exports. The present emphasis on sheltering through the use of import-restricting policy tools (Quadrant 3 of Figure 12) raises questions about its economic efficiency and potential effectiveness to improve the US trade balance in the long run (see Figure 13).

Porter (1986) has observed an increased globalization across industries. In this case, the overall position of the United States in Figure 13 is located in the fourth quadrant. In terms of Figure 11, this would imply that the United States is now shifting to the fourth quadrant instead of the third. Although jobs may be saved temporarily in such industries as steel and lumber, at a high cost for the general taxpayer

(Ohmae 1987), the trade balance effectiveness of such measures is questionable. Lawrence and Litan (1987) found that of sixteen major US industries receiving shelter since 1950, only one (the bicycle industry) was characterized by expansion after the elimination of protection. This research is consistent with our theoretical framework.

JAPANESE TRADE POLICY

In contrast to the United States, a non-free trade strategy was successfully implemented in Japan after World War II (Quadrant 3 of Figure 11). In particular, the import of manufactured goods was severely restricted. The Japanese government used an elaborate set of tariffs and nontariff barriers to limit foreign imports. A policy of selective granting of import licences was used by the Ministry of International Trade and Industry (MITI) for raw materials. This non-free trade strategy primarily served long-term FSA-developing purposes (with some exceptions, such as the sheltering strategy in the rice sector), with a gradual elimination of import restrictions.

One of the major industries selected for large-scale development by MITI after World War II was the steel industry. A so-called "industrial rationalization" strategy was implemented in order to assure the development of strong FSAs in the protected steel firms (McCraw and O'Brien 1986). Productivity improvements in the different firms became the main criterion used by MITI to allocate capacity expansion "rights." Such an FSA-developing strategy was, of course, conducive to the creation of a strong internationally competitive steel industry, since it stimulated intense domestic competition.

Similarly, Japanese industrial policies in the automobile sector were more "market promotional" than sheltering-oriented (Doz 1986; Tyson 1987). The automobile industry case also demonstrates that MITI could not engage in autonomous central planning. In 1961 MITI made a proposal to organize passenger car manufacturers into three specialized groups (regular passenger cars, minicars, and specialty cars) in order to improve scale economies. This proposal was rejected by the industry and domestic competition continued.

In other industries, MITI often set target dates when limitations on foreign competition would be abolished. In this way, Japanese firms were stimulated to adopt the most recent technological innovations in order to improve their competitiveness against foreign rivals after the elimination of Japanese trade barriers. Hence, import restrictions were merely a tool to encourage the development of strong FSAs, especially in manufacturing industries where dynamic scale economies were a prerequisite for international competitiveness.

During the 1970s and 1980s many of the previously dominant import-restricting tools of the non-free trade strategy have been eliminated. Although nontariff trade barriers still exist in many sectors, the average tariffs on industrial and mining products entering Japan were lower than American tariffs in 1982, and quantitative restrictions on imports existed for only five manufactured products (Yoffie 1986: 46). The Japanese government has also selectively eliminated import barriers faster than most other developed countries for products in which it chose not to engage in FSA-developing strategies.

As to export-promoting tools, these have also been reduced in comparison to the 1950s and 1960s, when numerous advantages were granted to Japanese firms with international activities. These included tax advantages, preferential financing, export insurance through MITI, and commercial bank credits at low interest rates. While export incentives remain extremely important, all special tax advantages had shifted to domestic projects by 1975, since the government perceived the existing FSAs of Japanese firms to be strong enough to compete internationally.

A related element is that this FSA-developing strategy could be successfully implemented only as a result of centralized coordination and choice, especially by MITI, which coordinated Japanese trade strategy in the postwar period. Japanese trade strategy forms an integrated part of an FSA-developing industrial policy (Morici 1984). MITI does not engage in centralized strategic trade planning, but it has a close working relationship with private business (through groups such as Keidanren) and other ministries such as the Ministry of Finance. Selectivity in protection is possible because "advantages" will only be given to specific firms and industries after extensive consultation with the private sector's industrial and trade organizations.

This structure is completely different from the American situation, whereby direct lobbying by individual firms or specific interest groups is much stronger (Ouchi 1984). In Figures 12 and 13, Japanese industries are situated in the first and second quadrants with FSA-developing strategies, which explains the overall effectiveness of Japanese trade policy. The rise of the Japanese computer and semiconductor industry after 1955 is perhaps the classic example of an FSA-developing strategy. Here, infant industry protection has led to the development of strong internationally competitive firms (ibid.) In generalizing about Japanese trade policy, Abegglen and Stalk (1985) have emphasized that, in most cases, no national champions are picked out by government; it is the marketplace that determines the "winning" and "losing" firms.

TRADE POLICY FOR THE NICs

The lessons for other Pacific Basin nations from the models developed here are to beware of the difficulties of policy implementation. The newly industrialized countries (NICs) like South Korea, Taiwan, Hong Kong, and Singapore are relatively small open trading economies. They do not have the large internal markets of either Japan or the United States, so a policy of export promotion is required. However, owing to the new US policy of administered protection, direct export subsidies and infant industry protection by the NICs are dangerous policies to pursue. Therefore the NICs must accept the discipline of operating a free trade strategy in Quadrant 1 of Figure 11, and be careful not to become trapped with the ineffective trade policy outcome of Quadrant 2. Another Pacific country, Canada, has been in pursuit of these types of open trade strategies in recent years.

The NICs can achieve their trade objectives, like Canada, by operating in Quadrant 2 of Figure 12; namely, an FSA-developing export-promotion strategy. Then, if their exports are in global industries, they will be equipped to survive in Quadrant 2 of Figure 13. All of this is easier said than done, but the implementation of successful trade strategies for the smaller partners in the Asia-Pacific region must always come as a result of understanding the policies of the two giants, Japan and the United States.

CONCLUSIONS AND NORMATIVE IMPLICATIONS

What are the normative implications of the above analysis for the United States? The first implication is that the American trade balance is not a good indicator of economic efficiency. Hence, the United States should not attempt to redesign its policy towards a non-free trade strategy. The administrative heritage of public policy structures and private sector views on the role of government is not conducive to the successful implementation of a Japanese-style, centrally coordinated, non-free trade strategy. Instead, selectivity is required, in the sense that a non-free trade strategy should only be conducted where it is clear that free trade policies have failed (perhaps because of protectionism of other countries). A non-free trade strategy should remain a secondary strategy, and if it is pursued, it should be a microefficiency oriented one. Protection should not be granted to industries whose survival may become completely dependent upon shelter.

The main problem associated with the present system of US decentralized administrative protection is that it provides shelter. It does not permit discrimination between protecting potential growth sectors and sunset industries that face an inevitable decline because of weakening FSAs. The escalating number of countervailing duty and antidumping cases suggests that a non-free trade strategy has become the new trade strategy of the United States. In turn, these nontariff barriers to trade, which are preventing foreign entry to the American market, would explain the enormous influx of foreign direct investment into the United States.

REFERENCES

Abegglen, James C., and George Stalk, Jr. (1985). *Kaisha: The Japanese Company*. New York: Basic Books

Brander, James A. (1986). "Rationales for Strategic Trade and Industrial Policy." In Paul Krugman, ed., *Strategic Trade Policy and the New International Economics;* 23–46. Cambridge, MA: MIT Press

Brander, James A. (1987). "Shaping Comparative Advantage: Trade Policy, Industrial Policy and Economic Performance." In Richard G. Lipsey and Wendy Dobson, eds., *Shaping Comparative Advantage:* 1–56. Toronto: C.D. Howe Institute

Brander, James A., and Barbara J. Spencer (1985). "Export Subsidies and International Market Share Rivalry." *Journal of International Economics* 18: 83–100

Destler, I.M. (1986). *American Trade Politics: System under Stress*. Washington, DC: Institute for International Economics

Doz, Yves L. (1986). "Government Policies and Global Industries." In Michael E. Porter, ed., *Competition in Global Industries*: 225–66. Boston, MA: Harvard Business School Press

Finger, J.M., H. Keith Hall, and Douglas Nelson (1982). "The Political Economy of Administered Protection." *American Economic Review* 72(3): 452–56

Hufbauer, Gary, and Joanna Erb (1985). *Subsidies in International Trade*. Cambridge, MA: MIT Press

Lawrence, Robert Z., and Robert E. Litan (1987). "Why Protectionism Doesn't Pay." *Harvard Business Review* 87(3): 6067

Leibenstein, M. (1976). *Beyond Economic Man*. Cambridge, MA: Harvard University Press

McCraw, Thomas K. (1986). "From Partners to Competitors: An Overview of the Period since World War II." In Thomas K. McCraw, ed., *America versus Japan*:1–34. Boston: Harvard Business School Press

—, and Patricia A. O'Brien (1986). "Production and Distribution: Competition Policy and Industry Structure." In Thomas K. McCraw, ed., *America versus Japan*:77–116. Boston: Harvard Business School Press

Morici, Peter (1984). *The Global Competitive Struggle: Challenges to the United States and Canada*. Toronto: C.D. Howe Institute

Ohmae, K. (1987). *Beyond National Borders*. Homewood, IL: Dow Jones: Irwin

Ouchi, William G. (1984). *The M-Form Society*. Reading, MA: Addison-Wesley

Porter, Michael E. (1980). *Competitive Strategy: Techniques for Analyzing Industries and Competitors*. New York: Free Press, Macmillan

Rugman, Alan M. (1981). *Inside the Multinationals: The Economics of Internal Markets*. London: Croom Helm, New York: Columbia University Press

Rugman, Alan M., and Andrew Anderson (1987a). *Administered Protection in America*. London: Croom Helm, New York: Methuen

— (1987b). "A Fishy Business: The Abuse of American Trade Law in the Atlantic Groundfish Case of 1985-1986." *Canadian Public Policy* 13(2): 152-64

Rugman, Alan M., and Alain Verbeke (1987a). "Strategic Management and Trade Policy." Dalhousie Discussion Papers in International Business, no. 69, Dalhousie University

— (1987b) "Bilateral Trade Liberalization and the Strategic Management of Multinational Enterprises." Dalhousie Discussion Papers in International Business, no. 70, Dalhousie University

— (1988c) "American Trade Policy and Corporate Strategy." Mimeo, June

Rugman, Alan M., and Samuel Porteous (1988). "The Softwood Lumber Decision of 1986: Broadening the Nature of U.S. Administered Protection." *Review of International Business Law* 2 (1): 35-58

Tyson, Laura (1987). "Creating Advantage: An Industrial Policy Perspective." In Richard G. Lipsey and Wendy Dobson, eds., *Shaping Comparative Advantage*: 65-82. Toronto: C.D. Howe Institute

Yoffie, David B. (1986). "Protecting World Markets." In Thomas K. McCraw, ed., *America versus Japan: 35-76*. Boston: Harvard Business School Press

CHAPTER EIGHT

Emerging Financial Centres in the Pacific

J. Colin Dodds

INTRODUCTION

The abandonment of gold convertibility in August 1971 by the United States and the demise of the Bretton-Woods system in 1973 with the introduction of a generalized float led to developments in exchange rate theory away from a preoccupation with trade flows as a major determinant towards a portfolio balance approach[1] creating incentives for capital flows. Exchange rates are now presumed to reflect the supply and demand for stocks of assets denominated in different currencies. Domestic fiscal and monetary policies can have an immediate effect on exchange rates, thus highlighting the interplay that exists in the balance of payments between current and capital accounts. The magnitude of capital flows provides challenges for world financial markets. With the end of the Pax Americana epoch (Bacha and Diaz 1982) and with it US hegemony in the world economy, we have witnessed the emergence of other centres of economic power, including the Pacific. The increased globalization and integration of world financial markets that has occurred (see, for example, Stockman 1988; Dodds 1989), and the volatility that continues to exist in them, has brought challenges and opportunities.

This chapter examines the emergence of financial centres in the Pacific by focusing on the requirements for a domestic and international centre and the emergence of Tokyo as a primary centre.

THE PACIFIC REGION AND THE CRITERIA FOR DEVELOPMENT OF FINANCIAL SYSTEMS

Japan has been successful in challenging the economic supremacy of North America and now plays a pivotal role in the economic success of the Pacific region, particularly in the Newly Industrializing Countries (NICs) and the ASEAN nations. There are some themes that run through the development and successes of these countries. Generally, they are regarded as export-oriented and outward-looking. What has emerged over the post-1973 period is that their economies have, for example, been able to withstand the economic turbulence with "sound" macroeconomic policy-making. Skully (1982) found them to be a model of successful monetization and financial deepening, with governments typically playing a key role. Their financial systems, important building blocks to their economic success, have been underdeveloped and largely closed, though increasingly there are relaxations in controls as well as rapid changes in the provision of financial markets.

Intra-regional trade and investment flows have led to greater integration of trade, with Japan playing a pivotal role in the shifting process of regional economic development.[2] The NICs in particular have been successful in building up balance-of-payment surpluses and foreign exchange reserves in response to changing factor availability and prices in the region that have had an impact on comparative advantage: the appreciation of the yen and the rise of US protectionism, principally against Japan. These countries have utilized exchange rate policy to peg to the dollar, in the case of Hong Kong, or appreciate only marginally against it. A float has not been a policy option (World Bank 1980), although as the financial systems develop in the region and become more integrated internationally as the normal market forces of arbitrage develop, then a float becomes a more attainable proposition. Certainly the experience of Japan illustrates this.

To understand the emergence of financial centres in the Pacific, let us at the outset examine the nature of domestic and international financial centres. A domestic financial system is made up of a network of financial markets where various types of economic units interact: companies, householders, financial institutions, the government, and, in an open economy, overseas residents. The financial system that has evolved in any particular country will have been molded by the needs of the participants in terms of the financial transactions engaged in, the degree of industrial and economic development, and the degree of state involvement.

Following Zysman (1983), we can recognize three types of systems: (1) a *capital market based* system where resources are allocated by market prices (for example, the United States); (2) a *credit-based* system with government administered prices (for example, Japan, at least prior to 1984); and (3) a *credit-based* system dominated by financial institutions (for example, West Germany).

Financial systems thus differ, though with the deregulation process, major structural changes are occurring within domestic systems. With the increased integration of world financial markets, a tendency to convergence will occur. In consequence, instead of representing a static picture, there is, in the main, a dynamic picture of a system reacting to and being influenced by its environment. Despite the differences that still exist, there is one essential function that all financial systems perform; it is described by Lavington (1932) as the "transfer of value." There are six key aspects[3] in this process without which the modern market economy could not function:

(1) the facilitation of the (immediate) means of payment — in ease and safety so that transactions can be made for goods and services;
(2) the facilitation of the transfer of savings from the surplus units to deficit units — in other words, the lending/borrowing process of new funds — which takes place in *primary* markets;
(3) the facilitation of the transfer of existing assets — real and monetary — among individual economic units via *secondary* markets. These markets, although not present for all financial claims, provide liquidity for lenders. The trend towards *securitization* reinforces the trading of these financial claims;
(4) the provision of markets for risk reduction (for example, forward, futures, options);
(5) the provision of financial services and financial innovations; and
(6) the provision of information.

In both theory and practice these aspects of the process are intertwined.

In developed economies, there are many markets within a financial system. For many developing countries, however, "commercial" banks dominate the sector. Nevertheless, in the ASEAN and Pacific region, the 1970s and 1980s have seen the development of financial institutions (including a wide range of specialized ones) and markets, including money, securities, and foreign exchange. Their evolution is the result of accidental circumstance and diverse causation. To move beyond the stage of being purely "domestic," they have shared common features, and developments in the world economy have brought them closer together — particularly via the technology available — and the competitive pressures have produced a greater uniformity in costs.

Table 60
Four Types of Offshore Financial Centres

Type of Centre	Source of Funds	Uses of Funds
Primary	World-wide	World-wide
Booking	Outside	Outside
Funding	Inside	Inside
Collection	Outside	Outside

Source: Park 1982

Park (1982) provides a typology to examine the relationship of domestic and international financial centres. It is reproduced below as Table 60.

Park's thesis is that the presence of economies of scale and externalities has led to the growth of International Financial Centres (IFCs). These centres, he argues, are playing an important integrated role on a regional and global basis, and he recognizes three distinguishing characteristics: (1) they deal in external currencies, and therefore there is an indirect linkage with the domestic system; (2) there is generally freedom of exchange control and taxes; and (3) primarily these markets are for nonresidents.

For the *Primary* Financial Centre, there will be a greater integration between the domestic and international systems, whereas for *Funding* Centres there will be greater segmentation. However, inevitably the two systems — international and domestic — are intertwined and the existence of an international sector will have a feedback relationship to the development of the country and region as a whole.

But a further set of prerequisites are necessary for the development of IFCs: (1) an openness and outward-looking approach to permit the movement of capital flows and entry of foreign banks and other financial institutions to permit the full spectrum of financial products to be developed. Financial markets can therefore be deeper, more liquid and more efficient; (2) a willingness of residents to hold and use money; (3) a willingness to innovate; (4) economic and political stability; and (5) a depth of knowledge and understanding on the part of the government and population of the needs of financial centres.

Until the 1960s, Hong Kong was the major regional financial centre for Southeast Asia. Its location, near South Korea, Japan, Taiwan, and the Philippines, gave it a locational advantage. Singapore has subsequently emerged as a major challenger, though essentially they are complementary in function, with Singapore acting as a funding centre and Hong Kong very active in other financial activities, including loan syndication.[4] Singapore's growth was based on exporting, and the role and structure of its financial sector was geared towards financing foreign trade. Its emergence as a regional financial centre and a model that other countries seek to emulate has been facilitated by an overlapping time zone advantage with Asia-Pacific centres and Europe, no withholding taxes, conscious government policy[5] (in contrast to Hong Kong), and the development needs of a growing economy. Singapore became the base for the Asian dollar market and the Asian bond market. Singapore has typically attracted offshore funds from outside the region (Europe and the Middle East), passing them to borrowers in the region, particularly the ASEAN countries.

The growth of these two financial centres has increased the efficiency of their own financial markets, but the linkage between domestic development and their role as international financial centres has been limited, partly because of their small geographical size. Nevertheless, their growth has led to better resource allocation across the Pacific region as a whole, at lower cost, and it has generated developments in the financial centres of other countries in the region as the funds are absorbed.

In the past few years, however, the dominance of Hong Kong and Singapore has been challenged with the emergence of Tokyo[6] as *the* financial centre for the region, rivalling New York and London. The growth of Tokyo is likely to be more complementary than competitive in its effect on these two regional centres. However, it has caused a major shift in the global economic balance to the Asia-Pacific region, complementing the growth achieved from that area in manufactured exports.

Up to the early 1980s, Manila had potential as an emerging financial centre[7] because of various steps taken to attract international business. One of its objectives was to provide incentives for the retention of capital in the Philippines. Political uncertainties and the country's large external debt (the 1987 Comprehensive Credit Policy Agreement is only restructuring) now militate against this. Various other emerging centres are possible in the future. Seoul, Taipei, Kuala Lumpur, and Bangkok are all at various stages of development with expanding financial sectors and increasing openness of markets. With stability in their domestic economic management and continued development of their financial institutions, they could develop as funding centres. As yet, however, they do not have all of the prerequisites mentioned earlier.

TOKYO AS A PRIMARY FINANCIAL CENTRE

Until recently, Tokyo would not have qualified as a Primary International Financial Centre on our criteria. Japan had achieved an internationalization of its economic base with a strong foreign trade performance, but its largely controlled and closed financial system — a building block for its economic success — has militated against the internationalization of its financial sector. Earlier the Tokyo financial system was identified as credit-based with strong government direction. This view is confirmed in the following passage from Ishi:

> The government regulation of the financial sector through institutional controls and the strict supervision of interest rates may well lead to an assessment of the Japanese financial system as one that is still undeveloped. One must be careful, however, not to carry this kind of argument too far, for the evolution of the present financial structure has not been a result of any inability to develop a system in which freely fluctuating interest rates determine the allocation of resources. Rather, there has been a conscious and clearly-defined policy on the part of monetary authorities in the construction of the present financial system.... [T]he process of internationalization is worth noting in the recent trends of Japan's financial institutions and market. In the past decade, the Japanese economy itself has been greatly internationalized, reflecting the sharp increase of exports, imports and overseas investments. Thus, Japanese financial institutions have recently made rapid progress in their international businesses and operations.... Today, international banking has become one of the main strategic targets of Japan's major banks.... [T]he operation of foreign banks in Japan has sharply increased in recent years ... [and] since Tokyo is expected to grow as an important international financial market, the operation of foreign banks is likely to increase further. (1982: 120-6)

The substance of this quotation, written about 1980-1, only hints at the emergence of Tokyo, though the strategic objective is clear. The Japanese financial sector was isolated with the limited use of yen to non-residents and insulated in its value from the full effects of market forces. The yen could not reflect the emerging strength of the Japanese economy. Investors, both Japanese and foreign, had relatively few yen-denominated instruments to attract them. In September 1982, the rules governing the issuance of yen-denominated securities by non-residents were liberalized, effective January 1983; but even as late as 1984 in Japan, the majority of interest rates were administered or at best determined by negotiations (for example, the issue of Government of Japan securities). However, in 1984, important yen-dollar negotiations were held covering three main areas: internationalization of the yen; access of foreign financial institutions to the Japanese market; and liberalization and deregulation of the domestic financial market.

Since that time, a series of changes in regulations affecting financial markets in Japan has occurred that has not only opened up some of

Table 61
International Bond Markets Issues (US $ billions)

	1983	1984	1985	1986	1987
Total issues	72.0	108.4	164.5	221.5	175.6
US dollar	39.2	68.8	99.4	121.7	62.8
Yen					
Euro	0.3	1.2	6.9	18.2	23.1
foreign	3.7	4.7	5.4	4.4	1.6
total	4.0	5.9	12.3	22.6	24.7
Swiss franc	14.0	13.1	14.9	23.1	24.0
Yen issues as a % of total issues	5.6	5.5	7.5	10.2	14.1

Source: BIS Annual Report, 1987 and 1988

the domestic financial system to foreign penetration, but also, more particularly, led to the establishment of a Euro-yen market. This was an important step in making the yen reflect Japan's position in the world economy. Table 61 details the Euro-yen bond issues by borrower since 1983; and what emerges is a clear increase in yen as a proportion of the total issues. Indeed, by 1987 the yen became the second-largest currency in the market. The increased participation of yen-denominated issues does require some qualification, since roughly 50 per cent have been swapped by issuers into other currencies because of restrictions on long-term borrowing domestically. Indeed, the whole swap market developed rapidly in 1987, only to fade following Black Monday in October 1987.

Japan cannot be regarded as fully participating in the world financial system without changes domestically. However, in the short-term capital market, there is already an emerging yen commercial paper market, but the absence of a treasury bill market limits the growth of the Japanese money market and also places constraints on the open market intervention by the Bank of Japan. The development of the yen-dominated bankers' acceptance market has been slow owing to restrictive procedures. The need for further risk management instruments, such as interest rate futures and currency futures, was recognized in December 1987, when the Financial System Research Council, an advisory body to the Banking Bureau, proposed the establishment of a *universal futures exchange*. The proposal adopted by the Japanese Finance Ministry is for the establishment of currency and short-term interest rate futures only. Nevertheless, the changes that will occur in broadening and deepening of capital markets in Japan will likely be accompanied by changes in regulations aimed at increasing the effi-

Table 62
International Bank Assets by Nationality of Banks*

Parent Country of Bank	December 1985 in US $ Billions	December 1985 % share of total	December 1986 in US $ Billions	December 1986 % share of total	December 1987 in US $ Billions	December 1987 % share total assets
France	244.0	9.0	289.6	8.4	375.5	8.6
Germany	191.2	7.0	270.0	7.8	347.9	7.9
Italy	113.2	4.2	145.1	4.2	185.0	4.2
Japan	707.2	26.1	1120.1	32.4	1552.1	35.4
Switzerland	109.2	4.0	152.0	4.4	196.1	4.5
United Kingdom	192.9	7.1	211.5	6.1	253.9	5.8
United States	590.2	21.7	597.2	17.3	647.6	14.8
Other	566.8	20.9	666.4	19.4	823.2	18.8
Total	2714.8	100.0	3454.0	100.0	4381.3	100.0

*This table shows the international assets that is, the cross-border assets in all currencies plus the foreign currency assets (vis-à-vis local residents) of banking offices located in the following seventeen countries: Austria, Belgium, Luxembourg, Canada, Denmark, Finland (as from the end of 1985), France, Germany, Ireland, Italy, Japan, the Netherlands, Spain, Sweden, Switzerland, the United Kingdom, and the United States (cross-border assets in domestic currency only). The international assets of US banks also include the cross-border assets reported by US bank branches in the Bahamas, the Cayman Islands, Panama, Hong Kong, and Singapore. The international assets in this table are classified according to the nationality of ownership of the reporting banks.

ciency of the system. In the meantime, the Japanese challenge abroad is apparent, since Japan now plays a pivotal role in international financial markets as a borrower, investor, and intermediary.

Table 62 presents comparative data on international bank assets, indicating that Japanese banks had 35.4 per cent of the total. If all cross-border positions between related offices are excluded, then the international assets of Japanese banks would be about three times that of the American banks. Japanese banks are also the largest foreign bank group in London (by size of balance sheet assets) and account for over 35 per cent of the international banking business there. The opening of the Japan Offshore Market in December 1986, in which Japanese banks play the dominant role, has led to a dramatic increase in activity, including that with other financial centres in Asia, particularly Hong Kong and Singapore. Some of this activity has been a rebooking of business to circumvent domestic regulations. The challenge does not end there, since Japanese securities companies, like the banks, play a dominant role, and in 1987 they were lead managers for 39 per cent of Euro-bond issues.

The Uruguay round of GATT negotiations is likely to focus on the service sector. This will lead to further reductions in regulations and controls, permitting the internationalization of many financial centres, including those in the Pacific. To respond to these challenges requires changes in regulation and attitude. In the United States, for example, the Treasury Department has recognized the need for "super banks" to compete more effectively with those of Japan and Europe. Creating them will require amendments to the Glass-Steagall Act of 1934 and the Bank Holding Act of 1956. Changes in these acts would promote the ownership of banks by industrial companies and would remove the separate pillars of a financial system, permitting the bringing together of underwriting and banking activity. This would simply regularize domestically what American banks have been doing internationally.

CONCLUSIONS

The Pacific has emerged as a major economic base in terms of exporting both capital and goods. In this region, Japan is playing a pivotal role as it moves in an evolutionary way with the shifting patterns of trade and investment. With the emergence of Tokyo and the increasing importance of Japanese banks and securities houses, North America and Europe both face a challenge that extends beyond the manufacturing sector to financial services. Japanese banks are already the largest in the world, and the yen is taking on an increasing international function. Both are a reflection of Japan's external account position and the steps taken to open up its financial markets. With the continuation of the process of deregulation in financial markets around the world, which may accelerate with the new GATT round, many financial markets in the ASEAN countries and NICs will become more open. If the "ladder of development" of the traded goods sector is repeated in the financial sector, then Japan will continue to play the dominant role in this area. Banks and other financial institutions from North America and Europe need to adapt to this new level of global competition (Lessard 1986), since they will need to recognize the integration of activities at home and abroad. In a study of Canadian financial institutions in Japan, Wright and Huggett (1987: 36) pointed to the need for banks to work together, something Japanese banks do as a matter of course, and the need to move into "newer creative money and capital market activities."

Just as Japan is seen to have developed a comparative advantage in many industrial sectors, it is quickly developing such an advantage in financial services. This is both a threat and a challenge. If, as some commentators (Kim and Young 1987) predict, we are now in the Pacific Century, then financial institutions from outside of the region wishing to participate will have to meet the challenge as well as the threat to their own domestic markets from Japanese financial institutions.

NOTES

1 The first moves in this were seen in the work of Mundell (1968) and Fleming (1962).
2 See Nemetz (this volume) on the concept of the "Ladder of Development" in the region.
3 Contrasts can be made between this set and those developed by Lee and Vertinsky (this volume).
4 For a discussion of the financial centres of Hong Kong, Singapore, and Manila, see Hewson (1986), and Lee and Vertinsky (this volume).
5 See Singapore's ten-year development plan.
6 For a review of Japan's financial markets, see Horne (1985).
7 For a recent review of some of the financial centres in Southeast Asia, see Skully (1984).

REFERENCES

Bacha, E.L., and C.F. Diaz (1982). "International Financial Intermediation: A Long and Tropical View." *Princeton Essays in International Finance,* no. 157: 33

Bank of England (1983). "Japanese Banks in London." *Quarterly Bulletin,* November: 518–24

BIS (1987). Annual Report of the Bank for International Settlement, June

Dodds, J.C. (1989). "Financial Aspects of Corporate Integration in the Pacific." PAMI Conference, Hawaii. Mimeo

Fleming, J.M. (1962). "Domestic Financial Policies under Fixed and Flexible Exchange Rates." *IMF Staff Papers* 9, September: 369–79

Hewson, John (1986). "The Internationalization of Banking." In Augustine H.H. Tan and Basant Kapur, eds., *Pacific Growth and Financial Interdependence*: 185–204. London: Allen and Unwin

Horne, James (1985). *Japan's Financial Markets*. London: Allen and Unwin

Ishi, H. (1982). "Financial Institutions and Markets in Japan." In M.T. Skully, ed., *Financial Institutions and Markets in the Far East*. New York: St. Martin's Press

Kim, W.C., and P.K. Young (1987). *The Pacific Challenge in International Business*. Ann Arbor: UMI Research Press

Lavington, F. (1932). *The English Capital Market*. London: Methuen

Lessard, D. (1986). "Finance and Global Competition: Exploiting Financial Scope and Coping with Volatile Exchange Rates." In Porter, M., ed., *Compe-*

tition in Global Industries:147–84. Boston: Harvard Business School Press
Mundell, Robert A. (1986). *International Economics*. New York: Macmillan
Park, Y.S. (1982). "The Economics of Offshore Financial Centers." *Columbia Journal of World Business*. Winter: 31–5
Sakakibara, Eisuke (1986). "The Internationalization of Tokyo's Financial Markets." In Augustine H.H. Tan and Basant Kapur, eds., *Pacific Growth and Financial Interdependence*:237–46. London: Allen and Unwin
Skully, M.T., ed. (1982). *Financial Institutions and Markets in the Far East*. New York: St. Martin's Press
— (1984). *Financial Institutions and Markets in South-East Asia*, New York: St. Martin's Press
Stockman, A.C. (1988). "On the Roles of International Financial Markets and Their Relevance for Economic Policy." *Journal of Money, Credit and Banking*. 20(3):531–49
Wright, L.W., and S. Huggett (1987). *A Yen for Profit: Canadian Financial Institutions in Japan*. Montreal: Institute for Research on Public Policy
World Bank (1980). "Exchange Rate Adjustment under Generalized Currency Floating: Comparative Analysis among Developing Countries." Staff paper no. 436
Zysman, J. (1983). *Governments, Markets and Growth: Financial Systems and the Politics of International Change*. Ithaca: Cornell University Press

CHAPTER NINE

Strategic Adjustment of International Financial Centres (IFCs) in Small Economies: A Comparative Study of Hong Kong and Singapore

Kam-Hon Lee and Ilan Vertinsky

INTRODUCTION

"A financial centre is generally defined as a central location where the financial transactions of an area are coordinated and cleared" (Reed 1981: 3). There are several reasons why financial transactions tend to be centralized geographically. Among the most important are: access to information stemming from proximity to rivals, complementary organizations, customers, and markets; the development of specialized technological and economic infrastructures, including markets for production factors and services; economies of density in interinstitutional transaction costs; increased liquidity associated with the development of large and efficient financial markets; specific inducements offered by governments that are not available elsewhere (for example, subsidies, tax and regulatory concessions, and so forth); and economies of scale.

The process of centralization, however, is constrained by some diseconomies that work to limit the geographical scope of a financial centre, at least for some types of transactions. Kindleberger (1974: 10–11) points out that regional centres have the advantage of access to information concerning local players and business customers. But, more importantly, centralization limits face-to-face contacts with primary customers of financial intermediation services. Centralization of financial transactions may also be constrained by national regulatory regimes and other forms of formal and informal discrimination against foreigners and/or foreign institutions.

Several recent developments are changing the economic calculus of the centralization of financial transactions, thus creating both opportunities and threats to the economic health of some of the traditional financial centres of the world. These threats and opportunities are especially pronounced for those financial centres that assumed international pre-eminence without the advantage of a large and stable national economic base. Two important Pacific Rim international financial centres that face the challenge of strategic adjustment and repositioning in international financial markets in this decade are Hong Kong and Singapore. In this chapter, we analyse the alternative strategies chosen in each of these two economies to face the changing environment and present the results and implications of a survey of top bankers in Hong Kong and Singapore with respect to the attributes each city must provide to enhance its position as an international financial centre.

THE CHANGING ENVIRONMENT

The world supply of money grew significantly in the last decade. This growth accelerated recently, reaching an annual rate of 20 per cent during 1985 compared with a rate of 11 per cent in 1981. The expansion of the world money supply was accompanied by a comparable growth in international financial markets. The international bond market, for example, grew from US $5 billion in 1970 to US $168 billion in 1985. Similarly, the Euro-bond market grew to nineteen times its original size during the same period. The trend towards globalization of financial markets is also well reflected in buying trends in equity markets. American investors held US $90 billion of foreign company shares in 1985 as opposed to US $21 billion in 1970, while foreigners held US $90 billion of US company shares in 1985 as opposed to US $36 billion in 1970.

Technological change in information processing and communications has led to greater integration between financial markets in geographically distant locations. Governments have responded to the globalization of financial markets by moving toward deregulation of national financial markets and providing more access to foreigners, thus accelerating the process of globalization (for example, the "big bang" in the UK in 1987). The integration of markets and the opportunities it created have brought about a trend toward around-the-clock operations. The extension of working hours has eroded some traditional time-zone advantages while creating others. A shift (temporary or permanent) toward debt "securitization" and a reduction in the role of traditional intermediaries, most notably banks, has created a stimulus for change in the strategies and management styles of the traditional financial institutions. Finally, the growing interdependence between financial markets and economies and the speed with which geographical financial flow patterns can alter are a source of variability and potential sharp discontinuities. (The size and speed of changing financial flow patterns make attempts to control them by single national actors infeasible, thus creating enormous uncertainties for even the largest economies.)

These changes in the environment mean that the strategic niches that Hong Kong and Singapore held in the past few decades may be exposed to competition resulting from further centralization (for example, competition from Tokyo) or the entrance of new regional competitors (such as Sydney or Melbourne) in the arena as rival IFCs. Before assessing the strategic positions and future options of Hong Kong and Singapore, it is useful to outline briefly current theories concerning the formation of IFCs, to provide a framework for our analysis.

THEORIES OF IFC FORMATION

Scholars have speculated about the patterns of growth of financial centres generally, and IFCs specifically. They have focused on alternative causes leading to the concentration of international and domestic financial activities in a particular place. Some scholars have focused upon the "derived demand" for financial intermediation. Thus trade, production, and investment patterns that create a surplus of funds and borrowing needs have been hypothesized to determine demand for financial intermediation (Vernon 1960).

Other scholars emphasized the "supply" side, that is, the ability to produce the services of international financial intermediation in a particular location at a competitive cost. Indeed, several authors have pointed out different important attributes of a financial centre that affect the quality and/or cost of producing financial services. For example, Ragazzi (1973) emphasized the importance of the existence of broad and efficient financial markets in the creation of an IFC. Kindleberger (1974) considered the externalities produced by the existence of a large banking sector in terms of specialization, joint facilities, and services of other industries such as printing, accounting, and legal services. He also emphasized the role of economies of scale that exist in financial markets owing to higher liquidity and consequent lower transaction costs.

Other scholars have focused upon attributes of a location that attract depositors or lenders (for example, derived demand for intermediation from "third" parties). Nadler et al. (1955) identified the following "necessary" conditions essential to the development of an IFC: (1) a currency system that is stable and sound, (2) constant substantial demand for and supply of the country's currency, (3) a national balance of payments that is reasonably well adjusted, (4) a sophisticated system of financial institutions, (5) a system of branch or subsidiary foreign financial institutions free to operate without undue restrictions and discrimination, (6) specialized institutions that supplement the role of commercial banking in foreign financial transactions, and (7) location of the principal office of the nation's central bank in the centre.

Probably the most comprehensive study to date of factors influencing the development of international banking and finance centres is by Goldberg et al. (1987). In a multitier study consisting of a comprehensive, cross-national review of forty-two countries as well as time-series studies of the US and Great Britain and a pooled cross-sectional, time-series analysis of IFC development in sixteen OECD nations, they obtained consistent relationships between attributes of IFCs and their national environments and measures of their size. The level of imports, real per capita GNP, saving rates, and offshore banking were significantly and positively associated with the size of an IFC. Interestingly, exports were found to be negatively related to the development of an IFC. This could be explained as the impact of neither exports nor imports alone, but of the financial imbalances created by trade deficits that provide the impetus to the growth of a financial centre. These results confirm the historical importance of demand for financial intermediation in the development of an IFC, rather than supply advantages.

The historical approach provides one with ex-post identification of conditions that facilitate the growth of IFCs, but it offers little insight into the possibility of deliberately developing or inducing the growth of a particular IFC and the strategy necessary to do so. Furthermore, while it is possible that demand variables dominated the past, supply variables could determine the competitive edge for future IFCs. Tan and Vertinsky (1987) investigated the circumstances and conditions under which alternative strategies for creating an IFC are feasible and effective. They concluded that: (1) marginal modification of supply advantages may shift the distribution of financial transaction concentrations within a national economy and affect, to some degree at least, the national pace of growth of international financial activities (mainly by enhancing agglomeration economies in the initial phase of growth); (2) an aggressive proactive policy requires a flexible, highly centralized financial system; and (3) important conditions for the success of proactive strategies are product innovation and sensitive adjustment to changing market environments. Specialization and product differentiation were identified as important strategic moves to ensure the resilience of IFC development in circumstances where existing demand-related advantages do not ensure the growth of an IFC.

In the following sections we attempt to assess the degree to which the growth of IFCs in Hong Kong and Singapore has been affected by demand pull, supply advantages, and deliberate public policies.

HONG KONG VERSUS SINGAPORE

An Historical Perspective on Two IFCs

Reed (1981), who studied the hierarchical structure of international banking centres and international financial centres from the beginning of this century, ranked Hong Kong as the fourth most important international banking centre in the year 1900, just behind London, New York, and Paris. With the exception of a period during World War II, Hong Kong consistently ranked as one of the top international banking centres throughout this century. In the Asia Pacific region, Hong Kong ranked as the preeminent banking centre until the early 1930s, when Yokohama outranked it. In 1935 Shanghai assumed the role of the preeminent regional centre. In 1940, Tokyo, Jakarta, and Hong Kong achieved the same rank. In 1947, Shanghai, Hong Kong, and Singapore emerged as the leading regional banking centres just behind London, New York, and Paris in the global ranking. In the late 1950s Tokyo assumed the role of the preeminent regional banking centre, while Hong Kong retained a position in the top ten banking centres in the global ranking. Reed's cluster analysis to identify a hierarchy of international financial centres yielded similar results.

The ranking that Reed generated using multivariate statistical methods corresponded well with information he obtained by interviewing a large sample of international finance executives who were asked to rank IFCs. The most significant difference between the rankings was the relatively higher ranks that Singapore and Hong Kong obtained in the interviews compared with a ranking based upon objective measures such as number of banks, financial assets, international linkages, and so forth. Reed (41) reports that "tradition, history, its importance to the People's Republic of China, and the large number of banks with offices there were cited as reasons for ranking Hong Kong highly."

Singapore, which was ranked among the top ten global financial centres by the panel of international officials, was classified by Reed's statistical analysis in the top ten only in 1947 and 1975. The interviewees, when asked why they ranked Singapore so highly, responded that their perception of Singapore's influence within the community of international financial centres may not be entirely accurate but that it was the centre of the "Asian dollar market." Singapore, an important deposit centre for the ASEAN countries, commanded the attention of the financial community through its innovation and aggressive pursuit of eminence as an international financial centre. These perceptions of each IFC form a basis for foreign direct investment decisions of financial service providers. An analysis of the resilience of each of these financial centres must contrast the role of Hong Kong with that of Singapore. Hong Kong has traditionally been a financial centre that handled transactions between China and the outside world as well as a large share of the financial transactions of the Overseas Chinese. Singapore has been an actively managed IFC, creating and defending a new niche as an international financial centre by expanding on its traditional role as a regional deposit centre.

Hong Kong and Singapore: Evolution of Present Financial Structures and Strategic Adjustments to Changing International Financial Markets

To assess the resilience of the financial systems in Hong Kong and Singapore, one must identify their natural and historical relative advantages as well as the strengths and weaknesses of their respective institutions of management.

The most important attributes of Hong Kong and Singapore that led to their emergence as financial centres were their locations and roles as regional, central ports and their ties to London — the world's financial centre. These attributes continue to provide a basis for the maintenance and growth of a financial centre in each of the cities. Both cities now rank among the world's most important ports. In 1986, Hong Kong's Kwai Chung container terminal ranked as the third-largest container port in the world, topped only by New York and Rotterdam. In the same year, Singapore was the second-largest cargo-handling port in the world. Both cities continue to enjoy their historical and cultural ties with England, providing westernized outposts in the Asia Pacific Rim, while maintaining and cultivating traditional informal ties to regional networks of business information and financial flows. Their evolution as financial and trade centres has been accompanied by the development of an accommodating communications infrastructure. Both cities, for example, have busy and well-serviced airports, efficient telecommunications systems, and significant computer service industries. Despite their relatively small populations and economies, both Hong Kong and Singapore are disproportionately significant in the realm of international trade. Exports in 1986 (including reexports) totalled Cdn $49.1 billion in Hong Kong and Cdn $31.1 billion in Singapore, while imports reached Cdn $49.2 billion and Cdn $35.3 billion respectively. Their position as regional trade centres in open economies creates derived demands for financial intermediation services. The presence of a critical mass of domestic and foreign banks has in turn created opportunities, rooted in economies of scale and centralization, for further development of the financial services sector in each city beyond the capacity indicated merely by derived demand for services from trade and domestic business transactions.

Indeed, in both cities the financial services sector is a significant direct contributor to national income and provides positive externalities to the development of other services (such as trade and communications) and investment ventures. The importance of the sector to the rapid development of each economy has meant that the respective governments pay close attention to the health of the sector. Their actions, however, have reflected differences in market opportunities, systems of government, and choice of strategies. The globalization of markets places the two cities in direct competition with each other, with Tokyo, increasingly viewed as an emerging world centre, and with other secondary regional centres such as Melbourne and Sydney. In the next two sections we analyse the niches that Hong Kong and Singapore have occupied historically in international financial markets and their strategic adjustments as they have attempted to cope with a changing world. We start with an analysis of the evolution of their regulatory structures and the philosophies of strategic management that they reflect.

Hong Kong

The territory of Hong Kong was acquired by Britain in three stages during the nineteenth century. The Island of Hong Kong was ceded in perpetuity under the Treaty of Nanking in 1842. Parts of the Kowloon Peninsula and Stonecutter's Island were acquired in 1860, while the New Territories were acquired on a ninety-nine-year lease in 1898. For the past four decades the People's Republic of China (PRC) has reasserted its claims for sovereignty over the entire territory and engaged in lengthy negotiations with Great Britain. During that time it established a significant presence in the financial sector of the city as well as in other aspects of its economic life. It is the benefit that the PRC derived from using Hong Kong as its channel to the outside world that offered the crown colony a certain measure of security and stability. Hong Kong's position as a world financial centre was also enhanced by the vigour of its own growing economy as well as the benefits of serving as the door to China.

The "opening" of the economy of the PRC to trade and investment with the West in the mid-1970s provided an added stimulus to the growth of the city as a financial centre (Jao 1983). The official signing in Beijing in late 1984 of the Sino-British agreement on Hong Kong meant the elimination of the immediate threats that failed negotiations could have brought about, although major uncertainties as to the fate of Hong Kong beyond 1997 remain, irrespective of the guaranties in the signed agreement. Thus, Hong Kong, while benefiting from its links with the People's Republic of China, must contend with the fact that its long-term political risks put constraints on the type and stability of financial flows that the city is likely to attract.

The regulatory regime of the financial sector that has emerged over the past decade reflects, in part, the views of the authorities about the attributes desired by those using Hong Kong's financial services. The present three-tier system of regulation of banking services reflects a flexible, "light touch" regulatory approach that evolved during the 1970s and 1980s. Though a formal ban was put on new banking licences from 1965 to 1972, the loose definition used to implement the ban permitted some overseas and local banks to open finance houses competing with licensed banks for deposits and banking services. In 1976 the government required the registration of these houses as registered deposit-taking companies (RDTCs). These RDTCs remained unregulated as to the interest rates they paid, in contrast to the licensed banks, which were regulated by a cartel that controlled interest rates. In 1981 non-licensed "banks" accounted for 36 per cent of total deposits. To reverse the trend, a new tier of deposit-taking companies was established—licensed deposit-taking companies (LDTCs). These were subjected to minimum paid-up capital requirements and a minimum tenure in the industry of three years. The moratorium on the issuing of new bank licences was lifted.

At the end of August 1981 there were 115 licensed banks in Hong Kong, with about 1200 branches. Eighty-one of the banks were foreign-owned. In March 1981, when the new legislation concerning deposit-taking companies was instituted, there were 342 such companies registered. Of these, about half were subsidiaries or joint ventures set up by foreign commercial banks, merchant banks, and investment houses. Subsequent to the reforms, a number of deposit-takers took advantage of the opportunity to become banks, and by June 1987, Hong Kong had 154 licensed banks, 35 licensed deposit-takers, and 248 registered deposit-takers.

The regulation of banks was delegated to the Hong Kong Association of Bankers. This association supervises banking standards and regulates charges and deposit interest rates. All licensed banks were required to be members.

The main thrust of government policy has been described as "positive non-intervention," a mix of light regulation designed both to ensure stable growth for the industry and to maintain a reputation for order sufficient to attract foreign banks and investors. Crises threatening the reputation or stability of the industry have been met by periodic reforms, the implementation of which ensured maximum flexibility and coordination with existing and potential providers of financial services.

Regular examinations of all banks and deposit-taking companies are carried out by the Office of the Commissioner of Banking and Deposit-Taking Companies. A number of bank collapses and problems in deposit-taking companies prompted the Hong Kong government to introduce new legislation in 1986. The new bill attempted to rationalize the regulation of banking services by providing a single regulatory framework for deposit-taking companies and banks, as well as by reinforcing the supervisory powers of the banking commissioner.

Less than a year after the introduction of this legislation, plans were announced to introduce new guidelines to tighten supervision. The major objective was to "bring the territory's financial system into line with other financial centres" (EIU 2/87:14). While tightening the regulatory regime on domestic companies, the government decided to liberalize the requirements for foreign banks wanting to establish banks in Hong Kong. "Both moves highlight the government's desire to integrate Hong Kong fully into the international financial community, enhance its reputation as a financial centre and demonstrate that it is a serious competitor with the Tokyo market" (ibid.). Searching for an "optimal" regulatory regime, the government is attempting to reconcile the conflicting interests of different existing and potential service providers. While some of the reconciliation process will result in modified guidelines and regulations, much of it is likely to be reflected in the process of "adaptive" implementation.

The attempt to balance demands for freedom and secrecy in the banking services sector against the need to defend a reputation for order and stability is characteristic of other sectors of the financial industry.

Periodic rationalization of natural growth processes, positive enhancement of the sector through removal of bottlenecks, and slow, reactive rather than proactive policies have also been essential characteristics of the role of the government in developing Hong Kong's stock and futures markets. The integration of the four separate exchanges into the unified Hong Kong Stock Exchange (opened in October 1986) took almost a decade to plan and implement. The supervisory structure was minimal and its style of implementation informal. The October 1987 global stock market crash ("Black Monday") led to a temporary closure of the market. The crash almost led to the collapse of the stock futures market; it was averted only by a government-arranged and financed bailout of losses.

The crisis triggered plans for reforms designed to maintain Hong Kong's reputation and update the regulatory structure in ways that meet the emerging global demands for adequate regulation. Despite a self-promoted image of Hong Kong as a laissez-faire international market, it is clear that it is in fact a market carefully guided to respond to and meet competition from other international financial centres. The niche these policies imply is one of minimal regulation adapted periodically to satisfy international standards and expectations within the framework of a stable, predictable legal framework. The desired minimum is constantly assessed informally (through consultation with the community of financial service providers) and through periodic formal reviews.

Singapore

In contrast to Hong Kong, Singapore has sought to exploit the benefits of a strong, stable, and proactive government to stimulate growth in the financial services sector. The natural locational advantages of time zone and central position on international trade routes have been exploited to their fullest by deliberate government policy. A stable political and economic infrastructure coupled with liberal monetary and fiscal policies turned Singapore into a regional deposit centre for the ASEAN countries. Using this position as a base and taking advantage of its developed technological and institutional infrastructure, Singapore has deliberately sought to create for itself a niche as an international financial centre.

The ten-year development plan of 1975 envisaged Singapore as an international financial centre. The government guided the development of Singapore as an IFC through the following measures: liberalization of regulations pertaining to the operations of foreign financial institutions; liberalization of exchange control regulations; provision of tax incentives for offshore-oriented financial services; creation of new financial markets through legislation, tax incentives, and direct participation, using government spending power and its influence on private spending; and facilitation of the introduction of new financial instruments.

The attraction of foreign financial companies to Singapore fostered the development of a pool of expertise in financial services and helped generate the benefits of concentrating financial services (that is, a higher level of liquidity, better access to information, and lower costs of interinstitutional transactions). The measures taken by the government led to an acceleration of growth rates of the banking and financial sector from 21 per cent in 1975 to 34 per cent in 1980. The share of the financial services sector in the gross domestic product grew from 7 per cent in 1975 to 10 per cent in 1984. In 1983 Singapore was served by 37 fully licensed commercial banks (of which 24 were foreign) and 13 restricted banks. In addition, there were 69 offshore banks, 69 representative offices of foreign banks, 49 merchant banks, 153 Asian Currency Units, 4 discount houses, 9 international money brokers, 79 insurance companies, and 34 finance companies (Tan 1985: 4). Favourable government policies were accompanied by public investment in the development of physical, technological, social, and institutional infrastructures conducive to the development of an IFC. In particular, the government established a sophisticated international communications system and developed an unambiguous, stable legal and regulatory framework. These activities and the pattern of consistent, rapid economic growth and political stability have sustained the role of Singapore as a pre-eminent IFC.

In 1984 and 1985, for the first time in many years, Singapore experienced a reversal in this pattern of growth. The recession was accompanied by a reduction in the growth of the financial services sector from 10.5 per cent in 1984 to 3.4 per cent in 1985. This fact and the recognition of the new trends in the international financial markets led the government to adopt new strategies aimed at renewing the growth of financial services. The global trend toward deregulation, and especially the liberalization of Japan's financial markets, poses threats to the traditional market niche that Singapore occupies, but it also creates opportunities. Seven potential, interlinked areas of growth identified by the Report of the Economic Committee in 1986 were as follows: risk management, funds management, capital markets, unlisted securities market, financial and commodity futures, financing of third-country trading, and reinsurance and captive insurance companies. The targets have been modified, but the strategic posture of the recommendations of the influential Economic Committee was consistent with the past pattern of actions adopted by the Singapore government.

The government is expected to create a fiscal and regulatory environment conducive to the development of a vibrant capital market with a wide range of tradable instruments. Product innovation, fiscal incentives, and a liberalized regulatory environment are to be accompanied by active efforts by the Monetary Authority of Singapore (MAS) to improve liquidity in local financial markets. Similarly, the recommendations envisage the use of some of the large amounts of compulsory individual savings controlled by the government to provide a domestic basis for a funds management industry. Finally, there is a clear recognition that the major asset of a financial centre lies in the expertise and ideas of its people. Thus, the private sector (the Association of Banks) and the public sector (the university) were called upon to develop the appropriate manpower by setting up a banking school to cater to the training needs of the ASEAN region.

The government also adopted a clear policy that facilitates the recruitment of foreign experts while fostering the growth of domestic expertise. Implementation in Singapore is swift. To implement the objectives proposed by the report, the Stock Exchange of Singapore Dealers Automated Quotation System opened on 18 February 1987. When this exchange did not obtain the critical mass to justify its existence, the government introduced a variety of measures to increase its liquidity and volume of transactions. Tax concessions were given to stimulate financial futures and gold-trading on the Simex (Singapore Metal Exchange). Similarly, tax concessions were introduced in the capital market for transactions involving non-residents. To encourage the orderly development of a bond market, liquidity requirements of banks were modified. To ensure an advantageous position in a twenty-four-hour global market, the Stock Exchange of Singapore was encouraged to negotiate an agreement with the authorities in London and New York that would allow shares quoted in these centres to be listed electronically in Singapore. If successful, Singapore would be the first exchange in the Asian time zone to do so, generating a major advantage over its Pacific rivals.

THE QUEST FOR A FUTURE NICHE

Formal public policy pronouncements provide a vision and facilitate some preconditions for the evolution of a financial centre. Past actions of regulators and service providers shape the strategic style of a centre. The actual niche that the centre occupies in international markets, however, depends to a large extent on the actions of those who actually provide financial services and compete in these markets. The niche that service providers expect their IFC to occupy is reflected in the profile of attributes they consider important for its growth. For this reason, studying the perceptions of Hong Kong and Singapore financial executives with regard to the importance of different attributes of the environment to the growth of the IFC may provide insights about the future niche of each centre's financial sector.

To obtain the data for such a study a three-page questionnaire was designed, and interviews with key bankers were conducted. The main part of the questionnaire was concerned with importance judgment (on five-point Likert-type scales) of attributes of a financial centre in terms of attribute contribution to centre growth. The attributes were those that may attract financial service providers by facilitating either supply (for example, low transaction costs, access to specialized labour markets, appropriate legal and political infrastructures, economies of scale through the existence of a large financial services sector) or demand (for example, finance of international trade and investment, proximity to a large base of borrowers and depositors) for financial intermediation. Attributes were identified on the basis of a literature search. Additional attributes were added on the basis of a pilot survey of both academic experts and practitioners. A total of fifty-three attributes were identified (see Appendix 1). Another part of the questionnaire requested the identification of the five most important of these attributes. A third section of the questionnaire was an unaided recall and ranking of the most important IFCs. The sample consisted of senior financial executives of banks with significant international activities. In each location the list of executives was developed through nomination of key local bankers. There were twenty-eight useful responses in Hong Kong and thirty-eight in Singapore (the respective response rates were above 60 per cent in Hong Kong and 70 per cent in Singapore).

The study showed a marked consensus between the two communities of bankers as to those attributes of a financial centre important for its success. Table 63 reports the attributes perceived to be the most important in contributing to the success of IFCs. When we computed the mean scores and arranged the attributes in descending order, the first twelve attributes identified as most important by the Hong Kong sample were exactly the same as those indicated by the judgments of the Singapore sample. However, the orderings of the attributes in the two samples were somewhat different.

The key attributes selected by the two methods — mean ranking

Table 63
12 Most Important Attributes Contributing to Success of IFCs as Perceived by Bankers in Hong Kong and Singapore (based on mean scores)

	Hong Kong[a]		Singapore[b]	
IFC Attribute	Rank	Mean Score[c]	Rank	Mean Score[c]
Well-developed communication links with the rest of the world	1	1.00	1	1.03
Organized and efficient domestic communication systems	2	1.46	3	1.47
Mature and sound legal system	3	1.54	8	1.55
Pool of expertise in legal services	3	1.54	11	1.63
Pool of expertise in financial services	5	1.57	4	1.50
Well-developed transportation with the rest of the world	5	1.57	7	1.53
Favourable taxation policy for nonresidents	5	1.57	12	1.68
History of political stability in this country	8	1.67	4	1.50
Access to opportunities to trade between diversified financial instruments	9	1.68	8	1.55
Environment where opportunities to implement innovative financial instruments are encouraged	10	1.70	4	1.50
Unambigious regulatory framework	11	1.75	2	1.39
Existence of a significant number of branches of the major international banks	12	1.86	10	1.61

[a] n = 28
[b] n = 38
[c] from 1 (very important) to 5 (not important)

(Table 63) and frequency of mention as one of the five most important attributes — were identical in eleven out of twelve cases in the combined sample.

Statistically significant differences ($p < 0.05$), however, were discovered between the importance ratings of Hong Kong and Singapore executives with regard to some important attributes. Executives in Singapore considered the following more important than Hong Kong executives: access to government financial decision-makers, convenient time zone, proximity to a large base of savers, ability of business community to communicate with policy-makers in the country's central bank, proximity to a large base of borrowers, an unambiguous regulatory framework, and an environment where opportunities to implement innovative financial instruments are encouraged.

The pattern and strong general consensus of ratings indicate that key attributes for obtaining a competitive edge in the new globalized international financial market in a relatively small economy are supply-oriented. The technological infrastructure (for example, a well-developed external and internal communication system) is paramount. An accommodating regulatory system and the existence of a pool of expertise are next in line. Linkages with the international financial service providers are also included in the list of top-ranked attributes of an IFC.

The differences in importance ratings provide, however, a clue about the different strategies each centre may assume. Service providers in Singapore indicated by their ratings the view that its future growth as a financial centre depends to a large extent on the continuation of the government's proactive management of its financial markets. Clarity of regulation and effective communications between service providers and regulators are important characteristics of a centre that attempts to position itself in a differentiated service niche through innovation. By contrast, Hong Kong executives, accustomed to the enhancing, but reactive management style of their IFC and aware of the limitations of public policy given Hong Kong's political position, seem to emphasize more cultural, environmental, and infrastructure advantages. In particular, they emphasized ties with the British legal system, the possession of legal expertise, and a favourable tax regime. The differences also show the higher perceived dependence of Singapore upon regional demands for financial intermediation (for example, proximity to borrowers and depositors of ASEAN). Many of Hong Kong's financial executives focused mainly upon new growth opportunities in world capital markets rather than those associated with China's trade and investment financing. These opportunities are being captured more and more by the PRC-owned Bank of China and its twelve sister banks (see Ko 1986; Jao 1983).

To obtain additional insight into possible relationships between an IFC's perceived preeminence and environmental attributes judged to be important for its success, we used correlation analysis. This methodology identifies the possible differentiating characteristics considered to contribute to the success of each city as an important IFC. The significant correlations for each community are presented in Table 64.

It appears that in Hong Kong those who value a more cosmopolitan business culture and language, minimal financial disclosure rules, and proximity to borrowers ranked the city higher than those who placed less importance upon these attributes. In Singapore, the local judgments of the preeminence of the city as an IFC are related to valuing proximity to other financial centres and a large base of savers and availability of inexpensive support services. Interviews with several bankers in each city confirmed our interpretation with regard to

Table 64
Correlations of IFC Preeminence Ratings and Importance of IFC Attributes by Local Service Providers

Hong Kong (n = 28)	
English is the working business language	0.52*
Access to political decision-makers by local and foreign financial institutions	0.47*
A country that requires a minimum degree of financial disclosure	0.39*
Openness of the local business community to foreigners	0.39*
Availability of inexpensive support services	0.36*
Proximity to a large base of borrowers	0.34*
A city with a well-developed post-secondary education system	0.34*
Singapore (n = 38)	
Proximity to other financial centres	0.35*
Proximity to a large base of savers	0.28**
Availability of inexpensive support services	0.27**

* significant at 0.05
** significant at 0.10

the nature of both financial centres and their likely attempts to position themselves in future markets.

Hong Kong was universally judged to be the more important financial centre. Its unique niche was identified by interviewees as stemming from: its British legal traditions and legal and financial expertise; its less constraining levels of regulation and disclosure; its role in the investment in and trade flows to and from the People's Republic of China, as well as the internal demands for financial intermediation (see also Jao 1983); its role as a prime financial centre for Overseas Chinese (see also Lee and Jao 1982; Bualek 1986; Chang 1986; and Lim 1986) — a role Singapore does not play because of its geographical position; and opportunities for abnormal profits resulting from the structure of the domestic banking market (see also Hanley et al. 1987). Some of the interviewees pointed out the fact that these conditions favoured movement of relatively short-term risk money to Hong Kong.

Singapore was identified as a financial centre that developed from an historical base as a regional deposit centre into an IFC mainly through the force of the will of its government to create a niche in international markets. This was achieved through innovation and diversification of financial instruments, and aggressive maintenance of a competitive edge by: the enhancement of the supply of support services, the creation and maintenance of liquidity, the importation of expertise, the development of domestic expertise, and the dynamic, adaptive maintenance of internationally competitive tax and regulatory cost regimes.

Indeed, we found our interviewees echoed Reed's contention that it is the high international profile of innovation and attempts at niche creation that explain Singapore's preeminent position, which exceeds its importance as judged by objective measures of stocks and flows.

CONCLUSION

Our comparison of Hong Kong and Singapore's strategies to defend and improve their traditional positions as preeminent IFCs in small economies results in two main conclusions. First, the globalization of markets can create opportunities for smaller IFCs if supply advantages (such as lower transaction costs, lower service costs, and lower taxes) can be maintained. In the past, growth of IFCs was motivated by demand advantages. Such demand advantages, and the centralization and agglomeration economies accompanying them, explain the increasing role of London, New York, and Tokyo in international financial markets. However, significant cost increases in these centres have created opportunities for low-cost competitors in several service areas. And second, IFCs in smaller economies may also create differentiated niches in international financial services markets by accommodating special market needs. Both Hong Kong, with its reactive, noninterventionist, market-sensitive strategy of environmental management and Singapore, with its proactive anticipation of a changing market environment, can respond effectively to changing needs that the more complex regulatory systems in other larger IFCs fail to identify or choose to ignore.

REFERENCES

Bualek, P. (1986). "The Growth and Development of Chinese Banks: Capitalists in Thailand (1932–1973)." Paper presented at the International Conference on Chinese Banking and Nation Building in Southeast Asia, Hong Kong, 10–11 October

Chang, C.Y. (1986). "Localization and Chinese Banking in South East Asia." Paper presented at the International Conference on Chinese Banking and Nation Building in Southeast Asia, Hong Kong, 10–11 October

Goldberg, M., R. Helsey, and M. Levi (1987). "Factors Influencing the Development of International Banking and Finance Centres: A Cross National and Historical Evaluation." Working paper, Faculty of Commerce and Business Administration, UBC, April

Hanley, T.H., J.M. Rosenberg, C.A. D'Arista, and N.A. Mitchell (1987). *The*

Hong Kong Banking System: An Intriguing Financial Services Center. New York: Salomon Brothers

Jao, Y.C. (1983). "Hong Kong's Role in Financing China's Modernization." In A.J. Youngson, ed., *Hong Kong and China: The Economic Nexus:* 77–103. Hong Kong: Oxford University Press

Kindleberger, C.P. (1974). *The Formation of Financial Centers: A Study in Comparative Economic History.* Princeton Studies in International Finance no. 36. Princeton: Princeton University Press

Ko, C. (1986). "Bank of China Outperforms Local Rivals." *South China Morning Post,* 13 January

Lee, S.Y., and Y.C. Jao (1982). *Financial Structures and Monetary Policies in Southeast Asia.* London: Macmillan

Lim, H. (1986). "Chinese Banking and Indonesia's Economic Development." Paper presented at the International Conference on Chinese Banking and Nation Building in Southeast Asia, Hong Kong, 10–11 October

Nadler, M., S. Heller, and S. S. Shipman (1955). *The Money Market and Its Institutions.* New York: Roland Press

Ragazzi, G. (1973). "Theories of Determinants of Foreign Direct Investment," *International Monetary Fund Staff Papers,* vol. 20, July: 471–98

Reed, H.C. (1981). *The Preeminence of International Financial Centers.* New York: Praeger

Singapore, Ministry of Trade and Industry (1986). *The Singapore Economy: New Directions.* Report of the Economic Committee, February

Tan, C.H. (1985). *Financial Markets and Institutions in Singapore.* 4th ed. Singapore: Singapore University Press

Tan, S., and I. Vertinsky (1987). "Strategic Management of International Financial Centers: A Tale of Two Cities." In S.J. Khoury, ed., *Recent Developments in International Banking and Finance.* vol. 2: 87–104. Lexington, MA. D.C. Heath

Vernon, R. (1960). *Metropolis: 1985.* Cambridge, MA: Harvard University Press

Additional Sources of Information

Economist Intelligence Unit (EIU) (1981–7). *Hong Kong and Macau.* Country Reports, annual and quarterly (up to no. 3, 1987)

—. *Singapore.* Country Reports, annual and quarterly (up to no. 3, 1987)

Hong Kong (1980–6). *Hong Kong Annual Reports.* Hong Kong: Government Printer

Lloyds Bank Group (1985/6). Economic Report: Hong Kong

Lloyds Bank Group (1985/6). Economic Report: Singapore

Price Waterhouse (1986). *Selected Financial Centres.* Summary of Banking and Tax Regulations, Canada

Appendix 1: Characteristics of IFCs

1 Size of domestic economy
2 Proximity to other financial centres
3 Well-developed communication links with the rest of the world
4 Favourable taxation policy for non-residents
5 Pool of expertise in legal services
6 Favourable domestic taxation policy
7 Organized and efficient domestic communication systems
8 Pool of expertise in language translation services
9 Access to government financial decision-makers by local and foreign financial institutions
10 Unambiguous regulatory framework
11 Well-developed computer systems
12 Cost of renting office space
13 Pool of expertise in financial services
14 Stability of domestic currency
15 Access to political decision-makers by local and foreign financial institutions
16 Maturity and stability of the domestic financial system
17 City with well-developed research institutes
18 English is the working business language
19 Availability of inexpensive support services (for example, office staff)
20 History of political stability in the country
21 Convenient international time zone
22 Proximity to a large base of savers
23 Well-established reputation in financial affairs
24 Well-developed transportation links with the rest of the world
25 Access of residents to international currency markets
26 Environment where opportunities to implement innovative financial instruments are encouraged
27 Country that requires a minimum degree of financial disclosure
28 History of financing and insuring international trade
29 Country that provides incentives for foreign investment
30 Existence of a recognized stock exchange
31 City with well-developed post-secondary educational systems
32 Strong diplomatic ties with other nations
33 City with cosmopolitan cultural characteristics
34 Favourable reserve requirements
35 Basic framework of statutory protection with a wide measure of self-regulation
36 Openness of the local business community to foreigners
37 Access of foreigners to domestic currency markets

38 Country with a strong industrial and economic base
39 Mature and sound legal system
40 Access and opportunities to trade between diversified financial instruments (e.g., bonds, stocks)
41 Proximity of a city to industrial and commercial centres
42 Volume of exports of a country
43 Existence of a significant number of branches of the major international banks
44 Existence of a significant number of headquarters of some major banks
45 Ability of the business community to communicate with policy-makers in the country's central bank
46 Convertibility of domestic currency
47 City with an attractive physical environment
48 Proximity to a large base of borrowers
49 Volume of imports of a country
50 High degree of diversification in deposit base and capital sources
51 Existence of a significant number of branch offices of trading companies
52 High degree of sectoral diversification among potential borrowers
53 Existence of a significant number of head offices of manufacturing companies

CHAPTER TEN

The Future of Pacific Ocean Minerals

Charles J. Johnson, Allen L. Clark, and Robert N. Yonover

INTRODUCTION

Although approximately twenty minerals are commercially produced from the shallow (less than 250 metres) continental margins of nations in the Asia-Pacific region, no commercial mining of marine mineral resources has taken place beyond the near-shore, shallow continental margins, even though more than US $600 million has been spent on evaluating deeper-water (800-5,500m) metal deposits.

Throughout much of the 1970s, there was substantial optimism that commercial mining of ocean-floor manganese nodules would begin in the 1980s. Major industry consortiums were formed to undertake exploration and research to evaluate the potential for commercial production of these nodules. Major assumptions behind these activities were that costs of production from land-based mines would increase, metal prices would rise in constant dollars, and/or competitive seabed-mining technologies would be developed. By the end of the 1970s, however, these assumptions increasingly appeared unlikely, and interest in deep-ocean mining declined dramatically. In the 1980s, crusts and sulfides replaced nodules as the mineral resources of greatest scientific interest and government-sponsored funding replaced private sector funding as the dominant source of research funds. While private sector funding of research and development (R&D) in a seabed nodule mining system has been almost nonexistent in the 1980s, government-sponsored R&D has continued, particularly in Japan, France, and West Germany. At present, the most ambitious program is directed by the Japanese government's Ministry of International Trade and Industry (MITI).

This chapter brings together the major technical and economic factors useful to nonspecialists interested in evaluating the status and possible future of deep-sea ocean mining in the Pacific. The chapter is divided into the following six sections: mineral resource characteristics; the plausible economics of ocean mining; the impact of ocean mining on metal markets; environmental impact of ocean mining; the future outlook for ocean mining in the Pacific; and conclusions.

MINERAL RESOURCE CHARACTERISTICS

There are three types of mineral deposits beyond the near shore that may be commercially developed within the next twenty years. The best-known deposits are ocean-floor manganese nodules (hereafter, nodules). In the first half of the 1980s two other ocean minerals occurrences, cobalt-rich manganese crusts (hereafter, crusts) and polymetallic sulfide deposits (hereafter, sulfides), have received relatively high levels of interest primarily by government and academic research groups. Our present understanding of the physical nature of these three resources is summarized in the following section.

Manganese Nodules

Nodules that are relatively rich in manganese, iron, nickel, copper, and cobalt are abundant over vast areas of the ocean floor. Nodules are typically potato-shaped and three to six centimetres in diameter; they have average metal grades of approximately 0.75 per cent nickel, 0.5 per cent copper, 0.25 per cent cobalt, and 20 per cent manganese. While nodules have been found in all the earth's oceans, the regions of highest potential and commercial interest to date are located in the Pacific Ocean at depths of four to five thousand metres. The richest known area for possible commercial mining is within the Clarion-Clipperton fracture zone located between Hawaii and Baja, California, as shown in Figure 14. This area covers about four million square kilometres, and about half of the area contains extensive nodule deposits. Assuming that 20 per cent of the nodules are recoverable, this area contains about two billion dry metric tons of nodules averaging about 1.3 per cent nickel, 1 per cent copper, 0.22 per cent cobalt, and 25 per cent manganese (McKelvey 1980). This quantity of nodules could support at least ten commercial-sized mining operations. If they are considered as part of the reserve base, the maximum tonnage of recoverable nodules from

Figure 14 Permissive Areas for Marine Mineral Resource Occurrences in the Pacific

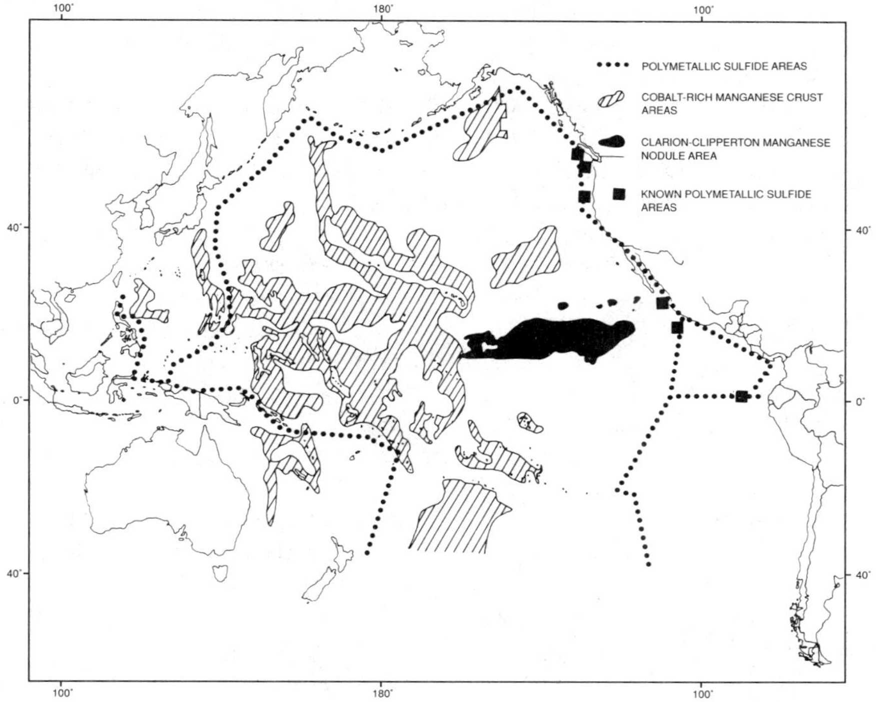

this area would increase the 1984 US Bureau of Mines estimates of world reserves by 50 per cent for cobalt, 25 per cent for nickel, and 5 per cent for copper and manganese.

Bottom photographs taken by the US Geological Survey on the SP *Lee Guyot* have indicated "several densely-packed nodule fields" (Hein et al. 1985). Nodule concentrations have also been noted in photographs of seamounts taken by the Hawaii Institute of Geophysics within the Hawaiian Exclusive Economic Zone (EEZ) and by Japanese researchers at a depth of twelve hundred metres in the Minami-Torishima area (Masuda, personal comm. 1988). Therefore, it is possible that nodule concentrations of commercial interest may exist in relatively shallow waters within the EEZ of one or more Pacific nations. These seamount nodule concentrations will probably have metal grades similar to seamount crusts.

Cobalt-Rich Manganese Crusts

Crusts are different from nodules in a number of physical aspects, the most important of which are metal grades, location, and their binding to the underlying substrate. Table 65 compares the typical grades of crusts and nodules.

The average metal grade of cobalt in crusts is over two times that of nodules, the grade of nickel is only about one-half that of nodules, and copper grades are about one-seventh that of nodules. Manganese grades are typically between 20 and 25 per cent for both nodules and crusts. For older crusts, those formed between nine and sixteen million years ago (Halbach et al. 1984), significant platinum values of up to about one gram per tonne with a few samples over two gm per tonne have been reported. The crusts of greatest commercial interest appear to be at depths of eight hundred to twenty-four hundred metres, compared with nodules located at depths of four to five thousand metres. The largest concentrations of nodules are found on soft ocean-floor sediments, whereas most crusts are attached to the hard rock substrate of seamounts. Crusts range in thickness from surface coatings of less than one millimetre and in rare instances have thicknesses more than ten centimetres. Crust deposits of greatest commercial interest are expected to be associated with seamounts that are about twenty-five million years and older and that are located between 15° S and 20° N latitude in the Pacific Ocean.

The most detailed study of crusts was undertaken near Johnston Island in 1984 by scientists on the West German research ship *Sonne*. A deposit averaging about three centimetres in thickness and containing in excess of ten million tonnes of crust was discovered on a gentle slope between about one thousand and eighteen hundred metres (Halbach 1984). Figure 14 shows areas of the Pacific where it is likely that seamounts of commercial interest may be located. Table 66 gives a relative ranking of the crust potential within the two-hundred-nautical-mile EEZs of Pacific Ocean countries and territories.

Polymetallic Sulfides

These deposits are of hydrothermal origin and are found along fracture zones on the ocean floor that are spreading apart at relatively rapid rates (up to fourteen centimetres per year). In general, sulfide deposits occur as vents, similar in appearance to stalagmite cones, and they may rise more than thirty metres from the ocean floor. The largest potential deposit discovered to date occurs approximately two hundred nautical miles east of the Galapagos Islands. Within this area a

Table 65
Typical Metal Grades of Nodules and Crusts

Metal	Nodules[a]	Crusts[b]
Cobalt (%)	0.27	0.63
Copper (%)	0.54	0.08
Manganese (%)	20.00	20.00
Nickel (%)	0.76	0.44
Platinum (gm/tonne)	n/a	0.40[c]

[a]Mckelvey et al. 1983
[b]Hein et al. 1987
[c]Based on a limited number of analyses (Halbach et al. 1984; Halbach 1984)

series of coalesced inactive sulfide vents occur intermittently for one kilometre along a fault and within a zone approximately twenty to two hundred metres wide (Malahoff 1982).

Table 67 shows the metal grades of the four major deposit types recognized to date. As Table 67 shows, the first type of deposit, such as that found in the Galapagos region, is high in cadmium, copper, and silver. The second type, such as that found at Juan de Fuca and Guaymas Basin, is high in silver and zinc. The third and fourth types of sulfide deposits are found at the Southern Explorer Ridge and at Axial Seamount of the Juan de Fuca region. The third type is high in zinc and copper, and the fourth is high in zinc and gold. Gold-bearing deposits have also been discovered in the Okinawan trough (Halbach

Table 66
Estimated Total Resource Potential of Crusts within the EEZs
of Pacific Ocean Countries and Territories

Pacific Area	Relative Ranking
Kiribati	High
Marshall Islands	High
Micronesia	High
Kingman-Palmyra	High
Johnston Island	Medium
Hawaii-Midway	Medium
French Polynesia	Medium
Northern Marianas	Medium
Wake	Medium
Howard-Baker	Low
Belau-Palau	Low
Jarvis	Low
Guam	Low
Samoa	Low

[a]Combination ranking from Clark et al. 1984, and Hein et al. 1987

Table 67
Metal Grades of Deep-Ocean Sulfide Deposits

Metal (grades)	Type 1[a]	Type 2[b]	Gold-Bearing Type 3[c]	Gold-Bearing Type 4[d]
Cadmium (g/mt)	31.0	n/a	0.4	0.5
Cobalt (%)	—	—	—	—
Copper (%)	5.0	1.0	8.5	0.4
Gold (g/mt)	0.1	0.1	0.7	4.9
Lead (%)	0.1	0.1	0.1	0.1
Manganese (%)	—	—	—	—
Nickel (%)	—	—	—	—
Platinum (g/mt)	—	—	—	—
Silver (g/mt)	10.0	300.0	0.1	0.2
Zinc (%)	0.1	30.0	9.0	22.7

[a]Galapagos; Bishcoff et al. 1983
[b]Guyamas Basin/Juan de Fuca Ridge; Broadus 1984
[c]Southern Explorer Ridge; Hannington et al. 1986
[d]Axial Seamount; Hannington et al. 1986
n/a not available

1989). There is potential for discovery of higher grade gold sulfide deposits than have been discovered to date.

Estimates by Mottl reported by Broadus (1984) indicate that the largest sulfide deposits will probably be about 30 million tonnes. Much larger deposits can be expected if the massive (marine) sulfide deposits that have been exposed on land are analogous to submarine sulfide deposits. For example, the Kuroko sulfide deposits of the Hokuroku District in Japan are estimated to contain 140 million tonnes of ore based on past production and estimated reserves (Tanimura et al. 1983).

Relatively little exploration has taken place for polymetallic sulfide vents; thus, the descriptions above may not accurately reflect the potential of this type of mineral occurrence. Exploration for sulfide sites began in the early 1980s, and to date only a few tens of millions of dollars appear to have been spent compared to hundreds of millions on nodules.

Discoveries of submarine hydrothermal vent fields in varied marine geologic environments suggest that potential sulfide-bearing vent systems are not limited to mid-ocean spreading centres and that they therefore can occur within the EEZs of many Pacific nations. Areas where occurrences are likely to be found are shown in Figure 14.

ECONOMICS OF OCEAN MINING

Of the three ocean mineral deposit types discussed in this chapter, it is only for nodules that R&D have advanced to the stage of detailed pilot-scale mining and -processing tests. It follows that the economic parameters pertaining to nodule mining are known with a much greater degree of reliability than are those of either crusts or sulfides. However, even in the case of the heavily studied nodules, economic analyses should be used with caution, since they probably do not accurately reflect the economics of a full-scale commercial operation or the full range of possible technological innovations.

The most likely mining system will probably include a highly efficient bottom-collecting device combined with a hydraulic system for lifting nodules through a six kilometre pipe to a surface ship. Such systems have been demonstrated with one-fifth scale mining systems by two mining consortia — Ocean Mining Associates and Ocean Management Incorporated (A.D. Little 1979). The nodules probably will be transported by 60,000 to 100,000 DWT ships to a shore-based processing plant for recovery of metals. The energy, freshwater, and space requirements for processing make processing of metals at sea highly unlikely.

There are two main nodule- and crust-processing alternatives, pyrometallurgical and hydrometallurgical options. It is not possible to predict which processing option will be selected for the first commercial development. There are a number of published estimates of nodule-mining and-processing costs (Flipse 1982; Nyhart et al. 1983: Arthur D. Little 1984; Johnson and Otto 1986), but only one estimate is known to have been published pertaining to the costs of crust mining and processing (State of Hawaii Department of Planning and Economic Development 1987; US Department of the Interior 1988).

Comparisons of nodule and crust projects should be based on commercial financial criteria using estimates of the internal rates of return for each project and the relative risks of each project. No detailed estimates have been attempted here because the results would probably be misleading due to the uncertainty of crust-mining economics.

Nodule projects are likely to be large, with annual ore production levels of two to four million tonnes and a total capital investment in the range of US $1.0 to US $2.0 billion. Crust projects will probably be constrained by the small size of the cobalt market (cobalt is the dominant metal in terms of value). Crust projects will probably produce from 0.7 to 1.5 million metric tonnes per year of ore and may have a total capital investment of US $0.5 to US $1.0 billion. Table 68 shows plausible revenue and cost estimates per tonne of dry ore produced by

Table 68
Rough Estimate of Capital and Operating Costs for Hypothetical Nodule and Crust-Mining and Processing Operations[a]
(1989 US $ per tonne of dry ore)

Cash flow	Nodules	Crusts
Metal sales revenue	240	260
Operating costs		
mining and transport	35–50	50–75
processing costs	90–120	90–130
Capital charge	60–100	100–150
Net profit	–30 to 55	–95 to 20

[a]Assumes processing by the pyrometallurgical method. Assumes a nodule operation of three million dry tonnes per year compared to a crust operation of one million dry tonnes per year. Above estimates are authors' estimates and are only useful as a broad indication of plausible costs. Taxes are not included. Technological breakthroughs may substantially reduce the costs

hypothetical nodule- and crust-mining and -processing operations. The estimates in Table 68 indicate that more favourable economics are expected for nodule operations than crust operations. However, a number of factors could reverse the comparisons. For example, it is likely that higher grade crust deposits will be discovered than assumed in the analysis. If so, the sales revenue for crusts would increase. In addition, there may be improvements in economies of scale if the crust-mining operation could be increased above one million dry tonnes.

About 65-75 per cent of both the capital and operating costs related to seabed nodule or crust mining and processing are associated with the land-based processing plant. However, most of the uncertainty is related to the actual mining and transport of the nodules and crusts from the seabed to the surface ship.

The admittedly rough estimates in Table 68 show too wide a range in profitability to attract active private sector interest. There is substantial potential for improving the mining and processing technologies, thereby reducing both overall costs and the uncertainty in the economics of seabed mining and processing.

Law of the Sea Treaty Implications for Mining Economics and Risk

The United Nations Law of the Sea Treaty signed in 1982 established fairly detailed terms for commercial deep-ocean mining. Private mining consortia have stated that the Law of the Sea Treaty is unacceptable in a number of areas including the requirement that mining technology be transferred to the UN established "Enterprise" and to developing countries when requested, and the lack of assurance that existing investors will be able to mine the sites they have been exploring (US General Accounting Office 1982). In addition to complaints voiced by the consortia, private international banks believe the Law of the Sea Treaty would not provide adequate protection for their loans in a number of areas (ibid.).

It is futile to try to predict whether or not private mining consortia will operate under the Law of the Sea Treaty in the future. However, it does appear that the treaty raises the risks perceived by investors and lenders, and their fears will be reflected in a higher profitability requirement. It is probable that before commercial scale seabed mining occurs, attempts will be made to modify the more contentious provisions of the Law of the Sea Treaty.

The discoveries in recent years of major crust deposits within the EEZs of selected Pacific countries may change fundamentally the commercial prospects for deep-ocean mining of nodules under the Law of the Sea Treaty. Mining of crusts and, perhaps, associated nodules may prove to be no more costly than deep-ocean mining of nodules. Because of the perceived lower risks of investing within the EEZs of some Pacific countries and territories, private sector investment might proceed first within the EEZ of one of the Pacific countries.

Countries having substantial past involvement in the development of prototype mining technologies include Canada, Finland, France, Germany (FRG), Japan, Soviet Union, United Kingdom, and the United States. In recent years, South Korea has become increasingly interested in the prospects for seabed nodule mining. Licence areas for the mining of deep-sea nodules from within the Clarion-Clipperton region of the Eastern Pacific (outside of the EEZ for any country) have been selected by a number of countries (FRG of Germany, France, Japan, United Kingdom, United States, and USSR) through an international working group on the "Law of the Sea Treaty." Crust and sulfide exploration/development has been restricted to reconnaissance mapping and dredging.

The Japanese have conducted preliminary surveys of nodule, crust, and sulfide deposits with long-term plans to become commercially active in the ocean mining arena. The present goal of the Japanese, through MITI, is to implement a pilot nodule-mining system, probably in the Clarion-Clipperton nodule region during the early 1990s (Ocean Development Office of Japan 1989).

The move by the United States to establish legislation to allow American mining consortia to mine nodules in countervention of the UN Law of the Sea Treaty is unlikely to reduce perceived risks to acceptable levels. Countries choosing to encourage the development of nodules in countervention of the treaty may face condemnation by most of the countries of the world. In addition to substantial political costs, there could be costs to private companies involved in any such consortium, such as restrictions on investment opportunities in countries that are signatories of the Law of the Sea Treaty. The obvious solutions to this dilemma are either to revise the mining provisions in the treaty or to accept its terms.

The most important crust deposits are expected to be located within the EEZ of Pacific nations, and, therefore, the risk associated with the terms of the Law of the Sea Treaty do not exist. Companies will face the technical risks of developing a commercial mining technology, and they will probably need to meet strict environmental guidelines. However, it may be easier to develop a legal regime acceptable to lenders in areas such as the US EEZ. It is also possible that a US-led consortium might be given some preferential treatment by the US government to encourage a commercial development of strategic mineral within the US EEZ.

IMPACT OF OCEAN MINING ON METAL MARKETS

It is not possible at present to predict the timing of the first commercial deep-ocean mining operations. However, given the lead time required to establish such a major and complex project, it is unlikely that a commercial mining operation could begin operation before the early part of the twenty-first century.

Table 69 shows the estimated impact of a single mining operation, for the various deposit types, on the world market in the year 2000. Crust operations are mainly cobalt operations, and, as is shown in Table 69, a single crust-mining operation would have the largest impact on the world supply of cobalt, adding 17 per cent to the world market size, while a single nodule operation would add 12 per cent.

As Table 70 shows, cobalt is primarily produced in Zaire and Zambia, which together accounted for 75 per cent of world mine production in 1988. Cobalt is considered by the United States government as one of the most important "strategic" minerals because of the lack of domestic supplies and the relatively high degree of concentration of output from countries that may, for political or economic reasons, restrict supplies and because of the critical role of cobalt in some high-technology and military applications. The implications of a classification of a metal as strategic are that governments are more likely to establish a stockpile, support research to provide substitutes, and/or provide incentives to develop new sources of supply. The US government is presently sup-

Table 69
Impact of a Single Marine Mining Operation on the World Market in the Year 2000[a]

Mineral	Market Size in Year 2000 (000 tonnes)	Nodules (%[b])		Crusts (%[b])	
Cadmium	23	—	—	—	—
Cobalt	45	5	12	8	17
Copper	15000	33	*	0	*
Gold[d]	56000[d]	—	—	—	—
Lead	7300	—	—	—	—
Manganese	12000	567	5	161	1
Nickel	1900	38	*	4	*
Platinum[c,d]	11000[d]	—	—	10[d]	*
Silver	20	—	—	—	—
Zinc	9400	—	—	—	—

Mineral	Sulfide 1 %[b]		Sulfide 2 %[b]		Sulfide 3 %[b]		Sulfide 4 %[b]	
Cadmium	.04	*	—	—	0	*	0	*
Cobalt	—	—	—	—	—	—	—	—
Copper	67	*	14	*	114	1	5	*
Gold[d]	0	*	0	*	16[d]	*	211[d]	*
Lead	0	*	0	*	0	*	3	*
Manganese	—	—	—	—	—	—	—	—
Nickel	—	—	—	—	—	—	—	—
Platinum[c]	—	—	—	—	—	—	—	—
Silver	.01	*	0.4	2	0	*	0	*
Zinc	0	*	405	4	126	1	306	3

[a]Market size based on projections from Bureau of Mines Bulletin 675 1985. Assumptions: single marine mining operations would recover for nodules — 3 million tonnes/year; for crusts — 1 million tonnes; for sulfides — 1.5 million tonnes on a dry basis and a variable recovery rate depending on grade and processing for individual ore types. Production in thousand tonnes except for gold and platinum, which are in thousand troy ounces

[b]Per cent of world production

[c]Platinum group metals used for world production estimates

[d]Thousand troy ounces

*Insignificant

porting research with respect to the crust and polymetallic sulfide potential within its two-hundred-mile EEZ, with the goal of encouraging private sector interest in commercial developments.

Sulfide deposits do not contain minerals generally considered to be of high strategic potential by the major industrialized nations. But from a marketing perspective, sulfide deposits face less risk in metal markets than either nodules or crusts. As can be seen from Table 67, significant sulfide occurrences are known that have relatively high grades of cadmium, copper, and silver; silver and zinc; copper and

Table 70
Major Producers of Cobalt, Copper, Manganese, and Nickel, 1988[a]

Cobalt		Copper	
Country	%[b]	Country	%[b]
Zaire	63	Other market[d]	18
Zambia	12	US	17
Canada	6	Chile	17
USSR	6	Other central[c]	12
Australia	4	Canada	8
Other central[c]	4	USSR	8
New Caledonia	2	Zaire	6
Other market[d]	2	Zambia	5
Finland	1	Peru	4
		Australia	3
		Philippines	2

Manganese		Nickel	
Country	%[b]	Country	%[b]
USSR	40	Canada	24
South Africa	14	USSR	23
Brazil	11	Other market[d]	14
Gabon	10	Australia	9
Australia	8	Indonesia	7
China	7	New Caledonia	7
India	6	Other central[c]	7
Mexico	2	South Africa	4
Other market[d]	2	China	3
Other central[c]	1		

[a]Derived from US Bureau of Mines, *Mineral Commodity Summaries* 1988
[b]Columns may not add up to 100% owing to rounding
[c]Other centrally planned economies
[d]Other market economies

zinc; and gold and zinc. Table 69 shows that the markets for copper, gold, and zinc are large and that there would not be a substantial impact on them from the commercial development of a seabed sulfide deposit.

ENVIRONMENTAL IMPACT OF OCEAN MINING

Mining of the ocean-floor presents a number of potential hazards to the ocean environment including the ocean-floor sediments, the overlying water column, and the ocean surface. Any mining of the ocean-floor will result in some disruption of the biota-containing substrate. Any dredging or mining process will probably also result in the generation of a plume of sediments in the water column above the mining area. Water temperature and photosynthesis processes (for example, food chain) may be affected by substantial generation of suspended particulates during mining.

The environmental impact of a specific mining venture will vary depending on the type of host substrate and the respective technologies used in mining and lifting ores to the ocean surface.

Nodules

Although nodules are commonly found in deep waters (four to five thousand m), which correlate to lower concentrations of biologic activity, the possibility of major disruptions to unique species warrants further investigation (US Department of the Interior 1988). Nodules are found resting on clay, and substantial plumes of suspended materials will probably be produced during mining. The preliminary conclusions of the DOMES study (NOAA 1981) are that the plumes created are not significant enough to prevent nodule mining based on environmental considerations.

Crusts

Crusts of greatest commercial potential appear to be located at depths of eight hundred to twenty-four hundred metres, which correspond to increased levels of biologic activity compared to the deep-water nodules (US Department of Interior 1988). Although it may be a more formidable technical challenge, the mining of crusts from hard substrate is expected to produce a much smaller particulate plume than is expected from mining nodules that rest on soft clay substrate. Preliminary studies supported by the State of Hawaii Department of Planning and Economic Development and the US Department of Interior Minerals Management System (1987) indicate that a relatively small plume will be generated during mining, with a more significant problem occurring if there is a loss of power to the ore lift system.

Sulfides

Sulfide deposits and their affiliated vent fields are found in moderate to deep water in narrow zones (typically less than a few kilometres). It is premature to evaluate the environmental consequences of possible commercial mining, however, because the biologic life associated with the few deposits examined to date appears to contain rare species; there are sensitive ecological issues that need to be evaluated prior to possible commercial mining activities.

Table 71
Gross Revenues from Marine Mining Operations
(one commercial operation)[a,b]

	Nodules		Crusts	
Metal	US $ millions	%	US $ millions	%
Cadmium	—	—	—	—
Cobalt	93	12	130	50
Copper	62	8	0	0
Gold	—	—	—	—
Lead	—	—	—	—
Manganese	350	46	99	38
Nickel	250	33	25	10
Platinum	—	—	4	2
Silver	—	—	—	—
Zinc	—	—	—	—
Total	755		258	

	Sulfides							
	Type 1		Type 2		Type 3		Type 4	
Metal	US $ millions	%	US $ millions	%	US $ millions	%	US $ millions	%
Cadmium	0.2	0	—	—	—	—	—	—
Cobalt								
Copper	130	97	25	5	210	65	9	3
Gold	—	—	—	—	6	2	74	20
Lead	—	—	—	—	—	—	—	—
Manganese	—	—	—	—	—	—	—	—
Nickel	—	—	—	—	—	—	—	—
Platinum	—	—	—	—	—	—	—	—
Silver	3	3	100	20	—	—	—	—
Zinc	—	—	370	75	110	34	280	77
Total	133		495		326		363	

[a]Assumed constant 1989 US $ prices as follows: cadmium $1.75/lb; cobalt $8.00/lb; copper $0.85/lb; gold $400/oz; lead $0.23/lb; manganese $0.28/lb; nickel $3.00/lb; platinum $400/oz; silver $8.00/oz; zinc $0.41/lb
[b]Same production levels as in Table 69

Sulfide deposits and their affiliated vent fields are found in moderate to deep water in narrow zones (typically less than a few kilometres). It is premature to evaluate the environmental consequences of possible commercial mining, however, because the biologic life associated with the few deposits examined to date appears to contain rare species; there are sensitive ecological issues that need to be evaluated prior to possible commercial mining activities.

larger waste streams into the atmosphere, and it produces a large tonnage of relatively stable, inert slag that appears suitable for landfill. The hydrometallurgical option generates a much larger amount of liquid wastes that may not be inert and limited amounts of material suitable for landfill.

FUTURE OUTLOOK FOR OCEAN MINERALS

It is generally agreed among analysts that no commercial development of nodules, crusts, or sulfides will be undertaken by private industry in the foreseeable future. The main constraining factors are large reserves in land-based mines, forecasts of relatively low growth rates in metal consumption, and a mining industry that became more cautious in the 1980s, particularly about investments in long-term, risky projects such as seabed mining. Our understanding of the complex interaction of changing technologies, economies, and politics with respect to long-term metals supply and demand remains quite imperfect. It is impossible to predict when commercial mining will occur. The recent discoveries of extensive cobalt-rich crust deposits and polymetallic sulfide deposits are a clear indication that major changes in our knowledge of the size, grade, and distribution of marine resources and the possible economics of their development are still occurring. In addition, the continued support by some government and private enterprises of the development of prototype mining technologies could result in the discovery of a commercial mining technology that would substantially improve the economics of seabed mining (see Table 71).

CONCLUSIONS

(1) Given the lead time required to develop a full-scale mining and processing operation, it is reasonable to conclude that no full-scale, private-sector financed commercial operation is likely to occur before the early part of the twenty-first century. A guess is that the first commercial operation could begin between fifteen and twenty-five years from today.

(2) Although crusts have a number of physical and locational characteristics that appear to make them favourable candidates for commercial mining, the continued support of prototype mining technology development for nodules suggests that commercial mining of nodules is likely to proceed before crust mining.

(3) Known sulfide deposits do not appear to have the size and grade

characteristics necessary for commercial development during this century. However, high-grade deposits, particularly gold, probably exist in much larger deposits than are known to date, and when they are discovered, they could provide a catalyst for commercial developments within the next fifteen to twenty-five years.

(4) The only market that would be influenced significantly by one mining operation would be the cobalt market, with cobalt-rich crusts having the largest impact. Indeed, more than one crust-mining operation would probably substantially depress cobalt prices in the year 2000.

(5) As shown in Table 66, the EEZs of a number of Pacific Island countries and territories are known or expected to have major crust deposits. Selected other Pacific countries are also likely to contain important crust deposits within their EEZs. The potential economic importance to small island countries is large, and the present state of knowledge about the extent of crust and other seabed resources is so limited that priority is justified in evaluating the potential of the EEZs of all Pacific countries and territories known to contain favourable geologic and physical environments for crust, nodule, and sulfide deposits.

(6) A single nodule or crust operation could significantly reduce the supply vulnerability for cobalt in the world market.

(7) The UN Law of the Sea Treaty increases the perceived risks of private mining consortiums and private lending institutions. As a result, commercial developments by private consortiums may be delayed unless changes are made to the treaty. Efforts to modify the treaty are probable in the 1990s.

(8) Recent interest by some governments in obtaining "pioneer" minesites under the UN Law of the Sea Treaty suggests that a commercial development might be supported by governments for a combination of strategic and political reasons.

(9) International consortiums are probable in order to spread the risks of seabed mining.

(10) Existing studies of the economics of seabed mining are based primarily on research undertaken in the 1970s, and they probably do not accurately reflect the economics of mining technologies that could be developed in the 1990s.

REFERENCES

Arthur D. Little, Inc. (1979). "Technological and Economic Assessment of Manganese Nodule Mining and Processing." Prepared for the US Department of the Interior

— (1984). "Technological and Cost Analyses of Manganese Nodule Processing Techniques and Their Significant Variations." Prepared for the US Department of Commerce, Contract No. NA83-SAC-00637

Bishcoff, J.L., R.J. Rosenbauer, P.J. Aruscabage, P.A. Baedecker, and J.G. Crock (1983). "Seafloor Massive Sulfide Deposits from 21 N, East Pacific Rise; Juan de Fuca Ridge; Galapagos Rift; Bulk Chemical Composition and Economic Implications." *Economic Geology*, 78:1711–20

Broadus, J.M. (1984). "Economic Significance of Marine Polymetallic Sulfides." Offshore Marine Resource Proceedings, Groupe d'Étude et de Recherche de Minéralisations au Large: 559–75

Callies, D.L., and C.J. Johnson (1985). "A Summary of Land and Environmental Laws and Business/Economic Factors Applicable to the Siting of a Manganese Nodule Processing Plant in the Pacific Basin/Rim: Australia, Canada, Colombia, Ecuador, Fiji, and the Philippines." Prepared for the US Department of Commerce, University of Hawaii Sea Grant No. NA81AA-D-00070

Clark, A., P. Humphrey, C. Johnson, and P. Chinn (1984). "A Resource Assessment of Cobalt-Rich Manganese Crust Potential within the Exclusive Economic Zones of US Trust and Affiliated Territories in the Pacific." Prepared for the US Minerals Management Service by the Resource Systems Institute, East-West Center, Honolulu

Clark, A., C. Johnson, and P. Chinn (1984). "Assessment of Cobalt-Rich Manganese Crusts in the Hawaiian, Johnston and Palmyra Islands' Exclusive Economic Zones." *Natural Resources Forum* 8(2):163–74

Halbach, P. (1984). Personal communication

—, D. Puteanus, and F.T. Manheim (1984). "Platinum Concentrations in Ferromanganese Seamount Crusts from the Central Pacific." *Naturwissenschaften* 71: S. 577

Hannington, M.D., J.M. Peter, and S.D. Scott (1986). "Gold in Seafloor Polymetallic Sulfide Deposits." *Economic Geology* 81:1867–83

Hein, J.R., et al. (1985). "Geological and Geochemical Data for Seamounts and Associated Ferromanganese Crusts in and near the Hawaiian, Johnston Island and Palmyra Island Exclusive Economic Zones." US Geological Survey Open File Report 85–292

Hein, J.R., et al. (1987). "Cobalt-Rich Ferromanganese Crusts from the Exclusive Economic Zone of the United States and Nodules from the Ocean Pacific." In D.W. Scholl, A.G. Grantz, and J.G. Vedder, eds., *Geology and Resource Potential of the Continental Margin of the Western North America and Adjacent Ocean Basins: Beaufort Sea to Baja California*: 753–71. Circum-Pacific Council for Energy and Mineral Resources Earth Science Series, vol. 6. Circum-Pacific Council for Energy and Mineral Resources, Houston

Johnson, C.J., and A. Clark (1985). "Potential of Pacific Ocean Nodule, Crust and Sulfide Mineral Deposits." *Natural Resources Forum* 9(3):179–86

Johnson, C.J., and J.M. Otto (1986). "Manganese Nodule Project Economics: Factors Relating to the Pacific Region." *Resources Policy*, March 1986: 17–28

Johnson, C.J., A. Clark, and J.M. Otto (1987). "Pacific Ocean Minerals: The Next Twenty Years." In Peter N. Nemetz, *The Pacific Rim: Investment, Development, and Trade*: 199–222. Vancouver: UBC Press

Malahoff, A. (1982). "A Comparison of the Massive Submarine Polymetallic Sulfides of the Galapagos Rift with Some Continental Deposits." *Marine Technology Society Journal* 16:38–45

McKelvey, V.E. (1980). "Seabed Minerals and Law of the Sea." *Science* 209, 25 July: 464–72

—, N.A. Wright, and R.W. Bowen (1983). *Analysis of the World Distribution of Metal-Rich Subsea Manganese Nodules*. US Geological Survey Circular 886

NOAA (1981). "Deep Seabed Mining. Final Programmatic Environmental Impact Statement." Washington, DC: Office of Ocean Minerals and Energy

Nyhart, J.D., M.S. Triantafyllou, J. Averback, A. Bliek, B. Sklar, M. Gillia, D. Kirkpatrick, J. Muggerridge, R. Nakagawa, J. Newman, and A. Will (1983). "A Pioneer Deep Ocean Mining Venture." Massachusetts Institute of Technology Sea Grant 83–14

Ocean Development Office of Japan (1989). "Japanese Activities in Deep Seabed Mineral Resources." Agency of Natural Resources and Energy, Ministry of International Trade and Industry (MITI)

Roskill Information Services (1982). *Roskill's Metals Databook*. London

State of Hawaii Department of Planning and Economic Development and US Department of the Interior Minerals Management Service (1987). "Mining Development Scenario for Cobalt-Rich Manganese Crusts in the Exclusive Economic Zones of the Hawaiian Archipelago and Johnson Island"

Tanimura S., J. Date, T. Takahashi, and H. Ohmoto (1983). "Stratigraphy and Structure of the Hokuroku District." In "The Kuroko and Related Volcanogenic Massive Sulfide Deposits." *Economic Geology*, monograph 5

US Bureau of Mines (1983, 1981). *Minerals Yearbook* vol. 3. Washington, DC: Government Printing Office

— (1988, 1985, 1983, 1982). *Mineral Commodity Summaries*. Washington, DC: Government Printing Office

US Department of Interior, Minerals Management Service and the State of Hawaii (1988). "Proposed Marine Mineral Lease Sale U.S. Exclusive Economic Zone Adjacent to Hawaii and Johnston Island." Draft Environmental Impact Statement, OCS EIS/EA, July

US General Accounting Office (1982). *Impediments to U.S. Involvement in Deep Ocean Can be Overcome*. EMD–82, 31

World Bureau of Metal Statistics (1984). *World Metal Statistics Yearbook 1984*. London

CHAPTER ELEVEN

Progress and Prospects for Energy Co-Operation in the Pacific Basin

Joy Dunkerley and Douglas Bohi

The Pacific Basin[1] has emerged as the most dynamic part of the world economy. Rates of economic growth have averaged over 5 per cent annually in this region in recent years compared with under 2 per cent for the world as a whole, and exports have expanded by 10 per cent per annum in contrast to a global figure of less than 3 per cent.[2] These achievements, plus high levels of investment, suggest that an increasingly large share of the world's economic activity will originate in the Pacific Basin.

In view of the region's emergence as a hub of economic activity, the question arises whether it should seek to establish institutions for the purpose of promoting regional economic co-operation somewhat analogous to those that have existed for years in Western Europe, Eastern Europe, and Latin America. Presumably, the benefits of regional co-operation would serve to enhance future regional economic prosperity and to promote regional prestige to balance that traditionally accorded the Atlantic Basin. On the other hand, the establishment of such institutions is not costless, and the benefits can be highly intangible or elusive. Furthermore, the benefits to be derived from region-wide co-operative schemes may not serve all member countries equally. Individual countries vary according to their interests and priorities and may find relatively little common ground on which to establish area-wide co-operation.

To investigate this question with respect to a specific economic issue, this chapter assesses the progress and potential for regional co-operation in energy. The energy price shocks of the 1970s demonstrated the importance of the energy sector to economic growth and stability in general. Moreover, it is commonly accepted that groups of countries acting co-operatively can achieve greater success in reducing the costs of energy supply disruptions than by acting independenly.[3] Thus, energy provides an example of a problem area that also serves as an incentive for co-operation. It is of interest to examine the extent of energy co-operation already achieved in the Pacific Basin and the prospects for building on these initiatives in the future. This will serve as a case study that may be suggestive of broader prospects for economic co-operation in the Pacific Basin.

In addressing this issue, we first describe existing energy co-operation efforts in the Pacific Basin and then analyse the nature of the benefits to be derived from co-operation. From the patterns that are revealed in existing co-operative efforts, we may deduce conclusions about the diversity of self-interests among individual countries and about gaps that remain to be addressed by future co-operative efforts. On the basis of this analysis, we then draw inferences about the prospects for future energy co-operation in the region.

CURRENT ENERGY CO-OPERATION ACTIVITIES

There is already in existence considerable energy co-operation activity in the Pacific Basin (see Table 72). This activity includes the work of organizations operating on both the regional and subregional level. Other energy co-operation initiatives are carried out within the region on a bilateral basis. Finally, many of the international organizations with global scope and responsibilities have developed special regional programs for the Asia-Pacific Region. Many of these organizations are intergovernmental, but there is also a significant number of private sector organizations and autonomous institutions established originally under governmental aegis but which have subsequently operated as independent entities.

Together these organizations (see Table 72) cover a wide range of activities — data development and analysis, technology transfer and training, research and development, trade and investment promotion, supply security, and environmental protection. In the lending carried out under co-operative arrangements, there is still a strong traditional emphasis on increasing supplies of conventional sources of energy, particularly electric power, although some shift away from power to oil, gas, and coal has taken place in recent years. At the same time, efforts have been made to extend the range of co-operative

Table 72
Activities of Pacific Basin Energy Co-operation Programs

Organization[a]	Training	Tech. ass.	Tech. transfer	Planning	Data coll. & analysis	Forum	Research & devel.	Scale econ.	National security	Trade	Lending	Environment
REGIONAL[b]												
ADB	X	X		X	X						X	
ESCAP	X	X	X	X	X							X
EPDC	X			X								
APO*	X											
AIT*	X		X	X	X		X					
EWC**	X			X	X	X						
CPCEMR					X							
PBEC**						X				X		
PECC**						X				X		
PENC**	X				X	X						
PAFTAD					X	X						
SUBREGIONAL												
ASEAN	X	X	X	X	X	X	X	X	X	X	X	X
SPRO	X	X	X	X		X	X	X	X		X	X
CCOP/AO	X	X										
& CCOP/SOPAC	X	X										
BILATERAL												
ODA	X										X	
Nuclear agreements	X		X							X		
US-Japan				X		X	X			X	X	
EXTRAREGIONAL												
World		X		X	X						X	
UNDP	X	X	X	X								
UNDTCD	X	X	X									
WEC					X	X						
LAEA	X	X	X									

activities to areas such as conservation, planning, energy enterprises, training, and research and development.

The extent of membership in organizations conducting energy co-operation programs varies considerably. Table 73 lists membership for regional and subregional organizations only. From this table it can be seen that a few organizations — notably the ADB, ESCAP, and the EWC[4] — have wide membership among Pacific Rim countries. None of these organizations, however, includes Pacific Rim countries in Latin America as members. The limited Latin American membership in Pacific Rim organizations is in non-governmental, professional organizations.

In the other organizations, membership is more selective either because it is specifically limited to certain countries (as in the case of ASEAN) or because the activities undertaken are of interest to only a limited number of countries. An example would be the PBNC, which is open in principle to representatives of all countries but which, in practice, is limited to countries with nuclear-generating facilities or with plans to install them.

BENEFITS OF CO-OPERATION AND THEIR RELATION TO THE OBJECTIVES OF EXISTING ORGANIZATIONS

Co-operation implies that there exist activities of mutual benefit to the interested parties that would not take place if left to private markets or to the actions of individual governments. If those same activities could be expected to occur in the absence of a co-operative agreement, there is no effective need for the agreement or for the organization established to administer the agreement. Thus, our analysis of the role of co-operation in the Pacific Basin and of the need for new or expanded agreements begins with a discussion of several reasons why co-operation may yield greater benefits than un-coordinated actions and how these rationales compare with the programs carried out by existing co-operative activities.

The economic benefits to be obtained from regional energy co-operation may arise from at least six sources. While interrelated, they can conveniently be discussed as distinct categories. They are: information; economies of scale effects; national security; promotion of investment; expansion of trade; and environmental improvements.

Information

International co-operation may be expected to enhance access to information. The advantages of co-operation arise because several aspects of

Table 73
Membership in Pacific Basin Programs

Countries	ADB[a]	AIT[b]	ECAP[c]	EWC[d]	CPCEMR[e]	PAFTAD[f]	PBNC[g]	PBEC[h]	PECC	ASEAN[i]	SPRO[j]	CCOP/AO[k]	CCOP/SOPAC
US	X	X	X	X	X	X	X	X	X				
Canada	X	X			X	X	X	X	X				
Mexico					X	X	X						
Ecuador					X								
Colombia					X								
Japan	X	X	X	X	X	X	X	X	X			X	
S. Korea	X	X	X	X	X	X	X	X	X			X	
Brunei			X	X	X					X			
Indonesia	X	X	X	X					X	X			
Philippines	X	X	X	X	X	X		X		X		X	
Singapore	X	X	X	X		X			X	X			
Thailand	X	X	X	X	X	X			X	X		X	
PRC			X	X	X		X						
Taiwan	X	X		X	X	X	X	X					
Australia	X	X	X	X	X	X	X	X	X		X		
New Zealand	X	X	X	X		X		X	X		X		X
Tuvalu			X	X							X		X
W. Samoa			X	X							X		X
Tonga	X		X	X							X		X
Fiji	X		X	X							X		X
Vanuatu	X		X	X	X						X		X
Kiribati			X	X							X		
Cook Islands	X		X	X							X		X
Naura			X	X							X		X
Niue			X	X							X		
Palau											X		
PNG	X		X	X							X		X
Solomon Is.	X		X	X							X		X

information have the character of a public good, where the benefits to be gained from information cannot be appropriated only by those who bear the cost of collecting it. The consequence is that information will not be collected in instances where the benefits outweigh collection costs if the costs must be borne individually. To enhance the flow of useful information, collection costs must be shared among the group of countries that will enjoy the benefits. In addition, individual countries will be inclined to participate more actively in supplying domestic information if they are members of a group effort to organize data collection. Finally, the need for co-operation recognizes that information flows less easily across political boundaries than within and that small and less lucrative markets may become especially isolated.

It is clear from Table 72 that one of the most common activities undertaken by the array of existing co-operative organizations in the Pacific Basin is in the area of information collection and dissemination. Nevertheless, some deficiencies remain in these activities. In the area of data collection, for example, there is a conspicuous lack of useful information of the breadth and detail collected by co-operating organizations in other regions such as the International Energy Agency for the industrial countries and the Latin American Energy Organization (OLADE). There is a similar and related lack of sophisticated economic-forecasting activity in many countries in the Pacific Basin and pertaining to the Pacific Basin as a whole. The development of an improved data base and forecasting methodology would greatly assist regional energy sector planning. This is an important consideration in the Pacific Region, since many of the new energy developments in coal, refinery upgrading, LNG, as well as electricity, are large scale and capital-intensive with both long lead times and long project lives.

Technology transfer, training, and technical assistance are other aspects of information flow. These appear to be popular objectives of the existing set of regional co-operative organizations. However, further activities seem warranted. Compressed natural gas in transport is a particularly fruitful area for regional co-operation, since the technology is well developed in New Zealand, and several other regional countries possess significant gas reserves which are far from end-use markets.

In this general area of technology transfer, training, and technical assistance, nuclear energy occupies a special place because of the multitude of problems requiring international solutions, including waste disposal, fuel enrichment, reactor safety, operator training, and questions of weapons proliferation. Co-operation in nuclear energy in the Pacific region takes place bilaterally and internationally, rather than regionally. Thus, there is a myriad of bilateral co-operative agreements linking the two large nuclear powers of the region, the US and Japan, with each other and with countries that have nuclear facilities (for example, Thailand, People's Republic of China, Indonesia, and Malaysia). The multiplicity of existing bilateral arrangements suggests the regionalization of nuclear technology and training, but this may be difficult to achieve on the governmental level because of political problems arising in trying to accommodate countries such as the People's Republic of China, Taiwan, and South Korea. On the international level, most Pacific countries participate in the work of the International Atomic Energy Agency. The sole regional initiative, however, is the series of conferences sponsored by the PBNC, a private sector organization.

The conduct, as distinguished from the transmission, of research and development is also carried out in several organizations. These include the AIT, the East-West Center, ASEAN, and the South Pacific Regional organizations. Much of this research is on topics closely related to the needs of the poorer countries, especially the South Pacific Islands (for example, new and renewable sources of energy such as wind power).

Research and development activities could be extended while still remaining focused on regional needs. One example is research into the development of compressed natural gas for stationary uses, such as pumps, which could increase the market for natural gas and, in some cases, improve refinery balance. Ocean Thermal Energy Conversion (OTEC) and geothermal energy have also been mentioned as appropriate areas of research because of their major potential in the Pacific Basin.

Economies of Scale

The second rationale for regional energy co-operation is economies of scale, a term that refers to the advantages of size in reducing the cost of producing, transporting, and purchasing energy and other commodities. This factor may include quantity discounts on large purchases that are made possible by bringing together several small countries and possibilities for implementing production technologies that enable unit production costs to fall as the rate of output rises. Also important is the influence of market power that may be exercised when several smaller countries join together in co-operative ventures. This factor is related to the national security argument for cooperation. Whereas an individual small oil-importing country may be ignored in a tight market environment, a collection of such countries will be more successful in bidding for their share of available world supplies.

All countries in the Pacific Basin can obtain some scale benefit by joining a regional co-operative, but for the larger countries the benefits may not be worth the trouble. Clearly, this consideration becomes more important the smaller the country; hence, the small countries in Oceania may attach great significance to this motive for co-operation. In addition, many of the advantages of co-operation depend on geographical proximity, for example, for production and transportation economies, and thus they are more important for co-operation among subgroups of the Pacific Basin than for the whole.

From Table 72 (column 8) it can be seen that there is relatively little activity in this category. The South Pacific Islands and ASEAN are the two major existing examples of regional co-operation to secure scale economies. For the South Pacific Islands, activities in this area have included efforts to secure quantity discounts on imported petroleum products by combining purchases. In recognition of the high import dependency and lack of conventional energy resources in South Pacific Islands, efforts are being made in ESCAP, AIT, and within the South Pacific regional organizations themselves to conduct research and development and to transfer the technology on wind energy, solar energy, and improved biomass stoves.

ASEAN member countries attempt to secure two benefits from economies of scale. The first is to create a market large enough for major industrial projects such as automobiles and fertilizer. So far, these projects have not included energy, but the same reasoning would apply to large-scale energy projects. The second, more appropriately discussed under "national security" (see below), is a variation on the "scale" argument involving efforts to reduce the effects of disruptions in the oil market by joint action.

National Security

The third rationale for co-operation, namely, national security, recognizes that countries can protect themselves from the risk of disruptions in energy supplies more effectively by acting together than if they act independently. This reasoning lies behind the formation of the International Energy Agency (whose membership is restricted to OECD countries), where member countries have agreed to share available oil supplies, reduce demand, and release stockpiled oil in the event of an oil emergency. For the Pacific Basin countries, particularly the smaller countries in the region, two aspects of co-operation would seem to be particularly useful: first, the use of collective market power to help attract supplies in a tight market; and second, joint management of oil stockpiles to reduce storage costs. Both are extensions of the economies of scale argument mentioned above, to be implemented in this case when an energy crisis occurs.

The only regional energy security arrangement in existence is that formed by the members of ASEAN, who have established an emergency oil-sharing agreement much like that of the IEA. Several of the larger Pacific Basin countries belong to the IEA, including Australia, Canada, Japan, New Zealand, and the United States. However, excluded from an energy security arrangement are South Korea and Taiwan, both of which are known to be concerned with supply security.

Although ASEAN members have apparently found it worthwhile to institute an oil-sharing arrangement, this action, as in the case of the IEA, is unlikely in practice to make member countries any better off in an emergency (Bohi and Toman 1986). The reason is that the agreement provides no additional incentives to increase collective oil stocks before a crisis or to reduce consumption after a crisis begins. An oil-sharing agreement of the IEA variety does not mean that more oil will be available or that it will be used more efficiently; on the contrary, the group may become worse off to the extent that individual countries are encouraged to free-ride on their neighbours.

Thus, while co-operation is a desirable way to lower the cost of implementing energy security policy, the Pacific Basin countries must take care to adopt a truly cost-effect approach to the problem. For example, a joint stockpiling agreement of the sort now under consideration in ASCOPE, which enables the group to lower storage costs, means that more oil could be stored at a given level of budgetary cost to each individual country.

Promotion of Investment

The fourth rationale for regional co-operation is to overcome the variety of barriers that impede the flow of investment among countries. This rationale is closely related to considerations of energy security. Emergency stockpiling and the like are useful instruments for energy security in the short term, but over the long term regional energy security can benefit from increasing regional energy supplies, thus reducing dependence on extraregional sources. Co-operative efforts may be required to obtain the seed money needed to attract private investment; otherwise, non-market goals, such as regional goodwill, would receive insufficient attention. International co-operation is also required to overcome political barriers to investment. Whether such barriers arise through narrow internal interests or national objectives, the process of international co-operation provides a broader perspective of compromise and negotiation to advance collective interests.

Several of these considerations are likely to be of relevance in the Pacific Basin. Though the Pacific Region includes both energy producers and exporters, the region as a whole is a net importer of energy products. Furthermore, energy consumption, though now increasing less rapidly than in the past, is still rising strongly so that large additional energy supplies from within the region will be needed if growing import dependence is to be avoided. The energy security motive is therefore a strong incentive to expand regional production. However, some of the richest resources are in poor countries that depend on foreign investment and expertise for their development. While part of this development will continue to be carried out on a bilateral basis, some of these resources, notably coal and LNG, can only be developed economically on a large-scale, integrated basis, which implies the need for long-term purchasing commitments from larger markets in the area, in particular Japan and, to a lesser extent, Taiwan and South Korea.

As can be seen from Table 72, there already exists some activity in the investment area. Lending for energy development is a major function for several organizations: the ADB, the World Bank, and the South Pacific Regional organizations, as well as bilateral aid agreements, all within a developmental framework. The private sector organizations (the PEBC and PECC) contribute to foreign investment by providing information on investment opportunities in member countries and by bringing investment barriers to the attention of governments in the region. CCOP/AO and CCOP/SOPAC provide geologic and survey material to help overcome one of the most important deterrents to oil investments in new areas — lack of geological data. ASCOPE has made a start by generating common rules for leasing offshore areas to developers and exchanging information on contract negotiations, arbitration, and contract performance. This is reported to be an area of co-operation that could be further developed. Another area for regional co-operation could be the establishment of machinery for the settlement of territorial disputes over resource ownership.

Expansion of Trade

Parallel to barriers to investment, the fifth rationale is the removal of barriers that impede the flow of energy trade in the region. As in the case of investment, political barriers to trade arise because of domestic interests or national objectives. International co-operation can provide a broader perspective to promote regional interests.

The promotion of trade is a major objective of the PECC and PBEC through providing information on trading opportunities to their members as well as by bringing trade barriers to the attention of governments in the region. Trade topics are also widely discussed in governmental and private councils between the US and Japan. A major ASEAN objective is the promotion of energy trade.

An important barrier to increased regional energy trade is the embargo on the export of most Alaskan oil (though not gas). At present, most Pacific Basin energy trade takes place either among countries in the West Rim or countries of the East Pacific Rim rather than trans-Pacific. The total value of intra-Pacific trade is US $69.4 billion, of which US $30.2 billion or 44 per cent is accounted for by trade among West Pacific Rim countries. The countries of the East Pacific Rim (US, Canada, Ecuador, Colombia, Mexico) account for 38 per cent (US $26.1 billion) of total intra-Pacific energy trade. Trans-Pacific energy trade, on the other hand, represents only 19 per cent of the total (at US $13.1 billion).

There is some logic to the subdivision of energy trade between East and West Rims, since each region is dominated by a major market, Japan and the United States. Both of these countries also import large quantities of energy from other parts of the world. However, given Japan's desire to diversify sources of energy supply away from the Middle East, there would appear to be potential for increasing trans-Pacific trade from the US and other East Rim countries, such as Colombia.

Another important barrier to regional energy trade arises from the desire to protect domestic petroleum-refining industries. Usually this means that countries discourage imports of regional products through import tariffs or quotas. Note, however, that the effect of limitations on refined product imports by one country will tend to make matters worse for its neighbours by lowering international product prices and encouraging imports to encroach even further on their domestic markets. In this case, import restrictions by one country may force others to adopt protective restrictions as well, possibly creating an environment that encourages nations to adopt a beggar-thy-neighbour trade policy. This example of interdependence among trading partners emphasizes the need to develop institutions to deal with the inevitable problems that develop as trade expands in the Pacific Basin region.

Environmental Improvement

A final rationale for co-operation concerns the environment, since production, transportation, and consumption of energy frequently create environmental pollution problems that transcend national boundaries. From Table 72 it can be seen that only a few organizations have environmental programs — the East-West Center, ESCAP, SPC and ASEAN — but membership in these organizations covers most of the countries. Some aspects of these programs, such as water and soil management, are not directly related to energy, but others, such as studies of deforestation at the East-West Center, marine pollution in both ASEAN and SPC, and the regulation of dumping of nuclear wastes, also in SPC, are energy/environment issues.

Some major energy/environment issues, such as nuclear waste disposal, do not appear to be receiving adequate attention even though this is clearly an issue that transcends national boundaries. Part of the reason is that it is usually assumed that the burden of waste disposal lies with the country creating the waste, and, so far, the problem is limited to Japan, South Korea, Taiwan, and the United States. At the same time, Pacific Islanders are greatly concerned about the use of Pacific sites for waste disposal, particularly since they neither benefit from nuclear power nor have a voice in international control organizations.[5] In addition to waste disposal, many environmental problems are localized in their impact but shared by many countries. These common problems suggest the benefits of pooled experience or even joint research development.

FUTURE DIRECTIONS FOR CO-OPERATION

The prospects for more comprehensive forms of economic co-operation on a region-wide basis may be suggested from the prospects for broadening energy co-operation to include more objectives and more countries. The information described above provides a basis for making inferences about future directions in energy co-operation.

As shown earlier, membership in the regional organizations differs considerably. It is to be expected that countries will differ in their perceptions of self-interests and that they will not attach the same importance to each potential objective of co-operation. Major dissimilarities in self-interest imply that specific co-operative initiatives cannot encompass all potential issues or all Pacific Basin countries. Similarly, the need for new co-operative initiatives may be subregional rather than all-encompassing to the extent that the Basin is composed of widely dissimilar groups.

Indeed, the pattern of co-operative activities that has developed so far supports these suppositions. The following matrix categorizes existing organizations according to whether they cover all objectives or selected objectives and all countries or some countries.

There are no organizations in category 1 that cover all the objectives and countries listed in Table 72. This is a reflection of the diversity of interests among the countries in the region.

The Pacific Basin countries are exceptionally diverse. They vary widely in size of population and economy, ranging from Japan and the US with populations of 122 and 244 million and GNPs of almost two and a half and five trillion dollars respectively, to a myriad of small independent nations with populations of under 1 million and GNPs of a few million dollars. There is also a wide diversity in living standards in these countries, ranging from well over US $10,000 per capita a year in the industrial nations to under US $500 in some of the poorer countries. These disparities in living standards reflect major differences in economic structure and a whole host of social indicators.

	All Objectives	**Selected Objective**	
	(1)		(2)
All countries of the region		ADB ESCAP CPCEMR	EWC APDC AIT
	(3)		(4)
Some countries of the region	ASEAN SPRO	PBEC PECC	PBNC PAFTAD

With regard to energy use, Pacific Basin countries also vary greatly. Energy consumption (see Table 74), ranges from under 100 kgoe per capita in Bangladesh (or perhaps twice as much if traditional fuels are included) to almost 7,000 kgoe in the US and Canada. There is also wide variation in energy import dependence (see Table 75). Of the twenty-four countries listed in Table 75, nine are net energy exporters, four are small importers (defined as importing less than one-quarter of total energy consumption), and eleven are large importers, in several cases importing 100 per cent of total commercial energy consumed.

Given this diversity, it is small wonder that there are no co-operative programs in the area that cover all objectives and include all countries. There is clearly not sufficient identity of interest to support such all-inclusive efforts.

There are, however, a number of organizations (category 2) that encompass all (non-Latin American) countries of the Pacific region. These programs are typically selective in their objectives and devoted

Table 74
Per Capita Levels of Commercial Energy Consumption, and GNP; Energy to GNP Ratio, 1986/7

Country	Comm. Energy Consumption per capita[a] (kgoe)	GNP per capita[b] (US$)	Energy/GNP (kgoe/$)	Population[b] (million)
N. AMERICA				
US	6,642	18,530	358	243.8
Canada	6,786	15,160	447	25.9
LAFTA				
Mexico	1,123	1,830	614	81.9
Ecuador	459	1,040	441	9.9
Colombia	545	1,240	440	29.5
Venezuela	2,366	3,230	733	18.3
DEVELOPED ASIA				
Japan	2,538	15,760	161	122.1
DEV. EAST ASIA				
Korea	1,137	2,690	423	42.1
Brunei	4,607	15,390	299	0.235
Indonesia	196	450	436	171.4
Malaysia	734	1,810	406	16.5
Philippines	172	590	292	58.4
Singapore	2,908	7,940	366	2.6
Thailand	315	850	371	53.6
PRC	494	290	1,703	1,068.5
OCEANIA & SOUTH PACIFIC ISLANDS				
Australia	4,690	11,100	423	16.2
New Zealand	2,737	7,750	353	3.3
W. Samoa	244	n.a.	n.a.	n.a.
Tonga	135	720	188	0.1
Fiji	270	1,570	172	0.722
Vanuatu	129	[c]	n.a.	0.15
Kiribati	92	480	192	0.066
SOUTH ASIA				
Bangladesh	43	160	269	106.1
India	190	300	633	797.5
Sri Lanka	212	400	530	16.4

Source: [a]1986 UN Yearbook of World Energy Statistics, Table 2
[b]*World Development Report 1989*, World Bank, Washington, DC 1989 pages 165/6
[c]GNP in low income range

to a subset of goals for which there is a wide measure of consensus. For example, all countries belong to the ADB in token of indisputable support for development assistance among the rich as well as the poorer countries of the region. Other activities which command

Table 75

1986 Production, Consumption of Commercial Energy, Energy Imports, Energy Exports, and Net Trade Position
(quantities in thousand metric tonnes of oil equivalent)

Country	Total production	Solids	Liquids	Gas	Primary elec.	Total* consumption	Energy imports	Energy exports	Net energy trade**	Level of trade depend. (%)[a]
N. AMERICA										
US	1,395,378	468,657	482,117	382,618	61,987	1,594,670	313,326	74,901	238,425	SI(15%)
Canada	220,556	33,011	83,775	70,927	32,843	174,349	31,372	78,733	-47,361	E
LAFTA										
Mexico	164,013	4,225	142,621	14,658	2,510	90,894	2,372	72,036	-69,664	E
Ecuador	15,116	0	14,644	101	371	4,428	418	10,713	-10,295	E
Colombia	28,743	7,252	15,836	3,960	1,694	15,987	883	11,295	-10,412	E
Venezuela	119,111	40	96,521	20,718	1,831	42,097	262	74,049	-73,787	E
DEVELOPED ASIA										
Japan	34,532	9,847	646	1,990	22,048	308,119	209,399	2,001	297,398	LI(97%)
DEV. EAST ASIA										
Korea, S	13,936	11,156	0	0	2,780	47,721	46,813	2,876	43,937	LI(92%)
Brunei	17,801	0	9,101	8,700	0	1,124	24	16,435	-16,411	E
Indonesia	99,580	1,207	71,007	26,743	623	33,237	6,364	70,418	-64,054	E
Malaysia	33,979	0	24,803	8,825	350	11,676	6,174	27,985	-21,811	E
Philippines	1,846	587	345	0	914	9,618	8,476	234	8,242	LI(86%)
Singapore	0	0	0	0	0	7,524	45,928	25,759	20,169	LI(100%)
Thailand	7,258	1,429	2,239	3,113	478	16,495	9,675	547	9,128	LI(94%)

Table 75 (continued)
1986 Production, Consumption of Commercial Energy, Energy Imports, Energy Exports, and Net Trade Position
(quantities in thousand metric tonnes of oil equivalent)

Country	Total production	Solids	Liquids	Gas	Primary elec.	Total* consumption	Energy imports	Energy exports	Net energy trade**	Level of trade depend. (%)[a]
OCEANIA										
Australia	126,003	83,347	27,606	13,645	1,406	74,567	7,342	58,510	-51,168	E
New Zealand	7,960	1,293	1,351	3,341	1,974	9,165	1,921	238	1,683	SI(18%)
Tuvalu	n.a.	—	—	—	—	n.a.	n.a.	n.a.	—	—
W. Samoa	2	0	0	0	2	40	38	0	38	LI(95%)
Tonga	0	0	0	0	0	15	15	0	15	LI(100%)
Fiji	29	0	0	0	29	200	342	77	265	LI(100%)
Vanuatu	0	0	0	0	0	19	39	0	39	LI(100%)
Kiribati	0	0	0	0	0	7	7	0	7	LI(100%)
SOUTH ASIA										
Bangladesh	2,920	0	97	2,784	39	4,480	1,855	0	1,855	SI(41.4%)
India	139,576	98,179	31,336	5,006	5,055	147,130	19,466	320	19,146	SI(13%)
Sri Lanka	227	0	0	0	227	1,331	1,845	108	1,737	LI(100%)

Source: 1988 UN Yearbook of World Energy Statistics

a Four levels of "trade dependence" have been defined based upon the percentage of total consumption composed by net energy trade:
E = net exporter
SI = small importer: ID 5 – 25%
LI = large importer: ID 25% and over
Numbers in parentheses are the calculated levels of "import dependence"

* Total consumption also includes stock changes, bunkers, and unallocated quantities
** Net energy trade signifies net imports

region-wide support (such as in the EWC, AIT, CPCEMR) are those concerned with the development and transmission of information. This objective has the added advantage of not usually involving a large financial commitment.

Category 3 consists of organizations that are comprehensive in their objectives but limited in membership. The outstanding example is the group of small South Pacific Island nations, which share many of the same problems and which stand to gain from important economies of scale by combining their efforts at information collection, research and development, and obtaining petroleum supplies.

ASEAN, while similarly comprehensive in objectives, consists of countries that in many important respects (for example, size and energy endowments) are quite diverse. In this case, shared perceptions of regional vulnerability as well as a desire to capture important economies of scale have been sufficient to overcome the differences existing among them.

Category 4 contains organizations with both limited membership and limited objectives. In practice, these are private sector business, professional, and scholarly organizations that draw their membership from the established industrial countries and the NICs; that is, countries with some similarity of economy and structure.

This suggests that, owing to the extreme diversity of member countries, there is little potential for the development of all-encompassing energy programs covering all objectives and all countries. Instead, two possible lines of development appear on the basis of past experience to be more realistic. First, the expansion of region-wide programs is likely limited to those objectives that now command, or can be reasonably expected to command, a wide measure of consensus. And, second, given regional diversity, there may be potential for a variety of subregional initiatives, especially in the Western Rim of the Basin.

CONCLUSIONS

Our analysis indicates that existing activities in energy co-operation correspond closely to the conceptual rationales for co-operation and that, by these criteria, the framework of existing activities can be judged to be inherently logical.

However, it appears that additional activities could with advantage be developed. These include:

— data development and improvement in forecasting methodology;
— research and development and technology transfer in areas of particular interest to the region such as CNG, nuclear energy, low-head

hydro, forestry, electricity load management and generating efficiency, Ocean Thermal Energy Conversion (OTEC), and geothermal energy;
— the technical assistance and training programs that must accompany such technology transfer;
— scale economies in production, transport, and purchase of energy;
— improvement in the short-term energy security of the many highly import-dependent countries of the region through stockpile policy;
— promotion of investment in regional energy projects in order to reduce dependence on supplies from outside the region;
— sharing of experience in foreign investment codes, contract negotiation and performance, and negotiation of territorial disputes;
— removal of barriers to increased energy trade, such as export of Alaskan gas and freer markets in petroleum products; and
— environmental protection and improvement, such as nuclear waste disposal and afforestation.

The further question arises as to how co-operation in these additional agenda items should be handled — by regional or subregional groupings. Our analysis suggests that it is not feasible in expanding energy co-operation to set up regional energy organizations covering all countries, but instead the objectives should be matched to the subset of countries that are most interested in them. We have seen that some agenda items command wide regional interest. These include investment in the development context, information development and dissemination, and environmental issues. This suggests that additional activities in these areas could be developed on a region-wide basis. Even so, there could be resistance within the region to the extension of some of these activities as the "easiest" of the agenda items are exhausted, new items become more controversial or of interest to fewer countries, and participation becomes more costly.

For the other agenda items, involving the removal of barriers to trade in energy products, national security, and scale issues, the logical path is through subregional groupings of countries with a strong identity of interests. In all areas there appears to be potential for the development of private as well as public sector institutions. In a word, our analysis suggests that further development in energy co-operation should appropriately take place in an evolutionary fashion, building on the present framework, which has been shown to be a logical response to the particular condition existing in the area.

The focus of this chapter has been on economic justifications for energy co-operation in the Pacific, yet there are also important non-economic considerations influencing the impetus to regional co-operation. The rapid growth of the Pacific Basin in a sluggish world economy has, for example, led to a growing political consciousness within the region that has become manifested in a desire to develop regional identity and increase the region's voice in global councils. Furthermore, as in the case of ASEAN, economic co-operation is carried out in a broader economic and political framework, wherein a balance is struck between the different priorities of co-operating countries. In this context, member countries may be willing to make sacrifices in one sector, such as energy, in the interest, of securing greater benefits in other sectors. Factors such as these could result in a more rapid expansion of energy co-operation than would otherwise be anticipated. Nonetheless, the most likely and logical path of co-operation in the absence of exceptional developments would appear to be to build in an evolutionary manner on the existing pattern of co-operation.

GLOSSARY

ADB	Asian Development Bank
AIT	Asian Institute of Technology
APDC	Asia and Pacific Development Center
APO	Asia Productivity Organization
ASEAN	Association of South East Asian Nations
CCOP/AO CCOP/SOPAC	Committee for Co-ordination of Joint Prospecting for Mineral Resources: in Asian Offshore Areas; in South Pacific Offshore Areas
CPCEMR	Circum-Pacific Council for Energy and Mineral Resources
ESCAP	Economic and Social Commission for Asia and the Pacific
EWC	Resource Systems Institute of the East-West Center
IAEA	International Atomic Energy Agency
PAFTAD	Pacific Trade and Development Conference
PBEC	Pacific Basin Economic Council
PBNC	Pacific Basin Nuclear Conference
PECC	Pacific Economic Co-ordination Conference
SPRO	South Pacific Regional Organization
UNDP	United Nations Development Program
UNDTCD	United Nations Department of Technical Co-operation for Development
WEC	World Energy Conference
World Bank	International Bank for Reconstruction and Development

NOTES

1 Includes in this instance other countries of Asia. For a definition of Pacific Basin countries, see Table 73.

2 See the World Bank Atlas or International Monetary Fund, *International Financial Statistics* for comparative economic data.

3 This principle provided the motivation for the creation of the International Energy Agency, an agreement among twenty-one members of the Organization for Economic Co-operation and Development to co-operate in response to another energy crisis. Australia, Japan, New Zealand, and the US are the only Pacific Basin countries that belong to the IEA; the institution is essentially an Atlantic Basin entity. For a description of the IAE and its origins, see Willrich and Conant 1977.

4 See glossary for a definition of acronyms.

5 Discussions of nuclear waste disposal issues and activities in the Pacific Basin are provided in Wakabayshi 1983a and b.

REFERENCES

Bohi, D.R., and M.A. Toman (1986). "Oil Supply Disruptions and the Role of the International Energy Agency." *Energy Journal* 7:37–50

Wakabayshi, Hiroaki (1983a). "Nuclear Waste Disposal Issues in the Asia-Pacific Region." WP-83-15, East-West Center, Honolulu, June

— (1983b). "Nuclear Waste Disposal: Philosophy and Strategy." WP-83-14, East-West Center, June

Willrich, M., and M. Conant (1977). "The International Energy Agency: An Interpretation and Assessment." *American Journal of International Law* 71:199–223

CHAPTER TWELVE

China and Japan: Energy Contrasts and Commonalities

Vaclav Smil

China and Japan, the two leading economic powers of Asia's Pacific Rim, present one of the sharpest imaginable socioeconomic contrasts of the late twentieth century — and yet their recent energy policies and realities have displayed a number of surprisingly similar attributes.

To a casual observer these commonalities are largely hidden by a multitude of obvious and enormous differences. On the one hand, there is China, the world's most populous nation (its 1.1 billion people account for more than one-fifth of humanity) with an extremely tumultuous modern history and still an overwhelmingly rural and poor society in urgent need of industrial modernization, a country ruled by a totalitarian regime.

On the other hand, with a population of only one-tenth that of China, there is Japan: a vibrant yet disciplined democracy with perhaps the world's most stable (and certainly most homogeneous) social environment, a highly urbanized and now also a very prosperous nation, generally seen as one of the great pioneers of advanced technology. Numbers can never tell the whole story, but Japan's 1988 per capita GNP surpassed US $20,000 — while China's was no more than US $350.

The real difference is undoubtedly smaller. Recent Japanese performance has been greatly inflated by favourable exchange rates, and the country's per capita GNP adjusted in terms of purchasing power parities is less than US $15,000 while the similarly adjusted Chinese rate is at least US $750. Still, the disparity is huge, and the measure serves as perhaps the most impressive, although inevitably imperfect, indicator of the existential gap separating the two nations.

The differences between China's and Japan's energetics, or system-wide pattern of energy acquisition and utilization, are equally fundamental. In fact, the two countries have such idiosyncratic patterns of energy use that it is impossible to find any close analogies even among the nations selected from the best generally matching categories (that is, comparing China with India and Japan with West Germany).

The disparity of resource endowment is overwhelming. China's coal reserves are the world's third largest after the United States and the USSR, and its total resources of solid fuels may be second, if not first. The country's hydroenergy potential, of which less than 5 per cent has been harnessed, is by far the world's largest. In comparison with these riches, hydrocarbon reserves are still relatively modest — in 1988 China was no larger than eleventh in worldwide ranking of these reserves — but there is a considerable potential for large discoveries, especially in the landlocked Xinjiang region.

Verified deposits of fissionable materials could support a capacity of fifteen gigawatts (GW) for three decades at full load. Finally, China's location and size provide it with one of the world's largest geothermal potentials (in many parts of the country but above all in Xizang) as well as with abundant opportunities for direct conversion of solar energy in the vast sunny northwestern interior.

In contrast, Japan's energy patrimony consists of a very limited quantity of poor coals, a mere trace of crude oil and natural gas (in spite of decades of diligent search), a helpful bit of hydroenergy (with increasing total energy consumption this electricity provides less than 5 per cent of all primary energy, compared to nearly 20 per cent thirty years ago), and a few locally useful geothermal fields.

Inevitably, economic expansion of post-1945 Japan had to be fuelled even more by large imports, while, at the same time, the People's Republic of China has been developing its rich energy resources in order not only to achieve self-sufficiency but also to emerge as a relatively small, but potentially much more important exporter of both coal and crude oil.

At the time of OPEC's first round of large price increases in 1973-4, the Chinese were just starting to export their waxy crude oil from the giant Daqing field, and although initial volumes were small, they grew rapidly. At the same time, the Japanese were buying nearly 90 per cent of their primary energy abroad, and these imports were dominated by crude oil purchases covering almost 70 per cent of the country's energy needs. No steam coal was imported at that time, and liquefied natural gas (LNG) imports from Alaska and Brunei accounted for less than 2 per cent of the total energy consumption.

Japan's inordinate addiction to crude oil emerged naturally and unavoidably. Crude oil became the principal energizer of the world's economic dash during the 1950s and 1960s owing to its ease of transportation, the widespread utility of its refined products, and, until 1972, a steadily declining real price. Other import choices would have been either uneconomical, such as coal, or technically impossible, such as reliance on renewable energies or on large-scale imports of LNG (this technique entered a limited commercial use only in the mid-1960s).

Still, Japan's 1973 share of primary energy consumption covered by crude oil was much higher than in any other rich industrialized country. Among the Big Seven, France came closest with 59 per cent, followed by Italy with 54 per cent. In contrast, China's search for oil was rewarded by the first big find only in 1959, and production from the giant Daqing oilfield in Heilongjiang started to make a real difference only in the late 1960s. By 1973, when Daqing was producing half of the country's total output, crude oil still covered no more than one-fifth of China's primary energy consumption. The country's dependence on coal (a bit over 70 per cent of the aggregate demand) was at that time matched or surpassed only by three European Communist nations with traditionally high coal extraction (Poland, East Germany, and Czechoslovakia).

The fundamental differences between Chinese and Japanese energetics extend beyond supply — resource endowment, degree of self-sufficiency, and make-up of the fuel deliveries — to utilization. The fourth crucial, and qualitatively the most telling, disparity between the two countries has been in conversion efficiency. No other advanced industrialized nation has been able to beat Japan's overall first thermodynamic law efficiency of about 57 per cent. This is the result of Japan's inordinately high reliance on liquid fuels (whose stationary combustion is more efficient than burning of coals), its relatively small shares of household and private transportation use, and its energy-efficient industries.

Although Japan is clearly an affluent consumer society, most Japanese households still do not enjoy the comforts of central house heating and cooling. Cold winter days are spent huddled around *kotatsu* (heated low tables) or under heavy blankets with foot warmers. Cooling during muggy summer days is largely left to the airy structure of traditional Japanese houses. And although the country has become the world's largest car producer, the rate of car ownership is still behind even the West European average (in 1987 Japanese owned 235 vehicles/1000 people while the US rate was 570 and the West German 446), and the frequency of driving is lower still.

In contrast, China's primary energy conversion efficiency of less than 30 per cent in the mid-1970s was unenviable even in comparison with the average performance of other large poor industrializing economies of Asia and Latin America. This large divergence in energy conversion efficiency was mirrored in the great disparity between China's and other countries' average energy intensity of national economic product. Two decades of China's Stalinist stress on heavy industry and chronic neglect of inherently less energy-intensive consumer goods manufacturing and service made this difference even worse. In 1973 China needed almost seventy megajoules (MJ) of primary energy for each US(1988)$ of its GNP, while Japan could do with just about eighteen MJ! For comparison, Canadians needed at that time about thirty MJ and Americans about twenty-eight MJ for each US(1988)$ of their respective GNPs.

When OPEC's sudden action ended the availability of low-priced crude oil in the winter of 1974, Japan was affected immediately and painfully; for the first time since 1945, GNP fell and inflation rose sharply. In yet another contrast, the Chinese expanded their crude oil extraction by 27 per cent in 1973 and by a further 20 per cent in 1974, and to attract Japanese investment, they started rumours about a new "Saudi Arabia" in the making. Top Japanese officials, including the later Prime Minister Yasuhiro Nakasone, were returning from China offering predictions of Chinese annual crude oil production surpassing four hundred million tonnes within a decade and Japan buying as much as one hundred million tonnes of this huge extraction.

However, the first decade of the new energy era did not bring such changes to Chinese and Japanese energetics. Soon, Chinese crude oil output started to stagnate; new onshore discoveries, with the exception of a relatively rich Zhongyuan oilfield, were bringing only smallish additions in production capacity. And offshore exploration, even after foreign oil companies were finally invited for geophysical reconnaissance and eventual drilling in 1979, has proceeded slowly, with only one major natural gas find south of Hainan and no major crude oil discoveries in the South China Sea by the end of 1984. And although Japanese crude oil imports from China increased from just 1 million tonnes in 1973 to 7.9 million tonnes in 1975, they stagnated afterwards around 7.5 million tonnes, and even by 1984 they did not surpass the 10 million tonne mark.

But other changes took place: shifts of surprising similarity that have demonstrated several essential commonalities guiding the development of energy systems in otherwise very disparate societies. OPEC did us all a great service in making crude oil a much more valued commodity. Although infrastructural inertia and the renewed decline of crude oil's real cost after 1974 kept the consumption of refined products rising for several years, the high prices of the second, Iranian (1979-81) round of increases eventually made the difference. Japan strove to lower its crude oil consumption in order to reduce its huge import costs; while China embarked on a nationwide program of oil savings to relieve, at least partially, chronic shortages of liquid fuels needed in farming and industrial production and to make more of the fuel available for the newly lucrative exports.

The savings have been impressive. In 1983 Japan's crude oil consumption was 16 per cent lower than in 1973, the year of the first *oiru shokku* (oil shock), and 19 per cent below the all-time peak reached in 1979. For the next four years oil consumption remained basically stable, declining only by a bit over 2 per cent by 1985 and gently rising to within 0.5 per cent of the 1983 level by 1987. The Japanese oil import bill was thus on a steady decline since its 1980 peak of US $58.9 billion and the global collapse of crude oil prices in 1986 pushed it to just US $24.1 billion in 1986 and US $27.4 billion in 1987. This means that recent Japanese oil costs were, in constant terms, only about one-third as high as during the peak cost year of 1980!

Chinese crude oil use went up sharply from 42 to 91 million tonnes between 1973 and 1983 — but all of this growth occurred before 1979, when the output of 106.15 million tonnes was a shade higher than in 1983. Afterwards, the steadily expanding production pushed the nationwide extraction over 130 million tonnes by 1986, leaving more oil for export (the shipments doubled between 1982 and 1986 to 30 million tonnes a year). Crude oil became a major source of the country's foreign exchange earnings. In the early 1980s it earned about one-fifth of the total, but by 1987 this proportion was reduced — owing to a combination of much lower oil prices and vastly expanded export of textile yarn and clothing — to just 9 per cent (US $3.7 billion).

The Japanese reduced their consumption of refined fuels by improving their already high conversion efficiencies, while in China the biggest performance boost came from a gradual withdrawal of the direct combustion of unrefined crude oil in power plants. Declining Japanese use of crude oil brought, inevitably, a substantial slowdown in growth rates of aggregate energy consumption, another common point shared with Chinese energetics. Between 1950 and 1973 Japanese primary energy use rose about 9.3 times, but the 1983 total was virtually identical with the 1973 aggregate. This represented a change from an exponential increase of almost 10 per cent a year to no growth rate at all. Chinese energy consumption kept growing fairly vigorously after 1973, but its annual exponential rise of 4.6 per cent between 1973 and 1983 was in marked contrast to the average 1950-73 growth rate of almost 11 per cent.

This great slowdown of annual consumption increments, shared not only by China and Japan but also by virtually all of the world's economies, translated into impressive declines in the energy intensity of the national product. Unlike many poor Asian, Latin American, and African countries, as well as most rich European nations, both the Japanese and the Chinese economies continued to grow at a relatively fast pace, so their efficiency gains look even better than those achieved elsewhere.

As already noted, in 1973 Japan and China needed about eighteen and nearly seventy MJ for each US(1988)$ of their respective GNPs. A decade later, the Japanese needed just 13 MJ, and the Chinese consumed about 55 MJ/US(1988)$. The Japanese improvement of about 27 per cent was the most remarkable achievement since their initial intensity was already the lowest in the whole industrialized world. It was made possible by a combination of numerous technical changes and process adjustments. For example, the chemical industry saved about 20 per cent of all energy by recovery of waste heat, and the cement industry's new efficient kilns brought roughly the same level of savings. There were also important structural shifts, most notably a decline of the steel industry.

The Chinese have reduced their energy use by finally adopting conservation techniques common elsewhere for decades. Still, their dismally high energy intensities leave a huge potential for further improvement. For example, the iron and steel industry, China's largest sectoral user of commercial energy still consumes nearly three times as much energy per tonne of finished steel as do the Japanese producers. Similarly, structural shifts have very far to go in China; during the first decade of Deng Xiaoping's reforms, China's industrial economy still remained Stalinist at heart. This perseverance of old habits is best illustrated by the fact that the single largest project in post- 1978 China is a giant iron and steel plant in Baoshan, just north of Shanghai.

With virtually unchanged primary energy consumption during most of the 1980s — 1987 demand was less than 2 per cent above the 1980 level — and with a vigorously expanding export-led economy, the Japanese have continued to lower the energy intensity of their national production, and the strengthening of the yen only accentuated these gains: in 1987 the Japanese economy needed only about eight MJ/US(1988)$ of GNP. Chinese improvements have also been substantial as the continuation of reformist trends led to rapid expansion of manufactured exports and to large gains in production of consumer goods and delivery of services. In 1987 the Chinese economy averaged perhaps as little as thirty MJ/US(1988)$.

The third most notable common trait of post-1973 Japanese and Chinese energetics has been the increased stress on coal. More than just the direction, the two countries also shared an experience of initially overly grandiose plans followed by much modified realities. During the 1960s Japan became a large importer of coking coal with 1970 shipments of 50.7 million tonnes, but deliveries of steam coal started only in the late 1970s. Japanese energy planners turned to coal in a major way only after the Iranian revolution, which caused a near-total loss of Japan's formerly single largest source of crude oil (32 per cent in 1973 and still 13 per cent in 1978).

Steam coal imports grew rapidly to 7.2 million tonnes in 1980 and 12.3 million tonnes in 1981. Forecasts of 1990 steam coal imports rose from the Institute of Energy Economics' estimate of 22 million tonnes in late 1976 to MITI's projection of 56 million tonnes in 1981, and the development of an enormous "coal chain" was to ensure these large deliveries. The Japan Coal Development Company foresaw a mixture of develop-and-import contracts, straight long-term purchases, and spot buys, involving projects on four continents, deals with a dozen major coal-producing countries (US, Canada, Australia, and China being the largest sources), and trading, banking, and research arrangements spanning the globe. Sanwa Bank prepared an estimate of the huge costs required to meet this switch to coal: about (1981) 7 trillion yen, the sum dominated by 5.6 trillion yen for twenty-two to twenty-three gigawatts (GW) in new coal-fired power plants and nearly 1 trillion yen going for 110 large coal carriers.

But almost as soon as these plans were announced, the stabilization of crude oil prices and much slower overall growth rates of energy consumption started to exert a strong moderating effect on future expansion of Japanese coals imports. By 1982 MITI's budget for the promotion of coal-fired electricity-generating stations was already cut by 40 per cent. The Japanese negotiators abroad started to show much less urgency and began to demand what Australians, Americans, and Canadians perceived as unreasonable conditions for participation in large-scale coal production projects. As the Japanese steam coal imports stabilized at around fifteen million tonnes a year, foreign coal producers noted increasing disparity between Japanese talk about long-term security of energy supplies and investment decisions based on the lowest fuel price.

Simply put, in the late 1980s, Japan, as the world's largest importer of energy, faced a situation where exporters of crude oil, steam coal, and natural gas were all eager to sell and where the composition of Japanese consumption made it possible to engage in major fuel substitutions. Unlike Americans, who consume some three-fifths of all liquid fuels for transportation (where they are difficult to substitute by other energy sources), the Japanese convert only a little over one-fifth of their crude oil into transport fuel. Oil consumed by power plants and industries can be relatively easily substituted by coal and natural gas — but given the relaxed state of the global oil market, there is no need to engage in any rapid switching. The shift from oil to coal is still underway, but its rate will be more moderate than predicted at the beginning of the decade.

The Chinese, with their already very high dependence on coal, found the further promotion of this fuel appealing on many grounds. The readily accessible reserves of high quality bituminous coals assure a possibility of rapid and relatively cheap development. In Shanxi province, China's richest repository of coal, reserves of over 200 billion tonnes of excellent quality are found in seams with an average thickness of 2.3 metres. Additional benefits of vigorous coal extraction include savings of valuable crude oil and export earnings from steam-coal shipments. But the Chinese had even more unrealistic goals than the Japanese. The initial expansion plan, announced by the Ministry of Coal Industry in 1978, was for doubling of the 1977 output in ten years to 1.1 billion tonnes and then doubling it again by the year 2000.

Fast forgotten, the 1978 fantasy was replaced in 1982 by a more realistic but still highly strenuous program of producing 1.2 billion tonnes a year by the end of the century. The most important ingredient of a serious Chinese commitment to higher reliance on coal must be the upgrading of existing primitive capacities. One comparison says it all: should the Chinese continue to produce their coal as they have done during the 1980s—with average raw coal output containing 30 per cent of rock or clay — then the annual output of 1.2 billion tonnes by the year 2000 would contain no less than 360 million tonnes of incombustible waste. Coal transportation already claims nearly one-half of China's railroad capacity, and burdening it with such a huge tonnage of waste would only increase its current inefficiency.

Given China's poverty and enormous developmental needs, greater reliance on abundant and relatively cheap coal makes sense, but many inherent limitations of such a higher reliance — ranging from exorbitant investment needs in opening new mines and installing new coal-cleaning and transportation capacities to environmental consequences (above all, the heavy air pollution burden in all Chinese cities) — have already lowered the most excessive plans, and they will most likely further moderate the current ones.

The last shared experience worth stressing here concerns the unfulfilled expectations for non-traditional non-fossil energies: nuclear electricity generation and renewable conversions. This excludes the most important traditional renewable conversion, since both countries have sizable hydroelectricity generating systems: Japan, with about thirty-four GW of installed capacity, has virtually no undeveloped large sites left, while China, with nearly thirty GW in 1987, has embarked on the most ambitious program of hydrogenerating construction in modern history, including plans for the world's largest station, Sanxia on the Changjiang.

Japan's nuclear electricity-generating industry has grown to a substantial size, but as in all other OECD nations with the exception of France, nuclear forecasts have been steadily decreasing. The MITI 1977 forecast for 1990 was sixty GW; by 1981 this dropped to fifty-one GW and, in 1982, the total was lowered yet again to forty-three GW — but the 1988 total was still short of thirty GW. The slowing growth in demand for electricity, a series of problems with the Tsuruga station, the country's well-known emotional ambivalence about nuclear generation, and the worldwide feeling of apprehension after the Chernobyl disaster combine to explain the declining trend and lowered expectations. On the other hand, MITI's calculations still show nuclear fission as the cheapest way to generate electricity, and the nuclear option remains an important asset in a country still so vulnerably dependent on huge imports of Middle Eastern oil.

At one time during the early 1980s the Chinese nuclear plans envisioned installed capacity up to 10 GW by the year 2000, a totally unrealistic proposition. After a few cycles of promotion and retrenchment, it appears that the first domestically built small (300 MW) and expensive Qinshan station near Shanghai and the joint Sino-French project — Dayawan in Guangdong (1.8 GW), which will deliver most of its electricity to nearby Hong Kong rather than to China's most electricity-short province — will be the only operating nuclear facilities by the middle of the next decade.

As for the novel renewable conversions, Japanese interest has been, by any measure, only a fraction of American and West European effort. Even geothermal generation, where the Japanese potential of up to 30 GW of installable capacity is among the world's highest, has been neglected. Plans for 3.5 GW by the year 1990 will not be met, and foreign critics have charged the Japanese with deliberate delays in order to let other countries do the expensive development work and then to buy licences for working techniques at a relatively low price. Should this be the real Japanese intent, then the country's research expenditures and commercialization efforts in solar and wind conversions would be even better examples.

In both cases, the outlays and tangible gains since 1973 have been negligible. Even the director of the Sunshine Project admitted that MITI is spending money just to show the willingness to look at new ideas. Any serious student of energy conversion must realize the major obstacles to large-scale commercialization of renewable technologies and should deplore the many questionable schemes that have received funding in post-1973 North America and Western Europe and that have produced exaggerated claims about imminent utility. Nevertheless, Japan's lack of pioneering spirit — especially when considering the country's utter dependence on energy imports — is surprising.

In contrast, the Chinese have tried much harder — but the results have been similarly marginal. Their efforts were born of necessity, aimed at improving inadequate urban supplies and, above all, at reducing massive rural energy shortages. Various Chinese sources claim that at least one-half of all rural families are short of fuel for up to six months each year. The biogas program was by far the largest effort to relieve these hardships; it started in Sichuan in the early 1970s and the total number of biogas digesters reached about seven million units by 1979. This is certainly not a high technology, but it is one that demands quality workmanship and proper management. Because methanogenic fermentation of animal and human wastes and crop residues requires strict absence of oxygen, the slightest leak in the structure will turn digesters into plain waste pits. And an efficient operation is impossible without adequate and balanced recharging with fermentable materials.

Shoddy construction, shortages of feedstocks, lack of careful management, and the mobilizational approach to popularization of the technique (with high targets for digester construction by a specified date) were the program's undoing. At least three million digesters were abandoned during the 1980s, and a large number of those remaining do not generate enough biogas to cook three meals a day even during summer (in the winter it is too cold for fermenting bacteria to survive anywhere but in southernmost China).

Since 1980 the Chinese have been encouraging planting of family fuelwood lots as a part of their de facto privatization of farming. This represents a return to a traditional renewable source of energy, which should fill an important need for cooking and heating energy but which can hardly be a base of rural modernization. Solar water heaters are now in use in many cities and in some rural areas of sunny interior provinces, but the total contribution of these devices is negligible on a national scale. No advances worth mentioning have been made in harvesting wind energy, and exploration of the country's rich geothermal resources consists of a relatively small (ten MW) station near Tibet's capital and a handful of tiny experimental installations in several Chinese provinces.

SUMMARY

Lessons from this brief review of some surprisingly similar experiences between China and Japan, the world's third and fourth largest energy consumers respectively, are worth summarizing in order to dispel the commonly held, but incorrect belief about the impenetrability of energy futures. Undoubtedly, post-1973 forecasting efforts have been overwhelming failures, but the record would improve if less attention were paid to formalities of modelling and more to the fundamental relationships of modern energetics, which are so well illustrated here by recent developments in the world's archetypal poor nation and its leading rich modernizer.

First, when prices rise enough, impressive conservation efforts and efficiency increases will follow. Real energy needs are clearly much lower than was thought for decades — be it in China, Japan, Canada, or France. The most encouraging finding in this respect is that the slack in the system is large enough even in the world's most energy-efficient economy. Large post-1973 Japanese efficiency gains demonstrated that it is realistic to talk not only about 10-20 per cent savings but about eventual national energy consumption decreases of up to 40 per cent in rich countries. In China, with its still rapidly growing population (recent years have seen net additions of about fifteen million people a year) and with its huge infrastructural (and hence necessarily more energy-intensive) needs, as in all poor nations, it would be difficult to do away with such large shares of existing consumption, but long-term opportunities for energy conservation are no less impressive.

Second, the right prices trigger substantial fuel substitutions, and on the North American continent only the excessive attachment to the gasoline-fuelled private car precludes the realization that crude oil can be replaced to a surprising extent by coals, gases, and, in due time, by other energy sources. Owing to their abundance and relatively low cost of production in large surface mines, coals are the most obvious choice for such substitutions, but the Chinese and Japanese experience — as well as the progress in North America and Europe — shows that the switch has to be a gently paced one. Only then will it be possible to eliminate or minimize undesirable effects, above all, environmental consequences, of higher reliance on solid fuels.

Third, while conservation, efficiency increases, and fuel substitutions are desirable and necessary realities, large-scale introduction of alternatives is not a sensible choice for at least the remainder of this century. New energy sources and conversions have always had slow penetration rates, and infrastructural inertia makes the established sources and processes preferable even after their costs rise drastically and their supply reliabilities become questionable. Development of new conversions should proceed steadily, but the delusions of fully nuclear or comfortably solar tomorrows have no place in such an effort; energy transitions last decades, and the coming move away from fossil fuels will be no exception.

The experience of Chinese and Japanese energetics during the fifteen years of the new, post-1973 energy era is thus clearly encouraging. There is still much room to do more with less, to deploy new mixtures of old sources, and to bring in new supplies gradually. The neo-Malthusian tones of many energy projections seem inappropriate — but the success will not be a matter of automatic transformation; it will require a great deal of devoted managerial effort, technical inventiveness, and social adjustments.

Every society can be thought of as a fleeting manifestation of its dominant energy conversions. Since these processes will be modified and substituted, the affected societies will change no less profoundly than the traditional agrarian societies switching to fossil fuels. China has not yet completed its transition to a fossil-fuelled society — while Japan is on the leading edge of the most efficient use of liquid and solid fuels. This gives the two countries many of their profoundly different socioeconomic features — but the quest for better satisfaction of coming needs leaves behind some surprisingly similar traces.

REFERENCES

Chinese and Japanese energy development during the 1980s can be followed in detail in these chronologically listed publications:

Smil, Vaclav (1981). "Energy Development in China." *Energy Policy* 9:113–26

Oshima, K., T. Suzuki, and T. Matsuno (1982). "Energy Issues and Policies in Japan." *Annual Review of Energy* 2:387–97

McKean, Margaret A. (1983). "Japan's Energy Policies." *Current History* 82:385–9, 392, 395

Fujime, K., and H. Kibune (1987). "Japan's Energy Supply-Demand Outlook up to 2000 and 2010." *Energy in Japan*: 41–97

Fukai, S.N. (1988). "Japan's Energy Policy." *Current History* 87:169–72, 182–4

Mossavar-Rahmani, B. (1988). "Japan's Oil Sector Outlook." *Annual Review of Energy* 13:185–213

Dorian, J.P., and D.G. Fridley (eds.) (1988). *China's Energy and Mineral Industries*. Boulder, CO: Westview Press

Smil, V. (1988). *Energy in China's Modernization Advances and Limitations*. Armonk, NY: M.E. Sharpe

CHAPTER THIRTEEN

The British Columbia Coal Industry

Harold Halvorson

This chapter examines the British Columbia coal industry and the importance of Pacific Rim markets. Before doing so, however, some general comments about the types of coal and their role in world trade are of value.

TYPES OF COAL

There are various types of coal, ranging from very low-grade lignite or brown coals through the better-quality bituminous or black coals to the highest-rank or anthracite coals. Lignite coals have low heat values (6300-8300 btu per lb.), low fixed carbon content (approximately 30 per cent), and high moisture content (25-35 per cent). Anthracite coals have high heat content (over 12,000 btu per lb.), high fixed carbon content (over 86 per cent), and low moisture and volatile content. The bituminous coals have properties between those of lignite and anthracite.

Western Canada possesses all grades of coal; however, only the bituminous coals are of interest here, since these dominate Canada's exports. Considerable lignite is mined in Saskatchewan, but it is used locally (in Saskatchewan and Manitoba) for power generation. A large quantity of a similar quality coal (subbituminous) is also mined in Alberta, but it is all consumed in "mine-mouth" power plants. No anthracite is produced in western Canada, although one such mine is under study in the northwestern British Columbia Groundhog coal formation. All the coal exported from western Canada is bituminous coal mined in the Rocky Mountains of British Columbia and Alberta.

Another common nomenclature used for coals divides them into thermal and coking types. Thermal coals, sometimes referred to as steam coals, are used for their heating value only, and their main use is for electricity generation. Other significant uses are for fuel in cement kilns and for generating steam for industrial purposes. All three ranks of coal, lignite, bituminous, and anthracite, can be and are used as thermal coals. What determines which type of coal is used in a specific application at a given location is the delivered cost of a btu of energy. Also important are the volatile matter and the sulphur content, the latter for environmental "acid rain" reasons. A good quality steam coal contains about 0.5 per cent sulphur and volatile matter approaching 30 per cent. BC coals meet the sulphur specification but generally contain too little volatile matter.

Coking coals, also called metallurgical coals, are used to make coke, virtually all of which is used in steel-making. Small quantities are used in foundries. Coking coals require rigid physical and chemical properties. To make coke, coking coals are heated in the absence of air until the fixed carbon in the coals "melts and fuses," producing coke with correct strength, porosity, and other physical properties. Only the better bituminous coals produce quality coke. Coking coals are premium coals and command a higher price than do thermal coals. For example, the current world price for good coking coal is roughly Cdn $60 per tonne loaded on a ship, while that of thermal coal is about 25 per cent less.

WORLD TRADE

Nearly all countries have exploitable coal deposits, and most coal consumed in the world does not cross international borders. For example, in 1986 the world production of coal was reported to be approximately 3.4 billion tonnes, while trade between countries was 339 million tonnes, or only 10 per cent of the total. The coal involved in world trade is largely bituminous, along with a small amount of anthracite. In 1986, of the coal traded, approximately 50 per cent was coking and 50 per cent thermal.

The number of countries involved in supplying coal to world trade is small. Table 76, summarizing world trade in 1986, demonstrates that the US, Australia, South Africa, and Canada supplied 90 per cent of the total ocean-borne trade. The remainder came from China, the USSR, Poland, West Germany, and a variety of smaller shippers. Asia (Japan, South Korea, and Taiwan) and Western Europe are the principal recipients of ocean-borne trade.

In summary, only a small fraction of the total coal consumed in the

Table 76
World Coal Trade in 1986 (million tonnes)

Exporter/importer	Western Europe	Japan	Other Asia	Eastern Europe	North America	South America	Total	% share
LOCAL TRADE (barge, rail, coastal ships)								
Poland	15.9			15.6			31.5	9
USSR	4.2			15.9			20.1	6
W. Europe	19.4			0.5			19.9	6
US					12.9		12.9	4
Canada					0.3		0.3	0.1
SUBTOTAL	39.5			32.0	13.2		84.7	25
OCEAN TRADE								
Australia	26.1	42.3	22.8		0.1	1.1	92.4	27
US	40.8	12.2	6.1	0.3		6.0	65.4	19
S. Africa	24.5	8.8	11.3		0.9		45.5	13
Canada	2.5	17.7	4.2			1.4	25.8	8
China		3.6	6.3			0.1	10.0	3
USSR		5.5					5.5	2
Colombia	3.7	0.2	0.3		0.7	0.3	5.2	2
Poland			0.4			2.6	3.0	1
Other		1.4					1.4	0.4
SUBTOTAL	97.6	91.7	51.4	0.3	1.7	11.5	254.2	75
TOTAL	137.1	91.7	51.4	32.3	14.9	11.5	338.9	100
% share	41	27	15	10	4	3	100	

world is traded among nations; there are two big consumers, Asia and the industrial nations of Western Europe, and four big suppliers, the US, Australia, South Africa, and Canada.

Thermal Coals

The principal importers of ocean-borne thermal coals, showing the 1986 share in per cent, are: Western Europe 49; Japan 18; S. Korea, Taiwan, Hong Kong 28. The principal suppliers are Australia, South Africa, and the US, whose 1986 per cent share is: Australia 35; South Africa 34; US 16; China 6; Colombia[1] 4; Canada 3.

In 1986, Canada exported only four million tonnes of thermal coal. This was from Cape Breton, Nova Scotia, sold in Europe, and from BC and Alberta, sold in the Far East and Europe.

Western Canada is a relatively minor factor in the world trade of thermal coal. BC exports of thermal coal offshore commenced in the early 1970s with the first oil shock, but they did not expand to the same extent as those of Australia, South Africa, and Colombia. Table

77 compares BC's growth in exports to other major exporters. From 1975 to 1981, BC's exports held static at about 0.5 million tonnes per year (tpy), while the combined exports of its four major competitors increased by a factor of 4.2. In the period 1982–4, new mines in the province and contracts, primarily with South Korea, increased BC shipments significantly. However, BC's exports now appear to have reached a plateau, while those of Australia and Colombia are still growing.

Data for Japan presented in Table 78 also demonstrate that western Canada (BC and Alberta) has not fared as well in the important Japanese market as has Australia. Japan began importing significant quantities of thermal coal in the late 1970s. Australia is its major supplier (with 65 per cent of the 1986 total), while Canada in 1986 supplied only 6 per cent.

The BC thermal coal producers, their published capacities, and estimated 1987 offshore shipments are summarized in Table 79. In 1987, the BC producers operated at roughly 40 per cent of design capacity. Most of the exports have come from three new mines, Greenhills, Line Creek, and Quintette. Balmer and Fording, although they have low production rates, have had and continue to have the capability to supply large amounts of exports from waste coal not suitable for sale as coking coal. Consequently, the capacities in Table 79 are understated.

BC thermal coals have not enjoyed wide acceptance in export markets. They are expensive because of the long rail haul and do not have volatile contents most desired by power plants — the biggest market by far. BC coals are and will continue to be purchased as a diversification strategy by major consumers. Little, if any, growth in exports over the 1987 level is likely. Thermal coal will therefore continue to be a minor component of the BC coal industry in spite of an expected good growth in the world trade of thermal coals.

Coking Coal

The dominant factors in the BC coal industry are coking coal and the Japanese steel industry. Coal production in BC commenced in the last century, but with the passing of the steam locomotive in the 1960s, the industry essentially collapsed. It was revived in the early 1970s when the Balmer and Fording mines were built to supply coking coal to Japan.

The world's largest importer of coking coal is Japan. In 1986, of a total of 134 million tonnes traded in offshore markets, Japan purchased 68 million tonnes, or 51 per cent of the total. Western Europe

Table 77
Comparison of BC Thermal Coal Exports with Those of Major Competitors
(million tonnes)

	1975	1976	1977	1978	1979	1980	1981	1982	1983	1984	1985	1986	1987	1988
Australia	3.4	3.0	3.7	5.2	5.7	8.9	10.2	12.8	18.4	28.8	38.1	40.2	44.2	41.9
S. Africa[a]	1.4	5.2	8.2	10.8	17.7	22.9	22.6	23.0	25.6	30.7	36.0	40.6	36.3	31.6
US[b]	12.8	10.5	10.7	8.7	12.8	24.3	40.8	36.9	24.4	21.6	28.2	25.9	26.5	29.2
Colombia	0.01	0.02	0.1	0.2	0.1	0.1	0.1	0.2	0.3	0.5	1.4	4.7	8.3	
BC[c]	0.6	0	0.5	0.5	0.2	0.5	1.0	1.4	1.2	3.4	3.6	2.6	2.6	2.4
	18.2	18.7	23.2	25.4	36.5	56.7	74.7	74.3	69.9	85.0	107.3	114.0	117.9	
BC share (%)	3.3	0.0	2.2	2.0	0.5	0.9	1.3	1.9	1.7	4.0	3.4	2.3	2.2	

Sources: AEC Resource Consultants Ltd., International Thermal Coal Market, 4th Quarter 1988; Australian Bureau of Statistics; *Coal Age*, March 1987; Coal Association of Canada, *1988 in Review*; Joint Coal Board, *Black Coal in Australia 1985–1986; Mining Magazine*, March 1988; Republic of Colombia, National Energy Study; Tex Report Ltd., *Coal 1988;* US National Coal Association; US Bureau of Mines, *Mineral Yearbook*

[a] Excludes anthracite
[b] Excludes anthracite; includes shipments to Canada
[c] Estimated: excludes rail/truck shipments to Canadian and US markets

purchased 39 per cent, and South Korea, Taiwan, and Brazil most of the remainder.

Steel companies buy a mixture of various hard, medium, and soft coking coals and blend them with indigenous coals and noncoking coals to make coke. The Japanese steel industry has mastered the blending of diverse coals to maximize coke quality while minimizing coal cost. By aggressive industrialization policies, Japan has been most successful in building up a major steel industry. Between 1966 and 1974 the production of crude steel in Japan increased by a factor of 2.4 from 48 to 117 million tonnes per year. Over the same period the country's imports of coking coal increased by a factor of 3.4 from eighteen to sixty-two million tonnes per year.

Over the 1966-74 period, Canada (that is, BC and Alberta) successfully captured an increasing share of the growing Japanese imports. In 1966 Canada supplied 0.8 million tonnes or 4.4 per cent of the total. By 1974 this had risen to 9.6 million tonnes or 15 per cent of total imports. This growth was met by the new Balmer and Fording mines in southeastern BC and the McIntyre, Luscar, and Coleman mines in Alberta. Over the 1974-83 period, Japanese production of crude steel levelled off, as did their requirements for imported coking coal.

As shown by Table 80, in the 1974 to 1983 period, Canada supplied a relatively constant tonnage to Japan of about ten million tpy. Australia, Japan's largest source, also maintained a relatively constant ton-

Table 78
Growth in Japanese Thermal Coal Imports (calendar years)
(million tonnes)

	Source of Coal						
Year	Australia	China	Canada	South Africa	USSR	US[a]	Total[b]
1971				0.001			0.001
1972	0.001					0.002	0.003
1973	0.001						0.001
1974	0.074	0.035			0.062	0.012	0.183
1975	0.213	0.123			0.040		0.376
1976	0.248	0.105			0.209		0.562
1977	0.433	0.190		0.021	0.231	0.004	0.879
1978	0.685	0.170		0.025	0.144		1.024
1979	1.000	0.256	0.013	0.021	0.117		1.407
1980	3.529	0.613	0.328	0.238	0.223	0.289	5.220
1981	5.676	1.188	1.140	1.263	0.255	2.119	11.641
1982	6.344	1.483	1.302	2.581	0.213	1.629	13.591
1983	7.646	1.712	0.555	2.618	0.418	0.930	13.919
1984	10.866	1.740	0.680	2.358	0.774	0.485	16.967
1985	13.608	1.299	0.784	3.168	0.963	0.958	20.696
1986	12.739	1.230	1.269	2.950	0.891	0.516	19.696
% share 1986	65	6	6	15	5	3	100

Source: 1988 *Coal Manual*

[a]Excludes anthracite (a high of 1.6 million tonnes in 1971 and running at about 1 million tpy during the period 1971–82

[b]Includes some minor shipments from other countries

Table 79
BC Thermal Coal Producers

Company	Mine	Start-up date	Present capacity (mill. tpy)	1987 exports (mill. tonnes)
SOUTHEASTERN BC				
Westar	Balmer	1975	1.6	1.4
	Greenhills	1984		
Fording	Fording	1975	0.3	0.6
Shell	Line Creek	1982	1.1	0.7
Esso[a]	Byron Creek	1974	1.8	0.2
NORTHEASTERN BC				
Quintette		1984	1.3	0
Bullmoose		1984	0.6	0
Total			6.7	2.9

[a]Exports in 1987 exclude approximately 0.5 million tonnes shipped to Ontario Hydro by rail on long-term contract.

Table 80
Sources of Japanese Coking Coal Imports

	1971	1972	1973	1974	1975	1976	1977	1978	1979	1980	1981	1982	1983	1984	1985	1986
COAL IMPORTED (million tonnes)																
Australia	16.6	20.6	24.9	22.8	22.8	26.0	26.0	24.5	26.0	25.8	29.1	25.4	25.3	29.8	30.3	29.2
US	18.5	16.5	16.5	25.4	22.4	17.5	15.2	8.9	13.5	19.2	21.5	23.9	14.1	15.3	12.8	11.7
Canada	6.6	7.7	10.3	9.6	10.7	10.3	10.8	10.9	10.5	10.6	9.6	9.5	9.6	15.4	16.8	16.3
South Africa		<0.1	0.1	0.1	0.2	0.8	2.3	2.4	2.2	2.9	3.0	3.3	2.9	4.6	4.5	5.0
China						<0.1	<0.1	0.3	0.8	1.0	1.2	1.4	1.2	2.0	2.1	2.3
USSR	2.5	2.5	2.7	3.2	3.1	3.0	2.9	2.3	2.2	1.9	1.1	1.1	1.1	1.7	2.9	4.4
Other	1.1	1.2	1.3	1.4	1.5	1.5	1.3	0.8	0.9	0.4	0.3	0.3		0.5	0.7	0.8
Total	45.3	48.5	55.8	62.5	60.7	59.1	58.5	50.1	56.1	61.8	65.8	64.9	54.2	69.3	70.1	69.7
DISTRIBUTION (%)																
Australia	37	42	45	37	37	44	44	49	46	42	44	39	47	43	43	42
US	41	34	30	41	37	30	26	18	24	31	33	37	26	22	18	17
Canada	14	16	18	15	18	17	19	22	19	17	14	14	18	22	24	23
Other	8	8	7	7	8	9	11	11	11	10	9	10	9	13	15	18
Total	100	100	100	100	100	100	100	100	100	100	100	100	100	100	100	100
Japanese crude steel production (mill. tonnes)			119	117	103	107	102	102	112	111	102	100	97	106	105	98

Source: Tex Report Ltd., *Coal 1988*

nage of approximately twenty-five million tpy. The swing supplier was the United States. Over the decade the smaller Japanese suppliers, Poland and West Germany, were phased out, while China, South Africa, New Zealand, and Indonesia entered the Japanese market. The USSR has maintained a relatively constant tonnage of approximately two million tpy. Over the period these small suppliers held 8 to 11 per cent of the Japanese business.

The US has been the swing supplier because its coking coal, on average, is the most expensive delivered in Japan. This high cost is demonstrated below, where the prices landed in Japan during December 1984 for the same grade of coking coal[2] are compared (US $ per tonne, CIF Japan): US 76.43; Canada 70.35; Australia 60.45; China 51.91; USSR 50.25.

In the 1980-1 period, decisions were made by the major suppliers to Japan to expand coking-coal capacities. This expansion was facilitated by the Japanese through long-term contracts and direct investment in new mines, and it was especially large in Australia and western Canada. Australia's announced plans equated to an increase in output for 1985 of twenty-seven million tpy; Canada's increase amounted to 13 million tonnes, a combined increase of 51 per cent. In BC, four new mines were added to the existing two. One new mine was built in Alberta. These mines are summarized in Table 81.

This new capacity came onstream in the 1982-4 period in the midst of a worldwide recession. Steel output was severely depressed as was coking-coal demand. The recession, coupled with new mine capacity, resulted in an oversupply of coking coal and downward pressure on prices. The principal impact was on the old mines, which suffered price and volume reductions. By 1986, some old mines were shipping only 50 per cent of originally contracted quantities to Japanese customers. To survive, such mines in western Canada diversified into other markets, Europe and the US Midwest principally, and they have managed to regain much, in most cases all, of their previous volumes. Generally, the recovery has been at the cost of absorbing freight costs to service distant customers.

The overall BC coking-coal industry is not producing an adequate return on investment. Some capacity is still threatened with closure. The Japanese steel mills and Quintette Mines Ltd. entered a price arbitration process in 1988 with the mills asking for the world price of approximately Cdn $60 per tonne; Quintette, for the escalated contract formula price of approximately Cdn $100 per tonne. The arbitration panel decided on a price of approximately Cdn $84 per tonne. This price will likely trigger a drastic rationalization of costs including

Table 81
Coking Coal Mines in Western Canada
(million tonnes per year)

Operator	Mine	Japanese equity (%)	Start-up	Capacity 1987	Production 1987
BC					
Westar	Balmer	33.4	1973	6.5	4.7
	Greenhills[a]	26.7	1983	2.1	2.4
Fording	Fording	nil	1974	6.0	4.6
Shell	Line Creek	nil	1983	1.1	1.1
Denison	Quintette	38.0	1984	5.0	4.7
Teck	Bullmoose	10.0	1984	1.7	1.7
SUBTOTAL				22.4	19.2
ALBERTA[b]					
Luscar	Cardinal River	nil	1972	3.3	1.6
Smoky River	Smoky River	nil	1970	2.0	0.9
Manalta	Gregg River	40.0	1983	2.1	1.7
SUBTOTAL				7.4	4.2
Total				29.8	23.4

[a] 20 per cent South Korea
[b] *Source:* Alberta Coal Industry Monthly Statistics

significant reductions in government royalties, surcharges, fuel and excise taxes, rail and port throughput charges, and bank-financing costs. Unless this is done, Quintette might close and, with it, perhaps the whole northeast coal development.

Based on generally accepted forecasts of Japanese crude steel production and the fraction made with coke, essentially no growth in Japanese demand for coking coals is foreseen. It is expected that the Japanese steel industry will use increasing proportions of weak-coking, lower-cost coals in their coking feed blend. Other markets for coking coal, South Korea, Taiwan, and South America, will grow but not to the extent that they will make significant inroads into the existing mine overcapacity in the major suppliers, Australia, US, and western Canada. In addition, a significant proportion of steel will continue to be made from scrap. The result of all these factors will be continued overcapacity, downward pressure on prices, and increasing competitiveness to capture other producers' customers.

What went wrong? Figure 15 demonstrates the main error: overly optimistic forecasts of Japanese crude steel production and hence coking-coal imports.

The decision to proceed with the northeast BC coal project and the expansions in the southeast were made in the 1980-2 period. Figure 15 shows that forecasts during that period concluded that Japanese

Figure 15 Forecasts of Japanese Crude Steel Production

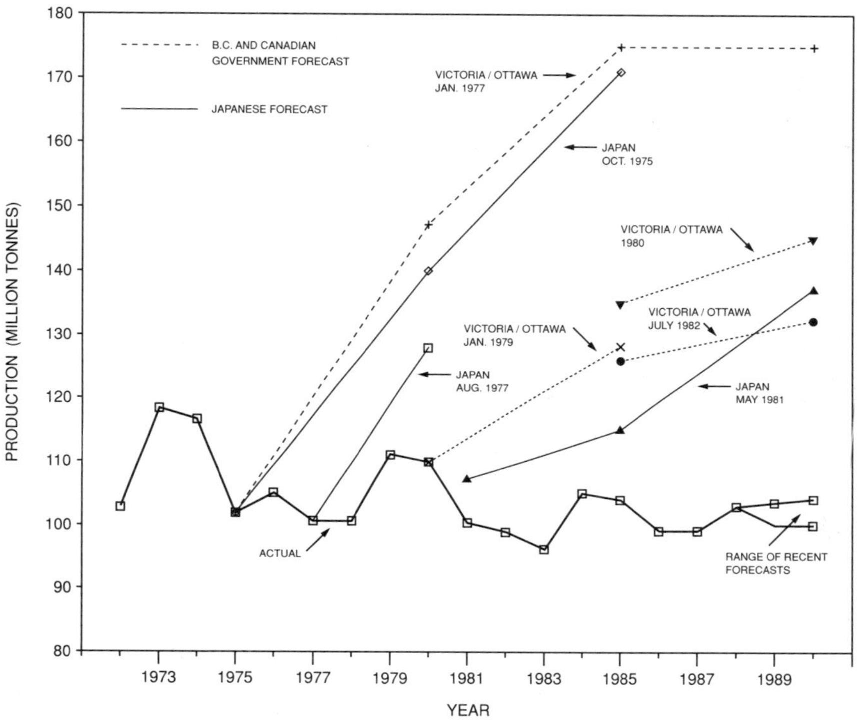

crude steel production would grow to approximately 140 million tonnes per year by 1990, a compounded growth rate of 1 per cent per year from the actual 1973 production of 119 million tpy. In fact, production in the period 1973-83 declined at a compounded rate of 2.1 per cent per year. Current forecasts call for Japanese crude steel production to hold in the 100 million tpy range into the 1990s.

A point to note in Figure 15 is that the Canadian/BC government forecasts lagged those being made in Japan. For example, the Japanese forecast for May 1981 was less optimistic than the Victoria/Ottawa forecast made in July 1982, over a year later. Subsequently, when Japanese companies and government agencies were forecasting crude steel production levels in 1983 in the 100 million tpy range, certain Canadian circles were dismissing such low forecasts as an attempt by the Japanese to effect lower coal prices. This greater optimism of Canadian forecasters is better demonstrated in Figure 16, where fore-

Figure 16 Forecasts of 1985 Japanese Crude Steel Production

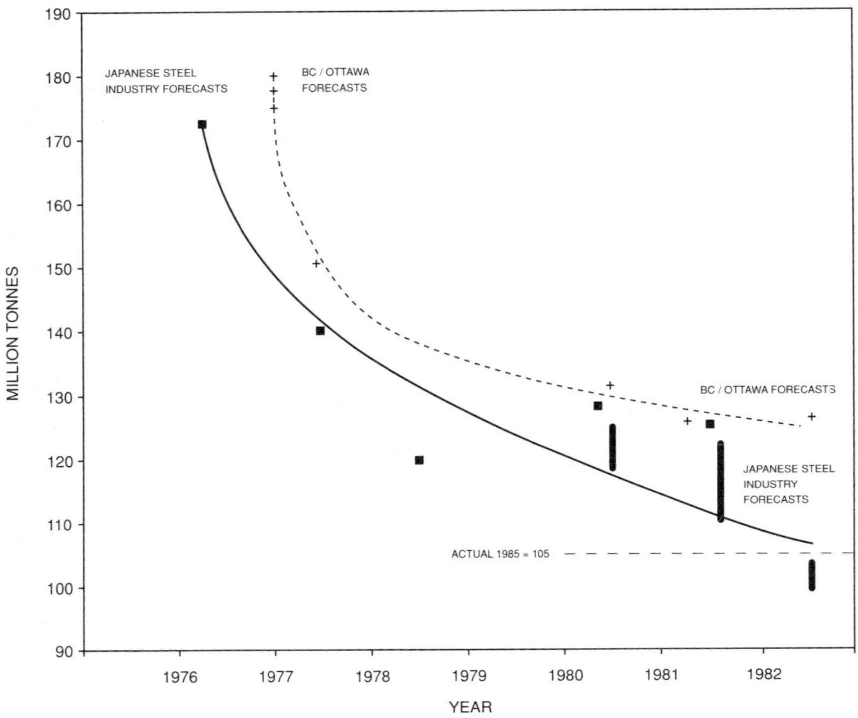

casts made in the period 1977-82 by both the Japanese steel industry and the BC/Canadian governments are compared for the year 1985. As 1985 approached, both the Japanese and Canadian forecasts declined. However, the Japanese forecasts declined at a faster rate. The Canadians seemed to ignore the decreasing Japanese forecasts, and northeast coal planning appeared to proceed on the basis of the more optimistic Canadian impressions of the Japanese coal market.

It must be remembered when reviewing the forecast shown in Figure 15 that even had the optimistic forecasts made in the 1980-2 period been realized, there was still too much coking-coal capacity built. It was possible as early as 1980 to foresee a glut of coking coal on world markets. The current low production levels of steel in Japan simply made what would have been a bad picture into a drastic one.

Figure 17 also demonstrates the optimism of government. The

Figure 17 Comparison of Government and Quintette Coal Ltd. Construction Contract Commitments

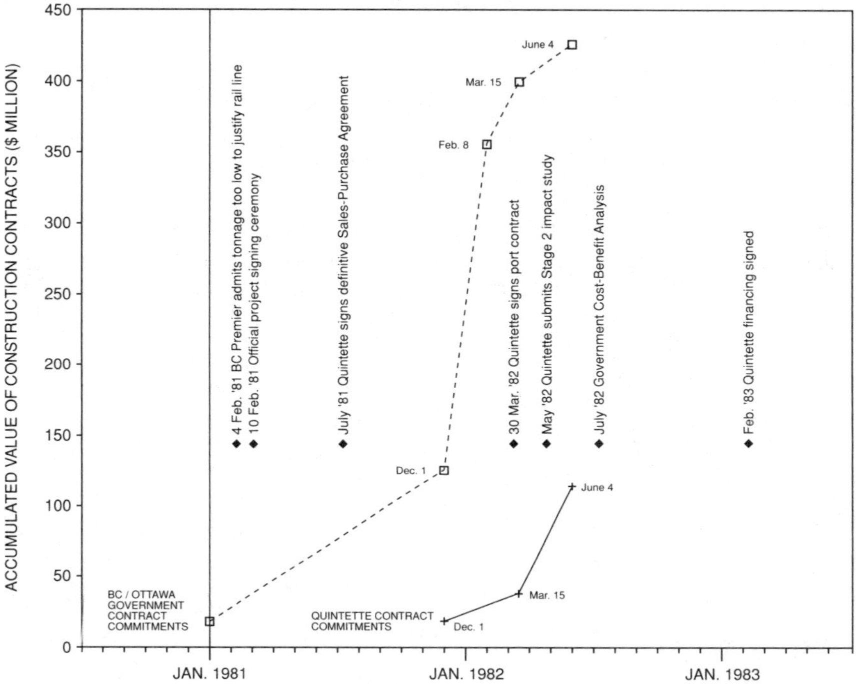

figure compares the rate of government commitments on infrastructure for the northeast coal project with those of Quintette Coal Ltd., the major mine in the project. Significant events are superimposed on these commitments. The BC and federal governments had committed almost $500 million *before* their cost-benefit analysis was completed.

CONCLUSION

The outlook for the British Columbia coal industry is not optimistic. The principal product, coking coal, will continue to depend primarily on the Japanese steel industry. Little if any growth in steel output by Japan is expected. Consequently, BC producers can expect a long period of overcapacity, downward pressure on prices, and increased aggressiveness by competitors to capture the business that exists. Closure of BC capacity is a distinct possibility.

Thermal coal has been a minor factor in the BC industry since the coal industry in the province was revived in the early 1970s. This situation will continue. Because of price and quality, offshore customers will likely continue to consider BC thermal coal primarily for reasons of diversification but prices will have to be competitive.

NOTES

1 Colombia, while not major in 1986, is a significant supplier today.

2 Eight per cent or more ash; less than 30 per cent volatile matter — the most common material produced in BC.

CHAPTER FOURTEEN

Capacity Stimulation Policies: A Possible Explanation for Excess Capacity in the Coal Industry

David L. Anderson

INTRODUCTION

The international coking-coal market is currently in a depressed state. Recent contract settlements between traditional suppliers in western Canada and the Japanese steel mills (JSM) support this contention. For example, most traditional producers recently signed agreements for FY 1987/8 that provide for reductions of approximately 10 and 30 per cent in price and quantity, respectively. Furthermore, pressure is also on the newer entrants to also accept price and, to a lesser extent, tonnage reductions.

The market situation of today stands in sharp contrast to the expectations held for this period by industry and government officials in the late 1970s. At that time, predictions of strong growth in steel demand led to the development of approximately twenty million tpa of additional export coking-coal capacity in the Pacific Rim. It should be noted that roughly half of this new capacity was located in western Canada and that the output of these mines was purchased by the JSM through long-term contractual arrangements.

Unfortunately, before most of the new mines commenced production, the Western world's steel industry entered a period of relative stagnation (Halvorson 1986). More importantly, the JSM suffered the same fate; in fact, the Japanese steel industry is now entering a period of retrenchment. In addition, technological developments are also helping to erode the market for hard coking coal. For example, as a result of research and development initiatives, Japanese steel producers are increasingly relying on weak and non-coking coals instead of traditional coking coal. Furthermore, the growing popularity of mini-mills is having a negative effect on the demand for coking coal. Hence, it is not surprising that the coking-coal industry is under severe financial pressure.

It is sometimes argued that the new mine developments of the early 1980s also played a significant role in creating the current situation facing suppliers. Indeed, some observers have suggested that the JSM set out to create an oversupply situation by "deliberately" overcontracting for coking-coal supplies. For example, Carl E. Bagge, then president of the National Coal Association, states:

> Then we can give attention to other problems we share, such as dealing with customers who deliberately encourage world over-production in order to play-off producers one against the other. (*Northern Miner* 1985a)

> The analysis found that by investment and encouragement you will have created by 1987 a world oversupply of coal in the neighbourhood of 24 million tons. While the American coal industry in good faith raised its own capital at high interest to serve a friend in need at a fair price, that friend was loaning money and technical assistance to others to create a 24 million ton oversupply and cutthroat practice. (Bagge 1984)

Similar views have been expressed in Australia and Canada. For instance, according to a lead editorial in the prestigious *Australian Financial Review* (1982) entitled "Japanese Mills Call the Tune":

> At the same time it is becoming increasingly clear in today's recession that the mills capitalized on the good times by encouraging massive industry-wide expansion in the production of Australian raw materials. . . . As the Australian coal trade surveys the bleak recessionary landscape, it is clear the Japanese mills have encouraged it to over-produce itself into a corner.

Furthermore, an Australian mining union brief states: "part of the problem of excess supply stems from the behaviour of consumers in encouraging, by their distribution of contracts, the creation of excess supply" (Mining Union National Liaison Committee 1983).

In Canada, the public debate on the "overcapacity" issue has been less intense and more recent than in Australia. Nevertheless, critics of the JSM's procurement strategy do exist. For example, Jack Morrish, president and CEO of Fording Coal, has been quoted as stating: "The major problem facing the Canadian coking coal producer is that of oversupply." The article adds: "Mr. Morrish placed the blame for the current oversupply situation squarely on the shoulders of the Japanese steel industry" (*Northern Miner* 1985b).

The advocates of the "deliberate" excess capacity thesis contend that, through a multitude of instruments, suppliers to the Japanese market were encouraged to build too much capacity. Consequently, it is unlikely that additional capacity will be required for another decade. During this time, excessive competition will ensure that the Japanese steel mills acquire coking-coal supplies at prices substantially below that required to generate an acceptable minimum rate of return on past investment.

The purpose of this chapter is to explore the supply stimulation thesis in some depth.[1] In particular, I shall focus on the decision-making environment of the 1976-82 period, within which I shall attempt to determine whether it was economically rational for the JSM to deliberately encourage overcapacity in the export coking-coal market. In order to undertake this task, I shall first discuss some conceptual issues. The chapter then provides an analysis of the demand and supply characteristics relevant to the oversupply debate. The penultimate section is devoted to a discussion of discriminatory reimbursement practices, and it concludes with a presentation of the policy implications of the findings.

DEFINITIONS AND DECISION RULES

In order to determine whether or not it is in the Japanese steel mills' interest to "deliberately" encourage excess capacity, we must first define the term. For the purposes of this chapter, "excess capacity" is defined, at any point in time, as the difference between existing capacity and that required to generate a minimum acceptable rate of return on the marginal mine. Rephrased, excess capacity represents the amount of productive capacity that must exist from the market in order that all remaining operations generate a rate of return equal to or in excess of each investor's hurdle rate.

If we assume that investors expect to earn at least a minimum acceptable rate of return, then "overcapacity" must be attributable to an investment "mistake." The mistake may be attributable to erroneous demand forecasts, failure to anticipate the impact of incremental capacity on market price, or other estimation problems. Consequently, suppliers may construct too much capacity, with the result that new investments will be unable to earn an acceptable minimum rate of return. Indeed, if the magnitude of the "error" is large enough, it is possible that some traditional producers will also fail to achieve a rate of return equal to their investor's risk-adjusted supply price of capital.

It is also possible that some investment "mistakes" are attributable to policy initiatives that distort the market signals facing producers. According to the proponents of this school of thought, private investors respond to these "misleading" signals and develop redundant incremental capacity. Consequently, the new projects fail to generate positive net benefits. In fact, if the market is sensitive to excess capacity, some traditional producers may be injured to such an extent that they too are unable to generate positive net benefits over the lifetime of the project. Although the remaining traditional producers will still earn a rate of return equal to or in excess of their shareholders' minimum acceptable level, the rate attained will be lower than what it would be in the absence of "excess capacity."

If the above scenario is plausible, it should attract the attention of public-sector decision-makers, since the situation is caused by market failure and hence provides an a priori rationale for government action (for example, see Boadway and Wildasin 1984). The nature of the problem is as follows: the presence of excess capacity can lead to the transfer of economic surplus from producers to consumers. Although this is not necessarily cause for concern in a closed economy, it is in an open economy, wherein the beneficiaries are foreigners and the losers are residents of the exporting country.

From the exporting nation's perspective, the problem is attributable to the failure of private decision-makers to incorporate all project-related benefits and costs into the decision calculus. Although such behaviour is rational, it does allow for a dichotomy to develop between the social and private net benefit calculations. Therefore, it is possible for the project to meet private-sector decision criteria and yet fail to provide positive net benefits to society.

For the purposes of this study, the dichotomy between private and social net benefit calculations can be attributed to two major but interrelated problems. First, if the world price for coking coal is influenced by the development of incremental capacity in the exporting nation, then the impact of these projects on traditional producers should be taken into consideration in the decision-making process. Obviously, private-sector developers will only do so to the extent that other mines within their corporate structures are affected. However, governments should consider those externalities that may render some or all of the new projects uneconomic from an economy-wide perspective.

An equally serious problem arises when the project (exclusive of externalities) is itself not economic, but is rendered so by the provision of implicit and/or explicit financial assistance. This assistance, which can take many forms, such as concessional finance, provision of quasi-dedicated infrastructure, and preferential price and tonnage treatment, allows the equity holders and commercial lenders to view the project as commercially viable. However, the project itself (all factors considered excluding externalities) may fail to pass traditional decision criteria. It is this phenomenon that serves as the focal point of this chapter. More explicitly, does it make sense for one or more consumers [henceforth called promoter(s)] to provide assistance to new mining projects and thereby stimulate the development of socially inefficient investment?[2]

From the preceding discussion, it is apparent that from the promoter's perspective, stimulation policies involve expected costs in addition to expected benefits. In addition to the provision of assistance at the capital stage to encourage construction, the promoter may also have to pay a premium during the operating stage to ensure that new producers survive in order to maintain downward pressure on the market and to avoid the longer-term political and financial ramifications of premature closure of dedicated projects.

It is apparent that supply stimulation policies will only be attractive to promoters if they yield expected positive net benefits. Rational decision-making suggests that such policies will be carried out to the point at which the expected marginal benefits equal the expected marginal costs. This suggests that the "excess" capacity debate should not be viewed as a question of ethics and morality, but as a matter of rational economic decision-making. In other words, does it make economic sense for the alleged promoter to initiate such practices? If it does, what options are open to exporters to protect their interests? Unfortunately, owing to time and space constraints, the remainder of this chapter focuses only on the former question and only with respect to Japanese and Canadian participants in the coking-coal trade. More explicitly, I shall attempt to see if it would have been in the JSMs' interests to have pursued supply stimulation policies in the late 1970s and early 1980s. This will be done, in part, by examining the characteristics of both the demand and supply side of the export coking-coal market, with particular emphasis on the Pacific Rim market.

DEMAND-SIDE CHARACTERISTICS

On the demand side of the market, the key factors are the consumer's market share, the role of regional markets, the price elasticity of demand, and future demand prospects. Let us look at each turn.

Market Share

The higher the proportion of a market controlled by the promoter, the greater the proportion of the resulting benefits it will be able to capture. Given that the promoter must expend funds to stimulate incremental capacity, it must also appropriate a substantial proportion of the benefits if the policy is to be successful from its perspective. The promoter's market share is also an important factor in limiting the options open to suppliers. If the demand side of the market is dominated by the promoter, the suppliers are placed, to some extent, in a take-it-or-leave-it situation.

In the case of coking coal, the consumer alleged to be stimulating capacity is a consortium of Japanese steel mills. They make most of their procurement decisions collectively and, hence, can be considered as a single buyer or promoter for purposes of this exercise (Anderson 1987; D'Cruz 1979; Catliff 1985). Since the mid-1960s, the JSM have dominated both their regional market and the international sea-borne export market. More specifically, between 1970 and 1983, the JSM held approximately 85-90 and 50-5 per cent of these markets, respectively. In the past few years their share of the Pacific Rim market has declined somewhat owing to the emergence of the Republic of Korea and Taiwan as aggressive steel producers. Nevertheless, the JSM have been, and still are, the dominant importers of coking coal in both the Pacific Rim and global markets.

The JSM's strong market position would have helped them institute successful capacity expansion policies. First, it would allow them to capture a substantial proportion of the benefits from falling prices. Second, the dominant market position enjoyed by the JSM in both the Pacific Rim and global markets severely constrained the options open to their natural suppliers, especially those in Australia and western Canada.

Regional Markets

Strong regional markets arise when transportation costs constitute a large proportion of the CIF price. Consequently, a supplier may be cost competitive in some markets and uncompetitive in others. Interestingly, it is in its "competitive" markets that a supplier is most vulnerable to supply stimulation practices. This follows from the fact that such a market is characterized by the presence of large locational rents which are up for capture.[3] This means that the promoter will attempt to drive the FOBT price in, say, Vancouver down to the level obtainable by Canadian producers from sales in other markets. The bargaining power of the seller is diminished and that of the promoter enhanced by the presence of excess supply.

Canadian coking-coal producers clearly face such a situation. They are cost competitive in the Pacific Rim market but face a substantial disadvantage in the European market (Barnett 1985a; Barnett 1985b). It must be noted that the Pacific Rim market constitutes roughly 60 per cent of the global sea-borne trade.

Both of these factors work to the promoter's advantage in an over-supply situation. For instance, it now becomes extremely difficult for Canadian exporters to divert supplies to other markets. If they do so by accepting an FOBT price that is lower than that offered by the JSM, they weaken their bargaining position vis-à-vis the JSM. That is, it becomes difficult to claim that the JSM are exploiting Canadian suppliers if these same suppliers willingly seek out new markets generating lower FOBT prices. Furthermore, Canadian suppliers face limited options as a result of both locational factors and the small size of the markets available outside the Pacific Rim.

Price Elasticity of Demand

The sensitivity of quantity demanded to a change in price is an important factor in determining the potential success of supply stimulation practices. More specifically, the less responsive is quantity demanded to price changes, the more the price must fall to clear the market of excess supply. Although price elasticity estimates for coking coal are not readily available, the prevailing view is that the short- and medium-term estimates are highly inelastic. This follows from the fact that coking coal constitutes only a fraction of the total costs of steel production. Furthermore, large-scale substitution away from hard coking coal to weak and non-coking coals can take three or more years to bring about. In addition, the substitution of mini-mills for BOF operations, which eliminate the need for coking coal, can take several years to complete.

On the other hand, the long-run price elasticity of demand for price increases is expected to be highly elastic. This follows from the above discussion: the long-run opportunities for steel producers to increase their utilization of weak and non-coking coals (Kinoshita 1986) and to replace their BOF operations with mini-mills (Pitler 1985). These factors serve to make coking-coal utilization much more sensitive to price increases in the long run than in the short to medium term.

Unfortunately for coking-coal producers, the long-run price elasticity of demand for declining prices is likely to be somewhat inelastic; indeed, the resulting estimate may not differ to any appreciable extent from its associated short- and medium-term counterparts. The reason for this lack of symmetry is the differential opportunities for substitution away from, and in favour of, coking coal. As shown above, if the price of coking coal increases, technological changes can be introduced that result in a substitution away from hard coking coal. However, if the price declines, there is likely to be little long-term impact on coking-coal utilization, especially in the Pacific Rim market. This is owing to the fact that since coking-coal costs are only a fraction of steel production costs, a decline in the price of coking coal will not materially increase the demand for steel and, hence, coking coal. More importantly, given the dominant role of BOF operations in the steel-making capacity of the Pacific Rim, there is limited potential for switching from the use of mini-mills back to the BOF process. In a similar fashion, given that the use of weak and noncoking coals was quite limited in the late 1970s and early 1980s, the potential for displacing inferior quality coals in the steel production process was severely constrained.

This discussion suggests that once an excess supply situation exists, declining prices cannot be relied on to generate new markets to absorb the troublesome excess capacity. Therefore, the excess capacity must be eradicated through either long-term demand growth or by way of mine closures.

Future Demand Prospects

The final demand-side issue to be considered is the role of demand forecasts in the supply stimulation process.[4] These are important since the JSM are likely to overstate their needs because the cost of underestimation is expected to be much greater than the cost of overestimation.[5] The role of expectations is important here, and the reader should recall that in the late 1970s and early 1980s, the JSM's raw materials procurement policy was heavily influenced by the 1973 and 1979 oil shocks and attempts by producers of some minerals to introduce supply management schemes. The resulting concern for security of supply was undoubtedly reinforced by the fact that, as we shall see below, the export coking-coal industry exhibits many of the textbook properties of an industry susceptible to oligopolistic practices. These fears may have been reinforced by the Australian resource diplomacy initiative of 1973-5, which was, to some extent, an attempt to counteract Japanese collective buying practices in the coking-coal market. Supply interruptions are of importance to the JSM since coking coal constitutes a necessary but only partial cost of steel production; hence, in the short to medium term, coking coal will continue to be purchased at prevailing levels even if its price rises significantly. Hence, the cost of allowing an undercapacity situation to develop is potentially large.

In fact, the generation of excess capacity may yield positive net benefits. In other situations, the cost of stimulating and sustaining excess capacity in Canada and Australia could be viewed as an insurance premium, the cost of which must be compared to the expected cost of operating in an environment characterized by a supply shortage. Nevertheless, at some point the insurance premium becomes too expensive vis-à-vis its alternative; this calculation is clearly affected by future demand expectations.

In summary, the analysis suggests that if the JSM was uncertain about their future coking-coal requirements, it was in their interest to pick high-side estimates, since the cost of estimation errors are non-symmetrical. Given the uncertainty surrounding the future of the steel industry in Japan in the 1976-82 period, the selection of "high-side" consumption estimates must have had some appeal.

SUPPLY-SIDE CHARACTERISTICS

Industrial Structure

If the supply side is characterized by relatively few providers, then consumers have, from a theoretical perspective, reason to be concerned about security of supply. The more important consumers can be expected to initiate defensive strategies. Perhaps the most likely response is to encourage the development of new productive capacity. It can be expected to reduce the supplier's ability to cartelize the industry. Let us now see if the Japanese steel industry had cause for such concerns with respect to the coking-coal industry.

Although this question cannot be answered with precision, the export coking-coal industry appears to display many of the characteristics of an oligopolistic industry.[6] Furthermore, because of the role of transportation costs, it is difficult for the JSM to find low-cost alternative sources of hard coking coal. This situation is exacerbated by the fact that the JSM are dominant in the Pacific Rim market and that demand for coking coal is price inelastic in the short to medium term. Hence, any large-scale attempt by the JSM to switch to non-traditional suppliers would have a dramatic impact on world price.

The above analysis suggests that if coking-coal producers sell collectively, they may be able to exercise considerable influence over the Pacific Rim coking-coal market. This follows from the fact that a small number of producers dominate this price inelastic market. More specifically, Canada, Australia, and the US jointly hold approximately 85 and 80 per cent of the Japanese and global sea-borne export markets respectively. Furthermore, the JSM can be expected to encounter problems in finding large quantities of alternative supplies that are both secure and low-cost.

Nevertheless, a closer examination of the supply side of the coking-coal market suggests that the initiation of a supply management scheme is highly unlikely and that if it were attempted, it would not likely succeed. There are two major constraints on cartelization activities in the coking-coal market. First, the long-run price elasticity of demand for price increases is expected to be moderately elastic because of the widespread availability of substitution opportunities. Hence, collusive behaviour could lead to an irreversible erosion of the market.[7] Second, although three nations dominate the export coking-coal market, production and capacity decisions are made by a large number of actors within each nation. Furthermore, coal producers, by and large, appear to be a fiercely independent lot. These factors, in conjunction with potential legal restraints, virtually preclude the possibility of effective cartelization of the export coking-coal industry.

Nevertheless, given the political and economic environment of the late 1970s, it is quite possible that the JSM did not readily dismiss the cartelization option. For instance, it has been reported that the JSM deliberately sought to restrict Australian producers to no more than 45 to 50 per cent of the Japanese coking-coal market in order to reduce Australia's market power. This same concern has also been raised to explain JSM's interest in higher-cost Canadian deposits. In this case, the premium price paid to Canadian producers can be interpreted as funds expended for purposes of reducing the probability of collusive supplier behaviour. More specifically, the creation of additional capacity is an important pre-emptive strike against the formation of cartelization initiatives, since it is much more difficult to devise long-lasting supply management schemes after the development of excess capacity than it is before the fact.[8]

Cost Structure

Perhaps the most important reason for expecting capacity stimulation policies to yield success in the export coking-coal market is that the industry cost structure makes it extremely vulnerable to such practices. Two attributes of the industry's cost structure are particularly attractive to prospective promoters: economies of scale and the average-variable to average-total cost ratio. Let us look at each in turn.

Open-cut coking-coal mines are highly capital-intensive and frequently display economies of scale throughout the relevant operating range. Therefore, if excess capacity arises in the industry, firms will suffer both declining prices and utilization rates. Some firms will respond by further dropping prices in order to capture increased sales; this outcome is particularly attractive since the existence of economies of scale means that unit costs can be reduced by increasing the utilization rate.

Although this strategy will be successful for the initial participants, it is doomed to failure if all producers adopt a similar strategy. This follows from the fact that the commodity is highly price inelastic; hence, price cuts will have a negligible impact on the aggregate quantity demanded. Therefore, since the price falls proportionally more than quantity increases, the inter-firm competition leads to declining industry revenues and profits.

In order to preclude destructive or cutthroat competition, sellers could act collectively. However, the coking-coal industry contains built-in incentives that operate to thwart and destroy supply management schemes. For instance, if the industry is characterized by excess capacity, each firm will receive a quota that represents some fraction of its full capacity. Unfortunately, it will always be in the interest of individual producers to slightly undercut the cartel price and, hence, increase their own capacity utilization rate. However, once this practice becomes known, others will be tempted to follow in order to protect their original market shares. If the process continues, the cartel quickly collapses. The result is that the industry is worse off after the introduction of competition than it was before it commenced; hence the label "destructive competition" (see Scherer 1980). This outcome can only be prevented by the use of policy measures precluding the operation of firms outside a supply management scheme. It is difficult to imagine that Canadian and US policy makers would ever adopt such measures.

The above discussion appears to apply, to a large extent, to the privately owned coking-coal industry of the Pacific Rim, which is prone to destructive competition. An industry with such a cost structure represents fertile ground for the introduction of supply stimulation policies. Given the JSM's extensive knowledge of the industry, it is difficult to imagine that they were unaware of the potential for such a policy initiative.

An equally important factor in facilitating a policy of deliberate overcapacity is the relationship of average variable to average total costs. If this ratio is significantly less than one, it will be exceedingly difficult to drive anyone out of the market. That is, since there is a large spread between average-variable and average-total cost, price must fall substantially from the level required to initially stimulate new capacity before it will be economically rational for mine operators to cease operations.

Equally relevant to the promoter is the fact that the average life of a mine is frequently twenty to thirty years; hence, once an excess supply situation is created in an industry characterized by relatively modern facilities, it can be expected to persist for a considerable period of time. It is apparent that the supply side of the Pacific Rim coal market possesses such attributes.

DISCRIMINATORY REIMBURSEMENT PRACTICES

It was previously stated that for promoters to create investment mistakes, they must distort normal market signals. The rationale for such intervention is that, otherwise, prospective projects would fail to meet conventional private-sector investment criteria, and hence would not be constructed.

This problem can be met in part by the provision of concessional finance, the purchase of project equity, the granting of bankable long-term contracts containing attractive price and tonnage terms, and the provision of assistance with infrastructure requirements. The promoter undertakes all of these activities on its own, or it may encourage others, such as host governments, to offer assistance, especially with respect to infrastructure.

Once the mines are in operation, however, the resulting excess capacity will depress prices and lead to tonnage cutbacks from individual suppliers. At this point, problems begin to mount for both the exporter and the promoter. Rephrased, if all producers receive similar treatment, a number of unwanted effects occur. For instance, the new entrants generally possess high cash-flow requirements; hence, they are likely to be the first group to experience financial difficulty and, thus, the first to exit from the market. This outcome is clearly unwanted by the promoter. First, it would reduce the level of excess capacity on the market and, subsequently, the degree of downward pressure on price. Second, if the promoter recognizes the possibility of additional coking-coal capacity being required in the forseeable future, it must be cognizant of the political ill-will generated by closure of dedicated mines and the additional risk premium that the financial community will require to compensate for the "obvious" risk associated with such projects.

One approach to this problem is to institute a differential compensation scheme. That is, new entrants will receive preferential treatment compared to that accorded traditional producers. In the preceding paragraph we saw how this practice could operate at the development stage. At the operating stage, the policy can be implemented by paying different prices for coal of essentially similar quality and by purchasing proportionally more coal from new entrants than from traditional producers. Given the capital-intensive nature of coking-coal mines, either route will confer substantial differential benefits.

The extent to which such a policy can be carried out is constrained by its expected costs versus expected benefits. The nature of the direct costs of initiating discriminatory reimbursements practices have been discussed above. The benefits are generated by the presence of prices below the level anticipated to prevail in the absence of the policy. This price spread is constrained in at least three ways. First, if it falls below the level required to cover average variable costs, some mines will close, thus reducing the downward pressure on the market. Second, if prices fall sharply, previously uncompetitive markets will become variable short- and medium-term alternatives at some point. Although transportation costs may deny producers the option of earning an acceptable rate of return on their investment, alternative markets may offer superior net cash-flow possibilities than does the Japanese market. Third, the ill will created by discriminatory treatment may generate long-run political and financial costs. This factor acquires more importance, the greater the likelihood that substantial additional capacity may be required in the foreseeable future.

In summary, the promoter must calculate the benefits and costs of discriminatory reimbursement practices at regular intervals over time. That is, even if it were deemed appropriate to confer special benefits on new entrants in order to entice them into the market, it may become too costly to continue to support them if market conditions change.

On the supply side, differential reimbursement practices are normally constrained by the ability of the aggrieved party to sell to non-discriminating buyers. However, this option is not a viable one for most coking-coal producers. They are severely constrained by the role of transportation costs and the dominant market position of the JSM. Rephrased, western Canadian sellers may face declining prices in the Pacific Rim but still not be tempted to pursue other markets zealously owing to the low FOBT price associated with such sales. This feature of the market allows the JSM considerable scope in exploiting an over capacity situation and allows them to institute discriminatory practices successfully. In addition, the dominant role of the JSM in the international coking-coal market, by definition, limits the options open to suppliers. Hence, their ability to expand markets in other areas through price competition is severely constrained. Similarly, price competition is constrained by the fact that if the available FOBT price from non-Japanese sales is less than that associated with JSM sales, the producers further erode their bargaining position vis-à-vis the Japanese steel mills.

It is apparent that the JSM have actively engaged in discriminatory reimbursement practices. Without getting into details, let it be said that differential price and tonnage practices have been widespread (Anderson 1986), as have concessionary financing arrangements. Such practices can be readily shown to work against the interests of coking-coal-exporting nations (see Smith 1982; Gaskin 1983).

POLICY IMPLICATIONS

This chapter has attempted to explore the proposition that the structure of the coking-coal market is conducive to the introduction of supply stimulation policies by the Japanese steel mills. The findings are generally in favour of the proposition. However, it must be stressed that it did not attempt to determine if the JSM deliberately pursued supply stimulation policies; instead, it only attempted to see if it might have been in their interests to do so.

The analysis indicated that the demand side of the market exhibits several important characteristics that facilitate the introduction of a successful supply stimulation policy. Among these important properties are: (1) the JSM are the dominant consumers in the Pacific Rim; (2) the Pacific Rim market is, in turn, the dominant regional market; (3) the price elasticity of demand displays the appropriate attributes, especially for declining prices; and (4) the JSM can be expected to overstate rather than understate their coking-coal requirements because of assymetric cost implications of forecasting errors.

Similarly, the supply side of the coking-coal market was found to be fertile ground for the introduction of policies encouraging excess capacity. For instance, the very fact that the supply side of the market is theoretically amenable to collective action can be expected to serve as a strong stimulant to the JSM to engage in defensive action. One such technique is to engage in a pre-emptive strike by encouraging excess capacity. In such an environment, producers are forced to operate from a position of weakness and are unlikely to be able to implement an effective international supply management scheme.

The cost structure of the coking-coal industry was found to possess two properties that are of crucial importance in determining the success of supply generation policies. The presence of economies of scale throughout the relevant operating range, in the presence of excess capacity and a price inelastic demand curve, renders the export coking-coal industry highly susceptible to destructive competition. In addition, the coking coal industry is highly capital-intensive. This property makes it very difficult to drive anyone out of the market. Therefore, destructive competition can be expected to continue either until demand increases sufficiently to absorb the available excess capacity or until a substantial amount of existing capacity becomes obsolete. Given the nature of the prevailing market forecasts and the relative youthfulness of most mines, neither event is likely to bring salvation to this beleaguered industry for a considerable period of time.

The mere existence of the properties described above serves as a necessary but not sufficient condition for the initiation of successful supply-generation practices. In order to make the policy yield economic benefits to its promoters, differential reimbursement practices were shown to be indespensible. The coking-coal industry is not only amenable to such practices but has indeed been the target of such JSM-inspired practices.

In summary, the available evidence, which is admittedly circumstantial in nature, suggests that in the late 1970s and early 1980s, it was in the JSM's interest to encourage excess supply through such practices as overcontracting. However, it cannot be proven that they deliberately sought to do so. Despite this qualifier, it must be stressed that such actions are entirely consistent with normal business behaviour. By doing so, they could pursue their twin objectives of enhancing security of supply and reducing costs in an efficient manner.

Although the suppliers are naturally bitter and resentful, they might better shift their attention from arguments of unfairness to those of market structure. That is, given the unique properties of both the demand and supply side of the coking-coal market, past "mistakes" are likely to be repeated as long as the buyers operate as a collective while the sellers operate in an uncoordinated, fiercely independent fashion.[9] Fortunately for Canada and its coking-coal producers, the future policy ramifications of this last statement, as well as the broader findings of this paper, are likely to be relatively modest. This follows from the proposition that the events of the past twenty years are not likely to repeat themselves. The rationale for this view is based on two key assumptions: first, the global demand for coking coal is expected to be stagnant over the next ten to twenty years; and second, the Japanese demand for hard coking coal is likely to decline over this time period owing to both declining steel production and increasing reliance on coking-coal-saving technologies.

Given these demand expectations, the export coking-coal industry will continue to be plagued by chronic overcapacity for a considerable period of time. Hence, it is difficult to see why it would be in any buyer's interest to try to stimulate new capacity now or in the foreseeable future. For instance, if current prices were to fall further, some existing producers could be expected to drop out of the market; this would largely negate the effect of the new capacity brought on stream at a substantial cost to the promoter. Furthermore, investors are likely to be quite leery of making additional investments in coking-coal operations, given current and future market expectations and the lessons learned from past events. Indeed, even governments may be more hesitant to provide infrastructure for primarily coal-based developments unless the spin-off benefits are deemed to be substantial.

Another demand-related reason for suggesting that the past will not repeat itself is the declining role of the JSM in both the Pacific Rim and international coking-coal markets. This phenomenon is expected to reveal itself with some force over the next decade as steel production increasingly shifts to newly industrialized nations such as the Republic of Korea, Taiwan, India, China, and Brazil. Therefore, since the JSM face the prospect of capturing a declining proportion of the benefits, they will be increasingly less inclined to engage in supply stimulation initiatives. Rephrased, why would the JSM pay the cost of stimulating additional excess capacity only to have steel makers in South Korea and Taiwan obtain a substantial share of the benefits? Indeed, such a policy would allow other Pacific Rim steel producers to obtain their input supplies at lower average CIF prices than the JSM, since the former would not have to pay a premium to the new entrants.

Notwithstanding the above analysis, modest benefits may be captured from government and industry initiatives designed to increase the level of information available to coking-coal exporters. Through such vehicles as study groups and producer associations, coking-coal producers may gain a better understanding of underlying market forces, especially those influencing critical variables such as capacity utilization and price. Although the "mistakes" of the late 1970s and early 1980s are unlikely to recur without strong evidence of increasing demand, an improvement in market transparency should lead to some mine closures and the preclusion of some additions to capacity. This should have a beneficial impact on price and on capacity utilization rates at individual mines. Furthermore, study groups and producers' associations may help preclude the worst abuses of coordinated bargaining, which characterize the demand side of the Japanese coking-coal market and, implicitly, the remaining markets of the Pacific Rim (see Anderson 1987; D'Cruz 1979).

The policy implications of this analysis for other resource sectors are also limited. With the obvious exception of liquefied natural gas and the possible exception of the thermal coal market, it is difficult to find other mineral markets possessing the characteristics suitable for the introduction of a deliberate oversupply strategy.[10] Although many minerals possess similar cost structures and prospects of declining markets, none faces a dominant buyer able and willing to pursue supply stimulation tactics aggressively.

To some extent this finding is encouraging to all elements of the Canadian mineral industry, since the obvious solution to the problem of "deliberate" oversupply creation is collective action. In other words, collective demand-side action, which is a necessary condition for rational supply generation policies, is best fought through collective selling responses. Canadian producers, with the exception of potash and sulphur producers, have generally shown themselves to be adverse to such solutions. They judge the cure to be worse than the disease. Fortunately, if the above analysis is correct, such choices will not have to be seriously entertained by most Canadian mineral producers and policy analysts as an instrument for counteracting supply generation policies.

NOTES

An earlier version of this chapter, entitled "Excess Capacity in the Coking Coal Industry: Possible Explanations," was delivered at the Canadian Institute of Mining and Metallurgy, Annual General Meeting, Toronto, 5 May 1987.

1 The remainder of this chapter draws heavily upon Anderson 1987.

2 It must be stressed that the term "promote," as used hereafter, refers exclusively to foreign-based organizations directly or indirectly promoting the development of additional coking-coal capacity. However, it should be acknowledged that domestic organizations, such as provincial governments, may also act to encourage non-economic investment. The likelihood and ramifications of such actions are largely ignored in this study.

3 This issue can be viewed as part of a bilateral monopoly bargaining situation. For details, in the context of the Japanese coal market, see Smith 1977.

4 This is an extremely controversial subject. The role of forecasting as an instrument in the supply stimulation debate lies outside the scope of this study. Interested readers should see Nemetz et al. 1984; Halvorson 1986; and Anderson 1987.

5 Historically the JSM overcontracted by approximately 15 to 20 per cent per annum to take account of probable supply interruptions, primarily attributable to strikes, and new mines taking longer to enter commercial production than anticipated. However, with the advent of tougher economic times, strike activity has declined substantially. Furthermore, since alternative markets are difficult to find, suppliers have not been tempted to undersupply the steel mills. Similarly, new mines came on stream on schedule, and the older operations have had time to resolve their production problems. Hence, part of the overcontracting debate may be the result of changing economic conditions. Nevertheless, this explanation does not address the events of the 1976-82 period, the focal point of this chapter.

6 For a coking-coal specific analysis, see Anderson 1987. For a general discussion, see Koch 1980; and Pindyck 1978.

7 An interesting discussion on this problem in the context of the tin market can be found in Tilton 1983.

8 Once excess supply is in place, capacity utilization must be explicitly or implicitly rationed across members. It is obviously much easier to operate a cartel if only price investment decisions must be addressed.
9 Although conventional economic and political wisdom in Canada is clearly against collective action, a number of researchers, institutions, and even politicians have suggested that, perhaps, collective action is a plausible policy in the export coal market, given the unique characteristics to be found on both the supply and demand side of the market. For example, see Maund 1984; Dyack 1985; Economic Council of Canada 1984:112; and Royal Commission on the Economic Union and Development Prospects for Canada 1985:473.
10 For an interesting discussion of the LNG Case, see Nemetz and Vertinsky 1984.

REFERENCES

Anderson, David L. (1986). "Marketing Arrangements for Western Canadian Coking Coal." *Canadian Public Policy*, September:473

— (1987). *An Analysis of Japanese Coking Coal Procurement Policies: The Canadian and Australian Experience*. Kingston: Centre for Resource Studies

Australian Financial Review (1982). "Japanese Mills Call the Tune." November

Bagge, Carl E. (1984). "The Samurai and the Cowboy: On the Road to Norfolk." Paper presented to the United States–Japan Coal Conference, San Francisco, 21 May:4

Barnett, Donald W. (1985a). "Rail Freight and the Cost of Australian and North American Export Coal." *Journal of Business Administration* 15(1–2): 175–201

— (1985b). "Export Coal Costs in Australia, Canada, South Africa and the USA." *Materials and Society* 9(4)

Boadway, Robin, and David E. Wildasin (1984). *Public Sector Economics*. 2d ed. Boston: Little, Brown

Catliff, Christopher E. (1985). "Japan's Government and Steel Industry Policies towards Coking Coal Procurement: The Implications of Industrial Restructuring for the *Northeast Coal Project*." MA thesis, UBC

D'Cruz, Joseph R. (1979). "Quasi Integration in Raw Material Markets: The Overseas Procurement of Coking Coal by the Japanese Steel Industry." DBA thesis, Harvard

Dyack, Brenda J. (1985). "Western Canada's Coal Industry: Status and Potential." Discussion Paper no. 278. Ottawa: Economic Council of Canada

Economic Council of Canada (1984). *Western Transition*. Ottawa: Supply and Services Canada

Gaskin, Maxwell (1983). *Organization and Structure of the Pacific Steam Coal Trade*. EAS Report G4. London: International Energy Agency, October

Halvorson, Harold (1986). "The British Columbia Coal Industry." *Journal of Business Administration* 16(1–2):293–306

Kinoshita, K. (1986). "Techniques of Utilization of Inferior Quality Coal at

Blast Furnaces and Coke Ovens and Future Trends." Paper delivered at the Canada/Japan Businessmen Cooperative Committee, Nagoya, Japan, May

Koch, James V. (1980). *Industrial Organization and Prices*. Englewood Cliffs, NJ: Prentice-Hall

Maund, Jacqueline K. (1984). "The Implications of Japanese Resource Procurement Strategy for Staple Resource Regions: An Examination of Coal Mining in Southeastern BC." MA thesis, UBC

Mining Unions National Liaison Committee (1983). Supplementary Paper no. 1. "Market Forces and the Coal Industry," April:11

Nemetz, Peter N., and I. Vertinksy, (1984). "Japan and the International Market for LNG." *Columbia Journal of World Business* 19(1):70–6

— and P. Vertinsky (1984). "Japan's Energy Strategy at the Crossroads." *Pacific Affairs* 57(4):553–76

Northern Miner (1985a). "N.A. Coal Producers Challenged Acid Rain." November:20

— (1985b). "Fording Grapples with Oversupply on Japanese Market." November:B6

Pindyck, Robert S. (1978). "Gains to Producers from the Cartelization of Exhaustible Resources." *Review of Economics and Statistics* 60(2):238–51

Pitler, P.K. (1985). "Steel Industry Process Technology Trends." *Materials and Society*: 9(2):147–59

Royal Commission on the Economic Union and Development Prospects for Canada (1985). *Report, Volume Two.* Ottawa: Supply and Services Canada

Scherer, F.M. (1980). *Industrial Market Structure and Economic Performance* . 2d ed. Boston: Houghton Mifflin

Smith, Ben (1977). "Bilateral Monopoly and Export Price Bargaining in the Resource Goods Trade." *Economic Record*, March:30–50

— (1982). "Bilateral Commercial Arrangements in the Energy Coal Trade." In Stuart Harris and Toyoaki Ikuta, eds., *Australia, Japan and the Energy Coal Trade*. Canberra: Australia-Japan Research Centre

Tilton, John E. (1983). "Material Substitution: Lessons from Tin-Using Industries." In John E. Tilton, ed., *Material Substitution: Lessons from Tin-Using Industries*:1–11. Washington: Resources for the Future

CHAPTER FIFTEEN

The Risk Transition and Nuclear Power: Evidence from Asia

Kirk R. Smith

Let us start by turning the clock back fifteen years and imagine ourselves at an energy conference just after the first oil shock. What would we have thought if some speaker had told us that in the next fifteen years the United States would hardly increase its total energy use in spite of substantial increases in population and economic activity? Or that, adjusted for inflation, the world oil price would be less in fifteen years than at present? That despite prognosis to the effect that natural gas would run out before oil even as early as the 1980s, globally there would in fact be more gas available than oil and that gas would be seen as a likely candidate to become the transition fuel into the twenty-first century? That woodfuel would become the most rapidly increasing energy source in the US? That wood burned in household heating stoves would be the chief source of air pollution in the US for some important pollutants? That the US and other industrial countries would have during much of that period a tremendous oversupply of electrical power plants and refineries?

In regard to nuclear power, we would have been equally sceptical to hear that not one further nuclear power plant would be successfully ordered, built, and put into operation in the US from this day onward and that the US breeder reactor program would be abandoned? As for the rest of the world, it would have hardly been credible that only three developing countries that did not already have nuclear power plants would build them in the next fifteen years or that two of these would have among the most intensive nuclear programs in the world.

While there were people advocating one or another of these directions in 1974, few would have seriously agreed with them as a set of predictions. Indeed, they would have seemed outrageous to many people.

Why were we wrong? On the supply side, many of us tended to think, for example, that the energy crisis was either a matter of geology or technology. Some of us spoke as if everything depended on whether or not there were sufficient reserves of fossil fuels or whether some particular energy technology, such as advanced nuclear power, was available. These are indeed important factors, but they are not the only ones. Among others that were recognized at the time is size: for example, power grids being large enough for an energy industry to take advantage of economies of scale. Another of these limiting nutrients for energy development, now more painfully obvious than then, is the ability to finance new energy systems, especially those that are highly capital-intensive.

The global experience of nuclear power during this period, however, illustrates some important factors that are not confined to geology, finances, or technology in the narrow sense. Outside the already industrialized countries, there are only two countries where nuclear power seems so far to have been a firm success: Taiwan and South Korea.

Each has had rapid development of nuclear power since 1974. Characterizing their economic development in general and nuclear development in particular — but not that of many other countries that have entered the field — are factors such as a dedicated and steadily productive workforce, an efficient level of professional management, national economic planning, and a means of achieving and maintaining societal consensus. Although they are now showing signs of eroding, these national organizational resources have been at least as valuable in the short term as more traditional domestic energy resources of oil and coal and, in the long term, substantially more valuable, as evidenced by Japan, the model of development in Asia.

Another area of the world that has also seen steady growth of nuclear power is Eastern Europe. There is a parallel with Northeast Asia, that is, Taiwan and South Korea, in that each of these areas had close connections to nations with active nuclear power programs. These special "client state" relationships allowed fairly easy transfer of financing and technology from the USSR in one case and the US in the other.

This chapter deals briefly with three issues: the role of electricity in economic development, the role of nuclear power within the electricity component of development, and the way nuclear power risks are perceived at different levels of development. The definition of development here is a narrow one — economic well-being (per capita income) — recognizing all the problems of its calculation and interpretation.

ELECTRICITY IN DEVELOPMENT

A comparison of world income with population reveals the phenomenon called by Harrison Brown the "fissioning" of human society. After World War II, by measures of average national income and consumption (energy, electricity, and steel), there came to be two major population groups: the poor countries, which had the majority of population but which were nevertheless distributed from the very poor to only slightly poor, and the rich countries with a similar distribution of their own. Few countries lay in the middle.

In this context, it is worth asking the following question: if all the world's income is divided by the total number of people, what is the average income and what country has such an average income? In 1986, the world's average was about US $3,100 per capita, about the same as Taiwan, with Greece next highest at US $3,700. According to the World Bank (which does not separately list the Eastern European countries), between US $3,700 and US $6,200 there was an income gap in which only two countries with a total of less than three million people were represented.

The bulk of the poor countries — for example, China and India, which represent a large fraction of the world's population — are slowly growing richer in per capita income. In recent years, they have even been growing slightly faster than the rich countries, so in that sense the relative gap has been slightly narrowing. Then there is a group of poor countries, mainly in Africa, which are becoming poorer, where per capita income is dropping. There are also several large and small Latin American economies that have had severe financial problems in recent years. Finally, there is a group of newly industrializing countries (often called NICs, but more recently renamed as NIEs, newly industrializing economies) that are growing quickly and transiting the gap between the two humps of the curve. These countries are mostly in Asia and include South Korea, Taiwan, Singapore, and Hong Kong.

The trend, then, is towards the appearance of three groups and two gaps. This is the result of a second "fissioning," in this case of the developing countries. By stagnation or actual decline, the desperately poor are becoming distinct from the bulk of the developing country population. While the older gap remains below the rich countries, it will become somewhat less distinct as the NIEs continue their transit.

Many developing countries would like to find that magical take-off point and experience the same kind of rapid economic growth that the NIEs have achieved. They would also like to do so by maintaining income equity, as have the Asian NIEs, particularly Taiwan. Indeed, some developing countries today have characteristics that make them look like Taiwan and South Korea in the 1950s when their development was just starting. Today, countries such as Malaysia already seem to be moving along such a growth course, with Thailand following behind. Electric power plays an important role in these efforts.

Economic development occurs, by definition, when the economy grows faster than population. In general, when this happens, energy use grows even faster, and electricity use grows faster than total energy consumption. Thus, electric power can sometimes be growing at fantastic rates — 15-20 per cent for years at a time, as in South Korea and Taiwan. This puts enormous pressure on the management of the power sector, on financing, and also, potentially, on the environment.

Among the surprises over the last fifteen years is the recognition that there is a relatively weak link between per capita income and total energy use, but a much stronger one with electricity consumption. There is some reason to think that the two may become less coupled in the future, however, because there seem to be numerous advances in electric efficiency that have not yet deeply penetrated many markets. There are also important temporal shifts in development patterns that affect fuel demand. Compared to the development period of the presently developed countries, for example, there is an earlier large demand for transport fuel in the presently developing countries. Nevertheless, substantial growth in power demand can be expected in most rapidly growing economies.

There is no question that there is a great potential demand in the developing countries for electric power. At early stages of development, most of the expressed demand is in irrigation and industry. When countries reach a stage achieved not long ago by Taiwan and South Korea, there is a shift in demand from industry to household and commercial and from winter to summer. The peak loads in recent years in Taiwan and South Korea, for example, are determined by air-conditioning. Because of geography, much of the Third World will eventually need air-conditioning. There is thus a tremendous potential demand for electric power and value to assuring its efficient generation and use.

The importance of the electric power sector for development can also be seen on the opposite side, that is, in the negative effects caused by lack of power availability. It is clear, for example, that the economies of India, China, and Turkey are severely constrained by the lack of sufficient electric power. Some of the major states of India experience

50 per cent average power cuts to their industrial sectors. There are investment repercussions, including, for example, flights of capital from power-poor areas of a country to relatively power-rich areas. Although determining "unmet demand" is not straightforward, the Chinese government estimates that its hope to increase the power system from about 100 GW in 1987 to 240 GW in 2000 will still leave it almost 20 per cent short.

The high growth rate of the electrical sector eats up tremendous quantities of capital. It is the largest consuming and investment sector in the economy in some nations, and it is the largest part of the energy sector in most nations. In Taiwan, for example, the power sector has annually soaked up 15-20 per cent of all fixed capital formation since 1974. It represents an even higher fraction of public sector investment, as in most of the five-year plans of India and China.

The importance of electric power can also be seen in the activities of international lending agencies, such as the World Bank. Of the US $10 billion lent for energy by the World Bank between 1979 and 1982, US $7.3 billion went for electrical power, even though the bank makes no nuclear power loans.

In summary, electric power investment in developing countries makes up 5-15 per cent of total capital formation, 15-25 per cent of public sector investment, and 65-90 per cent of development assistance in the energy sector. It is noteworthy, as Jyoti Parikh points out, that about 25 per cent of power equipment in developing countries must be imported. In the early 1980s this amounted to about US $10 billion — a significant fraction of the total oil bill for developing countries. Capital equipment is not usually mentioned as part of the energy import problem, but it actually plays a significant role in the balance of trade between many developing countries, even those that import most of their oil.

One implication is that improving the efficiency of the power sector can greatly improve overall economic performance. If the growth of power demand can be lowered or higher generating and transmission efficiencies can be achieved, tremendous amounts of capital can be saved just at a time when such developing countries most need it. Room for improvement can be seen in the low load factors that typify developing countries. In the Asia-Pacific region, for example, half the countries have system load factors of less than 60 per cent.

Developing countries also have bigger problems with power losses, that is, with electricity generated but never billed to a consumer. In the United States, Japan, and Taiwan, such power losses run about 5 to 6 per cent. Loss rates in developing countries run much higher. Many countries could save a whole year's investment in capital equipment and new supply if they could cut these power losses by 10 per cent or more.

One implication of these conditions is that the highest marginal return on investment in most developing countries' power systems is actually increased efficiency of the system: better management rather than new capacity. It is not clear, however, how much can be done with the power system in isolation from changes throughout the economy. Indeed, it is almost a tautology to say that developing countries generate and use electricity inefficiently, since they use all resources inefficiently, such as labour, capital, energy, and land.

Electric power has been the most important sector in dealing with the principal need generated by the oil shocks in most developing countries — moving away from oil, in particular imported oil. It is the power sector that has been the most successful in this task, partly because it is the most homogeneous and regulated sector and, therefore, the easiest for governments to get a handle on, to control. Also, most of the major substitutes for oil are in power generation, while few substitutes exist in transportation and other oil-using sectors. These substitutes include natural gas, coal, and nuclear and also the renewables, such as hydro, geothermal, and wind.

This oil substitution in the power sector, however, has some interesting effects on the international oil market. The big changes in the world oil picture that occurred in the 1970s were in the so-called "upstream" market, that is, in the production of oil, the ownership of oil fields, and the marketing of crude oil. The changes in the 1980s have been in the "downstream" market: in refining, in petrochemicals, and in product transport. OPEC countries, for example, have been building refineries because they want to be more dominant in the market for products as well as that for crude. As a result, there is relatively more product and less crude being traded internationally.

Stated simply, running a particular crude oil in a particular refinery will result, within fairly narrow limits, in a certain fraction of light products, such as gasoline, another fraction of middle distillates, such as kerosene and diesel, and another fraction of heavy products, such as the oil used in large power plants. If most of the substitutes for oil are in the power sector, however, then only the demand for heavy oil is actually being changed. Thus, there is not necessarily a decrease in overall demand for crude oil depending on the demand for other products.

It is possible to reduce the relative fraction of heavy oil produced by buying a different type of crude oil or by upgrading or building new refineries. Doing so is expensive, however, and requires an understanding of what may happen in the world product market before making decisions with long-term consequences. This prediction is difficult, for example, because the demand for the middle distillates, kerosene and diesel, is growing rapidly but erratically in developing countries. In summary, ownership and control of product transport and marketing are changing, complicating energy planning in developing countries. The largest pressures behind these changes come from the power sector.

Finally, electricity plays a critical role in what might be called the "dialectic of development," an important part of which is the tension between "top-down" and "bottom-up" development approaches. Should development proceed by having experts make analyses and governments institute programs that implement their plans downwards, or does development proceed from grassroots efforts to communicate needs and desires upwards? Ideally, of course, both processes operate. Electrical power sits in the centre of the dialectic because it is generated centrally but distributed to every household. Electric light in the village is a symbol of development, regardless of any economic benefit that may accrue from it. Consequently, there is great political pressure in many countries for rural electrification, regardless of cost. It is expensive to electrify locations with low loads: lights and a few small motors. But it is considered important in order to provide for basic human wants. This often places extreme financial and operational demands on power systems.

An important part of this dialectic relates to economics. Electrification schemes often do not recover their costs, and thus utilities in developing countries are continually seeking new capital. The World Bank believes they should charge the real costs of production to all their consumers, even their rural consumers, so that they can repay loans and improve economic efficiency. The politics are such, however, that it is impossible to set such rates in rural areas, for the poorest parts of the population. It seems there has to be a willingness to subsidize rural electrification; it will not pay for itself, at least not at this stage of development. Obviously, however, there are limits and important decisions to be made; for example, how much subsidy is justified.

NUCLEAR POWER IN DEVELOPMENT

Having briefly addressed the overall role of electricity in development, let us consider the role of nuclear power. Among its many disadvantages, nuclear power has two potential advantages: cost and energy security. Unfortunately, it is extremely difficult to determine and compare costs of power projects reliably, especially since these are spread over twenty years or more. Even though there are financial techniques for considering costs over time, they cannot make an evaluation that is truly independent of accounting practices, value judgments about future costs, and general economic conditions. Experience has shown how large the range within which the economic climate can change over such a period.

Using these techniques, however, it is possible to generalize that, over a thirty-year lifetime, a nuclear plant will be a bit cheaper than coal in many parts of the world. There are exceptions and qualifications, to be sure, particularly depending on location with respect to coal mines and the amount of non-plant infrastructure that is often required for nuclear plants in developing countries. In addition, this advantage has been steadily eroding in many parts of the world.

An important financial disadvantage to nuclear, however, is that the government or utility and the banks involved in the financing must initially spend much more money per year for a nuclear plant than for a coal plant. Construction times for nuclear power plants are estimated now at ten years. And it takes another twelve years or so until the annual expenses of the nuclear plant are actually less than the costs of a comparable coal plant. Of course, if all works as planned, after that twenty-two years there are savings from the nuclear system. But given economic uncertainties and the relative instability of many governments, this extra requirement for capital in the short term may be perceived as too daunting in spite of the results of standard economic calculations that may show long-term economic benefits for nuclear power.

Another factor that must be considered before purchasing a nuclear but not a coal plant is that, as pointed out by Alvin Weinberg, the nuclear industry is a global one. If an accident happens in a nuclear plant in India, news of it will be in the papers in Beijing, Tokyo, and New York. If an accident happens in a coal plant in India, however, few hear about it. And when a nuclear accident occurs, similar and sometimes even quite different plants will be closed down around the world, at least while immediate investigations are undertaken. A nuclear utility is vulnerable to the safety record of utilities everywhere else in the world and thus to factors outside its control. It is like the aircraft industry: if a DC-10 crashes in Chicago, all DC-10s around the world are grounded.

The accidents at Three Mile Island and Chernobyl, for example, have had, and will continue to have, negative impacts on the nuclear industry worldwide. It is paradoxical that this effect is almost inverse to the radiation dose received, that is, more impact in Western than in Eastern Europe and more in the US than in the USSR. It affects LDC perceptions as well, of course, as shown by the Philippines government's citation of Chernobyl as one of the factors in its decision not to begin operation of its essentially completed nuclear power plant. This global vulnerability translates into a financial penalty for nuclear power.

The global nature of nuclear power has expression also in regulation. When the Philippines, for example, was intending to embark on nuclear power, they were not in a position to establish a complete regulatory apparatus to cover all aspects of construction and operation. They intended to use the USNRC's regulations and updates, especially those covering the same type of reactor in the US. In other words, the American government (or any other nuclear exporter) essentially exports ongoing regulation as a part of nuclear technology export, as it does with aircraft. Not that it physically inspects the foreign systems, but the needed information is transferred as a result of the regulation of the same type of system in the US. In this case, a problem arose for the Philippines because the US cancelled the only reactor of that exact type being built, in Puerto Rico. While the cancellation was probably only a minor factor in the government's 1986 decision to abandon the plant, it illustrates the complexity of this global industry. It also illustrates one of the factors that the industry will need to address if nuclear power is to find an expanded role in many other developing countries.

How do things stand for nuclear power? There are several ways of looking at the question. One is by generating capacity. As shown in Table 82, early in 1989 there were about 310 GW in operation worldwide, of which LDCs account for less than 14 GW or about 4 per cent. Of that, 80 per cent is in two countries: South Korea and Taiwan. The total capacity in operation and in construction is about 400 GW globally, with about 23 GW in the LDCs, or 6 per cent, more than half of which is in South Korea and Taiwan.

Table 83 shows the relative amounts of nuclear power in individual LDCs. Although six nations have operating plants and three (China, Mexico, and Cuba) are currently building them, only one new developing country, Brazil, has put nuclear power into service since 1978. Of course, with any large project, and nuclear plants in particular, one should not count the chickens until they are hatched and running. For example, the Philippines' nuclear program was initiated after the first oil shock, and it completed its first unit in 1986. Now, however, with completely different economic, political, and energy situations than the 1970s, the government made a decision to abandon it, not to put it into operation. Iran was building four reactors at the time of the revolution that toppled the Shah in 1979, but since then their future

Table 82
Global Nuclear Power in Early 1989

Status	World	LDCs	LDC (%)	Asian NIEs % of LDCs
In operation	310 GW	13.9 GW	4	80
Under construction	88 GW	8.9 GW	10	10
Total	398 GW	22.8 GW	6	53

Source: World surveys in *Nuclear Engineering International* (8/88), *Nuclear News* (2/89), and International Atomic Energy Agency *Bulletin* 30 (3) 1988. Less developed countries (LDCs) are defined here to be non-European nations with less than the world mean per capita income ($2,900 in 1984). The nuclear Newly Industrializing Economies (NIEs) of Asia (Taiwan and Korea) account for a large fraction of total LDC nuclear power

Table 83
Nuclear Power in LDCs in Early 1989

Country	Year of first operation	GW	% of total LDC
In operation and under construction			
India	1969	2.9	13
Pakistan	1972	0.1	1
Argentina	1974	1.6	7
Korea	1978	7.2	31
Taiwan	1978	4.9	22
Brazil	1984	1.9	8
Mexico	(1989)	1.3	6
Cuba	(1990)	0.8	4
China	(1990)	2.1	9
Total		22.8	101[a]
Most likely by 2000			
Turkey			
Egypt			
Possible but unlikely by 2000			
Philippines and Iran (which have partially completed units in place), Bangladesh, Indonesia, Libya, Thailand			

This list does not include any Eastern European countries, most of which have nuclear power programs and several of which might be considered LDCs by some definitions. Nor does it include South Africa, which started the first of its two 920 MW units in 1984. See exclusions and data sources at bottom of Table 82.

[a]Column may not add up to 100% owing to rounding

has been uncertain. It has been reselling the uranium originally bought to fuel these reactors. Indeed, mainly as the result of their severe financial difficulties, neither Brazil nor Mexico is likely to pursue new nuclear projects in the near future and may even abandon their existing programs.

Table 84 shows three other measures of nuclear power. By number

Table 84
Global Comparison of National Commitments to Nuclear Power

Country	Number of operating units[a]	Per cent of electricity generated[b]	Economic intensity[c] (MW/$US billion GNP — 1983) Operating	Under construction
Korea	8	53	26	76
Spain	10	31	15	63
France	55	70	50	57
Hungary	4	39	18	53
Taiwan	6	49	80	47
Czechoslovakia	8	26	13	32
West Germany (FRG)	23	31	16	31
Switzerland	5	38	20	31
Canada	18	15	24	27
Belgium	7	66		26
Sweden	12	45	86	25
South Africa	2	5	0	25
US	108	18	20	20
USSR	57	11	17	18
Japan	36	31	15	14
East Germany (EDR)	5	10	9	13
UK	40	18	20	12
Argentina	2	13	14	10
Brazil	1	1	2	10
India	6	3	5	8
Mexico	0	0	0	7
Italy	2	0.1	4	6
China	0	0	0	1
Finland	4	37	49	0
Bulgaria	5	29	43	0
Yugoslavia	1	6	8	0
Netherlands	2	5	4	0

The countries are ranked according to the economic intensity of nuclear plants under construction.

[a]In early 1989; *Nuclear News*, April 1989

[b]In 1987; *Nuclear Engineering International*, June 1988

[c]Nuclear power plants operating or under construction as of 30 December 1983. From "World List of Nuclear Power Plants," *Nuclear News* (February 1984): 71–90; *International Financial Statistics* (Washington, DC: International Monetary Fund, September 1984); *Handbook of International Trade and Development Statistics 1983* (New York: UNCTAD 1983); *World Development Report 1984* (New York: Oxford University Press [for the World Bank] 1984)

of units, the US dominates with 108, about twice as many as its closest competitors, the USSR (57) and France (55). Next come other Western industrial countries, including Japan (36), but there are no developing countries until South Korea with eight, followed by India and Taiwan with six reactors apiece. By percentage of all electricity generated by nuclear plants, France and Belgium dominate, with close to 70 per cent. Next come Taiwan and South Korea, however, which are both close to 50 per cent. No other developing country has as much as 15 per cent.

There is also a fourth way of looking at nuclear power: in relation to the size of the economy as also shown in Table 84, that is, how many nuclear megawatts are there per billion dollars of the economy? This number indicates the relative financial commitment (or nuclear power intensity) of the nation. France is high on this list as well, but not the highest. The highest is Taiwan, when both operating and in-construction plants are included. Sweden is also high, as is South Korea.

It is instructive in this regard to compare three countries that are often seen to be similar in economic development patterns (although at different stages) — Japan, South Korea, and Taiwan. Japan has one of the oldest and largest nuclear power programs in a non-nuclear-weapons nation, and it built them while achieving high economic growth. How do the programs in Taiwan and South Korea, which started much later, compare with Japan's at a similar stage? It turns out that in comparable financial terms, South Korea and Taiwan have built nuclear power plants ten to fifteen times faster (megawatts per billion constant $ growth in GNP). This means that the financial and related vulnerabilities are also substantially higher.

As is well documented, past projections have nearly always anticipated a much larger swing to nuclear power than has thus far been the case worldwide. This is true both for the developed countries and the less developed countries. It can be argued, in fact, that only two countries that have recently entered the nuclear field have made a real success of nuclear power — South Korea and Taiwan — and that, in some respects, they have done better than the United States. As in Japan, their nuclear plants are built on time and at substantially lower unit cost, and they operate at higher capacity: evidence of their shared "energy" resource of good management.

Historically, there have been two approaches to nuclear development: exemplified by India and Taiwan. India's initial approach was to create its own industry, to import as little as possible. This decision, coupled with its refusal to sign the Non-Proliferation Treaty, effectively put it outside most of the world market in nuclear technology. Nevertheless, India was the first developing country to build a nuclear power plant (1969), although it has since been proceeding slower than it hoped. Because of the great need for new electric capacity, however, India has just concluded an agreement by which two 1.1 GW Soviet nuclear plants will be built. This decision marks a sharp change in policy and an even stronger commitment to nuclear power.

In Taiwan, on the other hand, a decision was made not to develop any of its own nuclear technology, but to import the most advanced and largest reactors possible in order to support its general industrial development. Because of its political situation, it has insisted on safeguards against weapons proliferation being written into bids for construction contracts and kept to US units. It apparently does not want even the remotest suspicion to interfere with development of energy security. As part of the effort, a great deal of technology transfer occurred from US companies. No units have been ordered since 1974, however, and Taipower is now faced with substantial public opposition in spite of following Japan's example of compensating local communities near nuclear power sites.

South Korea followed a similar, although not so extreme, path, by which it has been importing reactor technology in concert with technology transfer, but it did so from three countries: Canada, US, and France.

China has been pursuing a mixed path. It has an indigenous industry building a three hundred MW power reactor that is an upgrade of a submarine reactor and developing prototypes for four hundred MW(th) district heating reactors. In addition, it has ordered two French reactors to be built near Hong Kong, which will be basically "turnkey" projects. Like its northeast Asian neighbors, however, China expects a high degree of technology transfer so that it can become capable of providing a larger fraction of future plants on its own.

RISK TRANSITION

Economic development implies transitions of several kinds. Well documented, for example, are the demographic transition (changes in birth and death rates) and the energy transition (changes from noncommercial to commercial fuels), both of which signal profound societal transformations. Less well understood, but also of considerable importance, is the risk transition, which marks a shift in the relative significance of different hazards for human well-being. As shown in Figure 18, at low levels of economic development human health risk is dominated by what might be called "traditional" risks, in which poor rural environmental conditions play an important role. The health outcomes from these risks prominently involve epidemic, infectious, and intestinal diseases. Although this set of risks tends to decrease during economic development, it still dominates overall risk patterns in the developing world.

Figure 18 The Risk Transition

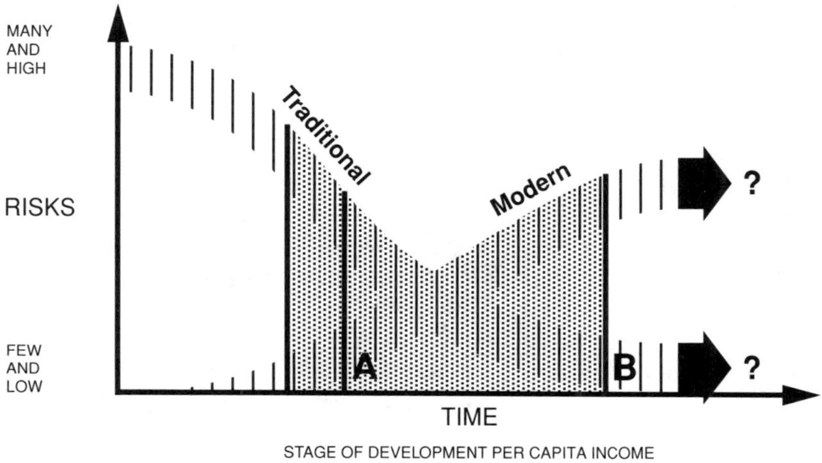

This generic illustration of the risk transition shows the decline of traditional and the rise of modern risks. The patterned area represents the period of risk overlap when there may be important interactions between traditional and modern risks. Point A marks the position of a typical developing country contemplating a nuclear power program, while Point B marks the risk pattern in a developed country.

During development, however, these traditional risks are gradually replaced by "modern" risks, which appear to rise with development. These are characterized by chronic diseases and cancers and are associated with environmental hazards related to agricultural modernization and industrialization.

This framework assists in understanding a number of aspects of societal behaviour related to risk, including providing plausible explanations for some of the "paradoxes of risk" that have perplexed many observers. For instance, there is a paradox seen in societies at point B in the figure that is often stated as follows: "Why have the richest and healthiest societies in human history become so worried about what, in global and historical terms, are extremely small individual and societal risks from modern technologies?" With reference to the figure, however, the concern can be explained by reasoning that people intuitively consider the risk-lowering as well as the risk-raising aspects of new technologies when making judgments. Even though formal risk assessment procedures are only well developed for determining gross risk-raising, it may be the perception of net risk (the difference between risk-raising and -lowering) that actually drives human judgment.

Thus, before reaching the level of economic development represented by point B, societies may have been willing to tolerate incremental increases in modern risk because they perceived that major reductions in traditional risks were still occurring. At point B, however, even relatively small increases in modern risks have become unacceptable because little additional traditional risk-lowering seems possible. In contrast, at point A it may be quite rational to undertake what, to some observers, may seem to be large modern risks in order to accelerate economic development with its attendant great risk-lowering.

Consider now the development history of the high-technology, high-visibility system nuclear power. Being high-technology, at levels of development too far to the left in Figure 18, the well-known limitations of grid size, personnel, financing, and regulation constrain nuclear development. At some point in development, however, these barriers can be overcome and nuclear power may appear quite attractive. This can be so even though nuclear power may be perceived to be a significant modern risk. The explanation, as introduced above, is that there is so much obvious risk-lowering occurring with new development, and being high-visibility, nuclear power is closely associated with development so that the perceived net risk is negative, that is risk-lowering. As development proceeds, however, the slope of reductions in traditional risk tapers off, thus shifting the perceived net risk against nuclear.

The way the risk transition is perceived by nations also depends on culture, history, international circumstances, and politics (for example, freedom of the press). Nevertheless, the recent public outcries in Taiwan that have combined with other factors to lead to what is essentially a moratorium on nuclear expansion would seem to fit well with this framework. Appropriately following behind, there are similar signs in South Korea, including demonstrations at low-level waste dumps. (Even Japan is experiencing the growth of serious anti-nuclear-power movements.) Indeed, such perceptions can run so high that they lead nations to undergo fairly large sacrifices rather than accept nuclear power, as is illustrated by the island of Luzon in the Philippines, which in early 1989 was undergoing severe power shortages with even worse expected by summer. The discomfort, inconvenience, economic loss, and cost of emergency gas turbines were apparently more acceptable than questioning the decision not to start their completed nuclear power plant.

Nuclear power's high visibility sometimes results in yet another type of risk — political. The Philippines' reactor seems to be permanently tainted by its association with the Marcos government, for example. Perhaps an even better example is found in the Pacific Islands, which, at first look, might seem far removed from nuclear power debates. Nuclear questions, however, actually dominate the environmental concerns of people throughout the Pacific. In Fiji and Tonga, for example, these issues have been at the top of the environmental agenda for both government and non-government groups. The reason, of course, is the history of nuclear-testing in the Pacific, initially by the US and UK and presently by France. Outside of Hiroshima and Nagasaki (and now perhaps the Ukraine), the Pacific Islands are the part of the world that has sustained the greatest damage from the nuclear age. In addition, the anti-nuclear and the anti-colonial (independence) movements coalesce in the Pacific. Even civilian nuclear power has created concerns in the Pacific Islands because of past US proposals to use Palmyra Island as a storage site for spent fuel and Japanese proposals to dump low-level radioactive waste at sea. Combined with the history of testing, failures in the resulting cleanup operations, and perceived coverups by the French and US governments, any such proposals run into strong political and emotional hostility in the Pacific. Risk analysis is almost meaningless in this context, as are attempts to distinguish civilian from military uses.

What about the most currently popular of the many risk issues that bear on nuclear power: global warming from fossil fuel combustion? In a first approximation, the impacts of climate change are similar to an increase in the frequency and severity of climate-related natural disasters: typhoons, droughts, floods, and storm surges. Such events are traditional risks in the framework described here, that is, they tend to decrease with development. The hurricane of a size that kills ten people in Florida will kill ten thousand in Bangladesh, for example. In the framework of Figure 18, therefore, climate change amounts to an addition to the traditional risk curve all along the development spectrum. The absolute impact will be greater in developing countries, but the relative impact may well be greater at the developed end of the spectrum. This factor could well act to shift to the right the point at which nuclear risk-raising is no longer balanced by its risk-lowering. It might increase the size of nuclear power's niche along the development spectrum.

CONCLUSION

In summary, except in the special conditions of Taiwan and South Korea, nuclear power has not found a major niche in the economic development of many poor nations. It is not dead, but it does not flourish. The places to watch during the next fifteen years are China and India, but it seems safe to say that growth will not be rapid. The extent to which concerns about climate change will affect nuclear power's growth rate in developing countries will largely depend on how much the developed countries are willing to pay to do something about it.

SELECTED BIBLIOGRAPHY

Brown, H. (1975). "Population Growth and Affluence: The Fissioning of Human Society." *Quarterly Journal of Economics* (89):236-46

Flavin, C. (1987). *Reassessing Nuclear Power: The Fallout from Chernobyl*. Worldwatch Paper no. 75. Washington, DC: Worldwatch Institute

Jones, D.W., A.P. Sanghvi, and E.L. Hillsman (1988). *The Impacts of Inadequate Electricity Supply in Developing Countries*. ORNL-6436, Oak Ridge National Lab, TN

Kadir, A., and Y.H. Kim (1985). "Electric Power Issues and Choices in the ASEAN Countries." Resource Systems Institute WP-85-19, East-West Center, Honolulu

Keepin, B., and G. Kats (1988). "Greenhouse Warming: Comparative Analysis of Nuclear and Efficiency Abatement Strategies." *Energy Policy* 16(6):538-61

Kim, Y.H., and K.R. Smith, eds. (1989). *Electricity in Economic Development: The Experience of Northeast Asia*. New York: Greenwood

Maeda, I. (1989). "The Nuclear Issue as Seen in Today's Perspective." (Japanese anti-nuclear movements.) *Energy in Japan* 97:33-41

Navarro, P. (1988). "Comparative Energy Policy: The Economics of Nuclear Power in Japan and the United States." *Energy Journal* 9(4):1-15

Nemetz, P.N., ed. (1987/8). "Selected Issues in Pacific Basin Development." A special issue of *Journal of Business Administration* 17(1&2)

Parikh, J. (1986). "Capital Goods for Energy Development: Power Equipment for Developing Countries." *Annual Review of Energy* 11:417-50

Smith, K.R., and F. Fesharaki, eds. (1986). *OPEC and Asia: The Changing Structure of the Oil Market*. New York: Pergamon. (See also the entire issue of *Energy* 11(4/5))

Smith, K.R. (1986). "Electric Power in Developing Countries: A Brief Exposition of Its Role in the Development Dialectic." In C. Chagas and U. Colombo, (eds.) *Energy for Survival and Development*: 242-71. Vatican: Pontifical Academy of Sciences

— (1988). "Perceptions of Risks Associated with Nuclear Power." *Energy Environment Monitor* (New Delhi) 4(1):61-70

— (1990). "The Risk Transition," *International Environmental Affairs* 2(3), in press

Surrey, J. (1988). "Nuclear Power: An Option for the Third World?" *Energy Policy* 16(5):461-79

Van Dyke, J., K.R. Smith, and S. Siwatibau (1984). "Nuclear Activities and the Pacific Islanders." *Energy* 9:733-50

World Bank (1982). "Energy Efficiency: Optimization of Electric Power Distribution System Losses." Energy Dept. Report no. 6. Washington, DC

— (1983a). *Energy Transition in Developing Countries*. Washington, DC

— (1983b). "Power System Load Management Technologies." Energy Dept. Paper no. 11, Washington, DC

— (1988). *World Development Report*. New York: Oxford University Press

Yuasa, T. (1989). "Nuclear Power Development in the World Since the Chernobyl Disaster." *Energy in Japan* (special edition): 65-81, February

Contributors

PETER N. NEMETZ, Associate Professor and former Chairman, Policy Analysis Division, Faculty of Commerce and Business Administration, University of British Columbia

YOKO SAZANAMI, Professor, Department of Economics, Keio University, Tokyo, Japan

TRACY REDIES, Commercial Accounts Manager, HongKong Bank of Canada, Vancouver, BC

RODNEY TYERS, Senior Lecturer in Economics, University of Adelaide

PRUE PHILLIPS, Research Fellow in Economics, Development Studies Center, The Research School of Pacific Studies, The Australian National University, Canberra

THEODORE PANAYOTOU, formerly Faculty of Economics and Business Administration, Kasetsart University, Bangkok, Thailand; currently with the Institute for International Development, Harvard University

GAVIN BOYD, Professor Emeritus of Political Science, Saint Mary's University, Halifax

ALLAN M. RUGMAN, Professor of International Business, Faculty of Management, University of Toronto

ALAIN VERBEKE, Visiting Research Fellow, Dalhousie University, Halifax

J. COLIN DODDS, Dean of Commerce, Saint Mary's University, Halifax

LAM-HON LEE, The Chinese University of Hong Kong

ILAN B. VERTINSKI, Vinod Sood Professor of International Business Studies, Director of the Centre for International Business Studies, and Director of the Forest Economics and Policy Analysis Research Unit, all of the University of British Columbia

CHARLES J. JOHNSON, Co-ordinator, Mineral Policy Program, East-West Resource Systems Institute, East-West Center, Honolulu, Hawaii

ALLEN L. CLARK, East-West Resource Systems Institute, East-West Center, Honolulu, Hawaii

ROBERT N. YONOVER, East-West Resource Systems Institute, East-West Center, Honolulu, Hawaii

JOY DUNKERLEY, Senior Analyst, Office of Technology Assessment, Washington, DC

DOUGLAS BOHI, Chief Economist, Federal Energy Regulatory Commission, Washington, DC

VACLAV SMIL, Professor, Department of Geography, University of Manitoba

HAROLD HALVORSON, Resource Consultant, Vancouver, BC

DAVID L. ANDERSON, Dean, School of Business, Queen's University, Kingston, Ontario

KIRK R. SMITH, East-West Center, Honolulu, Hawaii